76

HARVARD LAW SCHOOL STUDIES IN CRIMINOLOGY

# CRIMINAL CAREERS
# IN RETROSPECT

# CRIMINAL CAREERS
# IN RETROSPECT

SHELDON AND
ELEANOR GLUECK

NEW YORK

1943

Reprinted with the permission of
Sheldon and Eleanor T. Glueck

KRAUS REPRINT CORPORATION
New York
1966

Printed in U.S.A.

TO SAMUEL C. LAWRENCE

WHO FOR EIGHTEEN YEARS HAS EXPLORED WITH US
THE OBSCURE NOOKS AND CRANNIES OF PRISONERS'
LIVES AND HAS ENRICHED WITH HIS DISCOVERIES
OUR RECORDS OF THEIR PROGRESS

# PREFACE

THIS is the third in a series of follow-up studies of the careers of 510 offenders who had been inmates of the Massachusetts Reformatory and whose sentences from that institution expired in the years 1921 and 1922. In the first volume, entitled *500 Criminal Careers*,[1] which described the activities of these men prior to their commitment to the Reformatory, during their term of incarceration, and on parole, their careers were followed for a five-year span beyond the expiration of their Reformatory sentences. The second volume of the series, entitled *Later Criminal Careers*,[2] pursued the activities of the group over a second five-year span. In the present volume a third five-year period is embraced.

In the course of these researches we are becoming indebted to an ever widening circle of officials of both public and private agencies in Massachusetts and throughout the United States. It becomes more and more difficult for us, therefore, to express adequately our appreciation to the many persons who in one way or another have contributed to the data upon which these researches are based. In connection with the present volume we must, however, particularly thank the following agencies: the Massachusetts Departments of Correction, Public Safety, Public Welfare, Mental Health; the Massachusetts Board of Probation, the Boston Social Service Index, and the Federal Bureau of Prisons, for the continued assistance which they have rendered throughout. We want especially to express our appreciation to Commissioner Arthur Lyman of the Department of Correction, to Commissioner Albert B. Carter of the Board of Probation, to Mr. Roscoe C. Hill and Miss Carrie V. Moyer of the Department of Public Safety, to Miss Laura Woodberry of the Boston Social Service Index, and to Mr. James V. Bennett of the Federal Bureau of Prisons.

For advice about statistical problems arising during the course of the investigation, we are indebted to Dr. Edwin Bidwell Wilson, Professor of Vital Statistics at the Harvard School of Public Health, to Dr. Carl Seltzer, Research Associate in Anthropology at Harvard University, and to Dr. Lowell J. Reed, Professor of Biostatistics and Dean of the Johns Hopkins School of Hygiene and Public Health.

Our indebtedness to the members of our research staff grows with the years. To Mr. Samuel C. Lawrence, Mrs. Mildred P. Cunningham, and Mrs. Beatrice H. Scheff we are particularly grateful for their endless patience with the details of the study, their enthusiasm for the work, and their never ending

[1] New York, Alfred A. Knopf, 1930.    [2] New York, The Commonwealth Fund, 1937.

loyalty. Mr. Lawrence, who has been a member of our staff since we began our work in 1925, has reached the age of retirement but, fortunately for us, his connection did not terminate until the present work was completed. His association with us over eighteen years has been a source of inspiration not only to ourselves but to all the members of the staff.

We wish to express our thanks to the Commonwealth Fund which has financed the research and now sees fit to publish the results, to the Milton Fund of Harvard University which provided the money for statistical work, and to others who have rendered us assistance.

E. T. G.
S. G.

*Harvard Law School*
*February, 1943*

# CONTENTS

*PART I. Third Five-Year Follow-Up of "500 Criminal Careers"*

## PART II. *Response of Offenders to Peno-Correctional Treatment*

## PART III. Criminal Careers in Prospect

# CONTENTS

# PART I

# THIRD FIVE-YEAR FOLLOW-UP OF "500 CRIMINAL CAREERS"

# I

## INTRODUCTION

WHAT happens to criminals, and why? How do they behave during and after peno-correctional treatment? These questions, so crucial to an understanding of our peno-correctional system, were partially answered in two volumes dealing with former inmates of a reformatory. In *500 Criminal Careers,* published in 1930,[1] we traced the careers of youthful offenders during a five-year span following the expiration of their sentences from the Massachusetts Reformatory. As a foundation for that work we described the family and personal backgrounds of the offenders, indicating their outstanding traits and characteristics as determined by sociologic, psychologic, and psychiatric investigation. In *Later Criminal Careers,* published in 1937,[2] the careers of the same group were traced over a second five-year follow-up span. In the present work we are concerned with their conduct during the third five-year period which has elapsed since the expiration of their Reformatory sentences.

How has time dealt with them, and how have they dealt with time? Answers to these significant questions should throw much light on the nature of criminalism and the effectiveness of peno-correctional treatment, and should make it possible to determine in advance how offenders of varying make-up are likely to respond to the efforts of society to protect itself against their depredations. To answer these questions to the extent that our inquiry permits is the aim of the present work.

### Some Facts of Orientation

The average age of the ex-prisoners at the end of the first five years following the expiration of their sentences from the Reformatory was thirty years. They were thirty-five years old, on the average, at the end of the second five-year follow-up period, and forty at the end of the third.[3] The recruits to our criminal army originally numbered 510. They constituted all offenders whose sentences to the Reformatory had expired during the years 1921 and 1922.[4] The

---

[1] New York, Alfred A. Knopf.

[2] New York, The Commonwealth Fund.

[3] Sixty (13.7 per cent) of the men were, by the end of the third span (1936–1937), thirty-one to thirty-five years old; 211 (48.1 per cent) were thirty-six to forty; 106 (24.1 per cent) forty-one to forty-five; 45 (10.3 per cent) forty-six to fifty, and 17 (3.8 per cent) fifty-one or older. Appendix B, 3–2.

[4] The 510 men included in the original study were not in any way a specially selected group. Whether they are typical of the total of reformatory inmates throughout the United States is a question dependent upon variations in laws and sentencing practices in different parts of the

first follow-up span extended, therefore, in the case of some of the offenders to 1926 and of others to 1927. The second follow-up period ended in 1931 and 1932; the third, described in the present work, extended to the years 1936 and 1937. By the end of the first five years after their sentences to the Reformatory had been completed, 56 of the original 510 criminals had passed away—11 while still in the institution, 22 while on parole, 23 during the five years subsequent to the completion of their sentences. By the end of the second follow-up span death had claimed 15 more,[5] leaving 439 who were alive at the beginning of the third follow-up period.

## Family Background of Offenders

What were these offenders like prior to their commitment to the Reformatory? For a detailed picture, we refer the reader to *500 Criminal Careers*.[6] Here we present only the highlights and shadows, as sketched from that work.

The families from which the youths came were on the whole not of a kind who form the sinews of a healthy society. Comparison with the general population wherever possible disclosed them to be suffering from a widespread state of individual and social pathology. Their economic foundation for wholesome family life was, to say the least, shaky. Fifteen per cent of the families from which the men came were outright economic dependents; almost 60 per cent more were barely able to support themselves. Some 60 per cent of the families had been dealt with by various types of social-welfare agencies, which indicates the extent to which they were unable to manage their own affairs.

As a consequence of low economic status, the homes and neighborhoods in which the young offenders were reared were, on the whole, not conducive to socially acceptable life. Crowding, insanitary conditions, underworld influences (pool-rooms, dance-halls, saloons, houses of prostitution) and the relative absence of facilities for legitimate recreational outlets, excessive moving about without much opportunity to strike root in any one neighborhood— these were the cradles and forums in which our youths, with few exceptions, spent their formative years.

The educational assets for wholesome management of family life were, to put it mildly, meager. In only 13 per cent of the cases had one or both parents attended even grammar school. Further, family solidarity was far from prevalent. In 60 per cent of the cases an abnormal, frequently unhealthy, home

country. On the whole, and with regard to major considerations, it is our opinion, based on some comparisons made, that the sample herein described is fairly typical of reformatory inmates elsewhere. See *500 Criminal Careers*, pp. 8 *et seq.*, 165–166.

[5] Appendix B, 3–79a.

[6] Chaps. VI, VII, VIII, and IX.

situation existed by reason of the long or complete absence of one or both parents; in a large proportion of these cases (70 per cent) the rift in the home occurred when the young offenders were at the impressionable, formative years of fourteen or less. In addition to the youths whose homes had been broken by death, desertion, separation, divorce, illness, or imprisonment of parents, 24 per cent had not been given suitable parental oversight, because their mothers worked out or were intemperate or immoral. Added to all this is the fact that the subjects of our investigation came from families appreciably larger than the average, and also that the moral atmosphere of their boyhood homes was far from conducive to the development of wholesome ideals and aspirations. Over half the families contained members who had established an unenviable record of arrests or imprisonments for various crimes prior to the Reformatory sentence of the youths with whose destinies we are concerned; and an additional 30 per cent of the families contained members who were in fact delinquent and criminal, though for one reason or another they had escaped arrest.

Added to this gloomy picture of their background is the finding that they had among them two and one-half times the number of native-born persons of foreign or mixed parentage than is to be found in the general population, a factor contributing to the difficulty of adjustment between these children of the New World and their parents with their Old World standards, ideals, and customs.

Clearly, the soil from which our young offenders sprang was not favorable to their healthy growth.

### Personal Background of Offenders

Nor did the offenders themselves, who were committed to the Reformatory at the average age of twenty years, bring much to that experience by which to benefit from it. According to psychologic tests, only a third of the group were of normal intelligence, about half were of "dull" or "borderline" intellect; a fifth were feebleminded. Three per cent of the group had definite psychoses, 18 per cent were "psychopathic personalities," 9 per cent more were classified by the institution's psychiatrist as drug or alcoholic deteriorates or sex perverts, leaving 70 per cent without extreme mental disorder or distortion. Even among these, however, three-fifths displayed psychopathic or neuropathic traits and were described as peculiar personalities by the psychiatrists who examined them. Obviously there was an appreciable incidence of abnormality in the emotional-volitional make-up of our young offenders.

Nor were their early life experiences conducive to wholesome development. Over 80 per cent of them had left the parental home prior to sentence to the Reformatory, and for long periods, as well as for reasons reflecting a serious breach in parent-child relationships. Half of them left or were removed from the parental roof at the formative, impressionable years of fourteen and under; 40 per cent more at fifteen to eighteen years. In over a third of the cases the reason for leaving home was sentence to some penal or correctional institution, in 17 per cent it was the break-up of the home, in 9 per cent it was commitment to some non-penal institution or to the care of a public welfare organization; 6 per cent of the lads ran away from home.

There was very little difference between the educational status of the youths and their parents. Their academic retardation was considerably greater than that of the general school population, and their educational achievements much lower. Almost half the youths had completed their formal schooling by the time they were fourteen. The significance of this is emphasized in taking into account the fact that less than 10 per cent of the general Boston school population leaves school at so early an age.

There was little in their early occupational experiences upon which wholesome industrial careers could be built. The average age at which our youths began to work was slightly over fifteen. Almost 90 per cent of them were unskilled or semi-skilled workers upon their entrance to the Reformatory. Almost 60 per cent of them had not held a job for as long as a year prior to commitment. The work habits of over half the youths were poor, and their earnings were of course exceedingly low.

The nature of their early misbehavior was indicative of their probable development into unwholesome adulthood. By the time they were committed to the Reformatory, four-fifths of them had already experienced heterosexual relations,[7] almost half were in the habit of gambling, 40 per cent drank alcoholics, 95 per cent had undesirable companions. As a rule, more than one or two of these vicious influences were operative simultaneously during their pubertal and adolescent years. Together with these facts are the significant findings that no less than 85 per cent of the youths had never been absorbed into socially desirable organizations for the employment of leisure time, and that religious affiliation was the exception among them and not the rule.

Open conflict with the authorities of school or society (chiefly the latter) occurred before the age of fifteen in 27 per cent of the cases, and before the age of seventeen in 77 per cent. The average age of these youths at first arrest was slightly over sixteen years. More than four-fifths of them were arrested for offenses other than, and prior to, the one for which they had been sentenced to the Reformatory; and no fewer than 1,944 such offenses are definitely known to have been committed by the 510 youths, half of these being essentially major

[7] A fourth of the group were suffering from venereal diseases on their admission to the Reformatory.

crimes (largely felonies), half of a minor character. Over four-fifths of these arrests resulted in convictions. Forty per cent resulted in probation, 40 per cent in commitment to various penal or correctional institutions, the balance in fines and other dispositions. An average of over nineteen months had been spent in peno-correctional establishments by those who had been committed prior to sentence to the Reformatory. In fact, almost 10 per cent had served from one to four sentences in the Reformatory itself preceding the particular commitment which has furnished the point of departure for the study of the criminal careers of this group of offenders.

This, then, is a rough and necessarily incomplete sketch of the kind of youths we set out to study.[8] We have followed their careers for a considerable portion of the *via dolorosa*. We have played Boswell to them for three separate five-year follow-up spans. Although one of our present interests is to record and interpret the vicissitudes in their lives during the five years that have passed since the periods reported on in *500 Criminal Careers* and *Later Criminal Careers,* our major purpose in the present work is to determine their behavior during the various forms of peno-correctional treatment to which they have been subjected from the onset of their criminal careers, and to determine the trend of their behavior over the fifteen-year span following expiration of their sentences from the Reformatory. We want to know why it is that some of them responded better to certain forms of peno-correctional treatment than did others, why some reformed and others did not and whether it might have been possible to determine in advance of treatment what was the likelihood of their successful adjustment.

A word should be said about the methods which have been used in pursuit of the data on which the work is based. In the various follow-up investigations we have reported on, it has been our practice to interview the offenders themselves or their close relatives. Information obtained from them has been verified and supplemented from numerous other sources. In the study of the third five-year follow-up period we have not departed from this general plan, but the task was a little more difficult than in former years, because some of the men or their families have grown impatient with the repeated visitations; and our field investigators have been under considerable strain to maintain friendly, cooperative relations with them. The extent to which they succeeded, however, is evidenced by the fact that in 94.1 per cent of the cases the reaction of the men or their families to the continued investigations was entirely friendly, at least after adequate explanation was made of the reasons for them.[9]

[8] The interested reader is referred to *500 Criminal Careers* and *Later Criminal Careers* for details.

[9] Appendix C, 56.

It is worth noting that over half (53.5 per cent) of the 439 men living at the beginning of the third five-year span were personally interviewed by our investigators; in a fourth of the cases (24.8 per cent) the men themselves were not seen, but their close relatives (parents, wives, parents-in-law, brothers or sisters, aunts or uncles) were interviewed. In a few instances (1.8 per cent) where it was not possible to see either the men or their relatives, others in a position to know of their activities (police, probation officers, social workers, employers) were interviewed. In only a fifth of the cases (19.9 per cent) did we have to confine our investigations to consultation of records of public and private social welfare agencies or to correspondence with persons who knew the men and their families.

That the effort to secure interviews with the men themselves has borne increasing fruit is evidenced by the fact that during the first five-year span we succeeded in interviewing 40.5 per cent of the men, while in the second period the proportion rose to 49.6 per cent, and in the third to 53.5 per cent.[10]

It would be possible to write a chapter or two on the delicacy of the techniques required in approaching these men and their families and in maintaining friendly relations with them. These methods, as well as the techniques of verifying and amplifying the data secured from the offenders, have, however, already been sufficiently described in our previous works,[11] and it would serve no useful purpose to repeat them here.

### Scope of This Research

It has already been suggested that the following chapters are concerned not only with the behavior of the men during the fifteen years that have elapsed since the expiration of their sentences to the Massachusetts Reformatory, but also with their responses to the various forms of peno-correctional treatment to which they had been subjected from the onset of their delinquent careers until the present time. Comparison is made of the characteristics of those who reformed with those who continued to recidivate; and of those who behaved well during various peno-correctional treatments (probation, parole, correctional schools, reformatories, prisons, and jails) with those who did not. And, finally, a series of tentative prediction tables are presented that are based on the findings in this series of cases. From these, it will be seen that the probable behavior of any one of the 500 offenders both during various kinds of peno-correctional treatment and thereafter, and at various age spans up to about the

---

[10] Appendix C, 57.

[11] See *500 Criminal Careers*, Chap. V; *Later Criminal Careers*, Appendix A. See also *Five Hundred Delinquent Women* (New York, Alfred A. Knopf, 1934), Appendix A.

age of forty might have been determined in advance with a reasonable degree of reliability.

But first we shall look into the life stories of nine young offenders whose careers during boyhood, young adulthood, and through a first five-year follow-up period were presented in *500 Criminal Careers*.[12] These are now continued through a second and a third five-year follow-up span.

[12] Chap. IV, A Sheaf of Lives.

## II

## CRIMINAL CAREERS

THE life stories of nine criminals from among our original group of 510 delinquents should give the reader a realistic and intimate acquaintance with a variety of criminal careers. These stories span the years from birth beyond middle age. The statistical presentation in the succeeding chapters will indicate to what extent this sampling of personalities and patterns of criminality are typical of our army of 510 offenders.

The lives of these nine men were first described in *500 Criminal Careers*,[1] but their stories could not then go beyond the first five-year period following the expiration of their sentences to the Reformatory (which, as the reader will recall, furnished the point of departure not only for *500 Criminal Careers* but for the succeeding volume *Later Criminal Careers* and for the present work as well). We are now able to record the activities of these men during the second and third five-year periods that have elapsed since the expiration of their Reformatory sentences and even, in a few cases, beyond this span of years.

Each story is presented in two parts: Part I from birth to the end of the first five-year follow-up period (reproduced through the courtesy of the publisher with occasional minor literary changes from *500 Criminal Careers*); and Part II in which is told what has happened to them since (that is, at least during a span of ten more years).

### FRANK. PART I[2]

Frank was the oldest of six children of Italian parents. His father was a city laborer. Although none of the members of his immediate family had ever been in conflict with the law except his father, who had been arrested for gambling over thirty years before Frank's first conviction, two of his cousins were known criminals. The family just managed to make ends meet financially. Living conditions were always poor. There was much overcrowding. The children ran about the streets wholly uncontrolled.

Of his developmental history it is known that Frank, at the age of ten months, had spinal meningitis, followed by typhoid fever. When he was one year old, he suffered from convulsions, which recurred for a year but were apparently not diagnosed.

As a little child, Frank frequently ran away from home. When he was six

[1] New York, Alfred A. Knopf, 1930.
[2] In *500 Criminal Careers*, The Restless Spirit, p. 52.

years old, he was sent to a children's protectorate for three months and then returned home. At the age of eight he was arrested for truancy and was committed to a "parental school"[3] for one year. Very shortly after his return home, he was again arrested, this time for larceny of a team of horses, was sent back to the parental school for two years and, returning home, was soon thereafter once more arrested for larceny of a team and again committed to the parental school, this time for three years.

Frank had schooling until he was fourteen, at which age he had reached the seventh grade. He was, however, a continual truant; he did practically no work, spending most of his time at the moving-picture shows and baseball games. By the time he was fifteen years old, Frank smoked and chewed excessively, was habituated to beer and whisky, and was a confirmed, excessive masturbator.

At sixteen, some two years after his second release from the parental school, Frank was once more arrested for larceny of a team, and received a five-year "indeterminate" sentence to the Massachusetts Reformatory. Did this grave experience "reform" him? Did it at least frighten him and thereby act as a preventive? Evidently not, for during his parole from the Reformatory, Frank was again arrested for larceny of a team and received a new sentence to that institution. On these two sentences he served a total of fifty months.

Up to this stage in his career no diagnosis of Frank, no attempt to probe his motivations, had been made by any agency or institution that had dealt with him.

During his second parole from the Reformatory, in 1917, at the age of twenty, Frank was again arrested for larceny of a team. A psychiatric examination was thereupon ordered by the court. He remained in a mental hospital under observation for a month and was returned to the court with the diagnosis of "moron." He was then committed to a school for the feebleminded, where he was found to have a mental age of eleven years and one month and to be a "psychopathic delinquent." At the school for the feebleminded where he stayed only two months, Frank proved very troublesome and quarrelsome. He incited the other boys to rebellion and insubordination. He even planned an escape and ran off taking a dozen boys with him. Upon being captured he was transferred to a state hospital for the mentally ill. His sojourn at the hospital, where he was diagnosed as an imbecile, was almost as brief as his stay at the school for the feebleminded. After six months he escaped, ran away to New York City, remained there a week, and then returned home. Being captured, he was recommitted to the hospital; but two days later, on the promise of his father to supervise him carefully, Frank was released.

[3] An institution for habitual truants or "habitual school offenders."

His adventures in escaping the authorities were not yet ended; in fact they had just begun. After remaining home for three weeks, Frank was again committed to the state hospital by his father because of his refusal to work and his too frequent attendance at moving-picture shows. This time he remained for six months. But his entire being revolted at restraint. Once more he escaped, and wandered to a small town in New Hampshire, where he stayed for three weeks; he returned home, and after a week surrendered to the hospital authorities. But within a few days, at the request of his parents, these officials again released our turbulent wanderer.

Frank was now twenty-three years old. He stayed at home for a few weeks and then went to Fall River, where he lived with a cousin for a brief period. Then he joined a circus for a month, and shortly after returning to Fall River was arrested for burglarizing a jewelry store with an accomplice and was sentenced to a house of correction for one year. Because of two alleged attempts at suicide by hanging, Frank was transferred to a hospital for the criminal insane, where he remained for a year and a half and was then discharged. The report made on his discharge was: "Condition not improved. Diagnosis: mental deficiency."

Frank returned home, but not for long. Within a few months he became restless, got a job on a boat, and shipped to Havre and thence to Liverpool. There he served a month in jail for not having registered. Upon his release he signed up for a voyage to Genoa. Returning to Liverpool, he was sent home by the American Consul.

Two weeks after his return home, Frank was arrested for "larceny from the person." Again he was ordered by the court to a mental hospital for examination. There he remained for a month's observation and was then returned to the court with the cryptic diagnosis: "Not insane; moron." Upon this report the court sentenced Frank to the Reformatory for a third time.

Examined by the Reformatory physician, Frank was diagnosed as a psychopath and a moron. It was also found that he now needed treatment for syphilis. During this third stay in the institution whose graduates we are studying, Frank was extremely difficult to manage. He once swallowed ink and soap in a purported attempt at suicide.

Concerning his industrial experiences in the Reformatory, where he worked as an unskilled laborer, it was found that Frank "would work if he was handled right"—that is, "kidded along and made to believe what a good fellow he is and how strong he is; but even then he requires constant watchfulness."

This time Frank remained at the Reformatory for thirty-one months. During his stay he wrote to the Commissioner of Correction requesting transfer to a house of correction, so that "I could be near my people and they can come to see me. I should not be in a criminal institution. I should be in a state hospital for the insane. I have been in the X— School for the Feebleminded and in the D— State Hospital for the Insane, and the B— State Hospital for the Criminal Insane. P.S. And if I do not get transferred I will commit suicide and end it altogether. Please think it over."

As was said before, Frank made several apparent attempts at suicide. One of these consisted in banging his head against the wall, and another in trussing himself up with his suspenders. When the last attempt was discovered, it was noticed that there was no great amount of strain upon his neck, his feet were upon the floor, his breathing was natural, and there was no discoloration of the face. His excuse for these actions, as told to the Reformatory physician, was "that there is no use in living," that everybody is "down" on him, that he can't get along anywhere, and similar infantile expressions. He stated that he would kill the person responsible for his serving these sentences if he ever got a chance. The Reformatory psychiatrist found, however, that Frank was not mentally diseased (evidently believing him to be a malingerer), but "a low-grade, feebleminded person of the type who should be permanently segregated." And permanent segregation was perhaps the most sensible way to handle Frank's case, in the light of society's present limited facilities for coping with unusual personality problems.

But after thirty-one months in the Reformatory our turbulent spirit, now twenty-seven years old, was once more released on parole. Shortly thereafter he enlisted in the Army, and soon deserted. Then he enlisted in the Navy as an apprentice seaman, but received a dishonorable discharge two months later for being absent without leave.

During a leave from the Navy, Frank was sentenced to two years in a southern penitentiary. By this time his parole period from the Reformatory had run out.

Upon Frank's discharge from the penitentiary he again returned home. Soon thereafter, at the request of his family, he was again committed to a mental hospital and again a diagnosis of "psychopathic personality" was made. But no recommendation regarding treatment or institutional care was given and Frank was discharged to the care of his family. His stormy soul would not rest. He soon enlisted in the Marine Corps. While stationed in North Carolina, he overstayed his leave during one of his furloughs, and traveled to New Bedford, Massachusetts. A few months later he reported to the local naval station and there awaited general court martial. In the meantime he was committed to a naval hospital, where he received treatment for gonorrhoea. Within a short time he was discharged from the Marine Corps on the ground that "because of his mental calibre, it was believed that court martial proceedings for AWOL would serve no useful purpose."

Frank returned to his parents. Two months later he went to New York, where he again attempted to enlist in the Marine Corps, but was rejected in view of his prior undesirable discharges from the Navy and Marine Corps. Returning home, he was soon arrested for larceny of an automobile, having no license and no registration. For a fourth time he was sentenced to the Reformatory, where he remained but one month. This time he was diagnosed by the institution psychiatrist as a "responsible offender"[4] and "formerly a sex pervert." The psychiatrist was apparently impressed with the change in Frank, for he recorded of him: "This man's case is the most striking example in our records of the benefit to be derived from the regaining of self-control by a confirmed masturbator. Is very co-operative and willing to work, is studying bookkeeping, and is very proud of his achievement. Is very earnest in crediting his improvements to his mastery of his long habit of masturbation. Volunteers he has made up his mind it has not paid to steal."

But the superintendent of the Reformatory requested Frank's transfer to some other penal institution: "He is now 33 years of age and will be, as he always has been, a bad influence here. I recommend his removal and urge that it be immediate because if he breaks the rules, as he is quite likely to do any time, his removal thereafter will create a bad impression in the minds of others."

Frank was therefore transferred to a house of correction, but after staying there but one month he was committed to the Department for Defective Delinquents,[5] where he remained up to the end of the first follow-up period.

---

[4] "A person who shows capability of being a producer socially without assistance or supervision, that is, a person who can earn an honest living in open competition" (letter from Reformatory psychiatrist).

[5] In 1922 Massachusetts established a special institution for the "defective delinquent," defined in the statutes as a defendant who is "mentally defective," who, "after examination into his record, character and personality . . . has shown himself to be an habitual delinquent or shows tendencies toward becoming such," provided "such delinquency is or may become a menace to the public," and who "is not a proper subject for the schools for the feeble-minded or for commitment as an insane person" (General Laws, chap. 333, sec. 113). Commitment results only after the filing of an application therefor by "a district attorney, probation officer or officer of the department of correction, public welfare or mental diseases" "at any time prior to the final disposition of a case in which the court might commit an offender to the state prison, the reformatory for women, any jail or house of correction, the Massachusetts reformatory, the state farm, the industrial school for boys, the industrial school for girls, the Lyman school, any county training school, or to the custody of the department of public welfare, for any offense not punishable by death or imprisonment for life" (*ibid.*).

Frank's family, who were interviewed, thought him quite happy at the institution, as he had gradually adapted himself to the routine. Despite all the trouble they had had with him, they still looked upon him as an innocent, harmless, feebleminded boy and of course believed that he should be with them and that they were perfectly able to take care of him. They said that throughout his life Frank had had a "periodic mania for wandering," which would come on after a quiet spell, when he seemed inclined to work and to live peacefully. Then he would simply drift away and they would hear nothing from him for weeks at a time. His last sentence to the Reformatory was for stealing his sister's car. She told the investigator that Frank had always begged to be allowed to use it and that she had told him she would permit him to take it some time, provided he would have some friend with him who was a careful driver. On the occasion in question she was not at home and he used the car without her permission. Thinking that the auto had been stolen, she reported the fact to the police, and she supposes that if she had gone to the court and explained matters her brother would not have been returned to the Reformatory, but transferred to a house of correction and thence committed to the Department for Defective Delinquents.

In the case history as presented in *500 Criminal Careers* (page 56), we said:

If, as in all but two of the states, there were no provision for the commitment of mentally deficient criminals for a wholly unlimited time (even for life, if necessary), Frank would still be wandering from pillar to post, a social nuisance, and liability, a perplexed and misunderstood personality, clumsily trying to find his place in the sun.

Subsequent events show that we did not sufficiently take into account that there are ways of bringing about the release of even such inmates of an institution for defective delinquents who ought not to be at large, and that, at least in the case of Frank, incarceration for life or even for a considerable period was only a theoretical possibility. We were, however, correct in our prediction that without lifelong institutionalization, Frank would continue to be a socially expensive wanderer.

## FRANK. PART II

At the end of the first five-year follow-up period we thought Frank was settled for life in an institution for defective delinquents, but by the time four years of his commitment had passed, his overindulgent and affectionate mother and sisters began to clamor for his release. His married sister, representing the family (Frank's father had meanwhile passed away), engaged an attorney who made repeated attempts to have Frank sent home. The institutional authorities at first objected to his release because they felt that his conduct did not justify it. They reported him to be a "shifty, evasive, fickleminded individual with no sense of right and wrong . . . constantly in opposition to institutional rules and antagonistic to those in authority. . . . He must frequently be punished for fighting and for assault on other inmates. . . . He frequently threatens suicide although he never actually attempts more than drinking a bottle of ink following which he promptly notifies an employee of what he has done. . . . He responds reluctantly to disciplinary measures."

The family clamor persisted, however, and after a while the institutional officials began to feel that Frank might possibly be ready for return to the community. By the time he had been under their care for some six years they were ready to recommend him for parole. They had previously reported that Frank was a good tailor and capable shoe worker. "For the last two or three years he has been constantly decent. He has a home to go to and will live with his mother and married sister. He has been promised employment and under these conditions we feel that he should be given a trial." However, the parole board denied him parole. Meanwhile his lawyer had been active and managed to secure a final and absolute discharge for Frank through the Probate Court.

A position had been promised Frank by his sister's husband, but he kept it for only a few days and was soon asking assistance from a Prisoners' Aid Society. Since he was not on parole but had been given an unconditional release, no help was forthcoming and Frank was referred to an industrial aid society. Meanwhile the institution from which he had so recently been discharged was receiving complaints from parents of other defective delinquents that Frank had called on them requesting money which he claimed he would use to help to secure the release of their sons. The inadequacies in society's equipment for dealing with problems of this nature are glaringly shown by the statement of the institution authorities. "In view of the fact that he has been granted a final discharge from our department, his conduct will not be investigated. Were he on parole he would probably be returned to the institution." This would certainly have been the wisest course, but Frank was free and his excessively overprotective mother and married sister would have strenuously opposed his return.

Frank now went to the industrial aid society for assistance on the ground that he merely needed money for transportation to a nearby town where he claimed to have a position promised him in a mill. They told him it would be necessary to verify the job before he could be furnished with money for transportation. He agreed that his prospective employer be telegraphed to, but word soon came back that no such man had been hired; and Frank, meanwhile, went off and failed to return. He soon succumbed to his former habit of wandering.

By now Frank was forty years old. Despite the six years spent in an institution for defective delinquents quite isolated from the world outside and during an age span when the feeling of restlessness and the urge for new experience would normally have been reduced, he continued to crave adventure. The story of his comings and goings is an intricate one, because he would leave home with only enough money to begin his wanderings and would then have to beg his way, or through some social agency wire or telephone his family for funds to return home "for Christmas" or "to see my sick mother" or "to get a job that is waiting for me" or even "to go to a mental hospital for treatment."

Within a few months after his first departure from home, he was stranded in a small town in North Carolina and a local social agency assisted him in returning to his mother. Shortly thereafter he again left home, this time turning up in St. Louis where he was soon admitted to the city hospital as a mental patient. In view of the fact that he was not a resident of the state, a social agency tried to secure his return home and wished to arrange for his commitment to a mental hospital in his own state. Commitment papers were obtained and arrangements made for his return to Massachusetts with an attendant. However, all efforts to persuade Frank's family that he be sent to a mental hospital were of no avail. He was sent home, this time remaining with his mother and sister for three months. As usual, on each visit home, he was petted and pampered and furnished with new clothes and a small sum of money. He worked for a day now and then, making no effort whatsoever to obtain steady employment.

Frank's explanation for his excessive traveling about was that he hoped that changes of scene would benefit his mental condition. When he became weary of traveling by freight or highway he would go to a local hospital, explain his condition, rest for a few days, and then continue his wanderings.

Within three months of his last visit home, Frank again set off on his parasitic travels, this time turning up in Kansas City. Using his well-tried technique, he again asked for transportation home, this time presenting to a local welfare agency a complete history of his case written by himself and suggesting that if he were sent home his commitment to a mental hospital would be arranged. He was sent to a temporary home but did not remain there, applying instead to the psychiatric department of the general hospital for care. The doctors felt he was not sufficiently disturbed mentally to warrant keeping him, so they recommended his release. It was their opinion that while Frank might be psychopathic to some extent, he was just "a professional beggar and should be given no consideration."

After leaving the hospital in Kansas City, Frank continued to bum around, and was shortly arrested and committed to jail for two days on suspicion of burglary. Later he made his way through Kansas where he again spent a night in jail for vagrancy; then he "hopped freights" across the continent to California, where he was again held over night on suspicion of burglary. Winter was coming and Frank had a longing to get home for Christmas. A two months' trip eastward brought him there just in time for the holidays. He remained with his mother and sister for three months, then pawned some new clothes and disappeared toward the west. Soon he was heard from in southern California, where he had been picked up for vagrancy; a few weeks later in New Mexico; then in central Massachusetts, where he was jailed, soon released, and returned home. Shortly thereafter he was arrested for forgery and uttering and larceny, having secured $40 from a telegraph company on a forged money order. Frank's family employed counsel and urged him to appeal his sentence but he accepted a fifteen-month sentence to a house of correction. By this time he was forty-two years of age.

One month after parole, Frank was arrested for larceny from a building and was returned to the house of correction to complete the four months remaining on his sentence. Soon after, he wandered off again, this time turning up in Indiana where he was picked up for loitering. A month later found him in a small town in Pennsylvania where he was again arrested for vagrancy; shortly thereafter, in northern New York state he spent ten days in jail. Then, instead of returning home which he could have reached in a few hours by bus, he traveled southwest to Louisiana where he was arrested for larceny of a horse. The case was *nol prossed,* however, and two weeks later Frank turned up in Texas. Three months later he was in the state of Connecticut, two months thereafter in Massachusetts. At the end of the third five-year follow-up period, at the age of forty-five, Frank is serving a three months' sentence in a midwestern jail for vagrancy.

The cost to society of this "rolling stone," in terms of arrest, trial, imprisonment, hospitalization, and other expense, has been tremendous. The haphazardness and inefficiency of the machinery set up for dealing with cases of this kind are glaring. Yet Frank's family continue to be very tolerant of his comings and goings. The extent of their intelligence and sense of responsibility can be gauged by the fact that they explain his chronic *Wanderlust* on the ground that a few months before Frank was born, his mother had been greatly worried that her husband might have to make a trip! A sister, however, insists that Frank's difficulties are due to an attack of spinal meningitis when he was a year old.

If it were not for the blind devotion of his mother and sisters, it is likely that Frank would have been in even more serious trouble than he has been. He knows that he can return home whenever he wishes. His present home, though still in a crowded slum neighborhood, is nevertheless comfortable. The tenement is clean and cosy and is well furnished with modern appliances purchased on the instalment plan. His mother and a married sister and her husband occupy two connecting tenements. Another married sister lives around the corner. She has two young children who are frequent visitors at the maternal home.

Frank's relatives know they will always hear from him because he never fails to communicate with them when in need of funds. He wires collect, or telephones reversing the charges. They explain that when he returns home from one of these trips he is always disgracefully filthy. They then dress him up in a new suit, which he promptly disposes of for a few dollars, and he sets out again. They "thank God he doesn't want to get married; it would be the worst thing possible." At least he avoids alcohol, because drinking makes him sick. He has few friends but when he returns home from his various journeyings he amuses the family for days with stories of his experiences with other hoboes. During these brief periods at home he attends church regularly and avoids pool-rooms and gambling establishments. He does not hang about the corners and he has no friends in the neighborhood of his home. Occasionally he gets an odd job cleaning cars or helping a truckman. He spends most of his time eating and sleeping, is given money by the family for cigarettes and for movies. "We can't let the poor boy go about without a dollar in his pocket."

His family say Frank is boyish in his emotional reactions. They illustrate this by commenting that when his mother was sick he cried bitterly at the thought that she was going to die and that he would then not see her again until he too died. He is good-natured and affectionate. He helps his mother about the house and runs errands for her. He washes windows for the neighbors, repairs plumbing for them, and generally tries to make himself pleasant. There are, thus, some redeeming features in Frank's make-up; but it cannot be gainsaid that his being at large during all these years has cost society enormous sums both through his criminalistic activities and his failure to be self-supporting, and in the expense of hospitals, courts, prisons, and other institutions.

Exactly how his career will develop beyond this point, we do not know. That more than conjecture is possible, however, will be seen in Chapters XIV, XV, and XVI.

Our deductions from the career of Frank up to the end of the first five-year follow-up period have been proved essentially sound by the events of the following ten years. First, we said that no better illustration could be found of the as yet imperfect state of psychology and psychiatry as applied to the problems of delinquency and crime. To arrive at this conclusion one has only to recall the superficial generalities and the contradictions in the numerous diagnoses of his mental condition. After ten more years of following his career, it can still be said as in 500 *Criminal Careers,* that "not one of the numerous agencies that dealt with this wanderer seems to have studied him with sufficient thoroughness to understand and be able to explain the dynamics of his personality." Part of the difficulty springs, of course, from the still very imperfect state of psychiatry and psychology; but much of it arises from the fact that legislatures and courts have not yet been sufficiently enlightened to allow these disciplines to play an adequate role in certain aspects of criminal justice.

Next, we mentioned the lack of coordination of social and peno-correctional facilities. The entire case summary brings out in even more vivid form the unintegrated nature, the planlessness, of the facilities for the treatment of offenders of this type. It will be recalled that Frank's journeyings from pillar to post included sojourns in schools, hospitals, jails, prisons, and institutions for defective delinquents, contacts with public and private social welfare agencies, police, prosecutors, and courts, and even a visit to the American consul in a foreign port. Improper integration of relevant agencies had not a little to do with the wastefulness and the danger to society illustrated in this life story. At several stages in his career, Frank was discharged although all concerned knew that he required further incarceration. Most serious of these turnings loose upon society of one who should have been kept under long control were his discharge from the hospital for the criminal insane because of expiration of sentence, although the report clearly indicated that Frank's condition was not improved; and his discharge from the Reformatory because of the expiration of his sentence, although the psychiatrist recognized him to require permanent segregation. These instances, and the release by the probate court through intervention of a lawyer more interested in satisfying his client's family for a fee than in protecting society, indicate the crying need of more integrated, planful administration of criminal justice. They bring out, further, the need for a long-term, if not a complete, indeterminate sentence law, to take the place of the present only partially indeterminate sentences the weakness of which this case so graphically illustrates.

Finally, the story of Frank indicates what a harmful role can be played by ignorant and antisocial parents, and the fact that certain types of offenders soon learn to manipulate welfare institutions and agencies to their own selfish desires.

## JOHN. PART I[6]

John explains the genesis of his criminal career thus: "I never thought I would let myself go. Up to fifteen or sixteen I was about like other kids. I liked athletics and took part in them. I read books from the library, kept good hours, and all that. My parents took me out of school and put me to work and took all of my wages except fifty cents each week. I worked about a year, then I began going with a girl and she liked a good time. You can't give a girl a good time these days, even in N— (a small Massachusetts town), on fifty cents a week. The old man wouldn't give me any more. I was sore and had it on my mind: how could I make more money? One day along came a fellow I got acquainted with. He was a right guy [that is, a good thief; an intelligent, capable fellow who knows the business and will 'divvy with you and not do you dirt']. We put through a lot of jobs in N— and got away with it, and I have been at it ever since."

John's parents owned their home in N—. His father was foreman in a factory. His family had always just been able to make ends meet. John was one of three children. Up to the time of his misconduct no other member of the family had ever been known to be delinquent.

John did not work very long before he left home to roam about the country. He admits having first had heterosexual experiences at the age of fifteen. When he was sixteen years of age, John was arrested with a companion for breaking, entering, and larceny, and sent to a correctional school. Not long after his release, at the age of nineteen, he again began to roam about. During one of these freight-riding expeditions he had "dropped off a freight train in F— to look about the town and after staying there for about half an hour was on my way back to catch another freight into Boston when I was placed under arrest by a policeman. I pulled a loaded revolver out of my pocket and told him to stick his hands up. He did for the moment, but then he jumped at me and took the gun away." John was charged with being armed with a dangerous weapon and with assaulting and beating a police officer. It developed that this officer, in making his rounds on the previous morning, had heard suspicious noises in the rear of a factory and on investigation learned that John had been prowling around there. The assault and his arrest followed. John refused to give any explanation whatsoever regarding himself until after he had been sentenced to the Reformatory. The story there given by him was wholly false, and it was only with the aid of the police that his true identity was finally ascertained.

---

[6] In *500 Criminal Careers,* "Hard-boiled" John, p. 57.

John spent sixteen months in the Reformatory on this sentence. His physical condition was found to be good and he was designated a "responsible offender" of "dull normal" intelligence. For fifteen months he worked in the tailor shop. He violated institutional rules on an average of once in two and two-thirds months, which is much more frequent than the average for men in the institution. His offenses usually consisted of outbreaks of violence; he often fought with officers and inmates.

When John was released on parole he went home to live with his parents. His father secured a job for him as a roofer, which he held for three days. During that time he robbed his employer, taking about three hundred dollars' worth of jewelry. He left a note for his parents saying he was off to Texas. For some time he was a fugitive from justice. Finally he was trailed to Chicago and shortly thereafter was arrested by the police of his home town. He received a new sentence to the Reformatory, this time for larceny.

The parole officer characterized him as "a highwayman." John affected a wide-brimmed hat, a red bandanna handkerchief, and a belt with a revolver in it, and assumed the sobriquet of a western outlaw. During this second incarceration his conduct was as bad as formerly. Again he frequently assaulted inmates, refused to work, and was thoroughly incorrigible in every way. This time he spent twenty-eight months in the weaving shop.

Upon his second release from the Reformatory, John was twenty-three years old. He again began to travel about and soon was once more arrested for breaking, entering, and larceny. This time he was sentenced to the state prison for from ten to twelve years. During this term of imprisonment he made an unsuccessful attempt to escape.

When interviewed at the prison, John frankly stated he was an "outlaw," a professional thief by choice. "I feel that anything I can get away with is all right." He made it plain that he was not blaming anyone or any institution for his condition. He was eager not to "pass the buck." He admitted having done whatever he had been accused of "and a lot more." He took the attitude that crime was his business in life, deliberately entered into, and he expressed his intent to retain this view as long as he lived. Superficially, at least, he appeared to have no conventional moral standards and apparently, as far as property rights were concerned, he had absolutely no scruples.

He seemed to have no group loyalties whatsoever—for the state, the church, his prison associates, or even (and this is unusual among criminals) "the gang." He said that when he came out of the Reformatory, he met a good many fellows with whom he had become acquainted there, but they were "panhandlers." "They always wanted to borrow money from me. They would want me to go with them and do some petty stealing, but I got rid of them. Why should I be such a fool as to get into petty larceny? I have learned not to trust people. They say thieves won't do each other, but they will. I was with a fellow once, treated him white; and he did me dirt."

There was a note of bitterness in John's attitude: "I do not think that life is worth living. For humanity in general I have nothing but the utmost contempt." When pressed as to his reason for continuing in crime, John expressed his philosophy very frankly: "If I had all the money I wanted I would be just as honest as anybody. That is, if I had enough so I could do what I wanted to without working. I never liked work. I hate it and never will work. If I had money enough to travel all over the world and take my ease, nobody would be more honest than I. I have never committed a crime for the sake of doing the crime. Of course there is a certain 'kick' in driving up to a place in an automobile, putting through your job, and making your get-away. But there is not enough in it to attract me for the sake of the kick. I want the money. I have been in this game for ten years and am looking forward now to doing some big things when I get out. These fellows who do these small things are nothing but pikers. They don't know their business. You've got to do this thing the same as any other business. When I was caught before at one time I had about fourteen thousand dollars' worth of jewelry, but I didn't know any better than to go and see my girl, and cashed in only enough to pay my expenses to go to her, and they caught me." He pondered awhile and then: "They have schools here in the prison and I am going to get all the education I can get—not to reform myself, but to make myself more dangerous to society."

It is difficult to say how much of John's attitude was mere bravado. It would require a deep and time-consuming personality analysis to penetrate to the inner core of his motivations.

John was asked whether, if he had a son, he would train him to be a professional outlaw. "If I had a son," he snapped back, "I would wring his neck. Do you think I would ever be guilty of bringing a human being into the world?" This outburst he did not offer to elaborate.

John admits that during the periods when he was roaming about the country he had been committing crimes from coast to coast and had been in jails throughout the country. "I have been in them from coast to coast and — [a boys' industrial school] is the worst institution I have ever been in. When I came out, I carried marks on me that were from beatings I got there. I was treated rougher there than any prison I was ever in." John asserts he left this industrial school with a feeling of intense hatred toward society, and it is partly to this that he ascribes the continuance of his professional criminal career.

It may be said in closing that the psychiatrist at the state prison diagnosed John as a "moron" and a "psychopath."

## JOHN. PART II

At the end of the first five-year follow-up period John was still in prison determined, when he got out, to "do some big things. . . . These fellows who do these small things are nothing but pikers." Throughout the second five-year follow-up period, however, he had been kept in prison. He wrote to one of our investigators, "like many others in here—as we say—I am doing life on the installment plan. When I see my pal with twenty-five to thirty years I feel like a short-timer with only ten to twelve. I come up for parole in two and a half years but it doesn't mean a thing as I have one of the worst reps in here. This time I'll get my whole bit, eight years more." This was written two years after the beginning of the second five-year follow-up period, when John was twenty-nine years old.

During the second five-year span John made frequent attempts to escape and was often in solitary confinement. In fact he spent the best part of five years from the time he was twenty-nine until he was thirty-four (into the third five-year follow-up period) "in solitary." Usually he tried either to dig or saw his way out. Once he intended to dynamite his way to freedom, but was caught before the attempt was fulfilled. Although John was always caught, he never gave up hope that he would succeed the next time. The prison deputy stated that "John is of the type who will undoubtedly be in prison for life, because he cannot learn to conform even to the simplest of prison regulations and because he is extremely vengeful in his feeling against society."

During these years of confinement John had very little communication with anyone on the outside. His girl apparently did not keep in touch with him. He rarely heard from his father or married sister. A brother had long ago disappeared. John claimed to have two nieces who wrote him occasionally and with whom he hoped to make his home upon release. Our investigator kept in touch with John, writing him several times a year. For these attentions he was extremely grateful and would now and then write a letter revealing to the experienced observer something different from what was intended. "Since I wrote you last time my views have changed, my outlook and plans for the future are quite different, almost conventional. Perhaps I am getting older or perhaps I now realize the advantage of doing things correctly, or utilizing methods and agencies to achieve my gains of which I had not thought. . . . I may soon be out as my full time expires in thirty-four months. I hope to make connections which will be of use in the new future I plan, friends and acquaintances with business experience." From the above letter to our investigator, it might appear on the surface that John was changing for the better. But his conduct following his parole at the age of thirty-four, after spending ten years in prison, was not of the kind suggested by his letter.

In fact, only a couple of months before his parole he was punished for creating disturbances and disobeying orders. When his turn for parole came, it transpired that John did not know where his relatives were but stated his belief that they were still in the home town and that he hoped to live with them upon his release. He knew that his father and a cousin had been conducting a contracting business at the time of his sentence to prison and he was in a very vague way planning to enter this business. The institutional officials recorded that "because of his persistent previous criminal history and his great instability, his future looks extremely dubious." The warden, however, encouraged parole, because he could not "help feeling that John has been punished enough."

When he was finally paroled after serving ten years of a ten to twelve-year sentence, John planned to live with a "niece" and to rent a small farm for $300 which he had borrowed from another prisoner, promising to pay it back when he could. He had explained to his friend that this money would enable him not only to rent a farm but to marry and settle down. Meanwhile an investigation was made of John's proposed home and the parole agent reported that he could not approve it "because the so-called niece is a low-type person, the place is dirty, and she is the daughter of the man with whom John was arrested at the time of his commitment to this prison." The parole officials also disapproved the hiring of a farm by John as "a crazy scheme, for he does not know anything about farming." Further, when the parole agent looked into John's proposed marriage, he discovered that the parolee had never even met the young woman whom he intended to make his wife but that the marriage had been arranged through the mother of another convict who was known to be a "desperate character."

Meanwhile, John retained a lawyer who supposedly obtained employment for him as a factory hand at $10 a week and also arranged for him to board near his place of employment. John was released in care of his lawyer, but did not take the job to which he was supposed to go. Instead he went to his home town to visit his father and wrote to his parole agent, "I shall return shortly and hope to fulfill successfully the conditions of my release. To date I have conducted myself fairly well, and broken no law." Meantime the parole agent was unable to locate John's prospective employer. The lawyer to whom John had been released admitted he had not seen his client since the day of release, but he did know that John had reported to his employer that morning and immediately asked if he might have a week off to visit relatives.

John remained near his family for two weeks. His brother-in-law took him out on a job, sawing wood. John proved a first-class sawyer although he had never had any experience in this work. His brother-in-law felt that John "could make a good honest living in this if he would only stick to it," but John soon grew tired of the work, commenting that it was the first time he had ever sawed wood for a living and it would be the last. He left in a hurry one day without even waiting for his lunch and went to the home of a man with whom he had been arrested years ago and sentenced to prison. John's brother-in-law told how during this period John and his pal stole forty bushels of apples from him and sold them for $5, although the value was $40. The brother-in-law explained that John was eager for money to satisfy the demands of a girl.

All this had happened within one month after John's release from prison. Soon he was arrested in a Maine city by a railroad police officer for carrying a loaded revolver. It was also reported that there was reason to suspect that he had engaged in a number of hold-ups. The Maine police wrote that when he was picked up John had in his possession several skeleton keys, a small tool kit, and an old 22-caliber revolver. On his person were also found several newspaper clippings describing various hold-ups in which it was suspected he had been implicated. He was arraigned for larceny of railroad property and given thirty days in the county jail. For the commission of this offense John's parole was revoked, but he managed to escape the clutches of the authorities and thus avoided a return to prison.

John went back to the home of his friend, remaining there for a few months, but soon set out with another pal to wander through New York state plundering whatever he could. His family heard nothing of him for about eight months, when he turned up at home leaving a sawed-off shotgun and an automatic pistol with them for safekeeping. He then set out on a tour of New Hampshire with his pal, making his way by burglarizing.

After several months John returned to his home town for a brief period. His relatives reported that on each return home, John looked very prosperous and told stories of how he had many women friends, any one of whom could get as much money from him as she had the courage to demand. He vouchsafed that his main failing was "chasing around with wild women." His family got the impression that he had no idea of the value of money. Although he occasionally had large sums in his possession, he never attempted to provide for the future, and carried no insurance.

Very soon after his next departure from his home town, John met his death in a brawl with the police. He had been arrested for vagrancy in a nearby town because complaints had been received from neighbors that an unknown man was living in a shack and annoying and frightening children passing by. The police went for him and John consented to go with them to the police station, carrying with him a package wrapped in newspaper. This proved to be a sawed-off shotgun. One police officer was walking in front of John and one was beside him when suddenly John turned around and shouted "Hands up!" firing directly at the officer beside him. The other officer drew his gun, shot John, and knocked him senseless with the butt of his revolver. John was taken to the hospital where he soon died. The police officer whom John had shot died a day or two later.

Thus at the age of thirty-seven ended the career of "Hard-boiled John." His relatives evidently identified themselves more with their underworld relation than with the representatives of society, for in commenting on the tragedy, they said, "It's too bad that John wasn't quick enough to shoot the other cop."

It is difficult to say whether penetrating psychiatric insight would have laid bare the motivating mechanism of John's antisocial career. On the surface it seems that he represents one of a group of offenders who deliberately choose a life of crime. However, there is enough in even this sketchy account of his mental make-up and behavior to suggest that possibly there were some streaks of aberration in John's personality. At all events, the case again illustrates the need of more penetrating and continuing analysis of the personalities of offenders than prisoners usually receive at the hands of the part-time prison psychiatrist. What we said in *500 Criminal Careers* about this case is still essentially relevant, so far as all but a very few prisons are concerned:

Nothing less than a patient, penetrating course of friendly psychologic analysis followed by proof of personal interest and friendship can be expected to pierce the wall of defence and defiance which the prisoner has built up around him. But such procedure is unheard of in the modern prison, even where a psychiatrist is present. For he is concerned rather with the routine of examining and classifying inmates upon their admission than with the much more important therapeutic possibilities of the individual prisoner. Psychiatry, or any other art purporting to deal with the stresses and strains of the human mind, will get nowhere unless and until a serious effort is made to experiment with various forms of personality analysis of criminals and with different methods of psychotherapy and character reorientation. To call this man a psychopath and stop there is not the beginning, but the end, of wisdom.

The added events in John's antisocial life again show that, apart from a far better supervision of parolees than was given him, there is need for a long-term or wholly indeterminate sentence policy. Had this man been retained in prison, the shooting tragedy would not have occurred and society would have been protected from John's many aggressive crimes. Under the proposed policy, he might have been held in custody until he gave proof of having passed the stage of aggressive criminality. The recommendation of the warden that John be released because he had been "punished enough," which was adopted by the parole board despite its misgivings, discloses the persistence among prison men of the notion that the chief aim of the criminal law is and should be pain-suffering punishment, rather than the practical and scientific point of view that the length of incarceration should be governed first and foremost by the dangerousness of the offender.

In considering whether a wholly indeterminate sentence based on the idea of releasing offenders when they are no longer aggressively dangerous is feasible, we may ask the question whether John's continuous career of aggression might have been foretold. The reader will find Chapters XIV, XV, and XVI illuminating on that score.

Finally, this case again illustrates the fact that the families of criminals are inclined often to partake of the sentiments of the underworld rather than of legitimate society. This makes especially difficult the work of probation and parole officers. It demonstrates the great significance of the fact that correctional treatment of the "individual offender" very often means correctional treatment of an entire family.

## ARMAND AND ROBERT. PART I[7]

Armand and Robert are brothers, Armand being Robert's senior by four years. These youths are two in a family of eight children. They were both born in Massachusetts, of French-Canadian parents. The father, a carpenter, had steady work but earned small wages. The family had to plan closely to make ends meet. Because of their poor economic circumstances they were forced to live in a cheap tenement district, where the street influences were none too good.

Armand, the older brother, would stay away from school very often for any excuse whatsoever. By reason of these frequent absences he had to repeat several grades. He finally left school in the fifth grade at the age of thirteen, and soon thereafter went to work. He showed considerable capacity, but because he ran about the streets with a gang of youths who did not believe in working, he did not remain on the job steadily. He did, however, hold one job in a rubber factory for a year and a half, and became a semi-skilled factory hand.

He was introduced to heterosexual experiences at the age of fourteen.

When sixteen, Armand was arrested for the first time for stealing iron from the railroad, for which offense he paid a fine of three dollars. About a year later

[7] In *500 Criminal Careers*, Varied Fruits of the Same Tree, p. 61.

he was again arrested, this time for larceny of a bicycle, and placed on probation. During part of the probation period he worked well and kept away from his vicious companions. After a few months, however, he threw up his job and did not report regularly to his probation officer, who thereupon surrendered him to the court, which placed Armand on probation a second time. He again began to work, but lied to the probation officer about his place of employment. Finally he ran away from home, and his parents did not know where he was. They had tried very hard to keep him working steadily, but with no success.

When Armand was twenty, he was arrested for the offence for which he was sentenced to the Reformatory—breaking and entering a store with a companion, and stealing postage stamps. The other youth was placed on probation while Armand served twelve months of a five-year indeterminate sentence. The "examiner" at the institution, whose duty it was to interview newcomers, said of Armand that he was "very pleasant during the examination, answered intelligently, and had a good memory." However, he found the youth "somewhat lacking in maturity of thought," and concluded that "employment to which he is adapted and good associations might make a different fellow of him. They would seem to be the two greatest requisites for his doing well."

On examination by the Reformatory physician, Armand was found to be in fair physical condition, of "borderline" intelligence, and very suggestible. It was also the physician's opinion that the new inmate "is a thief of long training."

Armand was given no special schooling in a trade at the Reformatory; he was engaged wholly in unskilled work. He was spoken of as "a willing, industrious worker, is always willing to do more than he is told. His conduct has been excellent." He was assigned to the fourth grade in school and was advanced to the fifth. His conduct there was satisfactory in every way. He committed only occasional offenses while in the Reformatory—that is, an average of one offense in four months—and his violations of the rules were relatively minor, such as talking and "fooling."

Upon release at the age of twenty-one, Armand went to live with his family, with whom he remained for about a year, making occasional trips away from home to New York City, Philadelphia, and Maine, presumably to seek employment. While on parole he held jobs on an average of three months, working as a farm hand, watchman, restaurant hand, and painter, and in machine shops.

Thirteen months after his parole from the Reformatory, Armand's permit to be at liberty was revoked because he had left his home and employment and had not reported the fact to his parole officer. The warrant for his arrest was for some reason withdrawn, however. Soon thereafter Armand married and went to work in a factory at twenty-five dollars a week.

About a year later, at the age of twenty-three, Armand was again in trouble for larceny. A watch belonging to another employee in the factory where he worked was stolen. Armand was not arrested, but left the employ of this company. Two months later the watch was discovered in a pawnshop, and Armand was then arrested by the police, the case was dismissed, and upon revocation of his parole permit he was returned to the Reformatory, where he remained for nine months.

During his second stay at the institution Armand's wife made many pleas for his release, saying he had worked steadily and had been a good provider and a good father, and, somewhat inconsistently, that he had stolen the watch because she and their child were both starving. It is true that Armand had great financial stress during this period. His wife was not well and there were many doctor's bills, not only for her but for the baby, to whom he was very devoted.

Soon after Armand's second release on parole, he enlisted in the Navy, where he served for six months and was honorably discharged.

During the five-year period following expiration of his sentence from the Reformatory Armand proved himself a good husband and father. He worked off and on as a house painter, receiving very good wages; in dull spells he took jobs for other contractors. To add to his income he often worked evenings, and he spent what leisure time he had with his wife and two children. He was able to save enough to buy a small three-room cottage and a Ford. He tried to save enough money to go into business for himself. His wife, an American girl of English parentage, a rather energetic person, was evidently the "boss" of the household. She was very loyal to Armand, and during his second period in the Reformatory she worked in order to support their child. Interviewed at the close of the first follow-up period, Armand attributed his "reform" to her influence. After his second release from the Reformatory he altogether changed his way of using his leisure time. He ceased hanging about pool-rooms, and came to the conclusion that the pleasures such recreations offer are illusory. "My wife and my kids are my pleasure now." His wife, an Episcopalian, freely attended her own church while he, though nominally a Roman Catholic, rarely went to church.

At the close of the first follow-up period, Armand was thirty-three years of age. On looking back over his experiences he attributed his early delinquencies to misdirected leisure. He said that little by little the gang he went with got into the habit of doing things to annoy the police. They enjoyed it as a game, and largely in a spirit of fun they learned the habit of raiding fruit stands and stores. A little later he met a "really tough fellow" through these companionships, a youth completely given over to crime, who induced him to commit the larceny for which he was sent to the Reformatory. Armand said that the first time he was sent to the institution, he felt resentful because he had been punished much more severely than his companions; but he soon got over it because of the fair treatment he received at the Reformatory. He was convinced that the fact that he had a loyal wife and a home to which to return on his second release from the institution kept him from further crime.

Armand claimed he could not see that the Reformatory had anything to do with changing his way of living. "They revoked my parole and sent me back there a second time. That shows they didn't reform me, doesn't it?" He pointed out that he did not receive any industrial training at the Reformatory, since he was kept only on plain, rough labor. Nor did he regard his parole supervision as having been either constructive or helpful.

Earnestly he offered his opinion as to how to cope with the problem of delinquency: "You got to grab them out of the cradle!" This he elaborated: "Young boys in their play time contract wrong habits which, if uncorrected, lead to criminal conduct."

Meanwhile, when Robert, Armand's brother, was eleven years old, he was placed by his parents in a denominational children's protectorate because he so frequently truanted from school. There he remained for six months and was then returned home. His mother recalled that at that time the priest told her he did not think Robert was mentally normal. The boy attended school until he was fourteen, and largely because of his very frequent truancy he never got beyond the fourth grade. Beginning work at fourteen, Robert, like Armand, ran about the streets with boys whose influence was altogether unwholesome. He bunked out, often for the whole night. He showed that he did not have as much capacity for work as Armand, and loafed a good deal. The longest job he held was one for eight months in a rubber factory.

At the age of seventeen, Robert was arrested for larceny. The court imposed a six months' sentence to a house of correction, he "appealed," and in the superior court was placed on probation.[8] His brother, Armand, had two years previously received his first sentence to the Reformatory and was now out on parole. A few months after Robert was placed on probation, he too was sentenced to the Reformatory for breaking, entering, and larceny with two companions. They broke into a cellar, took a sweater, two pillows, and four yards of carpet—of a total value of ten dollars. The boys had also broken into a store at night and taken tobacco and cigarettes.

Robert spent eighteen months in the Reformatory on this sentence. The examiner there found he had "very little education, almost no memory, and his

---

[8] "Appeal" in Massachusetts consists of a retrial of the case in the upper criminal court. It is frequently resorted to by offenders, as it almost always results in a reduction of sentence.

mind operates very slowly. His moral development is as defective seemingly as his mental. He began his downward career as a truant. He has had a tendency to steal and has added to his criminal acquirements the bunking-out habit of the vagrant. Has little inclination or capacity for industrial pursuits. Regard him as a defective delinquent."

The mental examination disclosed Robert to be a "moron and a sex offender." He violated institutional rules occasionally—that is, on the average of once in seven months. His offenses were "gross carelessness," being out of place, malicious mischief, talking, causing disturbance in school, and others.

Robert was assigned to the "sloyd" class (manual training) and to the cloth department. He also worked for a time in the stockade. The instructor in the sloyd class said of him that he was "industrious, but of inferior capability and does not get along so well with this work as he should." In the cloth department, however, he was reported to be "an industrious and capable creel tender." His disposition and conduct were good. In the stockade he was found to be of average capability, quiet disposition, and good conduct.

During his parole period on this sentence, Robert was again arrested for breaking and entering, and this time received a six months' sentence to a house of correction, which he again appealed. In the superior court this case was "filed."[9] For some reason, Robert's parole permit was not revoked as the result of this offense and he was not returned to the Reformatory.

When Robert was nineteen, he was again found guilty of breaking and entering, was sentenced to a house of correction for six months, and again promptly appealed from this sentence to the superior court, which a month later sentenced him to the Reformatory. On this occasion he had forced open the door of an unoccupied house and taken from the premises lead pipe, faucets, and other articles.

On this sentence to the Reformatory, Robert remained for twenty-one months and was again placed in the cloth department, where he learned weaving. He was also given seven months' training in carpentry and again worked in the stockade. He proved willing and cheerful, but none of the occupations in which he was engaged ever required any great mental ability. He seemed dependable and courteous at all times. In the carpentry shop it was found that he was "capable along ordinary lines, but has little, if any, mechanical ability"; his conduct was good. While Robert was serving on this sentence, Armand was returned to the Reformatory for violation of his parole.

Upon his second release Robert went to live with his mother, and worked for a little over a month as a bolter in a ship-building plant. He then enlisted in

---

[9] The practice of "filing" cases can be greatly abused, although it is often necessary for legitimate reasons.

the Army and went overseas. After two years he was honorably discharged and a few months later re-enlisted. By that time his parole period had expired. Two years after his second enlistment he was dishonorably discharged because of "sentence to imprisonment by a civil court."

When Robert came out of the Army, he went to live with his mother. He now did odd jobs on coal and ice wagons and in pick and shovel work. For six years after his second release on parole he was not known to commit any offenses; and though he loafed a good deal and made some money "shooting craps" his conduct was not very bad. In 1925, however, at the age of twenty-seven, he was arrested for indecent exposure and received a four months' sentence to a house of correction. He was at the same time also charged with larceny and breaking and entering and was granted probation of six months on the larceny charge, and of two years on the charge of breaking and entering. His own account of the charge of indecent exposure was that, seized with the need of going to the toilet and finding the railway station locked, he went to the side of the station where he thought he wouldn't be seen, when a young lady saw him and called some boys and they had him arrested.

During his stay in the house of correction, Robert was examined by the Massachusetts Department of Mental Diseases[10] and was diagnosed as a moron. Close supervision by a social agency, with special effort to avoid old companions and surroundings, was recommended. It was asserted that Robert "does not appear to have any markedly vicious tendencies." A year after his release from the house of correction, however, he again received a sentence of a year for indecent exposure, there being numerous complaints against him on this score. For a few years previously Robert had no very close pals and seemed to prefer his own company. He was rather bashful with a group, especially where there were girls.

Interviewed by our investigator, Robert was found to be a large, heavy-set fellow, with dark hair and oily skin. He admitted he had loafed a good deal and spent his leisure time largely in pool-rooms. He said that while he was at

[10] In 1924 an act (Mass. General Laws, chap. 309) was passed in Massachusetts providing for the psychiatric examination by the Department of Mental Diseases of convicted prisoners serving over thirty days (except for non-payment of fine) in a house of correction or jail and those known to have served a prior sentence. The histories gathered by the Division for Examination of Prisoners of the Department of Mental Diseases are comprehensive, covering the school record and economic and social history of the prisoner, and embracing in addition psychiatric and psychologic, as well as physical and neurologic, findings. Copies of the case histories are forwarded to both the Department of Correction and the Probation Commission, together with recommendations for transfer or other treatment of the individual prisoner. Very often these examinations represent the first scientific attempt to understand the antisocial conduct of an offender of long standing. However, this work is no longer being done.

the Reformatory, the idea of "turning over a new leaf" gradually dawned upon him and that since leaving the institution he had tried hard to behave. His history, however, showed that, despite his good intentions, Robert might be regarded as a failure, not only from the point of view of criminality, but in other respects: he had not settled down to any steady work, had loafed a great deal, had left jobs without any thought of the future, and felt no responsibility whatsoever toward his parents or himself.

## ARMAND AND ROBERT. PART II

What has happened to the brothers Armand and Robert in the ten years which have elapsed since the end of the first five-year follow-up?

It is gratifying at the outset to record that Armand appears to have fulfilled his earlier promise. He has committed no crimes. He and his wife have remained loyal to each other. No trouble has resulted from their religious differences. He has permitted her to rear the children in her faith. They are devoted to the two children, a son and daughter, both born before the end of the first five-year follow-up period. They have given them close supervision and not permitted them to play far away from home.

Although the family have moved a few times in order to save rent or improve their living conditions, they have continued to live in a suburban area away from the crowding of large cities, something quite different from the dingy tenement-district environment of his boyhood. The family of four now occupy five rooms of a two-family house owned by Armand's mother-in-law. His wife's sister lives in the other apartment. The home is furnished with old-fashioned, but comfortable and substantial, furniture and with pictures. There is plenty of light and air, the house standing in the middle of a large field, where the children play with those of the neighbors.

Armand has continued his occupation of house painter, though at times, particularly during the industrial depression, this has offered but a precarious livelihood. On occasion, his business has been sufficient to warrant employment of several other painters, but more often he has worked alone. He has also occasionally found it necessary to seek factory work or to take a job as a fireman on a locomotive, in order to fill in during periods when the painting business was slow. It was not until the height of the depression in 1932, just before the end of the second follow-up period, that Armand had to turn to the public welfare authorities for temporary financial aid. He has always given his earnings to his wife, because he has implicit judgment in her ability to manage their finances. He insists, in fact, that she is a "better businessman" than he. She is watchful of opportunities to bring to his attention any prospects for painting jobs.

The family has not been able to put by any savings, although a small amount of insurance is carried.

Armand has very friendly relations with his wife's family who live in the neighborhood, but he rarely sees or hears from his own people. Forty-two years of age at the close of the third follow-up period, Armand is on the whole content with his lot in life—a good wife, two bright children, a comfortable little home, an old Ford. His daughter is already attending high school and his son is a student at a teachers' college. Although Armand spends most of his leisure time with his family, his wife, evidently a wise psychologist as well as a shrewd manager, allows him to devote his Saturday nights to his cronies in the neighborhood, with whom he enjoys playing cards. She feels that this slight gambling can do no harm, particularly since Armand keeps only $1.50 a week out of his earnings for himself. He does not drink.

Criminologists, psychiatrists, psychologists, and sociologists may probe for the complex causes of Armand's rehabilitation. He himself insists, simply, that his settling down in life is due to his wife, for whom he bears the utmost affection and respect.

Before commenting on this case, let us retrace the career of Armand's brother, Robert. While Robert was in the house of correction on the charge of indecent exposure, the first five-year follow-up period ended. He was then not quite thirty-four years old. The next ten years have hardly been as happily spent as those of his brother Armand. During the first few years of the second follow-up period Robert wandered about the eastern part of the United States picking up jobs as a woodsman but not holding any for more than a few weeks. In the course of these wanderings he was arrested twice, once for lewdness (exposing himself to children) for which he was confined for four months in jail and on another occasion for vagrancy (walking the railroad tracks), for which he was given ten days in jail. Except for these two arrests Robert managed to avoid the police. His relatives, however (mother, stepfather, and at least two of his brothers and one sister) all acknowledge that he has an abnormal sex trend which induces him to expose himself in public places and even to chase women in lonely sections of the country. They describe him as "a large, strong, rugged man but with the mind of a child."

For a short time Robert made his home with his mother and stepfather in the country. The stepfather had a small farm and offered Robert a chance to work there, but he soon quarreled with his stepfather and left home. During most of the second follow-up period he dropped in on his relatives only when in great need. Even his mother hesitated to keep him in her house any length of time because she feared he would get himself into an embarrassing situation with his stepfather's daughter. When Robert's parents moved back from the farm into the city he saw them more often. Although his family never knew just where he was, he managed to turn up at critical periods. For example, when his mother died (toward the end of the second follow-up period) Robert arrived for the funeral. One of Robert's brothers commented, "I hunted him all the evening and could not find him and then he appeared at the funeral. I don't know where he came from. When we returned from the cemetery he had already gone off and none of us knew where he went."

During these years Robert has barely earned $10 a week but at no time has he asked for assistance from public agencies. In this respect his case contrasts sharply with that of Frank (pp. 10 et seq.). Robert has always managed to get along somehow with the few dollars received from relatives.

After his mother's death, Robert began to call more often at the home of a married sister who had several small children of whom he was very fond. The sister, when interviewed, believed Robert to be mentally deranged and "growing worse."

At thirty-five, when Robert secured a job as a lumper for a coal company, he ceased drifting any distance away. He lived by himself in a rooming house but moved very often within one general neighborhood. His leisure time was spent with corner loafers. He frankly admitted sex irregularities and loafing in cheap restaurants. Except for the years spent drifting about the country, he has tended to make his home in crowded and dirty rooming-house areas among mixed ethnic groups. His brother-in-law commented that although Robert had never saved any money, he had shown a certain thriftiness in laying by money for an immediate need such as a new suit; he had a great knack, when he wanted to, of "gathering nickels and dimes and hanging on to them." This statement assumes significance when we see what happened to Robert a little later on. Meanwhile he carried no insurance nor did he ever assume any financial responsibility for anyone else. By the time he was thirty-six, Robert was earning about $12 a week and, for the first time in his life, holding on to a job he had secured on a coal delivery truck. He explained that he liked this work, because it kept him out of doors. Apparently the urge to wander over the countryside which he had in the earlier years had now ceased. In the past he would deliberately seek jobs as a casual laborer, admitting that he never stayed in one place more than six weeks. As soon as the work became somewhat monotonous, he would begin to think of traveling further. Sometimes, he told us, the urge to wander would attack him so severely and so suddenly that he would not even stop to collect his wages.

By the middle of the third follow-up span, Robert's inclination toward settling down to more conventional ways of life had become clear. When interviewed at this time he mentioned that in his rooming house there is a radio which he liked to listen to in the evenings; that he liked to go about "calling on folks," and that he spent one or two evenings a week at the home of his married sister. He also enjoyed a corner chat with his friends. He insisted he no longer indulged in any abnormal sexual activities. He told our investigator that he had gotten fed up with traveling about, not knowing where he would get his next meal; that the hardships of a hobo's life finally caused him to give up his travels. But he chose outdoor work because he liked fresh air and a job in which he had to move about a great deal. When asked about his plans for the future he expressed the ambition to become a mail carrier. Up to the end of the third follow-up period, however, he continued to work on a coal truck, had changed jobs only once, and then only because the wages offered him were higher. Eventually he earned $25 a week.

So at the end of the third five-year follow-up span, Robert, at thirty-nine, was steadily engaged as a laborer, the days of *Wanderlust* and overt abnormal sex expression evidently well behind him.

Our information about Robert extends three years beyond the end of the third follow-up period and is well worth recording. Shortly after the end of the period, Robert's sister introduced him to a young woman with two children who had recently been divorced from her husband. Robert became very much interested in her and they soon married and settled down in a neighboring city in a single house in a good residential section near a large park. Since Robert and his wife both worked (she was a forelady in a laundry) they have jointly made a good living. She has induced him to carry a $1,000 insurance policy. Robert comments that he would have married his wife twenty years sooner had he known her. Our investigator noticed that his stepchildren, fifteen and eighteen years old, call him "Daddy" and that the family relationships are entirely pleasant. Robert, like his brother Armand, turns over all his earnings to his wife who pays all the bills and manages the household affairs. They do not have a car, but his wife's brother frequently takes the family out riding. Robert comments that before marriage he used to like to hang about the street corners and would go with a gang of "tough nuts" and that he wasted his time. Since marriage he is content to stay at home evenings and read the newspapers and magazines and now feels that he "is getting something out of life." He does not attend church or belong to any clubs. He still has an idea that he would like to be a mail carrier or do similar work as long as it would keep him outdoors.

It should be said that Armand and Robert rarely if ever see each other. Armand considers Robert mentally deficient and Armand's wife has long felt that Robert is not a desirable person. When, however, Robert was in great need during the second follow-up period, Armand gave him a chance to earn a few dollars by helping him on painting jobs. Both brothers have settled down to conventional living, Armand at the age of twenty-six and Robert at thirty-seven. Robert's slower personality integration is perhaps due to the fact that he is of lower mentality than Armand.

In *500 Criminal Careers* the lives of these brothers had unrolled only through the first follow-up period, when Armand was twenty-seven years old and Robert twenty-four. At that time, Robert was still a wanderer and sexual offender. We then asked certain questions, the answers to which could not be fully given until a further segment of the life histories of these men was available. We asked, for instance (page 66):

In the light of their similar family background, early habits, and general environment, why should one brother turn out well, the other so poorly? In one case, of course, there was a loyal and capable wife, whose very attitude and wholesomeness probably encouraged good behaviour; in the other case there was a continued influence of street life and lack of loyalties and ideals of a worthy nature. But were there not also fundamental differences in innate mental equipment and personality?

We see more clearly now that there were these differences, certainly so far as intelligence is concerned; and, if one may draw an inference from the pathologic sexual behavior of Robert, there was also a difference in instinctual-emotional equipment. It is to be noted that Robert's settling down and abandonment of pathologic sex expression date several years prior to his stumbling upon the same good fortune as his brother in the form of an understanding and loyal spouse. Armand's wife seems to have played a considerable role in initiating her husband's good behavior; Robert's wife arrived on the scene after her prospective husband had already definitely abandoned his wanderer's irresponsible life and sexual misconduct; but she has doubtless acted as a prop in maintaining her husband on a socially acceptable road.

However, it seems quite clear that Robert achieved a socially adequate degree of personality integration at a much later chronologic age than did Armand. In two previous works[11] we have presented the theory of maturation as a basic explanation of the changes in criminal conduct with the passage of time. Analysis of numerous innate and acquired factors in the careers of our men up to the end of the first follow-up period and of a thousand boy delinquents through the third five-year span following their contact with a juvenile court, led to the conclusion that it is not arrival at any particular age span

---

[11] *Later Criminal Careers*, Chaps. IX, X, XIII; *Juvenile Delinquents Grown Up*, New York, The Commonwealth Fund, 1940, Chap. VIII, pp. 267–270.

but the achievement of a degree of maturity adequate to social adaptation, that seems reasonably to account for the abandonment of criminalistic ways. As we said in *Juvenile Delinquents Grown Up,*

Maturity is a complex concept. It embraces the development of a certain stage of physical, mental, and emotional capacity and stability, and a certain degree of integration of the personality. Common experience indicates that as the average person passes through different age spans there are changes in his development and in the integration or disintegration of his various physical, intellectual, emotional, and volitional-inhibitory powers. Normally, when he reaches chronologic adulthood the development and integration of his physical and mental powers make it easier for him to achieve a capacity for self-control, foresight, planfulness; to postpone immediate desires for later ones; to profit by experience; to develop perseverance, self-respect, regard for the opinion of his law-abiding fellows, and other similar attributes. These enable him to adapt successfully to the demands of society and to avoid drifting into, or persisting in, crime. However, individuals differ in their innate organization and in their early conditioning, so that development and integration of powers sufficient to be designated "maturity" are not always achieved at the expected age span.

As was indicated in *Later Criminal Careers,* the years from about twenty-five to thirty-five seem to be the most crucial in the lives of offenders, since during this age-zone there appears to occur the peak of a sifting-out process which differentiates those who mature normally from those who are inclined never to reach a stage of maturity sufficient to enable them to abandon criminalism, and who will either die as criminals or end their days in almshouses or on the streets. The offenders who are still criminalistic even at the relatively late age of thirty to thirty-five years (the highest age thus far reached by any of our former juvenile delinquents) are those whose pace of maturing is particularly slow, retarded, or otherwise erratic. Our comparison of the make-up and background of the men who have reformed and those who are still criminals confirms the suggestion made in *Later Criminal Careers* that, with the passage of the years, a differentiation seems to occur between the offenders whose delinquency and criminality are due more to adverse environmental and educational influences than to any deep-seated organismal weaknesses, and those whose inability to conform to the demands of a complex society is more nearly related to innate (and, partly, early-conditioned) abnormalities of the kind that set limits to the achievement of a socially adequate degree of maturity. The former, sooner or later, acquire the requisite degree of integration of intelligence, impulse, and behavior. The latter never achieve a stage of maturity requisite to lawful social adaptation. Despite their arrival at a high chronologic age, they continue to be criminalistic until physically and mentally "burned out." Misbehavior due to *un*integration gives way to misbehavior due to *dis*integration, until the organism runs down and finally stops.[12]

[12] *Juvenile Delinquents Grown Up,* pp. 267–269.

Whether the abandonment of criminalism at approximately the age when Robert settled down could have been foretold long before the event, is shown by his predictive score on p. 229, which should be compared with that of Frank, the first case described, whose behavior and background, and to some extent his intellectual make-up, partly resemble those of Robert. Frank, it will be recalled, is still antisocial; and at least one sign of his not having as yet achieved adequate maturity is the conviction of his family that though well beyond the middle forties Frank is still "boyish in his emotional reactions." This should be contrasted with the adult attitudes of Robert.

However, much more thorough personality studies than those contributed by the various psychiatrists and psychologists who had made merely routine examinations of Armand and Robert in institutions would be necessary to establish conclusively the differences in their innate equipment which might account for the variation in their pace of maturation. As we said of the two brothers in *500 Criminal Careers,* fundamental differences in innate mental equipment and personality should have been noted by the courts before whom these men originally appeared as boys. It will not be amiss to repeat the questions we there asked (page 67) : "Is some mental condition related to the sex offences of Robert, and if so, could it not have been discovered in childhood or later and somehow controlled?" We may ask, further, whether psychiatry and kindred disciplines can evolve techniques for hastening the maturation process. "Why are not the courts, before which Robert was brought for indecent exposure, equipped with psychiatric facilities for observation and report upon cases of this kind? Why do not our psychiatrists experiment in peno-correctional institutions with various forms of therapy? What, in general, should be the role of psychiatry and psychology in the administration of criminal justice?"

These questions are still vital and timely.

## ARTHUR. PART I[13]

When Arthur, an only child, was but a boy, his father, a coarse, crude, and brutal Pennsylvania coal miner of Dutch ancestry, died. Both parents were native-born, of Protestant faith. The father did not send the boy to school, but forced him to work in the mines. There Arthur, at thirteen, suffered a head injury, which a number of persons familiar with his early life believe may somehow have contributed to the boy's limited intellectual development. Upon the death of the father the home was broken up and the boy and his mother, a respectable and kindly woman, went to live in the home of a grandmother. It

[13] In *500 Criminal Careers,* The Mental Defective in a Protected Environment, p. 67.

was then that Arthur began to attend school. He got no farther than the fourth grade.

Leaving school at fourteen, Arthur began to work as a farm hand for a brief time, and then as a moving-picture-machine operator. His industrial activity was, however, very sporadic and irregular. He passed from occupation to occupation, but seemed unable to remain very long at any kind of work.

When Arthur was seventeen, his mother remarried, and he went to reside with her in Springfield, Massachusetts. The stepfather was very kind to the youth. He noted, however, that even at that time Arthur could hardly read or write. Shortly after his mother's remarriage Arthur was arrested for "breaking and entering and larceny," having stolen a bicycle. He was placed on probation for two years. The probation officer said that while under his supervision the youth acted very strangely. He would do things on the impulse of the moment and then be sorry he had done them. The probation officer seems to have been particularly planful in his work. He had Arthur examined by the school psychologist, who found that the youth was "a typical moron in intelligence." The probation officer "tried various occupations for this boy—electricity, work in a factory, on a farm; nothing seems to appeal to him." Finally it was arranged that he go to live on a farm, where he remained for a year. During that time it was rumored that the youth was committing petty larcenies in the neighborhood. Arthur complained that the farmer overworked him. "This boy," said the probation officer, "to my mind is more to be pitied than censured, because I feel that he should be confined in some institution not a penal institution, where they can take care of him for the rest of his life."

During his stay on the farm Arthur took from a shelf in the barn a shotgun belonging to the son of his employer, carried it to the woods, and hid it there. It was later found and returned to the owner. Arthur maintained that he had no intention of either selling or keeping the weapon, but had used it for shooting woodchucks. For this offense, however, he received a five-year indeterminate sentence to the Reformatory. The examiner there was of the opinion that Arthur "is of very inferior ability, because he had received only $15 monthly during his employment on the farm, and when he was a 'second-class' moving-picture operator he received but $12 weekly." He added that the latter "was the only work Arthur was interested in."

Upon examination at the Reformatory, Arthur's physical condition was found to be only fair. He was diagnosed as "a moron and over-suggestible." But the physician added that "with good supervision he might succeed."

Arthur remained in the Reformatory for sixteen months. He was given some training in the plumbing class and worked in the dining-room. The dining-room officer stated that he did not "consider Arthur mentally responsible, but that he does make an honest effort to do the work as well as it should be done. His principal difficulty has been his insistent talking, which it seems impossible for him to stop, and no warnings or repeated reports for this offense seem to have any effect on him." From the plumbing instructor the report was substantially the same. Arthur was considered "a fair worker, with very limited capacity." In the Reformatory school he was admitted to the fourth grade, but made very little progress. He committed institutional offenses as often as once every three weeks. His violations of the rules involved not only talking, but disobedience of orders, persistent shirking, gross carelessness, lying, insolence, inattention, and similar acts indicating his inability to adapt himself to the institutional routine.

After sixteen months, at the age of twenty-one, Arthur was paroled. It was arranged by the parole agent that he should go to New Haven, to live with his mother and stepfather who had recently moved from Springfield because of the mother's illness. During this parole period Arthur, with the assistance and encouragement of his family, made every effort to keep at work and to lead an honest life. He was occupied fairly regularly, doing odd jobs at painting and gardening, as a plumber's helper, and in a machine shop. He held these jobs on an average of three months. Whenever he was out of employment, he helped his parents at home, doing chores about the house. He finally succeeded in getting a "first-class" license as a moving-picture operator. He even attended an evening school to study reading and writing, an elementary class in electricity, and a swimming class. He joined a lodge. He attended church regularly. On several occasions he expressed his gratitude to the parole officer and the Reformatory. "I have been able to see how to live a better life," he once wrote. And again: "I like my work very much and I am so glad to be able to do it. I am at home with my parents and have no desire to leave them. We are very happy in the home, and I am content to stay there." His mother also was grateful. "Thanks for the training Arthur received," she once wrote. "He has got on the right road." Later she stated: "Arthur has been very good and the training he has received at the school has been a wonderful help such as put him on the right road for which I am very thankful." And again: "Arthur is a different boy since he came home. He attends church with us, he pledged to the church the sum of $25 per year for three years beside his regular offerings and I am very glad to say he has kept his promise. We hope he may build himself up this summer in the outdoors work, he is right aside the shore so can bathe. I do not think we ever will have cause to worry over him again and I must say it is a big load off my heart."

Such was the story of the rehabilitation of Arthur until three years after the beginning of his parole period. When he was twenty-four, the progress he had made was suddenly broken by his arrest for burglary. He had entered the home of a friend and had taken some small things. His mother then wrote to the parole officer: "It is with much sorrow I have to tell you Arthur has broken his parole. But he wants me to write and tell you. . . . I am sure you will agree with me prison is no place for a boy of his nature. He is kind and good only for that one fault. The training he got while in the Reformatory made a new boy of him it done more in them few months than I ever thought could be."

The public defender of New Haven wrote the Massachusetts parole board, asking that Arthur's parole permit should not be revoked: "The charge against him is serious in a way, yet there are some things connected with the facts that ought to mitigate the offense. First, he is mentally defective; and, second, his mother desires that he be given a chance on probation here. The Reverend X—, a minister, is interested in the boy and wishes to take charge of him as special probation officer."

Arthur was not returned to the Reformatory, but remained in New Haven and was carefully supervised, by both his parents and the minister. He continued to live with his parents and worked as an unskilled factory hand. Soon after the expiration of his parole period he married. Though he had been working fairly regularly, he had not been able to earn enough to tide him over during periods of unemployment. Both his parents and his wife's parents helped him during such times. He had been able to earn as much as $23 a week. Recently he moved with his wife and one child, three years of age, to a semirural section not far from New Haven, where they lived with the wife's married sister. His stepfather was of the conviction that Arthur's wife "is a darn sight too good for him." She was very devoted to her husband, although once or twice she had been tempted to leave him because of his inability to keep at work steadily. Previous to his marriage he had become interested in a girl of very inferior family who was known to be feebleminded, but this attachment was broken off at the time of his last arrest. His stepfather philosophized eugenically that "it would have been a misfortune to have two 'nuts' married."

Arthur was idle about a third of the time during the first five-year period. He was the kind of worker who is taken on only in rush times, and then only for brief periods. His stepfather saw that Arthur did quite well under direction in electrical work and in such jobs as setting up and repairing radios, for which he seemed to have a real liking. He even made a radio set of his own. The stepfather thought it unfortunate that the youth was not trained in work of that kind. It was his opinion that though the Reformatory helped Arthur somewhat, it did not give him suitable industrial oversight, as the authorities evidently had not ascertained his particular capabilities and given him proper vocational training. He had always been mechanically inclined and had tinkered a good deal with inventions, a fact that the Reformatory authorities should have recognized and built upon.

While the stepfather criticized the lack of vocational guidance at the Reformatory, he acknowledged that Arthur had greatly improved in health and general conduct since his stay in the institution; that he apparently did not learn any bad habits there; nor did he fall into bad company. Probably he did not follow up his Reformatory acquaintances because he immediately came to New Haven to live.

During the first five-year period Arthur and his wife attended church regularly, the pastor of this church being the one who had offered to supervise him during his last probation period. He spent his leisure time with his wife and did not hang around the streets. He was not arrested at all during the five years in question, and the police had no trouble with him. He was known to be good-natured, kind-hearted, and perfectly willing to work when he could get work. Neither the police nor his parents, wife, or minister, thought him likely to revert to crime again.

Arthur seemed to be able to get along very well in the community with such assistance as he was receiving from his family and friends. It will be noted that he attended evening school to take a course in electricity. It is possible that if, during his sixteen months in the institution, he had received the training that he really wanted, he would have been very much more successful industrially than he was during the first post-parole period. At all events, he seemed to have made a socially acceptable adjustment.

## ARTHUR. PART II

Arthur's successful adjustment to family life was short-lived, partly because he did not work steadily and, more important, because of sexual difficulties. Arthur's wife developed a feeling of repulsion for him because he was too aggressive sexually and was losing control with advancing years. However, for several years she tried to adapt herself to the situation without taking any drastic steps.

The family continued to live near New Haven. Because of Arthur's frequent unemployment, his wife decided to apply for a child to board. Their own youngster was already five years old and she felt she could easily take care of another child. However, the agency that made the investigation of her application was "very dubious about this home. Mrs. Z— has a very pleasing personality and is apparently very fond of children but the financial situation in the home is very questionable and it is doubtful whether it would be advisable to place a child here." So this means of additional income was denied. Arthur had been averaging only $10 or $12 a week over the past years since the end of the first follow-up period, in part-time employment by an upholsterer, but was finally discharged in the middle of the second five-year span. Arthur's wife went out of the home from time to time to do housework in order to supplement the very inadequate family income. Meanwhile a job paying $45 a month and meals was found for Arthur as an orderly in a local hospital. There he remained for a year and then was laid off.

A routine physical examination given by the hospital to prospective employees revealed that he had frequent headaches, nervousness, and tremors of the hands. A few months later while still in the hospital's employ, Arthur again complained of nervousness and tremors. It was thought at this time that a psychosis was developing and he was referred to a psychiatric clinic but did not go.

Since this last lay-off, which occurred in 1931 when Arthur was thirty-four years old, he has had only sporadic work. Financial aid was given the family by several local agencies. It became necessary for his wife to take a position as a matron in a theatre, a job which she has held steadily ever since and for which she gets $12.50 a week.

Arthur's wife began to express a desire to separate from her husband, not only because of her personal feeling of revulsion for him but because she was convinced he would be a bad influence on their little son. Shortly after the end of the second follow-up period she carried out her long-held wish to leave Arthur, taking the little boy with her. When the home was broken up, Arthur, then unemployed, found a room in a house of prostitution. He insists he had nothing whatsoever to do with the ménage but was merely a lodger.

After Arthur's wife left him, he drifted about in New Haven from one rooming house to another. His step-parents did not keep in close touch with him, because he had always shown an inclination to depend on them for aid. Arthur was supported by the welfare agencies and only now and then picked up a job. One summer he did chores at a hotel, earning $25 a month and board; for a few months he had a job as general helper in an automobile salesroom, earning $15 a week; occasionally he picked up an odd job of painting. But public support was necessary after his wife's departure.

After several months' lodging in the house of ill fame, Arthur moved to a much better neighborhood and on the whole had made his home in rather decent urban areas. He never made any attempt to contribute to the support of his boy but saw him occasionally, usually through an accidental meeting in the street. Arthur's step-parents considered him a "nut." They deeply regretted that his childhood head injury had not been handled by operation, as originally suggested by a surgeon. They were convinced that Arthur's defectiveness was the result of this accident and that it was too late now to do anything about it. Arthur's wife had hoped when she married him that she might make something of him. His family felt that if anyone could do this she had the capacity, but because of his increasing lack of self-control, particularly in the sexual sphere, and his growing indifference and deterioration as a worker, she finally became discouraged.

Arthur had avoided any trouble with the police and there was no reason to think that he had committed any offenses which might have brought him to official attention. In the previous few years he had been rather seclusive, and too lacking in ambition or initiative to make any plans for himself. He had come to depend on what guidance the social welfare agencies gave him. Left to his own devices, he drifted into a demoralizing environment, but he adapted himself well to a better one if someone else provided it for him. He was considered a harmless sort of defective in need of constant guidance.

Toward the end of the third follow-up period, Arthur's wife remarried and had no further contact with him. At forty-two, he was lodging with a respectable family who found him most acceptable. He happened to have a job in a restaurant working nights and earned $10 a week and his meals. He managed to carry a small amount of insurance but had no savings and was content to depend on the welfare agencies for aid during his very frequent periods of unemployment. Arthur's son visited him occasionally. Meanwhile Arthur's stepfather had died and there were no relatives who cared to keep in touch with him.

Our investigator, who interviewed Arthur on three different occasions, comments that the first of these three meetings, occurring when Arthur was about thirty, left the impression that he was then a "suppressed child"; on the occasion of the second interview, when Arthur was thirty-five, he appeared to be "a somewhat worried and resourceless dependent"; and on the occasion of the third contact, when Arthur was forty-two, he was "a young man just beginning to get the hang of things."

Whether early recognition of Arthur's evident special mechanical ability through proper vocational guidance in the Reformatory, and provision of training in the trade which appealed to him, would have been a sufficient source of stability to make him more of a success cannot now be said. At all events, his case illustrates the inadequacy of ordinary institutional diagnoses of mental conditions. In general intelligence, Arthur was apparently below par; but sometimes a special aptitude in a socially useful direction is able to compensate for general mental defect.

This case indicates that despite the efforts of a sober and intelligent wife, personality equipment, whether innate or affected by some trauma, may be inadequate for successful living in a highly complex and competitive society. Resort, whenever necessary, to the aid of social welfare agencies has taken the place of criminalism in other cases of this nature; but adaptation, both to marital life and industrial demands, has been only very imperfect in Arthur's case. His intervening success was in large measure due to the supporting influence of his wife and friends who helped to supervise him. Removal of these human props disclosed vividly the relative immaturity of Arthur. His prediction score on p. 229 of course foretells only whether or not he was destined to recidivate; it does not indicate his probable adaptation to family and industrial life.

## DENNIS. PART I[14]

The parents of Dennis are of Irish birth. He himself was born in this country. His father died when the boy was but seven years old, and the family were left in difficult financial circumstances. Dennis is the oldest of three children. His family say that he "always lacked common sense," that he was always "an easy mark," and that from earliest childhood they were unable to cope with and counteract the influences of the streets upon him. The two other children, a brother and a sister, showed no signs of delinquency, and Dennis has long been regarded as the black sheep of the family.

Dennis completed the first year of high school at fifteen, and shortly thereafter began to work as an errand boy. About this time, also, he was introduced to heterosexual experiences. Throughout his industrial career Dennis showed good capacity, and even ability to hold a job; but he appears to have made little effort to do so. Instead, he loafed and drank a good deal.

His first arrest occurred when he was nineteen. The charge was drunkenness, and he was "released."[15] Shortly afterwards he was arrested for larceny of a bicycle and was given six months' probation. Not long thereafter he was again arrested for larceny from a building, and the case was *nol prossed*.[16] When he was twenty-three, he was committed to the House of Correction for eight months, on a charge of assault and battery.

During his youth Dennis had acquired some industrial skill as a machinist's

[14] In *500 Criminal Careers*, The Alcoholic Turns Bootlegger, p. 71.

[15] In Massachusetts, probation officers are given authority to release, without court appearance, persons arrested for drunkenness, under certain circumstances and conditions (General Laws, chap. 272, sec. 46; *Probation Manual* published by the Massachusetts Commission on Probation, fourth edition, July 1921, pp. 46–47).

[16] The district attorney's "royal prerogative" to refuse to prosecute cases can be greatly abused.

helper and held two jobs for as long as a year and a half. When regularly employed, he seemed to have no trouble with the police.

At the age of twenty-four Dennis was arrested for breaking the plate-glass window of a shoe store and taking one shoe. He was under the influence of liquor at the time. For this offense he was sentenced to the Reformatory on a five-year indeterminate sentence. The examiner who talked with him upon his admission found him to be "very courteous and frank, a man of normal intelligence with a capacity to respond to training and amply capable of earning a good living. . . . He has much force of character and could do well if he would exert himself to do what he knows is right." The institution psychiatrist, however, diagnosed him as a "psychopath."

As he had had the equivalent of grammar-school education, Dennis was not compelled to attend the institutional school, but worked during part of his incarceration in the laundry and for part of the time in the shoe shop. He was also employed as a "runner," a position of trust, was found to be very efficient, and made an excellent record in every respect. He indulged in no misconduct whatsoever while in the institution. In asking the parole board to release him, he wrote: "I have seen that if I want to live as a human being should live, I will have to respect the laws of the state. I have profited by my stay here to know that I will have to do an honest day's work and give up drink if I want to gain the respect of decent people. My mother needs my help and I am determined to bring no more disgrace upon her. I am now a better man in every way than I was when I came here."

After twelve months in the Reformatory, where his conduct had been perfect, Dennis was released on parole and returned to his mother's home. He was now twenty-five years old. He went to work for a plumber and remained there for one year, earning thirteen dollars a week. Soon thereafter, however, he was arrested with a companion for larceny from a common carrier. The police officer saw two men seizing bundles from a parcel delivery wagon, and when Dennis and his companion were caught, a tussle ensued, so that the officer had to call for assistance. For this offense Dennis' permit to be at liberty was revoked and he was returned to the Reformatory, where he remained for four months. Again his conduct in the institution was perfect. Dennis wrote to the parole board: "I am behaving myself first rate and intend to do so in the future. I surely realize that I got the chance of a lifetime and I intend to grasp the opportunity now."

On his second release on parole Dennis worked for three months as a helper in a store. He soon began to drink, however, and within a few months was again arrested for larceny from a common carrier. The driver of an express company team apprehended Dennis after he had stolen three watches from the wagon, which was standing unguarded. Again Dennis was returned to the Reformatory, this time remaining six months. Once more his conduct in the institution was perfect.

With his usual promise of making good, Dennis was for a third time released on parole and worked for four months as a truckman, receiving $15 a week, when he was again arrested, this time for "larceny from the person." The complainant, an elderly gentleman on temporary release from a mental hospital, testified that he became ill on the street, and while he lay on the sidewalk awaiting the arrival of an ambulance, Dennis and a companion emerged from the crowds and picked his pockets, abstracting nine dollars. For the fourth time Dennis' parole permit was revoked and he was returned to the Reformatory, where he now remained eleven months. And again his conduct in the institution was perfect. Nine months of the eleven were spent at a prison camp[17] on Dennis' own request. In making his plea for transfer Dennis read the authorities an ingenious and not altogether unjustified lesson in penology, flavored with a dash of blarney:

Now gentlemen in dictating this letter to you I am not going to write three or four pages as do not think it necessary just a few lines and I think it will cover everything. Now I have been here only a little over two months having been revolked back here by the commissioners now this institution is alright for a man having been committed here the first or even the second time but after that to my way of thinking, it is only an unnecessary burden thrown upon the shoulders of the State. It has been the third time I have been sent back for violation of my parole in one way or an other. Now why not put me on one of the state farms where the state will gain more compensation and where I will derive more benefit morally and physically and be better capable to go out and meet the demands of the outside world when I am released. Esepecially now when all the world is clamering and crying for manual labor of one kind or another. Now I fully reliaze that I am only one of a number of others who are seeking this chance to make good hoping you gentlemen will consider my application favorably or that you will grant me an interview the next time you come to the reformatory.

On his fourth parole Dennis worked as a teamster, continuing to do so to the expiration of his parole period (a year and a half), earning $25 a week. His parole officer said of him: "He is not a bad fellow at all, but drinks morning, noon, and night, and would steal while under the influence of liquor."

[17] This prison camp no longer exists. It used to be operated on the plan of an "honor camp." Inmates found to be trustworthy in any of the county or state institutions were given opportunity to be transferred to the camp. The men were employed in outdoor work and thus had a chance to regain normal health and vigor. Most of them had served the greater part of their sentences before being transferred.

Dennis lived with his mother and sister for six months of his post-parole period, when he was again arrested for attempted larceny from the person. This time he received a suspended sentence to the house of correction. Two years later, at the age of thirty-two, being arrested for having morphine in his possession and for violating the liquor law, Dennis was sentenced for two years to the house of correction, from which place he was released in eighteen months. He again made his home with his mother and sister, this time for eleven months. Then he was once more arrested for larceny from the person and for being a vagabond, and was again sentenced to the house of correction, where he remained for six months.

Upon his release he went off to seek his fortune in a nearby city and was there arrested some two months later on suspicion of pickpocketing, but was released by the police. Thereupon he returned home and again took up his residence with his mother and sister. But soon he was again arrested. This time his offense was keeping and exposing liquor, and he was ordered to pay a fine of $75 and to serve four months in the house of correction. He appealed, and upon retrial in the superior court was fined $150. Six months later he was again arrested as a vagabond, but was found "not guilty."

The industrial career of Dennis was very sporadic. He worked as a truckman and then off and on in a shoe factory and at various odd jobs. He was most of the time engaged in bootlegging. He always paid his board when working. His mother and sister occupied the middle flat of a three-tenement wooden house in a crowded neighborhood of Irish and other nationalities. The district was quiet, neat, and reputable, and its inhabitants were laboring people.

At the end of the first five-year follow-up period Dennis was thirty-seven years old. He frankly stated that the hazard of being caught was worth taking; that one could be pretty sure of getting off with a fine, and that the fine was part of the expenses of the "business" (referring to the bootlegging trade). He admitted that his companions were largely such fellows as would patronize an illegal liquor shop; he looked upon it as good business to "be in with a sporting bunch." Among his companions were many with whom he became acquainted in the Reformatory and in the houses of correction. Though he had manifested a marked interest in reading while at the Reformatory, he did not follow up that interest.

He explained his misconduct by what he called the "force of circumstances," the lure of companionship and of "easy money," together with a lack of other interests, and the failure of all the institutions, including the Reformatory, to implant in him an "inspiration toward other ways of living." He admitted that the first time he was sent to the Reformatory he had the idea that he would thereafter "go straight," but that somehow he could not overcome the "circumstances" which he met with on the outside, and that his poor companionships and the lack of some inspiring influence after his release may account for his continued antisocial conduct. His attitude was that he did not intend ever hereafter to commit anything in the nature of a felony, but to stick to liquor selling, which he regarded as perfectly legitimate, "if you can get away with it"; merely a risky sort of business. The reason he gave for deciding to avoid felonious acts was "simply that it did not pay. You are pretty sure to get caught and sent away. Only a fool would keep on for ever doing that. Crime don't pay."

Our social worker who interviewed Dennis was of the opinion that this case was typical of the one child in a family who "goes wrong"; that upon the whole the boys and girls in the slum districts "muddle through" and make a remarkable success in life when one considers the handicaps in environment, disordered homes, and improper parental oversight under which they labor.

These persistent misdemeanors of the one delinquent in the family seem to indicate fundamental conative-emotional traits which made him more susceptible than the average child to the demoralizing influences about him.

## DENNIS. PART II

By the end of the first follow-up period Dennis had apparently become settled in a bootlegging business, but this was soon broken up by an arrest for possessing and selling drugs, for which he received a two-and-a-half year sentence to the house of correction. Meanwhile he had been making his home with a married sister who had several small children and with whom his mother was also boarding. Before this arrest Dennis was doing irregular work as a truckman. He paid board to his sister whenever he could, but this was very irregularly. Although when out of work Dennis would help his sister a little with the children, he was always out evenings and the family never knew where he spent his time; it was not in the neighborhood of his home, because local police said that they rarely saw him thereabouts. Dennis' mother often compared him with her other children, a daughter and a son, neither of whom had been in any difficulties. The whole family looked upon Dennis as the black sheep, but nevertheless remained loyal to him. In being questioned about the dangers of the bootlegging business, he commented that the hazard of arrest is worth taking because "one can be pretty sure of getting off with a fine . . . the fine is part of the expenses of the business and is taken care of by your backer."

Upon release from the house of correction, Dennis returned to his sister's home. He found a job in a shoe factory where he worked off and on for about a year. During this time his sister died and Dennis, never too eager for regular employment, began to devote himself to the care of his sister's children.

Whether he remained in his sister's home for so many years (throughout the three five-year follow-up periods) because of his devotion to the family or because he had become a confirmed drug addict and a fixed residence made it possible for him to secure the drug more readily from someone with whom he must have been dealing for a long time, is a question. The fact remains that when, toward the end of the first follow-up period, Dennis' sister died, he practically gave up all efforts to secure and keep employment and bore the brunt of the care of the four children, who at that time ranged in age from about five to ten years. Dennis' mother was not strong nor did she have great patience with them; and his brother-in-law, a fireman, was away from home a great part of the time and only too glad to entrust the care of the children to his mother-in-law and brother-in-law. Dennis drank occasionally, partly because of his association with bootleggers. However, he never permitted himself to get into a drunken state in the presence of his nieces and nephews, nor for that matter did he ever show any outward signs of addiction to drugs. He was very careful in his language and manners before them and his mother.

Dennis claimed he never felt the need for much companionship. He liked to be by himself and did not actively seek associates.

He admitted having picked pockets in order to secure money for "dope" and having become involved, now and then, in the sale of drugs. Other than this he insisted he had not been engaged in any criminal activities.

Interviewed before the end of the third follow-up period, Dennis was found to be a mild-mannered, easy-going individual and rather suggestible. Our investigator commented that "there is nothing he wants to do; there is nothing he wants to contribute either to other people or himself . . . An empty, healthy, well-set-up duffer."

For seven years (well into the third follow-up span), Dennis was not arrested. He insisted that after his release from the house of correction he no longer indulged in the use of heroin; that he "kicked it out," because it was not possible to secure the drug. This may or may not have been so. It seems doubtful, however, that after years of indulgence he was able to stop of his own accord without treatment, except for the deprivation of the drug that he had to undergo while at the house of correction.

Dennis must have been exceedingly careful in the use of drugs, because the police in his neighborhood were under the impression that for a number of years he had kept free of the habit. Prior to his last commitment to the house of correction they had known him to be a "cokie" and to belong to a gang who would break into stores or steal from carriers in order to secure money with which to buy drugs. It was the impression of the neighborhood police that he had since, however, kept himself free of the drug habit and of criminal activities and that even though not working, he had taken good care of himself and of his sister's children. He was not suspected in any way and one police officer commented that Dennis had been associating companionably with some of the better men in the neighborhood.

Seven years after the last arrest for violating the drug law which had resulted in sentence to the house of correction, Dennis was again arrested for peddling drugs. Once more he was sent to the house of correction from which, because of "queer conduct," he was transferred to a mental hospital for examination and then committed to a state mental hospital. The hospital authorities reported him to be suffering from a psychosis due to drugs, and their prognosis was "guarded." Dennis admitted to the hospital authorities that just prior to this arrest he had been taking forty to fifty grains of heroin daily. His legs were covered with scars from hypodermic needles.

Dennis' mother told our investigator that during the year prior to his last arrest, he would occasionally become dissatisfied with living at home and would take a room by himself in the neighborhood. During these periods he did not keep in touch with his family and they knew nothing of his activities. However, when he did return he would not seek companions but spent his time in the house reading. It was then that she began to notice that he was again using drugs; he no longer attempted to hide it.

Should Dennis, who is now fifty-five, be released from the state mental hospital where he has already been for almost five years (beyond the third follow-up period), it is doubtful whether his brother-in-law would welcome him home, because he is now finally convinced that Dennis is a confirmed drug addict and he would not want his children to come under their uncle's influence, particularly as he was in the habit of staying indoors for weeks at a time.

Our investigator has not interviewed him at the state hospital, because Dennis' mother says he refuses to talk to visitors, even relatives. "He pays no attention to anyone, doesn't care for the band concerts, and is always as far away from a crowd or person as he can get." The mother and brother-in-law think he is much better off at the hospital than he would be at home. They comment that he had been acting queerly at times during the two or three years prior to his commitment, particularly in his desire to be by himself.

Dennis represents a group of delinquents who ought to be frankly recognized as essentially medical cases. Jails and houses of correction are absurdly unsuited to meet the problems represented by chronic alcoholics and drug addicts. Abundant evidence exists that the role of ordinary imprisonment in preventing recidivism is very minor in the great majority of instances; in cases of this kind, it borders on the absurd to expect "reform" through imprisonment. One might as well expect punishment to cure tuberculosis. Many case records could be produced, each showing very many arrests and imprisonments of chronic alcoholics—a whole lifetime spent in shuffling and shuttling from saloon to police station, to court, to jail, and out again only to repeat the cycle at tremendous expense to society and tragic waste to the sick persons subjected to this inane procedure. For chronic alcoholics or drug addicts, treatment institutions that would stress physical, pharmaceutical, and mental hygiene therapeutics are necessary.

The forecast of Dennis' criminalistic behavior will be found on p. 230. Whether it would have been possible, at an early stage, to save enough of Dennis' personality for adequate integration is a question that can be answered only when society sets up suitable clinical and therapeutic facilities for those whose "crimes" (drunkenness, drug addiction, prostitution, vagrancy, and the like) are in all probability essentially manifestations of deep-rooted organismal abnormalities.

### JACK. PART I[18]

Jack is the oldest of six children. His parents are of Irish origin and came to America shortly after Jack's birth. The relationship of the parents was pleasant enough when the father was not intemperate. He was, however, frequently arrested for drunkenness and committed to both the house of correction and the state farm—the hostels of the vagrant and the alcoholic. A brother of Jack's has also been arrested several times for larceny and for drunkenness. The family suffered continuously from economic stress and were dependent upon the succor of numerous social agencies. The father rarely had steady employment because of his drinking habits. The home was very much overcrowded, since the mother kept lodgers. There was little, if any, parental oversight. To supplement the family income, Jack's mother frequently worked outside the home, doing washing and cleaning. The boy ran about the streets and was at fourteen introduced to heterosexual experiences, played dice, pool, and poker, and hung about cheap "billiard parlors." He left school in the fourth grade at the age of thirteen, and went away from home to seek employment in a small town in Connecticut, where he remained only two months before returning home.

At nineteen Jack married. Shortly thereafter he was arrested for the first time, for disturbing the peace, for which he paid a fine of $10. A year later he was in court for non-support of his wife. This case was placed on file. Two years thereafter, at twenty-two, he was again arrested for non-support, and

18 In 500 *Criminal Careers*, A Strong Motive for Self-Mastery, p. 75.

shortly after this he and his wife separated. Two years intervened before Jack was again arrested, this time for assault and battery, for which he again paid a fine of $10. Shortly afterwards he was picked up for robbery and sentenced to the house of correction for six months. Upon release he and his wife were reunited. But a year later, when Jack was twenty-six, he was once more in the toils for non-support and also for larceny; this time he received a suspended sentence to the house of correction. Within a few months he was arrested for drunkenness and shortly thereafter again for non-support, for which offenses he received probation.

Jack's industrial history during all this time was very irregular. He had worked as an errand boy; then for many years as teamster and longshoreman. From the time he first separated from his wife, he made several trips away from home, once to Maine, once overseas; he also took frequent freight-riding excursions.

Two weeks after the last charge of non-support, at the age of twenty-seven, Jack and a companion were arrested for assault with intent to rob and received a sentence of five years and a month to the Reformatory. They had assaulted a man in the vestibule of a house and took $35 in money and a pocketbook from his person. At that time the police stated that Jack had worked periodically as a longshoreman on the wharves, but spent most of his time drinking and loitering at the bar-rooms and corners and assaulting and robbing "drunks." It was a notorious fact that he did not support his wife and children.

Jack spent thirty-six months in the Reformatory. Mental examination there disclosed him to be "a moron and addicted to drink." As is often true of alcoholics, Jack blamed his wife for his misconduct.

He received training in the mills of the institution, worked as a fireman in the engineering department, and was found to be an extremely good and steady worker. He was then transferred to the Reformatory farm, where, as customary, he was to stay for a short period before his discharge. With only a brief term left to serve, Jack attempted an escape but was captured.

At the Reformatory he attended school where he proved to be extremely troublesome. His behavior elsewhere was also bad. He committed offenses as often as once in three months, among them being talking in dining-room and chapel, being out of place, disobedience of orders, fighting in shop. He became more amenable, however, as he grew accustomed to the routine and settled down to Reformatory life.

Released on parole, Jack went to live with his wife and two small children. This was during the first World War and he soon entered the merchant marine service. He again failed to provide for the support of his wife and children. A warrant was issued for his arrest, and his permit to be at liberty was revoked. On his return to the Reformatory he served three months before he was again released. Once more he took up his residence with his wife and children. During this time he was employed very irregularly as a teamster, fireman, longshoreman. His average earnings were $26 a week, and his average length of continuous work was three months. During the latter part of this parole period, however, he seemed to have settled down, showed himself to be a hard worker; and except for occasional lapses, when he "went on a bat," his conduct was good.

About eight months after the expiration of his parole period Jack was again arrested for drunkenness, and this time received a sentence of two months to the house of correction. Since then, until the end of the first follow-up period, his conduct was exemplary. He lived with his wife and children and supported his family throughout. His home was a very attractive upstairs flat of a two-family brick house, very comfortably furnished, clean and homelike, and showing evidence of substantial success. His children, a girl and a boy, seventeen and fifteen years of age, did not know of their father's penal experiences. They believed he had been away at sea. The home was situated on the brow of a hill in a crowded city neighborhood once occupied by upper middle-class people and in which Jack's parents and he himself had lived for many years. Jack had great pride in the neighborhood and clearly associated himself with it, considering himself a part of it in every way. He took care of his family without any help from anybody, but left financial matters entirely to his wife, who had begun to save a little of his earnings. Jack spent much of his leisure time at a neighborhood political and social club, whose quarters were on the opposite side of the street. The dues were very small, and there Jack met his neighbors and read and smoked, played pool, and chatted. By the close of the first follow-up period, the family had lived in the same home for six years and Jack, feeling rooted in the neighborhood, did not want to move.

At this stage, Jack's explanation for his remarkable change in conduct and for his industrial and family stability was as follows: "I have been on the water wagon ever since my last sentence to the house of correction. They kept me at the island ten days. I said to myself: 'You got to stop it or be a bum'; so I decided to stop it. I came home and I went to bed and I stayed in bed seven days and I made up my mind to stop, and I stopped—and that's all there was to it. A man can do about anything when he makes up his mind to do it."

Jack said that the restricted discipline and the regular life in the Reformatory "set him to thinking," and he was glad to have been sent there. However, he needed "another lesson" to make him stop drinking. But the chief factor in restoring Jack to normal life at this stage in his career appears to have been his spouse, a remarkably wholesome, vigorous, successful wife and mother. She had been loyal to Jack throughout and bound to make him "toe the mark." Certainly the good neighborhood influences must also be taken into account. Finally, as Jack's children were growing up, he evidently realized the necessity for changing his own mode of living if he would have their respect and that of his neighbors. At thirty-nine, at the end of the first follow-up period, Jack was a brickmason earning $44 a week. During periods of unemployment he would find work on the wharves as a longshoreman. He was certainly on the up grade.

## JACK. PART II

It would be gratifying to record that Jack continued on the up grade. For two years into the second follow-up period, he kept at work with regularity and his general situation remained as pictured up to the end of the first follow-up span. As long as his income was quite steady, there seemed to be no difficulty whatsoever. The family relationships were close, Jack's wife continued to be devoted to him and to the two children now quite well grown but still not married, and Jack participated in the neighborhood life where he felt very comfortable among his old cronies. But toward the middle of the second five-year period, when the industrial depression of 1929 began to be felt, it had its serious effect on the life of Jack and his family. He lost a job which he had held for some five years and had to return to longshoring which up to then he had resorted to only occasionally during brief periods of lay-offs from his regular work.

Jack's wife insists that it was renewed association with "drunks" and bootleggers on the wharves, and general discouragement over his inability to earn a living for his family, that caused him to succumb again to drink. Jack's first arrest after some seven years of wholesome living was for larceny of six cans of olive oil which he picked up on the wharves while in a semi-intoxicated state. For this he was placed on probation for six months. But even during this period of probation he was arrested twice, once for drunkenness, the second time for drunkenness and non-support, the latter charge being brought by his wife who thought that by turning him over to the police herself she might shock him out of his growing carelessness and lack of self-control.

But this was of little avail. At best Jack was able to earn only sixty cents an hour, and work was sporadic and uncertain. He had much idle time on his hands and spent most of it hanging around on the wharves with disreputable companions, waiting for a new shipload of goods to unload. Jack's wife and his son and daughter all were very tolerant of his relapse, somehow sensing that he was not deliberately trying to evade his responsibilities but was the victim of overwhelming circumstances. They tried to prop him up in every way possible, not only with affection but by getting the family doctor and priest to talk with him on occasion and to try to make him see the necessity of avoiding alcohol. He would respond well to such advances, and for brief periods would try to exercise sufficient self-control to avoid the habit; but always he succumbed again, because he was highly suggestible and unable to resist the urgings of a corner loafer to join him in a drink. And when under the influence of liquor Jack could not refuse the request of a friend for a few dollars, so that he was contributing less and less to the family support. Much against her will, his wife had to apply to public agencies for assistance. The daughter had married and was in no position to be of assistance, and the son, who had worked fairly steadily, was not able to do more than provide for his own support. However, just as soon as sufficient funds were provided for the most modest living, she would notify the welfare agencies that she no longer needed help.

In the latter half of the second follow-up period, Jack was committed to jail where he spent several months. On release, he was given $3.50 which, his wife complained, he promptly spent for liquor at the suggestion of several companions released with him. Very soon afterwards he was again arrested for drunkenness and returned to jail, being again released after a brief stay. Despite Jack's defections, the family clung together and a home was always awaiting him upon his release from jail.

During the third follow-up period, at the beginning of which Jack was forty-four years old, he was arrested on numerous occasions for drinking and non-support and again spent several terms in jail. Meanwhile the family fortunes were not improving. Jack's wife underwent an operation for a cataract, his daughter had by now two small children, and his son had also married and was having difficulty in supporting a wife and child. Jack's wife had to drop insurance policies amounting to $1,000, which she had been carrying on his life, one for $500 on herself and smaller ones on each child. Jack had always turned over all his earnings to her and she had paid the bills and handled all the family accounts. If not for her devotion and that of the children, there is no question but that Jack would have become one of the army of homeless vagrants.

Jack's strong family feeling is reflected in his deep emotional reaction to the death of his mother which occurred just before the end of the second follow-up period. He had always kept in close touch with her and with his brothers and sisters. During the year following her death, he was arrested even more often than previously. Occasionally he would wander away from home for brief periods usually going to the country to stay with his sister who lived on a farm. He did not remain away long, however, and would usually bring his earnings home, providing some fellow drunk did not get hold of him on pay day and "borrow" money.

For a time Jack's family began to wonder whether there was something wrong with him mentally, because when he was sitting around at home, he would sleep most of the time, he seemed listless and aged, and was generally deteriorating, even sometimes not seeming to recognize his friends. As his son put it, he seemed to be in a "fog." Jack's wife had for some time been contemplating moving away from the neighborhood where the family had lived for so many years. She decided against this, however, because she, Jack, and the children all felt rooted there and she did not think they could do better elsewhere on the small amount they could afford to pay for rent. "If he hasn't got the strength of mind enough to straighten out in his own home surroundings, there is little hope that he would do any better in some strange, poor neighborhood."

Somehow Jack's wife had managed to get by on his earnings from about two days' work a week. She had been able to save a few dollars a month by not heating the entire apartment. The family lived in the kitchen which served as dining-room and sitting-room. They continued to maintain this home even though both the son and daughter had married and no longer lived with them. During the second follow-up period, the daughter was able to help her parents a little, but the son himself had been forced to seek aid from welfare agencies.

At the end of the third five-year follow-up period, Jack was still indulging in drink, still working only two or three days a week, occasionally serving a short jail sentence. He was still on six-year probation on a charge of non-support made during the middle of the third five-year period.

We have information about Jack for two years beyond the third follow-up period. The story continues to be the same. Occasionally the family doctor, who is very severe with Jack, is able "to keep him on the water wagon" for a few months at a time. Jack is now fifty-one years old. Our field investigator who has seen him recently says that he now appears to be in better condition and more alert than he was a few years ago. There is no question but that he is a responsible earner when sober. As always, he leaves all financial matters to his wife. She has been able to resume about $500 of insurance, in order to provide burial expenses. "That's all I need," says Jack.

The story of Jack illustrates the fact that some personalities with strong impulses toward alcoholism are able for a long period of time to control their thirst. While in the case of Jack we again have the propping influence of a sympathetic and intelligent spouse, it is clear that the make-up of the individual has here been the predominant force. For, on the one hand, the abandonment of the early alcoholic indulgence seems to have been due to the achievement of an adequate degree of integration, that is, to intellectual-emotional maturity; and, on the other hand, despite the support given by wife and children, when this peak of integration had passed and early disintegration began to take place, the inclination toward alcoholic indulgence powerfully reasserted itself. Continued alcoholism had evidently weakened the controlling neurologic-psychologic mechanisms. It is true that Jack had been thrown in with alcoholic longshoremen, to contact with whom his wife attributes his decline; but it must be remembered that earlier he had been in institutions filled with alcoholics and yet was able to stop drinking for a long time. Hence the influence of "culture" must be accounted in this case as secondary to the influence of Jack's innate make-up in terms of maturation capacity. This is further borne out by the fact that both during his long abstinence and his period of renewed alcoholism, Jack lived in the same neighborhood and partook of the same culture.

What consultation of a predictive chart would have foretold about Jack's future will be seen on p. 231.

## PETER. PART I[19]

Peter's parents were Italians who kept a small grocery store in a crowded Italian neighborhood. He was the third of five children. When Peter was but four years old, his father was murdered in a brawl in a saloon during a card game. The moral character of the mother had always been very questionable, and less than two months after the death of her husband, she married again. The family lived in overcrowded quarters, the home consisting of two dark, extremely dirty rooms in the rear of the store. The children were neglected and ill behaved. They were often sent home from school because they were filthy. Even as very small youngsters they stole from their mother and from neighbors. They ran about the streets without any supervision whatsoever.

Shortly after the father's death the Society for the Prevention of Cruelty to Children became interested in the family since there had been much complaint of the neglect of the children. For example, the youngest child, while still an infant, was left strapped in a garret room all day while the mother tended the store.

Thus when Peter was a little over four years old, he, together with a brother and a sister, was placed in a children's protectorate. After only four months the children were all sent home because they proved unruly. Soon a public welfare agency placed the three boys, including Peter, in foster homes, and the other children remained with their mother.

[19] In *500 Criminal Careers*, A Drug Addict and His Background, p. 77.

While Peter was in a boarding home in the country his conduct was all that could be desired. He worked hard on the farm of his foster father and attended school and church regularly; and though he and his brother were a little "more difficult than most boys of this age," they nevertheless got along very well. He attended school until the age of fourteen when he was in the fifth grade. At fifteen, after three years in this home, his foster father died and the boy was sent back to his mother. This crisis seemed to be the definite turning point in Peter's life.

Soon after returning home, Peter, now beyond the juvenile-court age of sixteen, was arrested for running away. This case was "dismissed." He ran about the streets a good deal, wholly unsupervised, and at this early age he took to the use of drugs. He has been an addict and pedlar of drugs ever since. At seventeen he was arrested for violating the drug law, and his case was placed on file. Eight months later he was arrested for larceny, was released on bail, and defaulted. This case was later dismissed. Six months thereafter Peter was again arrested for larceny, and received a suspended sentence to jail. Within three months he was, however, again in the toils for larceny, was released on bail, and again defaulted.

Peter's only industrial experience had been in the home of his foster parents, where he did chores after school hours, ran errands, and helped his foster father in other ways. On return to his own home he worked in a "peanut place."

During all this time, not only was his mother known to be immoral but three brothers were confirmed drug addicts and a fourth had been sentenced for robbery. Peter claims it was the influence of his brothers that turned him to criminal acts after his return from the foster home.

When Peter was eighteen years old he committed the offense for which he was sent to the Reformatory—larceny of four gold bridge teeth, valued at $25, from the office of a dentist to whom he had gone for treatment. There was also a second charge against him—larceny of watches from a jewelry store. By that time Peter was known to the police as a confirmed "dope fiend," and it was believed that he used the money from his thefts to buy drugs.

Peter was in the Reformatory for eighteen months and was there diagnosed as a psychopath, drug addict, and moron. He was given fifteen months of training in the tailor shop. He committed offenses as frequently as once every five weeks—smoking in the yard, not keeping his room clean, fighting, persistent talking, causing disturbance, refusal to obey, being disorderly, quarreling.

During his first parole period he lived in his mother's home and worked very irregularly at various odd jobs. But six months after parole he was arrested in a nearby city for larceny of $20 and was returned to the Reformatory, where he now remained for four months. Upon his discharge he did not return home but boarded with a family nearby and worked for very brief periods as a shoe and furniture salesman and unskilled factory hand, and with an express company. All these jobs were held for a few days to a couple of weeks.

Nine months after his second release, at the age of twenty-two, Peter was again arrested for larceny from the person. The man from whom the money was taken had been in a saloon most of the afternoon, and about two o'clock Peter and his brother entered the saloon and walked along in front of the bar, looking everybody over. After a few minutes they went out through the pool-room attached to the saloon, and from there out into the street. At five o'clock the man for whom they were waiting, now under the influence of liquor, went from the bar-room into the pool-room, sat down at a table, laid his arms across it, and with his head resting on them fell asleep. Peter and his brother, who had been watching from the outside, came through the pool-room door and bought a sandwich, then took one of the chairs from the table at which the man was sitting, and sat down very close to him. The money was slipped out of the man's pocket by Peter, and he and his brother soon departed.

Peter was again returned to the Reformatory on a "revoke." This time he spent only one week there before being transferred to the prison camp and hospital because he was in such bad condition from the use of drugs that some treatment was deemed necessary. He was paroled after eleven months.

During his third parole period Peter again lived with his mother. But only one month after his parole, his permit to be at liberty was revoked because he had failed to report to the parole officer, had done no work since his release, and had been "hanging about" hotels. This time he spent eight and a half months at the Reformatory, again being transferred to the prison camp and hospital, from which he was paroled. Within a few months his permit to be at liberty was revoked because he had left home and had made false reports, and his conduct had been "indiscreet." He was not returned to the Reformatory, however, because he could not be found; and four years later the warrant for his return was withdrawn. It was later discovered that up to the end of his parole period he had been peddling drugs.

During the first five-year follow-up period Peter traveled about from city to city selling drugs. He returned to his mother's home occasionally and was always shielded by his family, who did not insist upon his paying board. He lived by his wits throughout this time, peddling drugs under the guise of selling neckties. He had for some years been suspected by the police of violating the Federal Narcotics Law, and was arrested twice on this charge, but released the first time because the grand jury found "No bill," while the second time the case was *nol prossed*. Finally, when Peter was thirty-one years old, suffi-cient evidence was found against him and he received a sentence of "one year and one day" to the house of correction for selling narcotic drugs. The sentence was, however, suspended and Peter was placed on probation.

## PETER. PART II

At the end of the first follow-up period Peter was rooming in Boston. Under the guise of peddling dry-goods, he was carrying on a brisk business in dis-pensing drugs (morphine and heroin). Although suspected by the local police he managed to evade detection until a year after the beginning of the second follow-up period, when he was again arrested for selling narcotic drugs and was given a suspended sentence.

Shortly thereafter he met a young divorcée, the mother of three children, who was working as a store clerk and who herself had a considerable record of arrests for larceny. She and Peter were greatly attracted to one another and lived together on and off for several years before they finally married shortly after the beginning of the third follow-up period. The three children of this woman had been in the care of her mother ever since the girl had separated from her husband. Although she and Peter continued to live in Massachusetts in towns not far away from Boston, neither of them kept in touch with their families. The young woman's mother expressed great disdain for Peter, and when asked what his occupation was she replied contemptuously, "I don't be-lieve it's much of anything most of the time." She did not want her daughter to associate with him.

In order to evade the police, Peter has used many aliases and given false addresses to his family and his friends. The police claim that he is so shrewd that they have had difficulty in "pinning anything on him."

After the couple had been associating for four years, Peter's friend was ar-rested for larceny from a department store and sentenced to a reformatory. Her sentence was, however, suspended and she was placed on probation. The police had reported that Peter had frequently been seen in department stores with this girl, that she was a notorious shoplifter and associated with women known to. be a bunch of gangsters' "molls," and that Peter was suspected of being part of this gang. Shortly thereafter she violated her probation. She and Peter were married and went off to New York City. Her whereabouts were unknown to the authorities but a warrant was issued for her arrest. Meanwhile the couple made their home in cheap hotels in the heart of the theatrical district of New York, where Peter with his wife's connivance continued in the drug traffic un-der the guise of peddling notions. Meanwhile both their families claimed not to know where they were and neither Peter nor his wife made any attempt whatsoever to contribute to the support of her children, who were still under the care of their maternal grandmother. Peter often went some distance away from New York through Connecticut, Rhode Island, and Massachusetts on his peddling expeditions, but throughout the third follow-up period he evaded the police.

Peter and his wife were attached to each other despite the strong disapproval of her mother. The latter rarely had an opportunity to interfere with their relationship, because most of the time she did not know where they were. Possibly the hazardous occupation in which the two were engaged (since marrying Peter, his wife had become involved in the drug traffic with him) helped to keep them together. It is known that a brother of Peter's was engaged in similar traffic, carrying on independently of Peter, and that other members of Peter's family were addicted to drugs.

We have information about Peter through a *fourth* five-year follow-up span. During this period he has been arrested for selling narcotics and committed to a federal penitentiary where he is now, at the age of forty-four, beginning a three-year sentence. Peter's wife was arrested with him and turned over to the Massachusetts authorities by whom she had been wanted for several years. At this time it was revealed that the couple retained a "drug ring" lawyer, which indicates how deeply they were involved in the drug traffic. Peter's wife was extradited to Massachusetts and returned to the reformatory.

Examined at the penitentiary, Peter was classified as a psychopathic personality, "prognosis guarded," and described as an "irresponsible, socially unstable individual . . . of dull normal intelligence." Peter and his wife correspond as often as permitted, and look forward to rejoining one another when their sentences have been served.

Peter is evidently but one representative of a family with questionable hereditary equipment and cultural standards. The case illustrates a tragedy well known to workers with neglected and delinquent children—the frequently favorable response of their wards to foster-home care for a brief period, only to relapse when returned to the old surroundings. Although finally diagnosed as a psychopathic personality, Peter certainly had enough intelligence and might also have possessed sufficiently sound emotional equipment to adapt legitimately to societal demands in the simple, protected surroundings of the boarding home in the small town to which he had been sent as a youth. That he did not possess adequate emotional integration to keep away from drugs in streets of the large city is apparent.

Thus, criminalistic behavior is a function of two sets of variables—the quality and degree of maturity of the individual, and the nature and pressure of the surroundings; it is the outcome of the interplay of a specifically constituted personality and a specifically constituted environment. Given even poor innate equipment, the individual need not resort to prohibited behavior in order to make an adaptation to social demands, provided the social demands are not excessive and the person is not propped up and protected in his efforts at adaptation. Subjected to complex and heavy pressures, the individual of limited innate equipment seeks adjustment to life in any way within his means, whether that way be legitimate or illegitimate.

At the present stage, Peter's problem is primarily medical—the cure, if possible, of the drug habit; but this drug habit is in turn based upon his psychopathic condition, and it is questionable whether that deep-rooted state is amenable to psychotherapy in his case.

Here, as in the case of chronic alcoholics, we have an illustration of the need of implementing the machinery of justice with institutions possessing an essentially medical, rather than a punitive or even "correctional," treatment program. While some progress in this direction has been made in the federal system and here and there in a few states, legislatures and the public generally are not yet sufficiently aware of the need.

## ANTONIO. PART I[20]

The parents of Antonio are Italians of good, healthy stock, who in the country of their birth had been small landowners. The father had a grammar-school education. When the family migrated to America, he learned the tailoring trade and established himself very soon in a small shop. The family have been in comfortable economic circumstances; there has rarely been any great financial stress; and they have been able to send their children to school.

Antonio is the second of eight children. The relationship of the parents to each other has been good and, except for the fact that one of Antonio's brothers was a school truant, there has been no known delinquency in the family.

Antonio's parents settled in New Haven. There the boy was born, and the family remained until he was seven years of age. They then moved to Boston, where they resided throughout Antonio's boyhood and young manhood. Antonio attended school until the seventh grade, which he left at thirteen. His school conduct was all that could be desired. He was found to be of normal mentality, with no sign of any mental disease.

Antonio began to work at fourteen, first as a stock-exchange messenger, then in a factory making mesh bags. He also had a little experience in an engraving plant and in a shoe factory; was an office boy; worked in a bowling alley; was a helper in a grocery store and in a garage. The average length of

[20] In *500 Criminal Careers*, A "Normal" Youth Who Found His Proper Niche in Life, p. 80.

his employment before he was sentenced to the Reformatory was two months, and he held his longest job for four months.

Soon after Antonio began to work, he fell in with a bad crowd of young boys, and from that time on his father found it difficult to control him. The boy had worked regularly enough and brought his pay home to his mother, thus contributing to his own support, until influenced by this group of companions.

Antonio committed his first offense of breaking and entering when fifteen years of age. On that charge he was committed to a correctional school. Shortly after his release, at the age of seventeen, he again committed the offense of breaking and entering. He burglarized a house, this time alone. He stole jewelry to the value of $450, sold one of the pieces the same night at a pawnshop, and was later arrested when trying to dispose of other portions of the loot. For this crime he was sentenced to the Reformatory, where he spent sixteen months. After interviewing the new inmate, the examiner of the institution noted in his records that Antonio "is rather of a secretive nature," and he ascribed the youth's course in life to pool-room and bowling-alley associations. "These companions, plus a pleasure-loving disposition and the additional influence of his correctional school associates, probably account for his downward drift."

While in the Reformatory on this sentence Antonio was assigned to the engraving plant for a brief period and at that time wrote his father: "I am working up in the engraver's all day now and I am learning more than I ever did before. When I get out I will be good enough to work at it. I would like to ask you is that job you got for me ready yet? If it is, write to me and let me know. I don't like to be wasting my time in here while I can be out helping the family."

During his parole on this sentence Antonio used to spend his evenings learning engraving. He looked about for an opening in this field, but was unable to find one. Shortly following his parole, after drawing his pay from the garage in which he had been working, and without paying his board to his parents or letting them know, Antonio left home. The following Christmas he returned, and soon thereafter, at the age of twenty-one, again committed the offense of breaking and entering, this time with two companions. For this crime he received a five-year indeterminate sentence to the Reformatory. On this occasion Antonio spent twenty-three months at the institution. He received training as a weaver, work which he did quite well; he also had some experience in carpentry, to which he was evidently not adapted; and was again given fifteen months of training in the engraving class, to which he responded exceptionally well. He was very industrious and much interested in the work, and the trade-school officer said of him that "he possesses skill and judgment in the work and is capable of making a good engraver."

Antonio had an almost perfect conduct record while in the Reformatory.

There was nothing of note about his physical condition, which was found to be extremely good.

During the second parole period Antonio lived with his parents, who moved to a better neighborhood, where he was necessarily separated from his old companions. He first secured a job as a helper in a store, but was so much interested in engraving work that he used to spend his evenings at it at home. He held his first job for only two months, however, and then secured a place as a machinist, which he held for four months. All the while he was looking about for an opening with an engraving concern. Finally he found this opportunity and was engaged in engraving throughout the remaining two and a half years of his parole period. The parole officer found the family very cooperative and glad to take any suggestions that he made to them concerning Antonio's behavior. Before the expiration of his parole the ex-prisoner wrote to his parole officer: "As long as I keep busy I'll never get into trouble." And a little later he wrote: "I am very glad to have learned the engraving trade at the Reformatory. Now that I have found the job that I like I am going to stick to it."

The first five-year follow-up history of Antonio was very creditable. He continued to live with his parents in a seven-room apartment in a modern stucco block of three-family houses. The neighborhood gave an atmosphere of village life and of wholesomeness. Throughout this period Antonio worked in engraving plants, earning from $35 to $45 a week. All of his employers who were interviewed commended him highly. He saved $700 and was hoping to marry as soon as he had sufficient funds to support a wife. His family felt that his second Reformatory experience was "the making of him," and Antonio was very grateful for having really learned during his second incarceration the trade of photoengraving and having been able to lead a quiet, regular life in the institution. He came out of the Reformatory with much ambition, fostered and developed because he succeeded in establishing himself in the occupation he most enjoyed. He was known to be an efficient and satisfactory worker in every respect. His leisure time was spent largely with his fiancée. He was a member of the Y.M.C.A., where he spent three evenings a week playing basketball. He attended church regularly. He had no trouble whatsoever with the police. His father believed that the fact that the family moved into a better neighborhood gave Antonio a chance to reorganize his leisure time and make new companionships.

Antonio said that during his second incarceration at the Reformatory "something led me to take it right." That something is, however, difficult for him to explain. "I made up my mind to get ahead and amount to something," he says simply. His father thinks he was naturally "a good boy who came back to himself" with the aid of the Reformatory. "It was all a wholesome thing for him, especially the trade."

### ANTONIO. PART II

Antonio has continued to be a credit to himself and his family. For four years of the second follow-up period he worked steadily as an engraver earning as much as $70 a week. He continued to live with his parents for a short time, but when his father died toward the middle of the second five-year period Antonio took a room in a good residential neighborhood in order to be near his work. He was saving money steadily and hoping to be able to marry the girl with whom he had been keeping company regularly. However, when the industrial depression began to be felt, it had its effect on Antonio's work. In 1931, a year before the end of the second follow-up period, he lost his job and moved into the home of his married sister of whom he was very fond. She lived in a two-family house in a good suburban neighborhood where Antonio had several friends.

Up to that time he had saved $2,000 and was also carrying insurance. Although the union which he had joined paid him some benefits during his unemployment, he had to use some of his savings because he felt obliged to pay board to his sister and did not wish to be a burden in any way to his relatives. Meanwhile he was keeping steady company with his fiancée. He admits that now and then he has had sexual relations with other girls, because "a man must have this sort of thing"; but he has been careful to avoid venereal infection. He says that he has on no occasion paid money for such experiences, but rather has taken the girl to supper or the theater. He claims he has never attempted sexual relations with his fiancée, because she is not the kind of girl who would tolerate this.

Before the end of the follow-up period Antonio found another job as an engraver, which gave him two or three days' work a week. This situation has continued throughout the third five-year period with only one change of employment. Antonio has throughout these years been able to earn as much as $50 a week. However, he feels that this work is not steady, and until he is satisfied that he has an absolutely permanent position he will not marry. He is again saving money. He does not carry as much insurance as he did formerly, but retains his union membership and carries a death benefit of $1,000.

Meanwhile Antonio's mother has died, but he is in close touch with all his brothers and sisters and still continues to make his home with his married sister. It is evident that Antonio is planful and ambitious and does not intend to establish a family until he feels he is well able to look after them. He is now, at the end of the third five-year period, forty-one years old.

We may profitably repeat what we said of this case at the close of the first follow-up period:

It seems that the combination of the co-operative functioning of intelligent parents with a family background of decent social standards, the discovery and fostering of an ambition, and a complete change of environment all contributed to the good result in this case. But Antonio himself feels that this explanation is not enough. What started the internal change? What was the "something" that led him to "take it right" the second time but not the first? What was it that caused him to make up his mind "to get ahead and amount to something"? Even this clean-cut case illustrates the inadequacy of any simple approach to what is essentially a complex problem, one that can be analyzed at different levels.[21]

To this statement may now be added the suggestion that Antonio's career is another illustration of the fact that the adverse influence of criminalistic associates or of a "delinquency culture" do not overcome the advantages of co-operative parents and a decent home and, most important, an adequate intellectual and temperamental equipment. Despite the ups and downs of delinquency and non-delinquency, despite his contacts with criminals both outside and inside the Reformatory, Antonio evidently had the intellectual and emotional make-up which, in the long run, enabled him to make socially acceptable adjustments to the demands of life even in a highly complex and competitive social organization. Although this is but a sketchy case summary, it indicates sufficiently that we are dealing with a mature, adult-minded person.

As we pointed out in *500 Criminal Careers,* the adventures of Antonio also speak eloquently of the great value of intelligent vocational guidance and painstaking trade instruction in any program for the rehabilitation of criminals. This fact has long been recognized in theory. It still has but little application in practice in most of the penal and so-called correctional institutions in this country.

The prediction of Antonio's conduct will be found on p. 231.

## COMMENT

The cases described are not necessarily typical, in all respects, of the group of 510 offenders originally reported on in *500 Criminal Careers,* whose lives we have now traced for at least fifteen years beyond the expiration of their

[21] *500 Criminal Careers,* p. 83.

sentences to a reformatory. We might have chosen others to illustrate various significant matters not brought out by these few lives. We have told their particular stories, because they are the men originally described in the chapter, A Sheaf of Lives, in *500 Criminal Careers;* and we thought it would be of greater interest to the reader to learn what had happened to them than to describe another series of cases.

Can at least some of the more significant issues and inferences drawn from these illustrative case summaries be supported by additional evidence from our mass of 510 cases? It is hoped that the data to be presented in the following pages will answer this question in the affirmative.

At the end of the fifteen-year follow-up span, the men whose careers have been described in this chapter range in age from thirty-six to fifty-one years, three of them being under forty, three between forty and forty-four, two between forty-five and forty-nine, and one just over fifty. In intelligence they range from normal to feebleminded; in affective make-up, from well-balanced to psychopathic or psychotic. There are among them alcoholics and drug addicts. Some have reformed, others have not. A few have continued to be seriously aggressive criminals; others have drifted into "nuisance crimes" or offenses presenting essentially medical problems. One has already met violent death. Of the reformed, one was about twenty-three when he settled into reasonably acceptable ways of life, another was twenty-six, a third twenty-eight, and a fourth thirty-seven. Three others, although not abandoning their criminalism, at least became minor offenders at approximately twenty-five, forty-one, and forty-four years of age.

There are a great many questions we should like to answer about the careers of the men included in this work. Some of them we believe we can answer; others we cannot because of the limitations in the data and the undeveloped state of the various disciplines involved in the study of criminalism. It is not amiss to point out, however, that this is the first time in the history of penology that the careers of a large number of criminals are described in detail from childhood well beyond maturity.[22] Although detailed studies of small groups of offenders[23] are illuminating, and there is much to be said for such highly intensive analyses of individual criminal careers, it is evident that reliable conclusions cannot be drawn from a few cases.

A basic question that we have sought to answer—one of both practical and theoretical implications—is whether at the time of their sentence to the Re-

---

[22] The reader is invited to consult, also, *Juvenile Delinquents Grown Up.*

[23] For example, Shaw, C. R., *The Jack Roller* (Chicago, University of Chicago Press, 1930) and Shaw, C. R., H. D. McKay, and J. F. McDonald, *Brothers in Crime* (Chicago, University of Chicago Press, 1938).

formatory, the behavior of these men could have been foretold, not only in the Reformatory but in the years following their release. Could the types of men have been indicated who would continue serious criminality throughout the fifteen years, who would change from the commission of aggressive crimes to less serious offenses, and who would abandon their criminal careers altogether? Could a fairly reliable prediction have been made of the age spans at which such fundamental changes in conduct would occur? Or, in these crucial matters, are we wise only after the event? These questions are of prime importance and we shall concern ourselves with them at some length in a later portion of this work.[24]

[24] See Chaps. XIV, XV, and XVI.

# III

## ENVIRONMENTAL CIRCUMSTANCES

Turning now to the mass trends in the careers of our men, we shall in this and several succeeding chapters indicate the ups and downs in the major aspects of their lives. In *Later Criminal Careers* we detailed the differences in their status as between the first five years following completion of the Reformatory sentence and the second five-year follow-up span. In the present work we shall focus attention on the differences between the second follow-up period and the third. The description of the men during the third period will of course be detailed; only the highlights of comparison with the two previous periods will be given in the text, reserving details for Appendix C (Period-Comparison Tables).

As in *Later Criminal Careers,* we have found it illuminating to make two approaches to these comparisons of status: the group method and the case-by-case method. Each is useful for particular purposes, and together they give a more correct description of the changes that have occurred from one five-year period to another than either affords alone. Mass comparisons are made between the periods under consideration to determine differences in the incidence of particular factors. In the case-by-case comparison, however, the changes in the status of particular individuals are indicated from period to period.

In the body of the book only the most significant data are presented; details are supplied in Appendices B, C, and D.

A word as to the tables and computations. All percentages are based on the number of cases in which information was both known and applicable. Consequently, the base figure on which the percentages have been computed changes somewhat from table to table. For the sake of smoother presentation, the number of "unknowns" in each factor is not stated in the text, except in a few instances where this group is so large as to necessitate unusual caution in interpreting the data. The exact number of unknown cases in each factor analyzed is shown in the appendices.

The sub-categories of each factor designated "inapplicable" pertain to men who spent most of one or another of the follow-up periods in institutions and regarding whom, therefore, certain data (for instance, character of home or neighborhood) are not relevant. The number of such cases is not recorded in the text, unless it is unusually large.

In connection with the case-by-case comparisons, attention is called to Appendix D, in which will be found the number of cases that were *unknown* or *inapplicable* in each period.

Of the original group of 510 men first reported upon in 500 *Criminal Careers*, 477 were living at the beginning of the first five-year follow-up period, 454 at the beginning of the second, and 439 at the beginning of the third. It is with these 439 survivors among the 510 delinquents with whom we are now primarily concerned.

We want first of all to know where they were living at the end of the third five-year span, and whether, during the five years of this third follow-up period, they had been in institutions (penal and non-penal). We want also to know for how long they had been removed from community life, whether they had moved about excessively, what their home and neighborhood conditions were like. We are concerned even more to determine whether there has been a change in their environmental circumstances as compared with their status during the first and second follow-up periods.

## Whereabouts

The first question we must answer is: Where were the 439 men at the end of the third period when our investigators went in search of them? Eighty-seven (19.8 per cent) of the men were residing in Boston and its immediate environs; 89 (20.3 per cent) were living in other cities and towns in Massachusetts; 117 (26.7 per cent) were making their homes in other states, while 5 (1.1 per cent) were living in foreign countries (Italy, Greece, Syria, and Poland). One man was a fugitive from justice, six were drifting about the land as hoboes, two were in the Army, 49 (11.2 per cent) were incarcerated in jails and prisons in various parts of the country, while 16 were in mental hospitals or hospitals for the chronically ill. Twenty-seven (6.2 per cent) of the 439 men died during the third period.[1]

The whereabouts of 40 men (9.1 per cent) were unknown at the end of the third follow-up period, although it is known where four of them were for at least a part of the time. In comparing the whereabouts of the group at the end

---

[1] This makes a total of 98 of the original 510 men who have passed away. Five of them were under twenty at the time of death, 25 were between twenty-one and twenty-five years old, 21 between twenty-six and thirty, 17 between thirty-one and thirty-five, 20 between thirty-six and forty, and 10 were forty-one and older. Appendix B, 3–79b.

The causes of death of these 98 men, in the order of incidence, were tuberculosis (24 cases), accidents (21), pneumonia or influenza (20), heart disease (8), acute alcoholism (5), kidney disease (4), intestinal infections (3).

In six cases other diseases, such as Hodgkin's disease and cerebral hemorrhage, resulted in death. Death was due to results of operations in three cases, to suicide in two cases; two men were "killed in action" with the police, and one was sent to the electric chair. Appendix B, 3–80.

of each period,[2] significant differences emerge, the most important of which is that a greater proportion of the men are now living outside of Massachusetts— 26.7 per cent as compared with 16.9 per cent at the end of the first five-year span and 23.8 per cent at the end of the second. The drop in the proportion of men found in penal institutions at the end of the first and second periods (17.8 per cent compared to 12.1 per cent) is not as marked in the third period (11.2 per cent). Of significance too is the gradual decrease in men who were fugitives from justice—6.5 per cent at the end of Period I, 0.7 per cent at the end of Period II, and 0.2 per cent at the end of Period III. The only other item of significance is the increase in the proportion of offenders found in hospitals for the mentally diseased or the chronically ill—3.6 per cent at the end of the third five-year span as compared with 1.5 per cent at the end of the first and 3.1 per cent at the end of the second period.[3]

It is clear that the changes in place of residence were not as marked between the second and third five-year periods as between the first and second.

*With Whom Living*

With whom were the men living at the end of the third five-year span? It will be recalled from the above statement of their whereabouts that a total of 67 of them were found to be either in penal institutions, in hospitals for the mentally diseased or chronically ill, or in the Army; 27 were dead, and the whereabouts of 40 were unknown. Of the remaining 305 men, 168 (55.8 per cent) were at the end of the third follow-up span making their homes with their wives and children; 67 (22 per cent) were living by themselves; 29 (9.6 per cent) with their parents; 13 (4.3 per cent) with brothers or sisters; 6 (2 per cent) with mistresses whom they say they intend to marry; another 6 in the homes of their employers; 7 (2.3 per cent) with relatives other than parents or siblings; 5 with their children. It is not known with whom 4 of the men were living at the close of the third follow-up period.

As would be expected, a lower proportion of the men were making their homes with their parents (9.6 per cent) than were doing so at the end of the first (16.5 per cent) and second five-year periods (15.1 per cent), but there was an increase in the proportion of men living with their wives and children— from 49.4 per cent at the end of Period I to 55.8 per cent at the end of Period III.[4]

---

[2] This means comparison of the 439 men still alive at the beginning of the third period with the 454 men living at the beginning of the second span and with the 477 living at the beginning of the third.

[3] See Appendix C, 2, for full details.

[4] Appendix C, 1. At the time of their commitment to the Reformatory, 357 (80.8 per cent) of the 454 men dealt with in *Later Criminal Careers* were found to have been making their homes

A case-by-case comparison of the whereabouts of the men at the end of the third as compared with the second five-year period will make the trend more specific:

(a) Of 72 men who, at the end of the second five-year span, were living with their parents, brothers and sisters, or other relatives, only 43.1 per cent were found to be residing with them by the end of the third; 19.4 per cent were living alone, an equal proportion with their wives and children, one man was making his home with an employer, 13.9 per cent were in institutions, and two had died.

(b) Of 164 men living with their wives and children at the end of the second period, 78.7 per cent were still doing so at the end of the third; while 4.3 per cent were living alone, 3.6 per cent in the homes of parents or other relatives, two with mistresses, one with his children, six were in institutions, and thirteen (7.9 per cent) had died.

(c) Three men who were making their homes with children at the end of the second five-year period (their wives having died or left the home) continued to do so in the third.

(d) Of seven men who were living with mistresses at the end of the second follow-up span, only one was still doing so at the close of the third, three were living with their wives and children, one man was living alone, and two were in institutions.

(e) Of eight men living in the homes of employers at the end of the second period, three were still doing so at the end of the third, one was making his home with his wife and children, three were living alone, and one had died.

(f) Of 61 men living alone at the end of the second five-year period, 34 (55.7 per cent) were still doing so at the close of the third, six were making their homes with parents, brothers and sisters, or other relatives, eight were living with their wives and children, two with mistresses, nine in institutions, and two had died.

(g) Of 71 men who were in institutions at the close of the second follow-up period, 40 (56.3 per cent) were still in institutions at the end of the third; five were living with parents, brothers and sisters, or other relatives; 11 were making their homes with wives and children; one was living with a mistress; one with an employer, four alone, and nine had died.[5]

This analysis shows that the major shift occurred among the men who were living with relatives (other than wives) at the close of the second period, more than half of them now making their homes with others. The men living with

with their parents, siblings, or other close relatives; 60 (13.6 per cent) were living alone; 24 (5.4 per cent) with wives and children. *Later Criminal Careers*, p. 20.

[5] Appendix D, 1.

their wives and children at the end of Period II largely continued to do so thereafter, while of those who were living alone in the second follow-up span, over half continued to do so.

### Length of Time in Community

Only half (52.8 per cent) of the men who survived the second follow-up period lived in the community throughout the third five-year span, meaning that they had not been confined in peno-correctional institutions or in mental hospitals or in hospitals for chronic ailments. A fourth (26.1 per cent) of the group lived in the community from thirty-six to sixty months, a tenth (9.5 per cent) twelve to thirty-six months, 4.8 per cent less than twelve months, while 6.8 per cent were not in the community at all during this period, but were confined for the entire sixty months either in peno-correctional or non-penal institutions. The average number of months during which they lived in the community was 48.14 (±.46).[6] This marks a slight but steady increase in average time spent in the community: 44.78 (±.53) months during the first follow-up period and 47.06 (±.51) during the second five-year period.[7]

A case-by-case comparison indicates changes in status more specifically:

(a) Of 30 men who were not in the community at all during the second five-year period, 15 maintained a like status in the third five-year span; the other half were in the community for a time though not throughout the period.

(b) Of 135 men who were in the community for only part of the second five-year span, 68.9 per cent were likewise at liberty for only part of the third follow-up period, 8.1 per cent were out of the community altogether, while 23 per cent remained outside of institutions throughout the third period.

(c) Of 220 men who were in the community throughout the second five-year period, 78.1 per cent maintained a like status in the third, while 21.4 per cent were at large for part of the period and only one had been removed from the community altogether.[8]

Of 188 men known to have spent less than the entire five years of the third period in the community, 175 had 180 institutional experiences of one kind or another. From among this number of institutional experiences, 157 (89.7 per cent) were spent in penal institutions, 17 (9.7 per cent) in hospitals for mental diseases, and six (3.4 per cent) in hospitals for chronic physical diseases.[9] Little change occurred in the proportion of men confined in institutions (penal or non-penal) during the third five-year span (44.2 per cent) as compared with the second, when 42.4 per cent were so confined; but this represents a slight

---

[6] For details see Appendix B, 3–11.　　　[7] Appendix C, 3.
[8] Appendix D, 2.　　　[9] Appendix B, 3–7.

falling off since the first five-year span[10] when 49.8 per cent of the men had been in institutions of one sort or another.

As we had found in *Later Criminal Careers* when comparing the status of the men in the first and second five-year spans, the following case-by-case comparison shows relatively little change between Period II and Period III:

(a) Of 224 men who had had no institutional experiences (penal or non-penal) during the second five-year span, 83 per cent likewise had none during the third, 17 per cent had one or more such experiences.

(b) Of 160 men who were in penal or non-penal institutions during the second follow-up period, 81.9 per cent continued to have such experiences during the third, while 18.1 per cent did not.[11]

*Mobility*

A high proportion of mobility reflects a lack of community and neighborhood ties. To what extent did the 439 men still alive at the beginning of the third five-year period move about from one place of residence to another? During Period III, 208 (58.9 per cent) did not move about excessively; that is, they remained in one place of residence for at least a year. The remaining 41.1 per cent of the men, however, failed to strike root in any one locality. Of the 145 men in this group, 22.8 per cent remained in the same general neighborhood but moved about very frequently (two or three times a year) within it; 26.9 per cent remained in one city but moved from one section of it to another as often as once a year, while 50.3 per cent moved from one city to another in their home state or moved about from one state to another. In this group are of course many men of the hobo type (see the case of Frank in the previous chapter) who are overtaken by a desire to roam the country and who pick up jobs here and there not as seasonal laborers but simply to earn a meal or a bed between freight-hopping expeditions.[12]

In comparing the mobility of our men during the third follow-up span, when they averaged thirty-five to forty years of age, with their status during the first and second periods, we see a steady decline in the proportion who moved excessively from one place of residence to another (54.2 per cent during the first span, 46.9 per cent during the second, 41.1 per cent during the third),[13] which reflects consistently greater stability.

The changes which have occurred in the mobility of the group in the third period as compared with the second are more clearly evident from the following analysis:

[10] Appendix C, 4.                          [11] Appendix D, 3.
[12] Appendix B, 3–15a.                      [13] Appendix C, 5.

(a) Of 182 men who did not move about excessively during the second span, only 13.7 per cent did do so during the third.

(b) However, of 142 men who had moved about excessively during the second period, 28.2 per cent did not do so during the third, indicating more clearly that the group as a whole were settling down.[14]

The growing stability of the group as a whole is further reflected in less shifting about from one household to another. During Period III, 60.8 per cent of the men, even though they may have moved about frequently, either remained with the same family group throughout or lived alone, while 12.8 per cent of the men made their homes in only two different households. (As an example of the latter, a man might have been living with his parents, then married and made his home with his wife, or he might have been living with his wife and children, deserted them and gone to live with a sister with whom he remained throughout the rest of the period.) A fourth (26.4 per cent) of the men, however, changed households three or more times during this period. (For example, a man may have been living alone at the beginning of the span, then made his home with a brother's family for several months, then wandered away and lived alone in rooming houses for a year, then gone to the home of a sister for a while, then married and remained with his wife.)[15] However, as already indicated, there has been an appreciable increase (from 39.2 per cent during the first five years, to 54.4 per cent during the second, to 60.8 per cent during the third)[16] in the proportion of men who have not shifted about from one household to another. More specifically:

(a) Of 170 men who had remained part of one household or lived alone throughout Period II, 78.8 per cent continued to do so during Period III.

(b) Of 29 men who were part of two or three households during the second period, 79.4 per cent remained in one family or lived by themselves throughout the third; 10.3 per cent lived in two or three different households, and another 10.3 per cent in four or more.

(c) Of 103 men who shifted about four or more times during the second five-year span, 34 per cent were part of one family group or lived alone throughout the third, 12.6 per cent shifted about two or three times, while 53.4 per cent continued to move from one household to another in the third period as they had done in the second.

On the whole, however, it is evident that there has been less shifting about in the third period than in the second, indicating, again, a growing stability.[17]

---

14 Appendix D, 4.
16 Appendix C, 6.

15 Appendix B, 3–17.
17 Appendix D, 5.

*Home Conditions*

In what kind of homes were these men living during the third span? A fourth (26.4 per cent) of them had homes which could be designated as *good*, because they were not crowded, were clean, decently furnished, and light; 31.7 per cent lived in homes that had to be designated as *poor*, in that they were overcrowded, dirty, and with shabby furnishings, or did not in other ways provide even a minimum of comfort; while 41.9 per cent of the men lived in homes that we have designated as *fair*, because though possessing some of the characteristics of good homes, they were nevertheless overcrowded or were in other respects uncomfortable.[18]

In comparing the homes of the men during the third follow-up span with those of the second and first, a decrease is evident in the proportion living in good homes since the second period (from 33.5 per cent in Period II to 26.4 per cent in Period III) and an increase in the proportion living in fair homes (from 35.7 per cent to 41.9 per cent). Evidently, the general improvement in the living conditions of these men in the second period as compared with the first (from 25.9 per cent to 33.5 per cent living in good homes) has not continued. This is probably assignable to the generally poor industrial conditions during the third five-year span[19] which made it impossible for some of the men to maintain the living standards they had achieved during the second period.[20]

The following analysis of changes which have occurred as between Periods II and III gives more detail:

(a) Of 102 men whose homes could be described as *good* in the second follow-up span, 73.5 per cent continued to live in good homes in the third, while 24.5 per cent now had only fair homes, and 2 per cent were downright poor.

(b) Of 109 men whose homes were *fair* during the second span, 76.2 per cent continued to be fair in the third, while 7.3 per cent were then good and 16.5 per cent dropped to poor.

(c) Of 86 men who lived in *poor* homes during the second five years, 80.3 per cent continued to be housed in such homes in the third span, 17.4 per cent had fair homes, and 2.3 per cent good homes.

It is evident that the men have not been able to maintain as good living standards in Period III as in the previous period.[21]

But the physical aspect of a home represents only one phase of life within it. Another is the general moral atmosphere as reflected in thrift, temperance, wholesome ideals, conformity to conventional sex standards, and freedom from

---

[18] Appendix B, 3–12.      [19] See Chap. V.

[20] Appendix C, 7. The second five-year span extended from 1926–1927 to 1931–1932; the third extended from 1931–1932 to 1936–1937.

[21] Appendix D, 6.

violations of law (except possibly such minor ones as the breaking of traffic regulations or license laws). Such home surroundings we would call *good*. We find that in Period III over a third (38.2 per cent) of the men were living in homes in which the moral atmosphere could be so designated. Another third (32.7 per cent) were members of households whose atmosphere might be deemed *fair*, because there was no positive effort to maintain standards of thrift, temperance, and wholesome ideals or, for that matter, not always strong positive disapproval of questionable behavior, but there was at least no conflict with the law on the part of any of those comprising the immediate family group. Even after fifteen years following completion of the Reformatory sentence, 29.1 per cent of the men still lived in *poor* households, those in which one or more of the members were delinquent or criminal or in which such conduct was lightly regarded if not often encouraged.[22] A decrease has, however, occurred in the proportion of men who were members of such households as compared with the second five-year span, when 37.1 per cent lived in homes of such low moral standards.[23]

A case-by-case analysis indicates the changes more clearly:

(a) Of 129 men who, during the second period, were part of households in which the moral atmosphere was *good,* 84.5 per cent continued to be part of such households during the third.

(b) Of 73 men who, in the second period, were part of households in which the moral atmosphere was *fair,* 71.2 per cent continued to be members of such households, 12.3 per cent of the men were now part of households whose moral tone was good while 16.5 per cent of the men had descended into homes of poor moral standards.

(c) Of 104 men who had previously lived in households of *poor* moral standards, two-thirds (66.4 per cent) continued to do so during the third follow-up period, 26.9 per cent were then members of households in which the moral standards were fair, and 6.7 per cent had become members of households in which the moral standards were good.[24]

## Neighborhood Conditions

In what kind of neighborhoods did our men make their homes during the third period? A third (33.9 per cent) of them lived for the most part in second-class residential areas of large cities, while 8.4 per cent lived mostly in modest residential suburbs. Another third (33.9 per cent) resided in what have been termed "interstitial areas," that is, neighborhoods that were once residential but have turned into business or factory areas, 11.6 per cent of the men lived

---

[22] Appendix B, 3–16a.　　　　[23] Appendix C, 9a.　　　　[24] Appendix D, 6a.

mostly in rural districts or in very small towns. An eighth of the group (12.2 per cent) moved about so frequently between urban and rural regions that the neighborhoods of their homes could only be designated as varied.[25]

In comparing the kind of neighborhoods in which our men generally made their homes during the three periods, we note a small but consistent increase in the proportion living in rural districts, from 6.7 per cent during the first five-year span, to 9.8 per cent during the second, to 11.6 per cent during the third. This increase, as will be shown below, derives not so much from the men who have lived in predominantly urban neighborhoods but from those who have shifted between urban and rural areas.[26] This is more clearly seen from the following analysis:

(a) Of 252 men who resided in *urban* areas during the second period, 92.5 per cent continued to do so during the third, 6.3 per cent shifted back and forth between urban and rural districts, while only three men (1.2 per cent) made their homes in rural districts throughout.

(b) Of 32 men who had lived in *rural* areas throughout the second period, 84.4 per cent continued to do so during the third, 3.1 per cent moved back and forth between urban and rural districts, 12.5 per cent became urbanites.

(c) Of 28 men who had moved between city and country during the second period, over half (57.2 per cent) continued to do so during the third, while 21.4 per cent became definitely city dwellers and an equal proportion remained in the city.[27]

Although some of the men lived in low rental residential neighborhoods, others in rapidly deteriorating areas of large cities, and still others in isolated rural sections, it is not enough to describe them in this way. We want to know the kind of influences by which the men were surrounded; whether in these neighborhoods there were street gangs, centers of vice, cheap commercialized dance-halls, disreputable restaurants, bar-rooms, pool-rooms, or other places where the underworld of vice and crime is likely to gather. As a matter of fact, only a tenth of the men lived in neighborhoods in which the surrounding influences could be designated as *good,* that is, in regions in which there were no street gangs, no centers of vice or crime within a radius of two square blocks in the city or a mile in the country, and where there were opportunities available for constructive recreation within easy walking distance, such as community centers under public or private auspices. Over half the group (55.7 per cent) lived mostly in neighborhoods which can be designated as *fair,* for although there were no vicious influences, they were lacking in outlets for the constructive use of leisure. A third (34.3 per cent) of the group generally made their homes in neighborhoods in which the influences are definitely *poor,* lo-

---

[25] Appendix B, 3–13.     [26] Appendix C, 8.     [27] Appendix D, 7.

cales combining all the vicious elements in which those who are easily susceptible to criminalistic stimuli can readily choose their antisocial companions and
activities.[28]

It is to be noted that while there was an appreciable decrease in the proportion of men generally making their homes in such poor neighborhoods, from
41.1 per cent during the first five-year span to 35.2 per cent during the second,
the situation has changed but little since the second five-year period. But the
proportion of men making their homes in really good neighborhoods has
dropped from 15.2 per cent during the first period, to 14.2 per cent during the
second, to 10 per cent during the third. This decline of residence in favorable
neighborhoods has been counterbalanced by a steady increase in the proportion of men making their homes in neighborhoods in which, although there
are no really vicious influences, there are no outlets for wholesome recreation
provided by the community (43.7 per cent, 50.6 per cent, and 55.7 per cent).
Possibly lower rentals in such regions explain this. The fact is, however, that
there is no significant movement toward the poorer neighborhoods. Deteriorating economic conditions during the years 1931–1937, embracing the third follow-up span, have made it impossible for these men to get into better districts,
but they are tending at least to move into areas in which the surrounding influences are not positively unwholesome.[29]

The following analysis brings out more clearly the changes in the neighborhood influences surrounding the homes of the men in Periods II and III:

(a) Of 44 men who lived in *good* neighborhoods during the second five-
year span, only 56.8 per cent did so during the third, when general industrial
conditions were bad; but only 9.1 per cent moved down into really poor neighborhoods, while 34.1 per cent made their homes in neighborhoods in which the
surrounding influences, though not constructive, were not definitely bad.

(b) Of 154 men who lived in *fair* neighborhoods during the second five-year
period, 83.8 per cent continued to do so during the third; but 4.5 per cent had
moved into good surroundings, while 11.7 per cent moved into neighborhoods
in which the environing influences were poor.

(c) Of 98 men who had lived during the second period in neighborhoods
in which the influences were *poor,* 77.6 per cent continued to do so during the
third, but 22.4 per cent had moved into fair neighborhoods. None of this group
moved into good neighborhoods during the third period.[30]

*Summary*

By combining the status of the men as regards the adequacy of the physical
condition of their homes, the moral atmosphere of their households, and the

[28] Appendix B, 3–14.        [29] Appendix C, 9.        [30] Appendix D, 8.

influences of the neighborhoods in which they lived, it is possible to summarize their environmental circumstances during the five-year span. A fourth of the men (23.2 per cent) can be designated as having *good* environmental circumstances; that is, their homes were adequate from a physical point of view to insure a minimum of comfort, the moral standards of their households were decent, and the neighborhood conditions were not unwholesome. In 44.1 per cent of the cases the environing circumstances were only *fair,* a designation applied to cases in which one or two of the constituents entering into the summary picture were not entirely favorable; while in 32.7 per cent of the cases the environmental circumstances were *poor,* which means that at least two of the three components of this summary were entirely unfavorable, the third only fair. Although we do not know what the status of the men was in this regard during the first five-year span, we can make comparison with the second five-year period. From this it is evident that there has been practically no change in the third as compared with the second period.[31] However, the trend may now be very slightly upward because in the fifth year of the third follow-up span there is a slight decrease in the proportion of men whose environmental circumstances can be described as poor, from 32.7 per cent during the first four years to 29.6 per cent in the fifth year.[32]

An analysis of the case-by-case changes that have occurred in the third period as compared with the second reveals the following:

(a) Of 77 men whose environmental circumstances could be described as *good* in the second five-year period, 76.6 per cent could be so designated in the third, while 22.1 per cent were then fair, and 1.3 per cent poor.

(b) Of 129 men whose environmental circumstances were *fair* during the second follow-up span, 76 per cent were likewise fair in the third, 14.7 per cent had dropped to poor; but 9.3 per cent were now good.

(c) Of 92 men whose environmental circumstances were definitely *poor* in the second period, 80.5 per cent continued to be such in the third, but 15.2 per cent became fair, and 4.3 per cent good.

It is evident, therefore, that despite the poor industrial conditions prevailing throughout the third period, there has been a slight improvement in the environmental circumstances of our men, even though those who had previously resided in good neighborhoods were not able completely to maintain this status during the third period.[33]

---

[31] Appendix C, 9b.     [32] Appendix B, 3–65a.     [33] Appendix D, 8a.

## IV

## FAMILY RELATIONS AND ASSUMPTION OF
## ECONOMIC RESPONSIBILITIES

W E now turn to a consideration of the relationships of our 439 men to
their wives, their children, and their close relatives, in an effort to determine whether they are maintaining a conventional pattern in these relationships. Are they happy in their married life? Are they attached to their children? Do they keep in touch with their relatives?

In the second portion of this chapter we shall be concerned with the problem
of whether or not these men are supporting themselves and their dependents
on at least a minimum subsistence level, or whether they lean on welfare agencies or relatives for partial or complete support.

### Marital Status and Conjugal Relations

By the end of the third follow-up period, when the men averaged forty
years of age, a third of the group (32.9 per cent) were still single, almost half
(46.5 per cent) were legally married and living with their wives, almost a fifth
(18.6 per cent) had separated or been divorced from their wives, while eight
men (2 per cent) had become widowers.[1]

In comparing this with the marital status of the men during the first and
second periods, we see a steady decrease in the proportion of single men, from
45.5 per cent at the end of the first span to 38.3 per cent at the end of the second, to 32.9 per cent at the end of the third.[2]

The changes which have occurred in the marital status of the men in the
third, as compared with the second period are more clearly indicated from the
following analysis:

(a) Of 153 men who had not married during the second period, 82.4 per
cent continued single in the third, while 15.7 per cent were married and living
with their wives at the end of the third period. Two, who had married, had
already separated from their wives and one had become a widower.

(b) Of 166 men who at the end of Period II were married and living with
their wives, 87.3 per cent were still doing so at the end of the third period, while
12.7 per cent were separated or divorced.

(c) Of 58 men who were separated or divorced at the end of the second period, 79.3 per cent had the same status at the end of the third; 17.2 per cent had

---

[1] For details see Appendix B, 3–20.        [2] Appendix C, 10.

remarried and were living with their wives and children, and two, though married, were widowers.

(d) Of five men who, while awaiting divorces, had illegally married other women and were living with them, all were now legally married to the same women.

(e) Of seven men who had been widowers at the end of the second five-year period, five had not remarried by the end of the third, while two were married and had already separated from their wives.[3]

It is evident from the foregoing analysis, that in addition to the steady increase in the proportion of married men, there has been an appreciable shifting about in marital relationships as indicated particularly by the divorces, separations, and remarriages.

Considering, next, the conjugal relations of the married men, we find that two-thirds of them (64.8 per cent) have been living compatibly with their wives throughout the third period, while in 15.5 per cent of the cases, although husband and wife were under the same roof, they were grossly incompatible, and indifferent or actually hostile to each other despite the fact that no open breach had yet occurred. In 19.7 per cent of the cases the men actually had separated from their wives during this period.[4] In comparing the conjugal relations of the men during the third five-year span with the first and second periods, we note a steady increase in the proportion whose conjugal relationships can be described as *good,* from 56 per cent in Period I, to 60.7 per cent in Period II, to 64.8 per cent in Period III. There has also been a decrease in the proportion of couples who *separated, deserted, or divorced,* from 27.6 per cent in Period I, to 24.4 per cent in Period II, to 19.7 per cent in Period III.[5] This consistent though slight decrease in marital break-ups tends to confirm the impression gained in the previous chapter that there is a growing stability on the part of the men, though not to the extent one would like to see.

The modifications with the passage of time are more specifically reflected in the following case-by-case analysis:

(a) Of 118 men who maintained *good* conjugal relationships in the second five-year period, 86.4 per cent continued to do so during the third; in 6.8 per cent the conjugal relations were fair; while in a like proportion they had deteriorated to poor.

(b) Of 28 men whose conjugal relationships were only *fair* during the second period, 50 per cent continued in this way in the third; in 17.9 per cent of the cases the relations of husband and wife had become good, while in 32.1 per cent an open breach occurred and the couples were separated or divorced.

[3] Appendix D, 9.     [4] For details see Appendix B, 3–22.     [5] Appendix C, 12.

(c) Of 25 men whose conjugal relationships were *poor* during the second period, 68 per cent continued to be so in the third, 16 per cent had become fair, and 16 per cent good.[6]

On the whole, therefore, the gains in the stability and happiness of the marital relation made in Period II were retained, if not somewhat improved.

## Assumption of Marital Responsibilities

Turning now to the question of whether these married men were meeting their responsibilities as husbands and fathers at least in the maintenance of a minimal standard of attachment and support, it is found that 65.2 per cent of the married men might be described as assuming their marital responsibilities. These men, in other words, have not during this third five-year period neglected or deserted their wives and children, or been unfaithful, or been physically or mentally abusive, and have made every reasonable effort to support their families without more than occasional aid from welfare agencies or relatives. A third of the men (34.8 per cent) did not, however, meet the above standard. Comparing the second and third periods we note a slight increase in the proportion assuming marital responsibilities, from 62.2 per cent in Period II, to 65.2 per cent in Period III.[7]

By the same standard that has been applied to the men, 88.2 per cent of their wives as contrasted to 65.2 per cent of the husbands, accepted their marital obligations during the third five-year span.[8] It would appear, therefore, that the marital difficulties which have occurred were to a greater extent due to the husbands than to their wives. This was the case, also, during the second five-year period, when about an equal proportion of wives assumed their marital responsibilities as did so during the third.[9] It should be mentioned in this connection that 71.1 per cent of the wives were found to be systematic, economical, clean and neat housekeepers, while the remaining 28.9 per cent were not efficient homemakers. The latter were careless, lazy, indifferent or wasteful, or suffered from temperamental difficulties which interfered with household routine, or were of such low mentality that they could not maintain wholesome standards of family life. In this regard the picture was about the same in the second five-year span.[10]

## Attitude toward Children

Of the 439 men living at the beginning of Period III, 267 were married and of these, 73 (27.3 per cent) had no children up to the end of the period. Of the 194

---

[6] Appendix D, 11.

[8] For details see Appendix B, 3–24.

[10] Appendix C, 12c.

[7] Appendix C, 12a.

[9] Appendix C, 12b.

who had children, 37.1 per cent were fathers of one child by the end of the third period, 19.6 per cent had two children, 16.5 per cent three, 11.9 per cent had four, 6.2 per cent were the fathers of five children, while 8.8 per cent had six or more. The average number of children per married man increased from 2.32 ($\pm$.08) at the end of the first five-year span to 2.46 ($\pm$.11) by the end of the second period, to 2.98 ($\pm$.09) by the close of the third.[11] During Period III the father's attitude toward his children can be described as *good* in 62.8 per cent of the cases, meaning that he had sincere affection for them; only *fair* in 16 per cent, the father being casual or indifferent in his attitude toward the children; and *poor* in 21.2 per cent, the fathers in these cases having shown no affection or evincing actual hostility toward the children.[12]

## Relation to Nearest Relatives

Considering, next, the matter of the attachment of the 439 men, whether married or not, to their nearest relatives, it is found that over half of them (56.4 per cent) kept in touch with their close relatives—their parents or brothers and sisters—because they were really attached to them, while the remainder (43.6 per cent) rarely communicated with their relatives or did so only when in need of assistance. There has been very little change in the attitude of the men toward their relatives during the three five-year periods. During the first span 54.2 per cent kept in touch with their parents, brothers, or sisters, in the second 52.2 per cent, in the third 56.4 per cent.[13]

A case-by-case analysis of the attachment of the men to their relatives in Period III as compared with Period II indicates that:

(a) Of 171 men who kept in touch with their nearest relatives and maintained a friendly relationship with them in Period II, 88.3 per cent continued to do so in the third follow-up span.

(b) Of 61 men who kept in touch with their relatives in Period II only when they were in need of help of one sort or another, 11.5 per cent resumed close family ties in Period III.

(c) Of 78 men who were entirely out of touch with their closest relatives in Period II, 23.1 per cent resumed friendly ties in Period III.[14]

Looking now on the other side of the picture, the attitude of the relatives toward the ex-inmates of the Reformatory, we find that a higher proportion of them were friendly and wanted to keep in touch with the men than of the

---

[11] Appendix C, 11. Of these children, four were known to have been conceived out of wedlock, though the parents married before the birth of the child, while two men were known to have children by women other than their wives and one who was unmarried had illegitimate children. Appendix B, 3–27. See also Appendix D, 10.

[12] Appendix B, 3–29a.　　　　[13] Appendix C, 13.　　　　[14] Appendix D, 12.

men themselves, namely, 66.6 per cent. However, 30.4 per cent of the closest kin were quite indifferent to the doings of their criminalistic relative and made no effort to keep in touch with him, and 3 per cent were hostile, or thoroughly disgusted with him, strongly disapproving of the offender and not wishing to have anything whatsoever to do with him.[15]

### Relations to Family

In view of the fact that not all the 439 men were married (131 men were still single), and that of those known to have been married at one time or another some were separated or divorced or were widowers while a few had illegitimate children, any inclusive description of their family relations during the third five-year span must refer to them all. We use as a standard of socially acceptable family relations the requirement that a man must not harm his family in any way that would be deemed injurious to the institution of family life. If married, he must not neglect or desert his wife or children, not have illicit relations with other women, not be abusive, nor continually away from home unless this is necessary to his business. If he has no obligations toward his wife because separation, desertion, or divorce occurred before the beginning of the third follow-up span but he does have children, he must assume his responsibilities toward them. If he has no children, or is a single man, he must keep in touch with his parents or brothers and sisters, and if living with them he must give evidence that he considers their home more than merely a convenient place in which to eat and sleep, that is, he must be an active participant in the life of the family.[16] If single, but a father, he must make provision for the care of his children.

It was found that 54.2 per cent of all the men met this minimum standard of socially acceptable family relationships during the third five-year span, while 45.8 per cent did not do so. There is a very slight increase in the proportion of men achieving this standard in the third period, as compared with the second, when 50 per cent of the men could be so classified.[17] That the trend is definitely upward, however, is evidenced in the fact that during the fifth year of the third span, 58.2 per cent of the men were meeting this standard of socially acceptable family life.[18] The total picture is one of marked improvement over the situation prior to the sentence of our men to the Reformatory, at which time the high proportion of 67.6 per cent had to be set down as failures in their family life.

[15] Appendix B, 3–18b.
[16] See Appendix A, *Definition of Terms,* Family Relationships.
[17] Appendix C, 14.          [18] Appendix B, 3–63a.

A case-by-case analysis reveals that:

(a) Of 172 men who were *successful* in their family relationships during the second five-year period, 87.8 per cent continued so in the third.

(b) Of 147 men who *failed* to meet the minimal standard in their interpersonal relations during the second span, 18.4 per cent met them during the third.

Clearly, there has been an improvement in the family life of the men in the third period as compared with the second.[19]

### Economic Condition

What alterations have taken place in the economic status of the men? During the third five-year span, we find that only 5.7 per cent can be described as being in *comfortable* circumstances, which means that they had accumulated resources sufficient to maintain themselves and their families for at least four months in the event of unemployment or illness. Half the group (50.7 per cent) were in *marginal* circumstances, that is, were living on daily earnings, accumulating little or nothing, and hovering on the border between self-support and dependency. These men might have had to resort to temporary assistance from social agencies or relatives in order to tide them over a brief critical period of a few days or even a month, but they were able to manage their own financial affairs with very little outside aid. The remaining 43.6 per cent were men partially or completely *dependent* on public or private welfare agencies or on relatives for support of themselves and, if married, of their wives and children. Of this group of 152, 108 (71.1 per cent) were dependent upon agencies or relatives not because of the depression but rather because of laziness or indifference toward supporting themselves or their families, while 44 (28.9 per cent) were entirely or partially dependent upon welfare agencies or relatives as a result of the industrial crisis which made it impossible for them to continue in employments they had engaged in previously and by which they had been able to support themselves and their families.[20] It is only by comparing the economic condition in the first and second periods with the third, that we see the significant change which has taken place. There has been an increase in dependency from 14.7 per cent in Period I, to 19.7 per cent in Period II up to 43.6 per cent in Period III.[21]

It is not surprising, therefore, to find that only a tenth of the men (10.8 per cent) had savings during the third five-year span, as contrasted with 23.8 per cent during the second.[22] However, on the whole, the men who carried insurance did not forfeit it to as great an extent as might have been expected. As

[19] Appendix D, 13.
[21] Appendix C, 17.
[20] For details see Appendix B, 3–33a.
[22] Appendix C, 16a.

the insurance policies were very small, in most cases under $500, they managed to keep these up. Less than half the men (45.1 per cent) carried insurance during the third five-year period, but this represents only a slight reduction compared with the 48.9 per cent insured in the second period.[23] Over four-fifths of those carrying insurance (82.9 per cent) paid for the policy out of their own earnings, their wives usually making the payments from the husband's income. Even if aid was being derived from social agencies or from work relief, a small amount was set aside to pay insurance premiums. In over a tenth of the cases (14.4 per cent) the premiums were paid for the men by their relatives and in four cases by employers or others. In this regard the status has practically remained unchanged since Period II.[24]

The shift that occurred in the economic condition of the men in Period III as compared with Period II is more clearly shown in the following case-by-case analysis:

(a) Of 34 men who were in *comfortable* economic circumstances during the second five-year period, only half continued in this status in the third, while 38.2 per cent dropped to marginal circumstances, and 11.8 per cent became dependents.

(b) Of 220 men who were formerly in *marginal* circumstances, 61.4 per cent retained this status in the third period, 37.2 per cent became dependents, and 1.4 per cent raised their status to comfortable circumstances.

(c) Of 67 men who were formerly in the *dependent* class, 86.6 per cent have continued as dependents in the third period.

It will be seen, therefore, that there has been a considerable lowering of the economic status of the men due largely to the poor industrial conditions prevailing during the third follow-up period.[25]

The influence of the depression on the lives of these men during the third five-year span is also evident in considering the proportion of them who had dependents in Period III as compared with the previous periods. Actually 72.5 per cent of them had dependents, that is, wives, children, and in a few cases parents whom they had to support. But it is to be noted that although the proportion having dependents increased from 67.3 per cent in Period I, to 69.1 per cent in Period II, to 72.5 per cent in Period III, this rise is so slight that it would not explain the greatly increased financial stress which has occurred in the group.[26]

A case-by-case analysis reveals the following:

(a) Of 102 men who had no dependents in the second five-year period, 32.4 per cent had them in the third.

[23] Appendix C, 18.          [24] Appendix C, 19.          [25] Appendix D, 16.
[26] Appendix C, 15.

(b) Of 227 men who had dependents in the second period, only 6.6 per cent had no dependents in the third.[27]

It should also be pointed out that when comparison is made of the disposition of earnings by these men during the first, second, and third periods, there is a steadily increasing proportion who are turning over their wages (little as they may be) to their wives: from 36.3 per cent in Period I and 41.8 per cent in Period II to 46.1 per cent in Period III.[28]

### Assistance from Social Service Agencies

The extent to which our men required assistance in the management of their personal affairs is reflected in the proportion who were aided by social agencies in one way or another during the third follow-up period, namely 59.4 per cent. Of the 212 men known to have been assisted by public and private welfare organizations, 68 of them were known to one agency, 59 to two, 55 to three or four, 18 to five or six, and 12 to seven or more.[29] A sharp increase occurred in the proportion of men dealt with by welfare agencies in the third period as compared with the first and second, from 25.4 per cent in the first to 41 per cent in the second to 59.4 per cent in the third.[30]

A case-by-case analysis of the changes in Period III as compared with Period II indicates the following:

(a) Of 189 men not known to social welfare agencies at all during the second five-year period, 40.7 per cent had to be dealt with by such organizations during the third.

(b) Of 135 men who had been clients of social agencies during the second follow-up span, only 13.3 per cent were not aided by them during the third.[31]

Two factors in the lives of the men account for this greater resort to the aid of social welfare organizations. First, their increasing burdens and responsibilities because of marriage and growing families, and secondly the industrial crisis which made it necessary for many men who were otherwise self-supporting to turn to relief agencies for help. Of the 212 men who had to resort to assistance, we find that 81.1 per cent were given direct financial relief, while 29.7 per cent received work relief of one sort or another. In a third of the group (32.1 per cent) free medical care was given to the men or their wives and children; in a tenth (9.4 per cent) mental hygiene treatment of one sort or another was provided for the men or their families; in 8 per cent of the cases agencies dealing with problems of childhood or adolescence had to step into the family situation; and in a few instances, questions of domestic relations and of industrial placement were handled by the agencies.

---

[27] Appendix D, 14.  [28] Appendix B, 3–34a; C, 16; D, 15.  [29] Appendix B, 3–35.
[30] Appendix C, 20.  [31] Appendix D, 17.

That the problem of furnishing relief to these men and their families has become acute is evidenced by the fact that during the third five-year span 81.1 per cent of those having to call upon social agencies for assistance did so because of need for monetary aid, as contrasted with 61.6 per cent during the second period. During the third span a far lower proportion of men and their families were turning to the agencies for medical aid (32.1 per cent in Period III as compared to 50.7 per cent in Period II), or for assistance in securing jobs (6.6 per cent in Period III and 19.9 per cent in Period II). There was however less resort to agencies for assistance with problems involving children (in 8 per cent of the cases in Period III and 13.7 per cent in Period II). Clearly, during the third follow-up span the problem of direct relief was the most pressing. Other needs were not stressed as much as they had been in previous years, yielding in importance to the urgent need of bread and butter.[32]

Analysis of the individual cases indicates that in 72 of the cases (20.5 per cent) there was no need for intervention by social welfare agencies either to furnish relief or to give other kinds of assistance to the men and their families. In 61 of the cases (17.3 per cent) whatever demands presented themselves among the men or their wives and children were adequately met by the welfare agencies, but in 62.2 per cent one or more needed services were not rendered, probably because the men and their families did not apply for them. This latter group comprises 219 cases. Their greatest need (in 72.2 per cent of instances) was for friendly supervision of their affairs. They would have profited greatly had some kindly and skilful social welfare worker conferred with them about their problems from time to time and given them some guidance. In a third of these 219 cases (32.4 per cent) the problem of furnishing mental hygiene treatment for the men, their wives or children was evident; another third of the group (30.6 per cent) were sorely in need of vocational guidance; 29.7 per cent should clearly have had their leisure time at least guided away from activities of a wasteful nature. In a fifth (20.1 per cent) of the group there were problems of family welfare which called for solution, mainly questions involving domestic relations.[33]

## Assumption of Economic Responsibilities

Over a third of the entire group (37.8 per cent) met their economic responsibilities by employment in legitimate occupations. This means that they managed to maintain themselves and their dependents, at least in marginal circumstances, with only occasional resort to public or private agencies or sporadic assistance from relatives. In addition, 7.5 per cent though meeting their economic obligations, were partly or wholly engaged in illicit occupations. Over

[32] Appendix C, 20a.                    [33] Appendix B, 3–60.

a third (36 per cent) deliberately evaded their economic responsibilities, these being men who could and should have been self-supporting even during this period of economic stress. This leaves a fifth of the group (18.7 per cent) who were actually unable to meet their economic obligations although they manifested willingness to do so. The bulk of this latter group were caught in the tide of the depression and were absolutely unable to make ends meet without resort to outside aid, while a small number (15 men in all) were unable to meet their obligations because of chronic illness.[34] That the group as a whole is beginning to pull itself out of this mire is evidenced by the fact that in the fifth year of the five-year period 42.5 per cent of the men were meeting their financial responsibilities in legitimate employment, as compared to 37.8 per cent during the first four years of this period.[35]

It is from a comparison of the assumption by these men of their economic obligations in the first and second follow-up periods with the third, that we can see the extent to which the industrial depression has brought about a decrease in their ability to shoulder their responsibilities even though they were willing to do so. We have excluded from consideration all men who were really victims of the depression but had manifested every willingness to support their families, or who absolutely could not do so because of chronic illness. On this basis there is indicated an increasing inability or unwillingness to meet economic responsibilities from 33.8 per cent in the first five-year span to 39.2 per cent in the second, and to 44.3 per cent in the third.[36]

The changes which have occurred in the third period as compared with the second become evident from the following analysis:

(a) Of 172 men who met their economic responsibilities by employment in legitimate occupations during the second five-year span, 59.9 per cent continued to do so during the third; 2.3 per cent though fulfilling their economic responsibilities, were doing so through illicit employment; 15.1 per cent neglected to shoulder their obligations through their own fault; while 22.7 per cent were unable, either because of the industrial conditions or because of chronic illness, to meet their responsibilities.

(b) Of 28 men who had fulfilled their economic obligations during the second period through earnings from illicit occupations, 50 per cent continued to do likewise during the third; 25 per cent were shouldering their responsibilities through legitimate occupations, 14.3 per cent neglected to meet their obligations through their own fault, while 10.7 per cent were unable to meet them though manifesting willingness to do so.

(c) Of 105 men who neglected their economic responsibilities in the second

[34] Appendix B, 3–31a.          [35] For details see Appendix B, 3–64.
[36] Appendix C, 21.

five-year span through their own fault, 76.2 per cent continued to avoid their obligations in the third period for the same reasons; 6.7 per cent were meeting their responsibilities in legitimate occupations and 1.9 per cent in illicit employment; while 15.2 per cent were unable to fulfill their economic responsibilities either because of industrial conditions or chronic illness.

(d) Of 11 men who were unable to meet their responsibilities during the second five-year period even though willing to do so, six were likewise unable to do so during the third period, two were assuming their obligations in earnings from legitimate occupations, one from illicit income, while two, though now able to meet their economic responsibilities, failed to do so through their own fault.[37]

## Summary

We have described the extent to which these men were dependent on the welfare agencies of the community for support and have seen that the bulk of such assistance was financial in character. We have indicated also that the industrial depression came to its peak during the third five-year follow-up period. We have seen, further, that there was a sharp rise in the proportion of men who became dependent on welfare agencies and relatives in this third period, but it has been evident, also, that there has been practically no increase in the proportion of men having dependents; nor has there been any significant decrease in the proportion carrying insurance. An increase has occurred in the proportion of men turning over their wages to their wives. We have also noted in the earlier part of this chapter that there appears to be a slight but growing stability in the family relations of these men.

On the whole the picture is one of somewhat improved family relationships but of greatly worsened economic status. The former is shown by the gains in the stability of the marital relations of the men and in their increasing assumption of family responsibilities. Their lower economic status is essentially a phenomenon of the industrial depression which characterized the third follow-up period and is evidenced by the more than doubling of the incidence of economic dependency since Period II, with an accompanying drop in savings and a rise in the proportion of men who had to seek assistance—largely direct financial support—from public welfare agencies.

[37] Appendix D, 18.

# V

## WORK AND USE OF LEISURE

### WORK

THE situation described in the two previous chapters indicates that our men, although seriously affected by the industrial depression, nevertheless seemed to have maintained the basic gains which had been made in the previous five-year span. What is the situation in respect to their industrial adjustment during the third follow-up period? At least a fifth of the entire group were engaged in work relief projects of one sort or another for portions of this period.[1] It should also be mentioned that a tenth were at no time during this five-year span engaged in private industry. In fact, only 15.5 per cent were in private employment throughout the entire span, 9.7 per cent were so employed for forty-eight to sixty months, 6.9 per cent for twenty-four to thirty-six months. Thus, a great majority of the group (57.1 per cent) were occupied in private industry for less than three years of the third five-year period.[2]

### Occupations and Skill

We now turn to a description of the occupations of the 439 men who were living at the beginning of the third period. In considering the kind of work these men were engaged in, we shall describe their jobs in private industry and not in work relief projects. The situation in which men are placed on such projects is so abnormal that it would not adequately describe their actual industrial status, but of course the changes wrought in their employment as a result of the depression period are taken into account throughout this chapter.

First we must note the fact that almost half the group (45.3 per cent) were unskilled laborers during the third five-year period, another 45 per cent were semi-skilled workers, while less than a tenth (9.7 per cent) were engaged in skilled occupations. Skill of occupation has been determined on the basis of the usual work in which a man has been engaged, or, if it was not possible to determine the usual occupation, on the basis of the highest degree of skill the man manifested in any of the jobs he held during the period. In comparing the occupational skill of the men during the third follow-up period with their skill during the second, when industrial conditions were more normal, it is not surprising to find an increase in the proportion of unskilled laborers, from 37.7 per cent to 45.3 per cent and a decrease in the proportion of skilled and semi-skilled workers. During this period of industrial depression men of

---

[1] Appendix B, 3–39c.                    [2] Appendix B, 3–36b.

greater capacity had to resort to less skilled employments in order to earn any sort of living. This becomes clearer in a consideration of the degree of skill of the men during this period.[3]

A case-by-case correlation of the skill of the men in Period III as compared with Period II reveals that:

(a) Of 101 men who were *unskilled* workers during Period II, 8.9 per cent were semi-skilled workers in Period III, but none had become skilled workers.

(b) Of 145 men who were *semi-skilled* in Period II, 74.5 per cent continued to engage in semi-skilled work, 2.1 per cent became skilled workers, but 23.4 per cent were employed in unskilled work.

(c) Of 35 men who had been employed in *skilled* occupations during the second period, 28.6 per cent resorted to semi-skilled work, none of the group being employed as unskilled laborers, however.

It is again evident, therefore, that the industrial depression has forced a considerable proportion of the men into less skilled employments than their capacities warranted.[4]

In Period III, 101 of the men (30 per cent) were usually engaged in rough labor and any kind of odd jobs they could pick up; 8.3 per cent usually worked as teamsters, truckmen, or chauffeurs; 11.6 per cent were factory hands; 9.5 per cent were generally engaged as salesmen, store clerks, or office workers, or were managing small stores of their own; 4.5 per cent were restaurant or hotel workers, usually cooks or waiters; 10 men (3 per cent) worked mostly as farm hands throughout the period. A sixth of the group (16.9 per cent) were working in skilled trades, as electricians, machinists, plumbers, carpenters, bricklayers, painters, gardeners. A small proportion of the men (7.7 per cent) were usually engaged in illicit occupations such as deriving profits from prostitution, drug selling, engaging in "nigger pool" rackets; while 4.7 per cent though working occasionally, were mostly idle throughout the period.

The proportion of men engaged in rough labor and odd jobs has increased from 21.9 per cent in the first period and 23.5 per cent in the second, to 30 per cent in the third. This is undoubtedly due to the fact that during this period of industrial depression men who were previously engaged in more skilled occupations had to turn to rough labor for a livelihood. There has been a slight though consistent decrease in the proportion of men usually occupied in skilled trades, from 22.6 per cent in the first period to 18.9 per cent in the second, and to 16.9 per cent in the third.[5]

A case-by-case analysis discloses more specifically the changes that have occurred in types of employment:

[3] Appendix C, 24.     [4] Appendix D, 21.
[5] Appendix C, 22.

(a) Of 72 men who were common laborers in Period II, 69.5 per cent continued to be such in Period III, 9.7 per cent remained idle during the third period through their own fault, one man usually made his living illicitly, six worked in factories, two became salesmen and store clerks, three worked in restaurants, one was a truckman, and two entered skilled trades.

(b) Of 11 men who were farm hands during the second follow-up period, seven continued to be so employed, and four turned to non-agricultural rough labor.

(c) Of 36 men who were trucksters, teamsters, or chauffeurs in the second period, 22 (60.9 per cent) continued to be so employed in the third, two entered skilled trades, two became salesmen, one worked in a factory, one on a farm, one in a restaurant, five were common laborers, and two earned their living in illicit occupations.

(d) Of 41 men who were factory hands in the second period, 25 (60 per cent) continued to work in factories during the third, five were now in skilled trades, one became a truckster, nine common laborers, and one earned his living illicitly.

(e) Of 26 men who were salesmen or store clerks in the second period, 18 continued in similar occupations during the third, one man went to work in a factory, one became a common laborer, five earned their living in illicit occupations, and one was idle through his own fault.

(f) Of 17 men who had previously worked in restaurants either as cooks, waiters, or dishwashers, nine remained in similar work, one went into a skilled trade, two became store clerks, one became a factory hand, one a truckster, two became common laborers, and one earned his living illicitly.

(g) Of 56 men who had been in skilled trades during the second period, 40 (71.3 per cent) continued in such work during the third, two became restaurant hands, three store clerks, one a factory hand, two trucksters or teamsters, seven became common laborers, and one was idle through his own fault.

(h) Of 16 men who were usually engaged in illicit occupations during the second five-year span, ten continued to be so engaged, one became a salesman, one was employed in a skilled trade, three were common laborers, and one was idle because of illness.

(i) Of 12 men who were generally loafing during the second period, five continued to do so in the third, two were engaged in illicit occupations, while five resorted to common labor.[6]

Turning now to the number of different types of work engaged in by these men during the third follow-up span, we find that a little over a third of the group (37.9 per cent) did only one kind of work, 17.8 per cent engaged in two

[6] Appendix D, 19.

different types of work during this period, while 44.3 per cent tried three or more types of occupation.[7] That two-fifths (37.9 per cent) engaged in one type of work is in marked contrast to the second five-year span, when the far higher incidence of 58 per cent were engaged in a single type of occupation; and the far lower proportion of 17.8 per cent tried three or more different types of occupations as compared with the 44.3 per cent during the third period. Again this must be charged to the exigencies of the abnormal industrial conditions prevailing during the third follow-up span.[8]

In regard to employment in illicit occupations, it should be said that only 20 men (6.1 per cent) of the group earned their living in illegitimate pursuits throughout the third period, while another 47 (14.4 per cent) resorted to illicit employment occasionally during spells of irregular employment or work relief. This totals a fifth of the group (20.5 per cent) who at one time or another during the third five-year span engaged in illicit pursuits. It is to be noted that there has occurred a slight increase in the proportion of men not resorting to illicit occupations for livelihood, from 76.5 per cent in the second five-year period to 79.5 per cent in the third. This again confirms the impression already gained that the growing stability which these men manifested during the second follow-up period as compared with the first has continued. Possibly it would have been greater if not for the severe strain placed on them by the rising industrial depression of the third period.[9]

A case-by-case analysis reveals that:

(a) Of 223 men who were not engaged in illicit occupations at all during the second five-year period, 93.7 per cent remained in this status during the third; but eleven men (4.9 per cent) earned their living in illegitimate pursuits for part of the period, while three did so throughout.

(b) Of 39 men who were engaged in illicit occupations for part of the second period, 41 per cent were similarly employed in the third period, while 15.4 per cent more were exploiting illegitimate occupations throughout the third period; but 43.6 per cent of the men turned to legitimate pursuits as a source of livelihood.

(c) Of 15 men who were engaged in illicit occupations throughout the second period, nine continued to be so employed in the third; while five more were engaged in them for part of the time and only one of the group earned an honest living throughout the third period.[10]

*Steadiness of Employment*

Considering, next, the stability of employment, it is found that over half the group who were engaged in private industry (53.4 per cent) held jobs on

---

[7] For details see Appendix B, 3–40a.     [8] Appendix C, 22a.
[9] Appendix C, 23.                        [10] Appendix D, 20.

an average of less than three months, but, on the other hand, over a fourth (27.3 per cent) retained their posts on an average of two to five years.[11] The entire group of men held jobs for an average of 18.14 ($\pm$.86) months. This represents practically no decrease in the average number of months during which men engaged in private industry held their jobs, for in Period II they worked on a job on the average of 19.7 ($\pm$.80) months, which is only a month longer than in Period III. Both these periods, however, indicate a marked improvement in the average length of time that jobs were held as compared with the first five-year span when the average was only 14.66 ($\pm$.58).[12]

A case-by-case analysis of the average length of time jobs were held in Periods II and III reflects more clearly the changes that actually occurred:

(a) Of 39 men who held jobs on the average of thirty-six or more months during the second period, 26 (66.7 per cent) were able, despite the industrial depression, to stick to their jobs for this length of time during the third period; eight (20.5 per cent) then held them for twelve to thirty-six months; three (7.7 per cent) three to twelve months, and two (5.1 per cent) for less than three months.

(b) Of 28 men who held jobs on the average of twelve to thirty-six months during the second period, over a third (35.7 per cent) were able to do so during Period III while less than a third (ten) held their jobs for even longer periods; but a fifth (six) were able to hold them on the average of only three to twelve months and four (14.3 per cent) for less than three months.

(c) Of 24 men who held their jobs on the average of three to twelve months during the second period, over half (thirteen) were able to maintain this average during the third span, while three held their jobs twelve to thirty-six months and only one (4.1 per cent) for thirty-six or more months. Only seven of the men could not maintain the average length of employment they had achieved during the previous period, holding jobs for less than three months.

(d) Of 73 men who kept their jobs on an average of less than three months during the second follow-up period, 95.9 per cent maintained this low average during the third.[13]

The longest period of time the group as a whole held jobs during the third follow-up period is 20.90 ($\pm$.76) months.[14] This indicates a reduction of about two and one-half months since the second period; but in both the second and third spans the men held jobs longer than during the first, when the average was only 18.38 ($\pm$.63) months.[15] This again reflects their growing stability in employment, although job limitations during the industrial depression resulted in some falling off in the good record they had made in the second five-year period.

[11] For details see Appendix B, 3–43.   [12] Appendix C, 31.   [13] Appendix D, 28.
[14] For details see Appendix B, 3–44.   [15] Appendix C, 32.

More specifically:

(a) Of 60 men who held a job for as long as thirty-six or more months during the second follow-up period, two-thirds (65 per cent) did equally well during the third.

(b) Of 56 men who held a job for as long as twelve to thirty-six months in the second period, over half (55.3 per cent) were able to do this or better during the third, while 44.7 per cent held their longest jobs for less than that time.

(c) Of 36 men who stuck to their jobs for not more than three to twelve months during the second period, almost two-thirds (61.1 per cent) managed to do this or better during the third, while 38.9 per cent held their longest jobs for less time.

(d) Of 58 men who continued on the same job for less than three months during the second period, three-fourths (75.9 per cent) did no better during the third, but 24.1 per cent were able to hold a job for a longer time.[16]

The continuity of employment of these men is best summarized in the following way: A fifth of the group (62) may be described as *regularly employed* during the third five-year period, which means there were very few if any breaks in their work. A third of the group (109) may be designated as *fairly regular workers;* that is, men who despite periods of unemployment did have sustained work. But almost a half of the men (123) were *irregular workers,* having frequent or long protracted periods of unemployment and no periods of sustained work. As it is steadiness of employment which has been so seriously affected by the abnormal industrial conditions prevailing during this span, we are not surprised by an increase in the proportion of men irregularly employed, from 37.8 per cent in Period II to 46.1 per cent in Period III.[17]

The following case-by-case analysis is revealing:

(a) Of 87 men who were *regularly* employed during the second period, only 49 (56.3 per cent) were able to maintain this degree of steadiness during the third, 27 (31 per cent) were then employed only fairly regularly, 9 (10.4 per cent) were irregularly employed, and two men were illicitly employed.

(b) Of 96 men who were *fairly regularly employed,* over half (54.2 per cent) were able to maintain this relative degree of steadiness in employment; while a tenth (11.5 per cent) were regularly employed; but 31.3 per cent were now irregular workers and a few were engaged in illicit occupations.

(c) Of 100 men who were either *irregularly employed or engaged in illicit occupations* in Period II, 89 per cent continued as such during the third period, only ten men worked with a fair degree of regularity, while one man had pulled himself up to regular employment.[18]

[16] Appendix D, 29.     [17] Appendix C, 30.
[18] Appendix D, 27.

*Earnings*

In regard to wages received during the third five-year span, we would expect a falling off as compared with the previous periods. The average weekly wage of the group in the third span was only $19.20 (±.57);[19] while in the first five-year period it had been $26.60 (±.43) and in the second, $25.25 (±.44).[20] Not only has there occurred a drop in the average earnings of the group but also in the highest wage, which averaged $23.70 (±.56)[21] in Period III as compared with $30.30 (±.48) in the first and $32 (±.47)[22] in the second period. Again it should be pointed out that this decrease is not due to any deterioration in the men themselves, but rather to the general industrial conditions prevailing during the period.

The change in earnings in Period III as compared with Period II is more clearly seen from the following analysis:

(a) Of 25 men who in the second follow-up period had earned more than $35 per week, on an average, only ten were able to maintain this substantial wage during the third period, while eight dropped to the $25-$30 a week level, and seven to earnings of less than $25.

(b) Of 54 men who in the second period were averaging $25 to $35 weekly, sixteen (29.6 per cent) remained in this wage group during the third period, six earned more, while 32 (59.3 per cent) received less than $25 a week.

(c) Of 86 men who averaged less than $25 a week in Period II, 91.9 per cent remained in this low wage group during the third period, while six were able to earn between $25 and $35, and one averaged $35.[23]

A case-by-case comparison of the highest wage earned during the third period with that earned during the second further indicates the drop in wages:

(a) Of 82 men who had earned $35 or more a week in the second period, only 41.5 per cent ever earned as much as this during the third.

(b) Of 60 men who earned as much as $25 to $35 during the second period, only 53.3 per cent earned as much as this during the third.

(c) Of 79 men who averaged less than $25 during the second period, only 15.2 per cent earned more than this during the third.

It is evident, therefore, that wage scales were lower in the third period. This is due to the industrial depression and not to any real lessening of the earning capacity of the men.[24]

*Work Habits*

Regardless of the decreasing opportunities for steady and skilled or semi-skilled occupations, we find that 42.9 per cent of the men had *good* work habits

[19] For details see Appendix B, 3–41.    [20] Appendix C, 26.
[21] For details see Appendix B, 3–42.    [22] Appendix C, 27.
[23] Appendix D, 23.                       [24] Appendix D, 24.

during the third follow-up period, that is, they were reliable workers and altogether an asset to their employers; a fourth of the group (25.5 per cent) were *fair* workers, for though permitting their work to be interrupted by periodic drinking, the drug habit, occasional vagabondage, or sheer laziness, they showed some underlying qualities of reliability. Less than a third of the men (31.6 per cent) must be described as *poor* workers, that is to say, as unreliable, dishonest, unstable, ambitionless, wayward, or engaged in illegitimate occupations. This last group are out-and-out industrial liabilities, many of them unemployables. In comparing their status as workers in Period III with the second and first periods, we find further confirmation of the evidence that has already emerged, an increasing stability in the group despite the industrial pressures, because the proportion of men with good work habits has increased from 35.1 per cent in the first five-year span to 41.2 per cent in the second and to 42.9 per cent in the third. There has, however, also been a gain in the ranks of poor workers from 25.9 per cent in the second period to 31.6 per cent in the third, this improvement occurring largely among the men described as having fair work habits.[25]

More specifically:

(a) Of 117 men whose work habits had been *good* during Period II, 84.6 per cent continued likewise in the third period, while the work habits of thirteen (11.1 per cent) were only fair and of five (4.3 per cent) poor.

(b) Of 99 men whose work habits were *fair* during the second period, 51.5 per cent continued to be fair during the third, 20.2 per cent had improved, while 28.3 per cent had become worse.

(c) Of 66 men whose work habits were *poor* during Period II, 80.3 per cent continued likewise in the third period, but the work habits of seven (10.6 per cent) were now fair, while a tenth of the men, six (9.1 per cent) were now assets to their employers.[26]

A comparison of the proportion of men who left their jobs through their own fault shows a consistent decline from 53.2 per cent in the first follow-up period, to 44.2 per cent in the second, and down to 39.3 per cent in the third.[27] This supports the conclusion that our men, though experiencing greater unemployment and a decline in the incidence of skilled employments, have not, on the whole, deteriorated as a result of the industrial depression.

More light is thrown on this by the following case-by-case analysis:

(a) Of 97 men who left their jobs during the second follow-up period through their own fault, a fourth (27.8 per cent) changed employments during the third period for reasons not reflecting on them personally.

(b) Of 96 men who in Period II left jobs for reasons not reflecting upon

[25] Appendix C, 28.        [26] Appendix D, 25.        [27] Appendix C, 29.

them personally, only 13.5 per cent could be charged in the third period with leaving jobs through any fault of their own.[28]

### Industrial Adjustment

To describe fairly the industrial adjustment of these men during the third follow-up period it is necessary to combine data regarding their work habits and their steadiness of occupation, eliminating those who were not in private employment for most of this five-year span. Of the balance, a fifth (20.2 per cent) were *industrial successes,* being regular workers with good work habits; somewhat over a third (37.5 per cent) can be labeled *partial successes,* either because they had good work habits but were not regularly employed, or were regularly employed but did not have good work habits; and 42.3 per cent were definitely *industrial failures,* in that their work habits were poor and they did not work regularly or were engaged in illicit occupations.[29] Despite the fact that more of them were industrial failures in Period III (42.3 per cent) than in Period II (37.3 per cent),[30] which is accounted for by the effects of the industrial depression, nevertheless by the fifth year of the third five-year span they were already climbing out of the depression years as reflected by a growing adjustment in industrial life.[31]

A case-by-case comparison indicates that:

(a) Of 75 men whose industrial adjustment was *good* during the second five-year period, less than two-thirds (62.7 per cent) continued to be well adjusted industrially during the third.

(b) Of 102 men whose industrial adjustment was *fair* during the second period, well over half (59.8 per cent) continued fair in the third, and 11.8 per cent made a good adjustment; but a fourth (28.4 per cent) were now poorly adjusted in industry.

(c) Of 95 men whose industrial adjustment was *poor* during the second period, 85.3 per cent continued poor in the third, but 12.6 per cent became fair and 2.1 per cent good.[32]

### Summary

In reviewing these findings, one gets a general picture of progress in industrial life, despite the pressures of the economic decline. True, there was a decrease in the proportion of men who obtained employment in private industry and an increase in the incidence of work relief. True, also, the percentage engaged in skilled occupations declined, as did the average length of

---

[28] Appendix D, 26.
[30] Appendix C, 33.
[32] Appendix D, 30.

[29] For details see Appendix B, 3–34b.
[31] Appendix B, 3–63b.

holding jobs, the regularity of employment, and the weekly wages. But such unfavorable trends were not excessive and are largely to be laid at the door of the depression rather than to be charged to the men themselves. Such a conclusion is supported by the material increase since Period II in the proportion of men engaged in more than one type of work, something compelled by the general industrial decline. The substantial retention of the gains made during Period II, however, is evident in the decline, slight though it is, in the proportion of men resorting to illicit means of gaining a living. That the depression has not resulted in an increase in illicit occupations among these men is strong proof of their growing stability. This steadying and maturing of the group is further reflected in the increase in the proportion of good workers among them, slight though it is. Despite the tensions imposed by the industrial decline, the good work habits previously established have continued. A further evidence of the retention of the gains previously made, and even of a slight improvement over the situation in the preceding period, is the decline in the proportion of men who left their jobs through any fault of their own.

## USE OF LEISURE

We have analyzed the environmental conditions under which our men lived during the third follow-up period, their relationship to wife, children, and other members of the family, their assumption of economic responsibilities, and their adjustment in industry. Before turning to the central question of the extent to which the group continued to commit crime during the third period, we shall give some consideration to their companionships, haunts, and recreational activities.

### Companionships and Haunts

To what extent did these men associate with questionable companions during the third period? Over half the group (55.7 per cent) made companions of people with whom association might lead to delinquency at any time,—street corner loafers, habitués of cheap pool-rooms, drunks, men and women who live by their wits, professional gamblers and others of such ilk. Because of the bad industrial conditions prevailing during this third five-year span, one might have expected an increase in association with questionable companions during this period. But such is not the case. There has actually been a decrease, from 68.8 per cent in the first follow-up span to 63 per cent in the second and to 55.7 per cent in the third.[33] There has also been a decrease in association with definitely criminalistic gangs, from 7 per cent in Period II to 3.5 per cent in Period

---

[33] Appendix C, 34.

III, together with an increase from 40.4 per cent in Period II to 52.6 per cent in Period III, of men who, in their leisure time did not associate either with gangs or with crowds of men (a gang being distinguished from a crowd by being organized for a definite anti-social purpose and having specific leadership). In other words, there is becoming apparent a marked tendency away from group leisure-time activities.[34]

More specifically:

(a) Of 118 men whose companions were not of doubtful character during the second five-year period, only 8.5 per cent later had bad companions.

(b) Of 180 men who indulged in harmful companionships during Period II, 15.6 per cent had ceased associating with such companions in the third period.[35]

In regard to places in which their leisure time was spent, over half the group (184), as might be expected from the above findings regarding companionships, were habitués of places distinctly questionable in character, such as bootlegging joints, gambling dens, houses of ill fame, and other disreputable resorts. A third of the men (112) frequented places in which the influences, although not affirmative, were however not likely to prove harmful, since the great majority of patrons are not there for illicit purposes—public, commercialized dance-halls, skating-rinks, bowling-alleys, beaches. Only a tenth of the group (39) spent any of their leisure time in places of constructive recreation such as community centers, public libraries, Y.M.C.A.'s, or similarly well-planned and supervised organizations for the use of leisure time. Here again in comparing the haunts of the men during this third follow-up span with the first and second, we note a consistent decline in the proportion employing their leisure time in disreputable places—from 68.1 per cent in Period I to 61.5 per cent in Period II and to 54.9 per cent in Period III.[36] This is further borne out by a slight decline in the proportion of men hanging about street corners or idling aimlessly in front of stores, from 48.7 per cent in Period II to 44.9 per cent in Period III.[37]

More specifically:

(a) Of 121 men whose usual haunts during the second period were of a harmless nature, 9.1 per cent now spent their leisure time in questionable places.

(b) Of 170 men whose haunts were harmful during the second five-year span, 13.5 per cent were no longer idling about in such places during the third five-year period.[38]

---

[34] Appendix C, 35a.  
[36] Appendix C, 35.  
[38] Appendix D, 32.  

[35] Appendix D, 31.  
[37] Appendix C, 35b.

*Constructive Activities*

At no time in their careers has this group of men shown any inclination toward membership in such organizations as clubs, lodges, secret fraternities, trade unions, mutual benefit societies, and the like. During the third follow-up span, 85.5 per cent belonged to no legitimate organizations of any kind. However, a very slight increase is to be noted in organization membership, from 11.9 per cent in the first five-year span to 13.8 per cent in the second, up to 14.5 per cent in the third.[39] As the men grew older and settled a little more into neighborhood life (it will be recalled that mobility has been less in this period than before, and household stability greater) they showed a slightly greater inclination to join clubs and other organizations.

This is reflected in the following analysis:

(a) Of 239 men who had not belonged to clubs or organizations during the second period, 6.7 per cent joined them during the third.

(b) Of 44 men who had been members of clubs or organizations of one sort or another during the second period, thirteen (29.5 per cent) had dropped their membership in the third.[40]

This pattern does not seem to cover church attendance, however; for during the third follow-up span two-thirds of the men did not attend church at all, a fourth attended now and then, especially on holy days, while less than a tenth went to church regularly. In comparing the proportion of men in each span who entirely neglected their church duties, we find an increasing proportion of non-attenders, from 43.3 per cent in the first span to 47.6 per cent in the second, and up to 66.1 per cent in the third. It may well be that the discouragements attendant upon difficulties in finding work during this period, with their resultant economic pressures, partly explain this sharp rise in neglect of religious duties.[41]

More detailed analysis of church attendance shows that:

(a) Of 30 men who had attended church regularly during the second five-year period, 23.3 per cent later became irregular attendants and 6.7 per cent did not attend at all.

(b) Of 100 men who had attended irregularly during the second period, 58 per cent continued to do so during the third, only 7 per cent became regular attendants, while 35 per cent no longer went to a place of worship.

(c) Of 119 who did not attend church at all during the second period, 5 per cent were attending irregularly during the third.[42]

Although our men are of very low educational status (it will be recalled that

---

[39] Appendix C, 36.  [40] Appendix D, 33.

[41] Appendix C, 37.  [42] Appendix D, 34.

by far the highest proportion of them did not finish common school, only 3.3 per cent of the entire group made any attempt to further themselves educationally by attending night school or taking correspondence courses. A rise in this respect had occurred in Period II as compared with the first five-year span (from 3.9 per cent to 5.6 per cent) but the drop to 3.3 per cent in the third period probably reflects, in part, the discouragements due to the poor industrial conditions and the sheer struggle for existence.[43]

More specifically:

(a) Of 270 men who did not participate in educational activities of any sort during the second five-year period, only two men were doing so in the third.

(b) Of 17 men who took advantage of educational activities during Period II, only nine were still doing so during the third.[44]

## Summary

By way of summary, it may be said that over half the men (57.4 per cent) utilized their leisure time *harmfully* during the third five-year span (i.e., they were indulging in forms of recreation which might lead to criminal conduct, such as membership in gangs, association with bootleggers, prostitutes, loafers, drug addicts, gamblers); while a third (39.9 per cent) may be described as making *negative* use of their leisure time (i.e., although they were not engaging in harmful activities, they were not utilizing their leisure constructively). Only 2.7 per cent of the entire group employed their spare time in a *constructive* way, either as members of well-supervised social groups or by furthering themselves culturally or vocationally in their spare hours.[45] It should be said, however, that the trend in the last year of the five-year span has been away from harmful use of leisure, for only 49.5 per cent of the men were misusing their spare time in the fifth year, as compared with 57.4 per cent during the first four years.[46] This improvement in use of leisure has been consistent, for in the first follow-up period 69.4 per cent of the men used their spare time harmfully, a proportion which dropped to 65.8 per cent in the second period and to 57.4 per cent in the third.[47]

Despite the industrial crisis, therefore, these men have shown gains in the nature of their companionships, in their places of recreation, in their membership in clubs and organizations, and, generally, in their use of leisure time.

This is further reflected in the following analysis:

(a) Of 195 men who used their leisure time harmfully during the second follow-up period 14.9 per cent were not doing so during the third.

---

[43] Appendix C, 38.
[44] Appendix D, 35.
[45] For details see Appendix B, 3–46a.
[46] Appendix B, 3–65b.
[47] Appendix C, 39.

(b) Of 117 who previously had not been using their leisure time harmfully, only ten (8.5 per cent) resorted to harmful outlets in the third period.[48]

That the improvement in use of leisure time has not been marked in Period III should be considered in the light of the handicaps and discouragements these men had to undergo during the economic depression and the generally pessimistic psychology it has engendered.

[48] Appendix D, 36.

## VI

## CRIMINAL CONDUCT

WE now turn to the most important aspect of this follow-up study, the criminal conduct of our men during the third five-year span. In *Later Criminal Careers* it was shown that a considerable improvement in the behavior of the group occurred in the second period as compared with the first. This was revealed in an appreciable decrease in the proportion of criminals as well as in the commission of serious offenses among the men who continued to be delinquent. A crucial question is whether this improvement has continued. To answer it, we must focus attention in some detail on what changes have actually taken place.

### Number and Frequency of Arrests

First of all it should be stated that 208 men were arrested in Period III, which represents 57 per cent of the group about whom the information was known and applicable, as compared with 55.1 per cent arrested in Period II and 70.7 per cent in Period I.[1] Thus the decrease in arrests in the second follow-up period has been maintained in the third.

During this third five-year span the average number of arrests among the 208 men arrested was 3.56 ($\pm$.11). The average number of arrests among those arrested has, however, not varied greatly in the three periods: it was 3.30 ($\pm$.11) in the first five-year span and 3.71 ($\pm$.12) in the second.[2]

In regard to the frequency of arrests among the men arrested more than once during the third follow-up period, arrests occurred on the average of once in 12.92 ($\pm$.41) months.[3] Here, too, as in the number of arrests among those arrested, there has not occurred any marked change, for in the first five-year period the men were arrested on an average of once in 13.94 ($\pm$.42) months and in the second, once in 12.5 ($\pm$.45) months.[4]

A case-by-case comparison reveals the following:

(a) Of 54 men who were arrested on an average of less than once a year during the second follow-up span, 75.9 per cent were arrested just as frequently during the third, while the remainder were taken into police custody less frequently.

(b) Of 28 men previously arrested on an average of once in one to two years, eight (28.6 per cent) were in the third period arrested as often as this,

<hr>

[1] Appendix C, 40a.

[3] For details see Appendix B, 3-55.

[2] Appendix C, 40a.

[4] Appendix C, 41.

seventeen (60.7 per cent) more often, and only three (10.7 per cent) less frequently.

(c) Of nine men who had been arrested on an average of only once in two or more years during the second period, three were not arrested any more frequently, six were.

As this analysis refers only to men arrested more than once in either the second or third five-year span, it is necessarily incomplete.[5]

### Nature of Arrests

The group of 208 men were arrested 985 times, the nature of arrests in the order of incidence being 57.7 per cent for drunkenness, 17.7 per cent for offenses against the public health, safety, or policy (e.g., being "idle and disorderly," vagrancy, disturbing the peace, violation of license or gaming laws, etc.); 12 per cent were arrested for offenses against property (burglary, larceny, and the like), 4.4 per cent for offenses against the person, 3.8 per cent for offenses against family and children (non-support, desertion), 2.3 per cent for offenses against chastity (largely pathological sex crimes), and 1.1 per cent for the use or sale of drugs. In comparing the offenses committed by the men in this period with those of the two previous five-year spans, the most significant change that has occurred is in the decrease in offenses against property, from 26 per cent in the first period, to 17.3 per cent in the second, and to 12 per cent in the third; and the increase in arrests for drunkenness, from 41.4 per cent in the first period, to 51.3 per cent in the second, and to 57.7 per cent in the third.[6]

It is evident, therefore, that although there has been no change in the proportion of men arrested in the third period as compared with the second, nor any appreciable change in the frequency of arrests among those arrested, there has nevertheless occurred a decrease in the proportion of arrests against property, despite the stringencies of the industrial depression.[7] This decrease in property crimes has apparently been absorbed largely by an increase in the proportion of arrests for drunkenness. Now let us see whether these changes in the nature of the arrests reflect a change in the offenders themselves.

Of 208 men arrested one or more times during the third follow-up span, 49.5 per cent were arrested one or more times for drunkenness, 44.7 per cent for crimes against the public health, public safety, and the like; 35.6 per cent were arrested one or more times for crimes against property. Over a tenth of these men (12 per cent) were arrested for crimes against the person, 8.7 per cent for

---

[5] Appendix D, 37.                    [6] Appendix C, 40.

[7] It may be that police were more loath to arrest during the height of the depression, but this influence cannot have been marked when the police dealt with men known to be criminals of long standing.

sex offenses, 7.7 per cent for offenses against the family, and 3.9 per cent for use or sale of drugs. In comparing this with the offenses for which the men had been arrested during the second follow-up period, there has been a decrease in the proportion of men arrested for crimes against property, from 43 per cent in the second period to 35.6 per cent in the third; but the proportion of men arrested for drunkenness has remained the same (50.5 per cent during the second period, and 49.5 per cent during the third). The only other change which has occurred is in the proportion of those arrested for crimes against the family, which have dropped from 10.5 per cent in the second five-year span to 7.7 per cent in the third. This finding is in harmony with what we have already learned about the increasing marital stability of the men in the third period as compared with the second.[8] Otherwise, like proportions of men were arrested one or more times for the various offenses mentioned.[9]

Although the proportion of men arrested for drunkenness remains about the same as it was in the second period, more of the men were actually drinking to excess in the third period than in the second or becoming intoxicated in public more frequently; for 61.4 per cent of all men with habits in conflict with the law were drunkards in Period III as compared with 51.3 per cent in Period II.[10] It might be mentioned in passing that there had been a reduction in the proportion of drunkards in the second five-year span as compared with the first (from 56.9 per cent in Period I to 51.3 per cent in Period II).[11] The increase in the amount of drinking in Period III may be due to the discouragements brought about by the industrial depression, as well as to some deterioration in the group which occurred with the wear and tear of age and extended indulgence.

### Predominant Offense

It need not be labored that the nature of the delinquency of offenders can obviously not be judged solely by the offenses for which they were actually arrested. It is a well-known fact that there are variations in police activities in different communities at different times and that an investigation into a man's conduct based only upon his record of arrests is inconclusive. In each case, therefore, we have not only examined the official records of courts, police, probation and parole departments, fingerprint files, and other sources of official information, but have made a thorough study of each man's behavior history to discover conduct for which he might have been apprehended by official agencies of the law but which, for one reason or another, escaped their attention. By taking into account not only those men who actually were arrested or came

[8] See Chap. IV.                              [9] Appendix C, 40b.
[10] Appendix B, 3–49.                         [11] Appendix C, 43.

to official notice in other ways (as by dishonorable discharge from the Army or Navy), but also those who committed offenses for which they might have been apprehended (and 14.3 per cent of the men fell into this category),[12] we have been able to determine the *predominant offense* (i.e., the type most characteristically committed) of each man who was delinquent during the third follow-up span. This procedure applied to all three periods has enabled us to note the differences that have occurred in the usual type of offense which the group committed during the third five-year period as compared with the first and second. The total number of delinquents (official and non-official) in Period III was 238. The predominant offense of over a third of this number (36.1 per cent) in the third five-year span was drunkenness. Next in order were those who chiefly committed offenses against the public health, safety, and welfare (22.3 per cent). Then came offenders against property (18.5 per cent); next, a small group (7.2 per cent) who shifted from one type of offense to another to such an extent that their pattern of crime could only be described as "varied." A small group (6.7 per cent) typically committed offenses against family and children, 4.6 per cent usually were sex offenders, 2.5 per cent were mainly drug sellers or users, and 2.1 per cent generally committed offenses against the person.

Although a comparison of the arrests during the three periods and the types of offenses for which the men were apprehended is significant, a comparison of their predominant offenses is perhaps more truly revealing. The decrease in offenders against property is substantiated by the fact that during the first follow-up period 33.3 per cent of the men chiefly committed such offenses; during the second, 20.7 per cent; and during the third, 18.5 per cent. In regard to drunkenness as a predominant offense there has been no appreciable change in the third period as compared with the second (36.1 per cent as compared to 37.2 per cent); but both periods represent a marked increase in the proportion of such offenders as compared with the first five-year span, when only 25.7 per cent were mainly drunkards. Another change worth noting, although the total number of cases involved is not large, is a doubling in the third period of men who were predominantly offenders against the family (from 3.9 per cent in the first period and 3.3 per cent in the second up to 6.7 per cent during the third). While, as was shown in a prior chapter, there has been on the whole a growing stability in the marital relationships of the men, there is no doubt that in a small number of cases some break-down in family solidarity has occurred. The only other difference is in the proportion of those who usually committed offenses against the public welfare, which rose from 13.2 per cent in Period I and 12.8 per cent in Period II up to 22.3 per cent in Period III. As these of-

[12] Appendix C, 51.

fenses are largely in the nature of vagrancy and begging, this increase is mostly explainable by the difficult industrial conditions prevailing during this period, associated with the growing effects of old age in some cases.[13]

A case-by-case analysis reveals the following:

(a) Of 110 men who were *non-criminal* in the second period, 82.7 per cent continued to have a clean record during the third, while 17.3 per cent committed offenses of one sort or another. Of the nineteen men in this group whose status was ascertainable for both periods, three committed offenses against property during the third span, four committed offenses against family and children, the crimes of six were predominantly offenses against public health, safety, and policy; four were chiefly drunkards, one committed crimes against the person, and the offenses of one have to be described as "varied."

(b) Of 35 men who in the second period usually committed *crimes against property*, 22 men have continued to commit such crimes; the offenses of one man during the third period were predominantly sex crimes; those of four men were crimes against public welfare and the like; of one, drunkenness; of three, varied offenses; four of these second-period property offenders became non-delinquents during the third follow-up span.

(c) Of 13 men who in the second period were predominantly *sex offenders*, four have continued to commit such crimes during the third, another four usually committed offenses against the public welfare, one developed into a chronic drunkard, one committed varied offenses, and three men became non-offenders.

(d) Of seven men who usually committed *offenses against family and children* in the second period, six continued to do so in the third, while one man became a non-delinquent.

(e) Of 29 men who formerly committed *crimes against the public welfare*, 19 continued to do so in the third, three usually violated laws against drunkenness, while seven abandoned criminality.

(f) Of 87 men who were predominantly *drunkards* or committed offenses in the second period resulting from drunkenness, 67 (77.1 per cent) have continued in similar offenses during the third five years, 10 men were then primarily committing offenses against the public welfare, one man was usually charged with offenses against family and children, three were engaging in crimes against property, one man was committing crimes against the person while five men had become non-offenders.

(g) Of six men who were formerly *drug sellers*, five continued to commit similar offenses during the third five-year period and one became a drunkard.

[13] Appendix C, 42.

(h) The one man who in Period II had typically committed *offenses against the person* continued to do so in the third.

(i) Of 38 men who committed *varied offenses* during the second period, only ten did likewise in the third. Eight settled into drunkenness as their typical offense, six into crimes against property, three into crimes against the family, an equal number into crimes against public welfare; two were committing primarily sex crimes; one became an offender against the person; while five became non-criminals.[14]

## Use of Aliases; Associates in Crime

One indication that possibly our men have become less criminalistic in the third span as compared with the first and second is the fact that of those who were arrested, 28.2 per cent used aliases during the third period,[15] while during the first and second follow-up spans a considerably higher proportion (38 per cent and 39.9 per cent) had attempted to hide their identity in this way.[16]

More specifically:

(a) Of 52 men who had used aliases during the second period, 63.5 per cent continued to do so in the third.

(b) Of 84 men who though arrested did not use aliases in the second period, only eight did so in the third.[17]

The change for the better is also reflected in the fact that 70.3 per cent of those arrested had committed their offenses alone rather than in company with others,[18] a marked decrease in group crime, as is shown by the fact that during the previous five years only 57.3 per cent had been lone offenders.[19] That there has been an increase in the proportion of men committing offenses alone is in consonance with the finding in the previous chapter (on use of leisure) that with the passage of the years there has been a lessening tendency on the part of the men to belong to gangs and to hang about with street crowds, more and more of them spending their spare time either alone or with their families.

## Number and Frequency of Convictions

Having determined the nature of the offenses committed by these men, let us now consider how their arrests were disposed of and the number and kind of their peno-correctional experiences. Of 208 men arrested during the third five-year span, 10.7 per cent were not convicted at all, 29.3 per cent had but one

---

[14] Appendix D, 38.

[15] Since many of the offenders were vagrants and alcoholic deteriorates.

[16] Appendix C, 52.                              [17] Appendix D, 44.

[18] For details see Appendix B, 3–57a.

[19] Appendix C, 53. Information on this point is not available for the first five-year period.

conviction, 21 per cent were convicted twice, 17.6 per cent three or four times, 10.3 per cent five, six, or seven times, and 11.1 per cent were convicted eight or more times. The average number of convictions among those arrested during Period III was 2.79 ($\pm$.11), this marking little change over the years; for during the first span those arrested had been convicted on an average of 2.43 ($\pm$.09) times and during the second, 3.05 ($\pm$.12) times.[20]

Among 155 men arrested more than once, convictions occurred on an average of once every 17.06 ($\pm$.57) months.[21] This is a slight and probably not significant decrease in the frequency of convictions as compared with the first and second five-year spans, when convictions occurred on the average of once in 16.58 ($\pm$.52) months and once in 15.65 ($\pm$.48) months, respectively.[22]

Detailed analysis of the 86 men who were convicted more than once in both periods reveals that:

(a) Of 46 men convicted more often than once a year in Period II, 35 were found guilty as frequently in the third five-year period, while eleven were convicted less often.

(b) Of 22 men who had previously been convicted once in one to two years, six were convicted with this degree of frequency in the third period, while eleven were found guilty more frequently, and five less often.

(c) Of 18 men previously convicted only once in two or more years, six were as infrequently convicted during the third five-year span, twelve more frequently.

As in the case-by-case comparison of arrests in Periods II and III, which includes only those men who were arrested more than once in both periods, so in this comparison of frequency of convictions, which refers only to the men who were convicted more than once in both periods, the findings must not be interpreted as giving a picture of the changes in behavior of the entire group of delinquents.[23]

### Nature of Dispositions

How were the 985 arrests disposed of? A third (32.9 per cent) resulted in convictions and commitments to peno-correctional institutions; a sixth (17.4 per cent) were followed by probation (including probation with suspended sentence); 10.1 per cent resulted in fines and 2.5 per cent in commitment to jail for non-payment of fine; following one arrest, restitution was ordered. In a tenth of the arrests (11.7 per cent) the cases were "filed"; 5.2 per cent of ar-

---

[20] Appendix C, 44a. In *Later Criminal Careers*, p. 66, the average number of convictions occurring in Periods I and II had been incorrectly reported as 3.14 and 1.69 respectively.

[21] For details see Appendix B, 3–56.      [22] Appendix C, 45.

[23] Appendix D, 39.

rests on charges of drunkenness resulted in release by the probation officer; 1.8 per cent of arrests resulted in *nol prossing* of the cases, while almost a fifth of all the arrests (18.3 per cent) were disposed of by a finding of "not guilty" and the accused were released without further charges.

In comparing the dispositions of arrests in the third follow-up period with the previous periods, it is evident that the most noteworthy changes have occurred in releases on probation, imposition of fines, and in findings of not guilty. Probations increased from 13.6 per cent in both Periods I and II to 17.4 per cent in the third five-year span,[24] while the imposition of fines decreased from 22.8 per cent in the first period to 16.7 per cent in the second, to only 10.1 per cent in the third. Releases after a finding of not guilty increased from 11.4 per cent in the first period, to 12.9 per cent in the second, up to 18.3 per cent in the third.[25]

Of the 208 men arrested during the third five-year span, 62 per cent were committed to reformatories, prisons, or jails at one time or another during that period. Over a third of the group (37 per cent) had the benefit of probation during this span; 28.4 per cent were fined, 6.3 per cent were committed to jail for short periods for non-payment of fine. The cases of a fourth of those arrested (27.4 per cent) were filed, one man was ordered to make restitution, 12 per cent were released by the probation officer without court appearance, the cases of 6.7 per cent were *nol prossed,* while the high proportion of 41.8 per cent were found not guilty and charges against them dismissed. In comparing the court experiences of those arrested in the third period with those taken into custody in the second, we find an increase in the proportion of arrested men committed to penal institutions (from 55.5 per cent to 62 per cent) and also a small increase in the proportion placed on probation (from 32.5 per cent in Period II to 37 per cent in Period III). But there was a decrease in the proportion of men who were fined following arrest (from 38 per cent in the second period to 28.4 per cent in the third) and also a decrease of those whose cases were filed (from 35 per cent to 27.4 per cent). There was also a drop in the fraction of the group who were released by a probation officer (from 15.5 per cent in the second five-year span to 12 per cent in the third).[26] It would appear, therefore, by the increase in the proportion of men experiencing commitment and the decrease in fines, that courts were becoming more severe with the men because of their long-continued records of criminality; although, as will be seen later, by far the largest proportion of commitments were to institutions for short-term offenders (largely for drunkenness and vagrancy).

[24] This runs counter to the expected decrease in probation as offenders lengthen their criminal records.

[25] Appendix C, 44.                    [26] Appendix C, 44b.

*Peno-Correctional Experiences*

In considering the peno-correctional experiences of the 439 men living at the beginning of the third follow-up period, we included not only the commitments which were made within this third span but those which, though occurring in the second five years, extended into the third follow-up period. On this basis, 157 men (40.4 per cent of the total) had peno-correctional experiences during the third span. Of these, 42.7 per cent had one such experience, a fifth of the group (20.4 per cent) had two, 24.8 per cent had three or four, and 12.1 per cent served five or more sentences in peno-correctional institutions. The average was 2.72 (±.11) penal experiences per man. Comparison with previous periods indicates that the changes which have occurred are slight; for in Period I, 43.5 per cent of the men had penal experiences, in Period II the proportion fell to 36.8 per cent, but in Period III it increased slightly to 40.4 per cent. This increase is probably due to the rise in drunkenness among our offenders and to resort by judges to the sentencing of such chronic offenders to jails and houses of correction. The average number of penal experiences increased very slightly, from 2.22 (±.08) in Period I to 2.72 (±.12) in the second five-year span and 2.72 (±.11) in the third.[27]

From a case-by-case comparison we see that:

(a) Of 235 men who had had no penal experiences in the second five-year span, 16.6 per cent underwent one or more imprisonments during the third.

(b) Of 141 men who had had one or more penal experiences in the previous period, 20.6 per cent did not have any during the third span.[28]

Of the 157 men spending any time in peno-correctional institutions during the third period, 28.7 per cent were incarcerated for a total of less than five months, 12.1 per cent for five to ten months, 16.6 per cent for ten to twenty months, 12.7 per cent for twenty to thirty months, 8.9 per cent for thirty to forty months, 5.7 per cent for forty to fifty, 6.4 per cent for fifty to sixty, while less than a tenth of the group (8.9 per cent) were held in peno-correctional institutions throughout the sixty-month period. The average number of months spent behind walls during this five-year span was 23.30 (±.87).[29] In comparing this with the number of months spent by the men in penal institutions during the first and second periods, we find that the proportion is about the same as it was in the first five years, when the average number of months of incarceration was 23.70 (±.78), but is a decrease from the number of months behind walls during the second follow-up span, when the average was 27.50 (±.98).[30] Again this reflects the fact that in the third span judges were resort-

---

[27] Appendix C, 46.

[28] Appendix D, 40. See also Appendix D, 41.

[29] For details see Appendix B, 3–10.   [30] Appendix C, 49.

ing to short-term institutions for these men to a greater degree than before, and this view is confirmed below.

One hundred and fifty-seven men had 387 penal experiences (exclusive of commitments for non-payment of fine) during the third follow-up period. Of these, 322 were imposed during the third five-year span while 65 had been imposed in previous stages and continued for part or all of the third five-year period. Of the 387 penal experiences noted, only two were in reformatories, due, of course, to age limitations on commitment to such institutions. A fourth of the penal experiences (25.1 per cent) were in prisons, while the high proportion of 74.4 per cent were in institutions for short-term offenders (jails, houses of correction, and state farms).

In comparing this with penal experiences in the first and second five-year spans, we note an increase in the proportion of incarcerations in institutions for short-term offenders, from 60.1 per cent in Period I, to 67.7 per cent in Period II, and to 74.4 per cent in Period III.[31] This seems to confirm our previously expressed supposition that judges are tending to commit these men to jail for short periods rather than sending more of them to prison. A chief reason, of course, is the fact that as these men grew older serious crimes decreased and a marked rise occurred in the proportion of drunkards and offenders against the public welfare, health, morals, and safety.

Two-thirds (63.6 per cent) of the incarcerations during this period were in institutions within Massachusetts. Of those outside the Commonwealth, one incarceration occurred in Canada and three in European countries. In comparing places of incarceration during the three periods, we find that there has been an increase in imprisonments outside the state, from 26.9 per cent during the first five-year period to 28.7 per cent during the second, and up to 36.4 per cent in the third.[32] This means that the delinquents among our men were moving about the country more excessively than they had before.

*Seriousness of Offense*

For some purposes it is convenient to classify the men into *serious offenders, minor offenders,* and *non-offenders.*[33] The proportion of serious delinquents, after dropping markedly from 51 per cent during the first five-year span to 38 per cent during the second, continued downward to 30.4 per cent during the

[31] Appendix C, 47.                    [32] Appendix C, 48.

[33] Serious—refers essentially to felonies (property crimes, pathological sex offenses and rape, homicide, escape or rescue). See *500 Criminal Careers,* pp. 354, 355, 356 for details.

Minor—refers to such offenses as drunkenness, vagrancy, begging, violation of liquor laws, lewd and lascivious cohabitation, fornication, non-support, assault and battery, disturbing the peace, peddling without license. From *Later Criminal Careers,* p. 252.

third; while the incidence of minor offenders has increased slightly from 29.1 per cent in the first period to 31.9 per cent in the second up to 38.8 per cent in the third.[34] The proportion of 30.8 per cent of non-offenders, though remaining the same as it had been in the second period, nevertheless represents an improvement over the first five-year span, at which time only 19.9 per cent were found to be non-offenders.[35] However, it should be mentioned that 21 men now included among the delinquents may really be considered to belong to the non-delinquent group. They are men who had reformed at least five years before the beginning of the third five-year period but who temporarily relapsed into crime during the third period for a very brief time for reasons revealed in Chapter VIII. This would raise the proportion of non-delinquents during the third five-year span from 30.8 per cent to 37.2 per cent. These men very quickly resumed the straight and narrow path after briefly straying from the fold. This is reflected in the fact that in the *fifth* year of the third follow-up span, 41.8 per cent of the entire group were non-delinquent as compared to only 30.8 per cent in the first four years of the total period. This finding of the relatively high proportion of 41.8 per cent non-criminal in the fifth year of our check-up is further evidence of the general trend toward a decline in the incidence of criminality in our men.[36]

From a case-by-case analysis we see more clearly the changes that have occurred:

[34] Of 118 men who were judged to be *serious offenders* during the third five-year span 92 (78 per cent) were placed in this group because they had actually been convicted of major crimes; three, though arrested for serious offenses and not convicted, nevertheless had a proven course of major criminality; five were included in the category because, though not arrested, they had been committing serious crimes for which they might well have come to the attention of legal authorities, and 18 (15.3 per cent) were classed as serious offenders because they were in penal institutions for most of the third five-year span on prison sentences for major crimes imposed in a previous period. Of the 151 men described as *minor offenders* during the third five-year period, 105 (69.5 per cent) were placed in such category because they were convicted for petty offenses; 15 men (9.9 per cent) were included therein because they were actually arrested for minor offenses and though not convicted had a proven course of minor delinquencies for which they might have been convicted had they come to the attention of the police; and 31 men (20.6 per cent) were in this group who, though not arrested, committed minor offenses for which they too might well have been arrested. Appendix B, 3–66.

[35] Appendix C, 54. It is to be noted that in presenting the proportions of delinquents and non-delinquents in *500 Criminal Careers* and *Later Criminal Careers,* we omitted from consideration those men who were institutionalized during a particular period on a sentence which had been imposed in a previous period, because we felt at the time that one could not really judge whether, had these men been free, they would have committed offenses or not. However, we have now included such men among the serious offenders in each period because legally they must be so considered even though the offense itself which resulted in the incarceration occurred in a previous period.

[36] Appendix B, 3–57b and 3–61.

(a) Of 107 men who had been *serious offenders* during the second five-year period, 62.6 per cent continued to be such during the third, 29 per cent became minor offenders, while 8.4 per cent abandoned crime altogether.

(b) Of 117 men who had been *minor offenders* in the second period, 78.6 per cent continued as such in the third, 6.9 per cent reverted to serious crime, while 14.5 per cent became *non-offenders*.

(c) Of 117 men who had been *non-offenders* during the second follow-up span, 78.6 per cent continued to be law-abiding while 17.9 per cent reverted to minor offenses and only 3.5 per cent to serious crime.[37]

## Delinquency in Children of Offenders

It has been of incidental interest to determine whether any of the children of our men are beginning to show signs of delinquency. Although many of these youngsters are still under juvenile court age, and many of the families are still incomplete, we have nevertheless been able to determine that at least 26.5 per cent of the children who were already of juvenile court age during the third period are manifesting signs of delinquency as reflected either in arrests or in the type of behavior which might lead to arrest at any time.[38] It is impossible to say to what extent this disturbingly high incidence of delinquency in the second (and frequently in the third) generation[39] is attributable to Nature or Nurture. Something frequently forgotten should be pointed out, however, that the *milieu* in which children are reared is in large measure itself the product of sub-standard biologic equipment on the part of the parents. Thus "environment" can hardly be sharply distinguished from "heredity." That a family culture in which crime among the parents is not an uncommon phenomenon may readily influence the behavior of the children adversely, cannot be denied; but it must also not be overlooked that culture is neither fixed, nor born, nor maintained in a vacuum. It changes; and although partially acquired through social inheritance, it is also partially modified by each new generation. And the biologic make-up and natural behavior tendencies of the parents undoubtedly contribute to the kind of home life to which the children are subjected.

## Behavior in Third Five-Year Period

It has already been indicated in the report of the arrests of these men and also of their predominant offenses that not as many of them were serious criminals (i.e., committing essentially felonies) in Period III as in previous years. Ac-

---

[37] Appendix D, 45. See also Appendix D, 42 and Appendix D, 43.

[38] Appendix B, 3–29b.

[39] It will be recalled that over half the families of our men contained members who had been arrested or imprisoned for various crimes prior to the sentence of our men to the Reformatory.

tually less than a third of the group (30.4 per cent) could be so characterized, while 38.8 per cent were minor offenders (drunkards, vagrants, non-support-ers, adulterers), and 30.8 per cent were non-offenders.[40]

### Behavior During Fifteen-Year Follow-up Span

Turning now to the behavior of the entire group of 510 men with whom this investigation originally started (the men whose sentences to the Reforma-tory expired in the years 1921 or 1922 and whose conduct during fifteen years beyond that time has been investigated), we can summarize their conduct over the whole stretch of these years. It is necessary, first, to eliminate 41 (8 per cent) of the 510 men about whose behavior we have no information whatsoever during the fifteen years, one man who was in a mental hospital throughout the period, and 50 (9.8 per cent) men whose conduct could not be adequately classified for the entire term, because they died within the first ten years of the fifteen-year span and up to the time of death had continued to be serious offenders. There is, of course, no conclusive evidence that these latter would have continued to be serious offenders had they lived or would have become minor offenders or eventually reformed entirely. Though their continuance as serious offenders for years after they had left the Reformatory raises the supposition that they would not have later reformed, it seems better to err on the side of caution and omit these cases from consideration in describing the conduct of the men during the fifteen-year span. After eliminating the above 92 men from consideration, we find that *135 (32.3 per cent) of the 418 men whose behavior over the entire fifteen-year span can be adequately described, persisted in serious criminality throughout the three follow-up periods; one man has been a minor offender since the very beginning of the first five-year follow-up span; while 121 men (28.9 per cent) although they had not reformed up to the end of the fifteen years, nevertheless became minor offenders. During the fifteen-year span 140 (33.5 per cent) of the men reformed entirely; and 21 men (5 per cent) though they had abandoned criminalism during either the first or second five-year span, relapsed into criminal ways for a very brief time during the third, and then again became non-criminals.*

At approximately what ages did these changes in behavior occur? Of the 140 men who reformed altogether, 18 (12.9 per cent) were under twenty-one years old when they abandoned a career of crime, 38 (27.2 per cent) were twenty-one to twenty-seven years of age, 45 (32.1 per cent) were twenty-seven to thirty-three years old, and 39 (27.8 per cent) reached thirty-three years or more before their reformation.[41] In the case of the 121 men who progressed

---

[40] Appendix C, 54.

[41] The striking fact that 60 per cent of the wholly reformed group and 56 per cent of the men

from serious to minor criminality, the transformation occurred when the men were under twenty-one years of age in nine instances (7.4 per cent), when they were between twenty-one and twenty-seven in 44 (36.4 per cent) of the cases, when twenty-seven to thirty-three in 46 (38 per cent), and not until they were thirty-three or older in 22 (18.2 per cent). The majority of the men therefore did not improve until well along in adulthood. Of the 21 men who had reformed during the first or second period, and suffered a temporary lapse from good behavior in the third, the relapse into crime occurred when five were under thirty-three years old and the remaining sixteen were older.[42]

The above analysis describes briefly the behavior of the 510 men over the fifteen-year period that has elapsed since the expiration of their sentences to the Reformatory. It is possible to proceed a step further, however, and indicate the approximate age at which their behavior changed from serious to minor criminality, whether in the first or second five-year span or even after the end of the third follow-up period. Of the 510 offenders originally included, 320 have to be eliminated from any consideration of change from serious to minor delinquency either because they continued to be serious offenders throughout the fifteen-year span or up to the time of death; or because they did not become minor delinquents before reforming entirely; or because it could not be determined whether they had shifted from serious to minor delinquency. This leaves 190 of the original group of 510 men whose behavior is known to the end of the fifteen-year follow-up span, and whose misconduct clearly changed from serious to minor delinquency. Of these 190 men, 25 (13.1 per cent) were under twenty-one years of age when this change occurred; 36 (18.9 per cent) were between twenty-one and twenty-four years old; 39 (20.5 per cent) were between twenty-four and twenty-seven years of age. Forty of the men (21.1 per cent) were between twenty-seven and thirty years old when they became minor offenders; 23 men (12.1 per cent) were between thirty and thirty-three years of age; 11 men (5.8 per cent) were between thirty-three and thirty-six; 7 men (3.7 per cent) were between thirty-six and thirty-nine; 5 men (2.6 per cent) were between thirty-nine and forty-two; and 4 men (2.2 per cent) were forty-two years or older.[43] Thus, about half the group were well along into adulthood, i.e., twenty-seven years or older, when they became minor offenders. The average age of the 190 offenders at change from commission of serious to minor delinquency was 26.74 (±.28) years.

who improved to the extent of becoming minor instead of serious offenders did not reform or change from serious to minor crime until they were twenty-seven or older, should be borne in mind in considering the reference to delayed maturation on p. 292.

[42] Appendix B, 3–67 and 3–69.          [43] Appendix B, 3–68.

## Summary

Once again, and this time in regard to that aspect of their total behavior which is our prime interest in this study—criminalism—we have noted some improvement. This is shown primarily by the increase in non-delinquents from 19.9 per cent in Period I to 30.1 per cent in Period II and 30.8 per cent in the third follow-up span to 41.8 per cent in the fifth year of Period III; and by the rise in the incidence of minor offenders from 29.1 per cent in Period I to 31.9 per cent in Period II and to 38.8 per cent in Period III.

Some elements in the picture have, however, either not changed or have slightly deteriorated. Not only has the proportion of those arrested during the three periods not varied markedly, but the average number of arrests and the frequency of arrests among those arrested have shown little change in the three follow-up periods. Perhaps partially attributable to the depression, as well as to growing mental deterioration, there has been an increase in the incidence of arrests for drunkenness. Since the proportion of men arrested for drunkenness has remained stationary we have here an intensification of this form of delinquency among the same group of offenders rather than any substantial addition to their ranks. While the incidence of those who were predominantly drunkards has not materially changed during the last two periods, the proportion in both spans is appreciably higher than it was during the first follow-up period.

Again, although relatively few men were predominantly committing crimes against the family, the percentage in this group practically doubled in the third period as compared with the two preceding spans. So, also, the incidence of offenders who typically committed crimes against the public health, safety, and welfare (petty offenses) was markedly higher in the third period than in the preceding two. These increases in certain types of offenses involve violations of law of a kind that would reflect both the stresses of the depression period on selected groups of men and the premature disintegrating effects of rapid aging beyond the peak of relatively early chronologic adulthood.

Compensating for these elements of deterioration there is the marked improvement reflected in the decrease in incidence of arrests for property crimes, despite the depression. Another possible reflection of improvement in conduct is the substantial reduction in the percentage of men who sought to conceal their identity behind aliases. This may, however, partially express a growing intellectual inability to resort to aliases rather than a conscientious unwillingness to do so. So, also, an element of improvement may be found in the reduction in the incidence of offenders who committed their crimes with others, something that harmonizes with previous findings as to the lessening tendency of the men to hang around with gangs and street crowds.

A slight decrease has occurred also in the frequency of convictions, particularly as contrasted with the first five-year follow-up period. Acquittals have appreciably increased over the two preceding periods, but sentences to institutions (largely short-term) have increased. On the other hand, the proportion of men sentenced to prisons and jails and the average number of penal experiences have changed little from preceding periods. But the average time spent behind walls was less than in Period II, although equal to that of Period I. There was a substantial increase in sentences to short-term institutions, reflecting the rise in commission of petty offenses.

Obviously, the improvement in the third over the second period is less marked than between the second and first. The curve has tended to flatten out. Taking into account the added stress of the industrial depression, however, it is legitimate to characterize the behavior of our men as showing some improvement since the second follow-up period.

## VII

## DIFFERENCES BETWEEN REFORMED AND UNRE-
## FORMED, AND SERIOUS AND MINOR
## OFFENDERS

IN the previous chapters we have described the environmental conditions surrounding our men, their family relationships and assumption of economic responsibilities, their industrial history, their use of leisure time, and their criminal conduct not only in the third five-year period which followed the expiration of their sentences to the Reformatory, but during the first and second periods. We have been able from this to see clearly the trend in their behavior. As this has followed the same general pattern already described in *500 Criminal Careers* and *Later Criminal Careers* in which it was indicated that on the whole, with the passage of time, improvement in behavior occurs, and that this is due largely to maturation, there seems to be no need to make any further analysis of the influence of maturation on reform. The interested reader is asked to consult Chapter X of *Later Criminal Careers* and also Chapter VIII of *Juvenile Delinquents Grown Up* in which the place of maturation in the reformative process has already been discussed.

In view of the fact that we have now covered a fifteen-year follow-up span in the lives of our original group of 510 offenders each of whom served at least one term in the Reformatory, it should be revealing (a) to compare the family and personal background of those who reformed during this fifteen-year span and remained non-delinquent, with those who continued to be criminals (whether serious or minor offenders); and (b) to compare the characteristics of those who remained serious offenders throughout the fifteen years with those who at one time or another during that period became and remained minor offenders.

It will be recalled that of the original group of 510 men, seventy-one had died before the beginning of the third five-year span and of course there were a number (twelve) whose criminal history was not entirely known throughout the three follow-up periods. Limiting ourselves, therefore, to those whose conduct was ascertainable for all three of the five-year spans after the expiration of sentence to the Reformatory, there are 140 men who became non-delinquent at some time during the fifteen-year period and remained so to the end, 135 who were persistently serious offenders throughout the fifteen-year period, 121 men who though originally serious offenders became minor offenders at some time during the fifteen years and remained so to the end of the period, and 21 who had become non-delinquent at some point within the first ten years of the fifteen-year span, but temporarily recidivated during the third five-year follow-up period. We are concerned with this latter group in the next chapter, in which they will be compared with the permanently reformed.

In the meantime, let us turn to a comparison of twenty-seven factors reflecting the family and personal background[1] of the 140 men who reformed at one time or another during the fifteen-year span and remained non-delinquent to its end and the 256 men who continued to be either serious or minor offenders throughout the fifteen years. Of these latter, 135 were continually engaged in serious crimes while 121 became minor offenders at some time during the fifteen-year span and remained so to the end.

### Resemblances between Reformed and Unreformed

There are a number of pre-reformatory factors in which those who reformed and those who continued to recidivate *resemble each other* in their family and personal background. Of course, none of the following neutral factors can explain their difference in conduct after completion of sentence to the Reformatory.

Regarding their family background, first of all, the reformed and unreformed come from families of equal size. They were to a like extent exposed to the hazards of conflicting cultural backgrounds, as similar proportions of them were native-born sons one or both of whose parents had been born abroad. They were to an equal extent sons of parents of limited educational attainments. Their fathers had, in like proportions, been skilled, semi-skilled, and unskilled workers.

As to the youths themselves, those who reformed and those who continued to be criminalistic during the fifteen-year span were of like nativity. Both groups occupied the same relative birth rank among their brothers and sisters. They shared good health to an equal extent. Both those who reformed and those who continued to be delinquent had the same amount of schooling. The one group was no more retarded in school than the other.

In regard to bad habits and use of leisure time, they likewise resembled each other; they had unwholesome habits to the same extent and used their leisure time equally harmfully. The reformed and those who remained delinquent attended church with equal irregularity. The two groups began to work at an equally early age and both were subjected to equally frequent changes of environment in that they moved about excessively from one place of residence to another in the years prior to their commitment to the Reformatory.

---

[1] For a listing of these factors, the reader is referred to Chap. X, p. 161.

### Differences between Reformed and Unreformed

The *differences*[2] in their family and personal background prior to their commitment to the Reformatory are summarized in Table 1.

TABLE I. PRE-REFORMATORY DIFFERENCES IN FAMILY AND PERSONAL BACKGROUND OF REFORMED (140)* AND UNREFORMED OFFENDERS (256)*

| Factors of difference† | Percentage of unreformed in fifteen-year follow-up span | Percentage of reformed in fifteen-year follow-up span |
|---|---|---|
| Other members of family delinquent | 79.1 (220)‡ | 62.5 (112) |
| Parents economically dependent | 17.7 (237) | 10.9 (128) |
| Mothers worked outside home | 28.5 (235) | 24.6 (126) |
| Families were clients of social agencies | 57.4 (216) | 47.7 (111) |
| Homes broken by death, desertion, separation or divorce of parents | 81.9 (254) | 75.0 (136) |
| Parents incompatible | 39.5 (228) | 31.2 (125) |
| Offenders mentally defective | 22.0 (236) | 15.2 (132) |
| Offenders showed evidence of mental pathology | 49.3 (203) | 16.5 (109) |
| Offenders truanted from school§ | 60.6 (94) | 42.2 (45) |
| Offenders were first delinquent under age fourteen | 43.6 (256) | 34.3 (140) |
| Offenders first left home under age fourteen | 45.9 (205) | 34.5 (113) |
| Offenders were unskilled workers | 60.0 (256) | 52.9 (138) |
| Offenders had poor work habits | 58.0 (193) | 44.9 (109) |
| Offenders did not meet their economic responsibilities | 90.4 (198) | 71.1 (114) |
| Offenders had no affectional ties to parents and siblings | 72.4 (228) | 56.0 (116) |

* Maximum number of cases on which observations were possible.
† The factors of difference are presented in the order of their discussion in the text.
‡ In this and subsequent tables, parenthesized numbers refer to known cases on which percentages are based.
§ Although observations on school truancy are limited to less than half the total number of cases, the figures are nevertheless presented for whatever they may be worth. The direction of difference is consistent with other differences revealed in the table. However, we recognize that caution is necessary in the interpretation of these particular data.

An examination of Table 1 reveals, first of all, that the men who continued to be criminals came, to a greater extent than those who reformed, from families which contained other members who were also delinquent or criminal. The continuing offenders were, to a greater extent than those who reformed, sons of parents who had been economically dependent, having had to rely for

[2] In this and succeeding chapters in which comparisons are made between two series of cases, a difference of 4 per cent or more in the incidence of sub-categories of the compared groups is sufficient for our purposes to indicate the *trend* or *direction* of differences. It is evident from the tables presented in this and the succeeding chapters (Chaps. VIII, X, XI, and XII) that not all the listed differences would stand the test of statistical significance to the extent of being three times their probable error or twice the standard error. But because of the internal consistency of the differences as a totality, they are important for the purpose of indicating general trends of difference.

long periods upon outside sources (largely relief agencies) for support. This economic differentiation is further reflected in the finding that a slightly higher proportion of the mothers of those who continued to be delinquent had to work outside their homes than is true of the mothers of the youths who became non-offenders. The families of the men who continued to commit crimes during the fifteen-year period had not been as well able as the families of the reformed to manage their own affairs. This is reflected in the finding that a greater proportion of the former had been clients of various kinds of social welfare agencies that helped them with a wide variety of problems.

The greater environmental stress in which the continuing offenders had been reared is further shown in the finding that more of them than of the reformed had been reared in either broken homes or homes otherwise inadequate to the wholesome development of children. That their parents had lived together less harmoniously than the parents of the youths who became non-delinquent is shown by the fact that more of the continuing offenders than of those who reformed were sons of parents who had been grossly incompatible in their marital relationships.

Considering next the differences in the youths themselves, we find first of all that among those who continued to be delinquent during the fifteen-year span there was a higher proportion of mental deficients than among those who became non-delinquent. A much greater difference is noted among the reformed and unreformed in the extent to which they had been found by psychiatrists to be burdened with mental pathology of one kind or another. In view of these findings it seems logical (despite the relatively small number of cases on which the fact was known) that a higher proportion of those who remained criminal had actually been school truants than is true of those who became non-offenders.

Indicating that the original delinquency of those who continued to be offenders is closer to the roots of their biologic make-up than the misconduct of those who ultimately reformed is the finding that a greater proportion of the former were under fourteen years of age when they first showed signs of delinquent conduct than of those who ultimately reformed. The earlier misbehavior manifestations of the unreformed are further reflected in the finding that more of those who persisted in crime had first left the parental roof when they were under fourteen years of age as compared with those who reformed.

Considering now the differences in the work history of the two groups of offenders, we find, first, that those who continued to be delinquent had less industrial skill than did those who ultimately reformed. Furthermore their work habits were poorer, for more of those who continued to be criminalistic were found to be liabilities to their employers in the years prior to their commitment to the Reformatory than of those who ultimately abandoned crime.

The more severe behavior difficulties of the former are further reflected in the finding that a considerably greater proportion of those who persisted in criminality during the fifteen-year span following expiration of their sentences from the Reformatory had neglected to meet their economic obligations to their families than of those who ultimately reformed.

Finally, more of those who continued to be offenders had had no affectional ties to their families in the years prior to their commitment to the Reformatory than of those who reformed entirely.

### Resemblances between Serious and Minor Offenders

Considering next the similarities of those men who persisted in serious delinquency throughout the fifteen-year span and those who at one time or another during these years became minor offenders and remained so, we find that there are a great many factors in which the serious and minor offenders *resemble* each other; and therefore it is not among them that any explanation for the differences in their later behavior should be sought.

First of all as to their family background, the serious and minor delinquents were sons of parents of similarly limited educational attainments. The two groups had been reared in homes from which the mothers were in like proportion absent during the day because gainfully employed outside. The two groups came from families who were compelled to an equal extent to resort to help from various kinds of social agencies, indicating that they were to like degree unable to manage their own affairs.

The serious and minor offenders had been subjected to a similar extent to the possibilities of culture conflict between themselves and their families, for they were in like proportion native-born sons one or both of whose parents were foreign-born. Their childhood homes were to an equal extent either inadequate to the wholesome rearing of children or actually broken by death, desertion, separation, or divorce of the parents.

Turning now to the youths themselves, those who were persistently serious offenders throughout the fifteen-year period and those who became and remained minor offenders to the end, were of like nativity. They occupied the same birth rank among their siblings. They further resembled each other in their physical condition in youth, in their intelligence level, and in the extent to which they were burdened with mental pathology of one kind or another.

In regard to their school history, also, the serious offenders and those who became and remained minor offenders had a similar amount of schooling; the offenders of one group were as much behind grade for their age as the other, and they had truanted from school to a like extent. As to their occupational status, they were to an equal extent unskilled workers and had similarly poor work habits.

The two groups were equally neglectful of their economic responsibilities to their families and were in like proportion emotionally unattached to their families. The continuously serious offenders and those who became minor offenders resembled each other, also, in the extent of their bad habits and of their harmful use of leisure. The two groups had attended church with equal irregularity. Finally, the two groups had first shown signs of delinquent conduct at an equally early age.

## Differences between Serious and Minor Offenders

But there are a number of factors in which the continuing serious offenders and the minor offenders *differ* from each other in their family and personal background. These are summarized in Table 2. First, a greater proportion of

TABLE 2. PRE-REFORMATORY DIFFERENCES IN FAMILY AND PERSONAL BACKGROUND
OF SERIOUS (135)* AND MINOR OFFENDERS (121)*

| Factors of difference† | Percentage of continuing serious offenders in fifteen-year follow-up span | Percentage of those who became minor offenders in fifteen-year follow-up span |
|---|---|---|
| Offender is an only child | 9.6 (135) | 4.1 (121) |
| Other members of family delinquent | 85.1 (114) | 72.6 (106) |
| Parents separated or divorced | 26.7 (120) | 17.6 (108) |
| Parents in marginal or dependent economic circumstances | 65.3 (124) | 77.9 (113) |
| Fathers skilled or semi-skilled workers | 73.9 (119) | 61.3 (111) |
| Offenders under fifteen when began to work | 50.0 (128) | 40.5 (116) |
| Offenders first left home under age fourteen | 50.9 (114) | 39.6 (91) |
| Offenders moved about excessively | 49.3 (134) | 39.8 (118) |

* Maximum number of cases on which observations were possible.
† The factors of difference are presented in the order of their discussion in the text.

those who persisted in serious delinquency were only children (and probably therefore more "spoiled" by their parents) than were those who subsequently became minor offenders. A higher proportion of the persistently serious offenders came from families which contained other delinquent or criminal members than is the case among minor offenders. They had the greater burden also of being the sons of parents whose marital association was even more unhappy than of the parents of those who became minor offenders; for more of the persistently serious than of the minor offenders were sons of parents whose conjugal relationships were poor (which means that their parents had actually separated).

Apparently, however, the persistently serious offenders came from homes of better economic circumstances than those who became minor offenders, for a higher proportion of them than of those who became minor offenders were sons of parents not constantly on the borderline of dependency. This is possibly due to the fact previously noted that a larger proportion of serious offenders were only sons than of those who subsequently became and remained minor offenders and these smaller families were easier to support. The better economic condition of the parents of the persistently serious offenders is possibly also due to the fact that a higher proportion of fathers of the serious offenders were semi-skilled or skilled workers than of the fathers of those who became minor delinquents.

Turning now to differences in the employment history of the serious and minor offenders, we find that the former were younger than the latter when they began to work, half the serious offenders having been under fifteen when they entered gainful employment, as compared with two-fifths of those who became minor offenders. Likewise the persistently serious offenders had, to a greater extent than the minor, left the parental roof when under fourteen. And, finally, proportionally more of those who have persisted in serious crime had moved about excessively prior to their commitment to the Reformatory than of those who subsequently became minor offenders.

## Comment

Any inferences to be drawn from this comparison of the characteristics of (a) those who ultimately reformed and those who did not and (b) of those who remained serious offenders and those who became minor offenders must be considered in the light of two limitations. First is the fact that certain personal and situational characteristics may have been omitted which in subsequent researches may prove of great significance in differentiating the ultimate behavior of offenders. The reader who is familiar with 500 *Criminal Careers* will perhaps recall[3] that we were limited in our choice of background factors to those which had been originally gathered by the Reformatory's investigators. Coming to these data, as we did, so many years after the event, and having to verify and supplement them, the scope of our investigation has necessarily been narrower than we should have liked. Nevertheless, the factors we have been able to compare appear to be meaningful.

A further caution in interpreting these findings has to do with the limita-

---

[3] See Chap. V describing the method of that research.

tions in the psychological and psychiatric data at our disposal about our group of offenders. Obviously these are not as intensive and thorough as we should like to have had.[4] On the other hand, their significance is enhanced by the fact that at the time the tests were applied and the psychiatric diagnoses made, neither the psychologists and psychiatrists nor we ourselves had anticipated a subsequent series of follow-up studies.

Despite the limitations of our materials, there is a significant consistency in the findings resulting from the comparisons we have presented. It is obvious that those who reformed were better circumstanced than those who continued to recidivate in that they were reared in a less criminalistic environment, in homes of slightly better economic status, and of greater family solidarity. They also had the further advantage of somewhat higher intelligence, greater emotional stability, and fewer distortions of personality. They were better behaved in school, having truanted to a far lesser extent than those who have persisted in criminality. Further, those who reformed did not leave their parental homes quite as early as those who continued to be delinquent, and they had closer family ties. Nor did they begin to show delinquent tendencies quite as early in life. Another evidence of their better mental equipment is that they had greater industrial skill and better work habits prior to commitment to the Reformatory than those who have continued to recidivate. And finally they had met their economic obligations to their families somewhat more effectively than those who continued to commit crimes.

Although some of the distinctions between those who ultimately reformed and those who have continued to be delinquent are not marked, the comparison of their background does reveal a general difference both in their make-up and in their environment. Apparently, in this difference the biologic factors loom as more significant than the environmental. This is evident not only in the considerable differentiation between the reformed and unreformed as regards mental and emotional abnormalities but, indirectly, in the striking finding that a paramount environmental influence, namely culture conflict, engendered by differences in the nativity of parents and sons, has been found to be a neutral one. There are other environmental resemblances which

---

[4] In a study which we have recently undertaken of a large series of young offenders, we will not have to base any of our findings, as in this and in our previous researches, upon background data originally gathered by others and necessarily limited by their concepts of what is and what is not important in the investigation of an offender. Incidentally, of course, it should be remembered that the scope and nature of data to be gathered for a specific research are quite different from those gathered in a cursory investigation following the commitment of an offender to a peno-correctional institution. We are, in this new research, in a position ourselves to make the examination of the offenders and their backgrounds with a staff of experts especially trained for this purpose.

strengthen our conclusion that the differences between the reformed and un-reformed are more biologic in character than they are environmental. For example, both groups of youths had the same amount of schooling and were equally retarded in school.[5] They had used their leisure time equally harmfully, had been irregular church attendants to the same extent, had been subjected to the hazards of street trades at an early age, and to equally varied neighborhood influences as reflected by their frequent changes of residence.

Some or all of these factors obviously may have been operative in the genesis of their delinquencies, but they are neutral so far as ultimate differentiation of their behavior is concerned.

That the biologic differences between the reformed and unreformed have to do with their mental and emotional make-up rather than with their physical condition is suggested in the finding that the reformed and unreformed did not differ in the state of their health at the time of commitment to the Reformatory.

Now as to the differences between the persistently serious criminals and those who became minor offenders, we have seen that the two groups resemble each other in many ways, but by and large the serious offenders are not so favorably circumstanced as the minor: more of the serious offenders came from families containing other members who were delinquent; a greater proportion of them were sons of parents whose conjugal relations were poor; they had moved about more excessively than those who became petty offenders; and they had left their parental homes at an earlier age and also began to work sooner than the minor offenders. On the other hand, the persistently serious criminals were to a slightly greater extent than the minor, the only children in the household and possibly because of this the economic stress of their homes was not quite so great. It would appear, however, that on the whole the youths who eventually became minor delinquents were sons of more wholesome and stable families.

It must be borne in mind that the distinction between serious and minor offenses is essentially that between felonies and petty offenses. The latter include predominantly drunkenness, vagrancy, family neglect, and offenses against the public welfare. Minor offenders are not aggressive criminals; nor are they essentially the kind who persist in criminal careers with deliberation and by choice. Rather they are irresponsible persons of low energy and little planfulness. However, there is not so much difference between the serious and minor offenders as between those who ultimately reformed and those who persisted in crime, whether serious or minor in character.

[5] Retardation depends, of course, upon both innate mental deficiency and various environmental factors.

## VIII

## REASONS FOR RELAPSE INTO DELINQUENCY

IT will be recalled that 21 of the men who had presumably reformed by the end of the second follow-up period reverted to criminal behavior either of a minor or serious nature for a brief time during the third five-year span. Although the immediate reasons for this may emerge from some of the case illustrations which follow later in the chapter, it would be well to make a comparison of the men who reformed entirely at some time during the fifteen-year span and have remained non-delinquent to the end of the period (140 cases in all) with those who temporarily relapsed into criminal behavior after at least five years of non-delinquency (21 cases in all). From such a comparison of the background of these men we may derive some clues to the less obvious reasons for reversion to criminality than are manifest in what seem to be, from the case illustrations, the immediate precipitating causes.

### Resemblances between Reformed and Temporary Recidivists

In a number of ways those who relapsed into criminalism after at least five years of non-delinquent behavior entirely resemble those who had reformed at some time during the fifteen-year span and remained non-criminal to the end. In none of these factors of resemblance can we seek an explanation for the relapse of 21 men into criminal conduct.

The two groups *resemble* each other in the size of the families from which they came; in the extent to which their families contain other criminalistic members; in the limited educational achievements of their parents; and in the extent to which their mothers worked outside the home.

As to the youths themselves, those who remained non-offenders and those who relapsed temporarily into criminal conduct resemble each other in nativity, a like proportion of both being native-born and a like proportion foreign-born.

They further resemble each other in their physical condition in youth, in their intelligence, and in the extent to which they were free of mental pathology as determined at the time of commitment to the Reformatory.

As to their school and work history, there are also a number of resemblances between those whose reform lasted throughout the fifteen years and those who recidivated temporarily. The two groups had about the same amount of schooling; they entered gainful employment at about the same age; they had about the same degree of industrial skill, and the same incidence of good or bad work habits.

Those who remained non-offenders and those who relapsed temporarily into criminal conduct met their economic obligations to their families to a similar extent and also were in parallel degree attached to their families. The two groups had bad habits to a like extent; a similar proportion of both groups had used their leisure time harmfully prior to their commitment to the Reformatory; and they attended church with an equal degree of irregularity.

The two groups further resembled each other in that they first showed delinquent tendencies at about the same age.

## Differences between Reformed and Temporary Recidivists

The trend of *differences* between those who remained non-criminal and those who reverted to minor or serious crime at some time beyond the first five-year span is evident in Table 3.

TABLE 3. PRE-REFORMATORY DIFFERENCES IN FAMILY AND PERSONAL BACKGROUND OF TEMPORARY RECIDIVISTS (21)* AND REFORMED OFFENDERS (140)*

| Factors of difference† | Percentage of offenders who reformed before beginning of third five-year follow-up period but relapsed into delinquency in the third five-year span | Percentage of offenders who reformed before beginning of third five-year follow-up period and remained non-offenders in the third five-year span |
|---|---|---|
| Offenders reared in broken homes | 77.8 (18)‡ | 50.7 (136) |
| Parents separated or divorced | 26.3 (19) | 18.4 (125) |
| Offenders exposed to culture conflict (native born of one or two foreign born parents) | 65.0 (20) | 53.0 (134) |
| Families were clients of social agencies | 80.0 (15) | 47.7 (111) |
| Parents in marginal or dependent economic circumstances | 82.4 (17) | 71.1 (128) |
| Fathers unskilled workers | 44.4 (18) | 38.6 (127) |
| Offenders were school truants§ | 70.0 (10) | 42.2 (45) |
| Offenders were retarded two or more years in school | 81.2 (16) | 73.9 (111) |
| Offenders first left home under age fourteen | 50.0 (12) | 34.5 (113) |
| Offenders moved about excessively | 65.0 (20) | 45.3 (139) |

* Maximum number of cases on which observations were possible.
† The factors of difference are presented in the order of their discussion in the text.
‡ As to the significance of the percentage differences, see note 2, p. 127.
§ See note, Table 1, re truancy figures.

We find first of all certain differentia in regard to the home background of the two groups under comparison. Those who relapsed into crime, even though only for a brief time, were to a greater extent the products of broken homes than those who remained non-criminal. Further, they were to a greater extent sons of parents whose conjugal relationships had been poor when the boys were growing up. They had been more exposed in their youth than the continuously non-criminal to the dangers inherent in conflicting cultural backgrounds, for a higher proportion of those who temporarily recidivated were the native-born sons of one or two foreign-born parents than were those who remained non-criminals.

The greater inadequacy of their general social background is further reflected in the finding that four-fifths of the families of the youths who temporarily reverted to criminal conduct had been dealt with by various kinds of social welfare agencies during boyhood, as compared with only half the families of the youths who remained non-criminal. Supporting this finding of an excess of families who required propping is the fact that a higher proportion of the youths who temporarily recidivated had been reared in homes of low economic status than is true of the youths who remained non-criminal. This finding is consistent with the fact that a somewhat higher proportion of the fathers of the youths who relapsed temporarily had been unskilled workers than of the fathers of those who remained non-offenders.

Turning now to the youths themselves, we find that more of those on whom these data were available and who relapsed into criminalism had been school truants than is true of those who continued to be non-criminal throughout; and that a slightly higher proportion of the former than of the latter had been retarded two or more years in school, and this despite the fact that both groups were of the same intelligence level.

Those who temporarily reverted to criminality were somewhat younger when they first left the parental roof than were those who had reformed entirely, a half of the former being under fourteen when they departed from home as compared with a third of those who remained non-delinquents throughout the fifteen-year span. Not only had they left home earlier, but they had also moved about more from place to place than was the case with those who remained non-delinquent.

From this it becomes evident that on the whole the environment in which those had been reared who relapsed into criminalism was less favorable than that of the men who were consistently non-criminal, and we may fairly assume that the influence of this early environment persisted into their later life so that when they had to face crises they were unable to meet them as well as the youths who had not been quite so burdened.

*Case Illustrations of Temporary Recidivists*

A few illustrations will bring out more clearly some of the precipitating causes of relapse into criminality.

*Henry* had settled down following a second parole from the Reformatory to which he had been returned because of the commission of larceny of an automobile. Shortly after this, at the age of twenty-three, he married and has since worked steadily and been a devoted husband and father. During the first follow-up period he was an auto repairman, earning about $40 a week. During the second five years he continued to be steadily employed not only as an auto mechanic but as an auto salesman, earning as much as $60 a week. The family (the couple have a daughter) lived in a good residential district, kept in close touch with their relatives, spent their leisure time together in wholesome ways, and lived comfortably. In the third follow-up period, when the effects of the industrial depression began to be felt, this reflected itself in Henry's earning capacity and steadiness of employment. He lost his job as an auto mechanic and had to earn a precarious living by selling automobiles on a commission basis at a time when sales were slow. His earnings fell first to $25 a week and then to $15. The family had to move to cheaper quarters in order to save rent. Henry's wife became ill and things went from bad to worse with him. He was finally forced, much against his will, to apply for aid to a social agency. They supplemented his income with money for groceries and paid medical bills for his wife. In desperation, because money was needed at home, Henry embezzled $50 from his employer, who brought a complaint against him. The charge was soon withdrawn because the offender made restitution. The whole case was dismissed on the grounds of "business carelessness."

A few days after Henry's arrest for embezzlement and on the very day when the complaint was withdrawn, Henry committed adultery with a negress to whom he paid a dollar. There is some suggestion that he had been unable to have sexual contact with his wife during this period because of her illness; and apparently the excitement of the whole episode and his relief in having the complaint on the embezzlement charge withdrawn, caused him to give vent to his pent-up emotions.

Several years have now passed since this event. Henry has again found steady work, and all goes well.

*Philip* has a continuous record for drunkenness since the age of twenty. He has also frequently committed larcenies, always while under the influence of liquor. He married before his sentence to the Reformatory and gave as his reasons for desiring parole that he wished to support his wife and child in an attempt to stop her divorce proceedings. Meanwhile his wife did get a divorce, but when Philip was released he began to woo her again. He bought a small piece of land and built a house on it, purchased a horse and wagon, and began a trucking business. Meanwhile he worked for several employers and was usually discharged because of drinking and committing petty larceny when under the influence of liquor. Having established a home, he remarried his divorced wife.

During the first five-year follow-up period he worked off and on for contractors, masons, and in factories, carrying on his trucking business when other work was scarce. At best he was barely eking out a living and found it necessary to sell his house a year after the beginning of the first follow-up period, for $400. Throughout this time he continued to be lazy, drank heavily, and was not able to support his family properly. Meanwhile, two more children were born.

After leaving the farm the family moved into a cheap tenement in a slum neighborhood. During the second five-year period Philip continued to drink, often indulging in sprees "with the boys." The family had to be supported by welfare agencies. Meanwhile Philip's wife was known to be carrying on an affair with a boarder. This proved very disturbing to Philip and he apparently realized that if he did not get a grip on himself he would lose her again. What went on in Philip's mind we do not know, but when he stopped drinking in the fifth year of the second follow-up period he gave as the reason the fact that he had stomach discomfort and that liquor nauseated him.

At this time the famiy moved away from the tenement into a three-family house in a reasonably good suburban neighborhood, leaving the boarder behind. Philip began to show a little more initiative in supporting his family, and spent his evenings at home. He ceased meeting with fellow "drunks," although he continued to be a very irregular worker. He at least turned his money over to his wife, however, instead of spending it for liquor.

For four years of the third follow-up span, Philip did not drink. The family remained in the home just described and Philip's wife did not carry on with her former "boy friend" until the fourth year of the third follow-up span. Then, because of very bad economic conditions, she again took him as a boarder, and the affair which had been smouldering for several years burst into flame. Philip's wife began to grow discontented with him and finally took her children and left home. Meanwhile, Philip had to move into a cheap rooming house and manage by himself as best he could. He was extremely unhappy and discouraged and at this time began to drink again, so that after a period of five years free of liquor and of the commission of any other offenses which were the result of drinking, Philip returned to his old ways.

We have some information about what has happened since the end of the third five-year span. Philip's wife has secured a divorce and married the boarder. A year and a half has already elapsed since the end of the third five-year period and Philip is still drinking and has on one occasion committed burglary while under the influence of liquor.

So, at the age of forty-three, Philip reverts to his old habits and when questioned about this, says that this is all due to family difficulties, that he becomes easily discouraged, and that liquor helps him forget his troubles.

While still on parole, *Joseph* married and quickly settled down. To the end of the second follow-up period he supported his wife and two children in modest circumstances. He was an unskilled laborer, worked fairly steadily, and earned about $20 a week. The family lived in a comfortable two-family house and kept in touch with relatives; and Joseph spent most of his leisure time with his wife and children. Until well into the third period he got along reasonably well, managing to have work as a laborer; but because of the industrial depression he had to drop his insurance policy and was forced to ask assistance from public welfare agencies. In order to make ends meet, his family had to move into a cheaper neighborhood where, according to the police, the moral standards were not so good as they had been in the previous home.

Meanwhile Joseph's wife began to run about town a good deal and loaf in bar-rooms. Whether this was the precipitating cause of his own indulgence in alcoholism is not clear, but the fact is that when Joseph was arrested for drunkenness with another man and placed in jail, he accused his companion of running around with his wife. Joseph and his companion had got into a street brawl while under the influence of liquor. This was evidently Joseph's way of taking it out on the man who had become too familiar with his wife. In jail, on the morning following Joseph's accusation of him, the man hanged himself in his cell. For this Joseph was not held responsible. However, since this tragic episode there has been no further difficulty. Joseph does drink occasionally but not to excess. Although he has had to accept public assistance, he resents this and hopes to regain work in private employment soon.

Following a second release from the Reformatory where he had been sent for the crime of larceny, *Peter* married and settled down with his wife in a modest but comfortable three-family house. He worked quite steadily as a shoe salesman, occasionally supplementing his income by promoting dances. At his regular work he was earning about $35 a week, during the first five-year span. During this period five children were born to Peter and his wife. He assumed his responsibilities very well, and as the family increased in size, Peter appeared to be able to take on the additional obligations.

During the second five-year period four more children were born to the couple. They moved into larger quarters in a fairly decent residential neighborhood, and Peter was saving a little money and carrying insurance. He continued to be a shoe salesman and at odd times to promote dances and theatrical performances. Until the depression Peter was earning about $30 a week. However, toward the end of the second follow-up period he began to feel the effects of the industrial slump and in the third five-year span he had only very irregular work as a shoe salesman and found it necessary to try to earn a living in what had previously been his "side line," the promotion of entertainments.

By now Peter was the father of twelve children. He and his wife had been getting along very well, had both been assuming their family responsibilities, and were very much attached to their children. Though it was necessary for them to apply for aid to the local welfare agencies, they both resented this very much.

Toward the middle of the third period, as Peter was becoming more and more involved in the business of promoting entertainments, he was going about a great deal to sporty night clubs in connection with this work, and he began to drink a little for the sake of sociability. Also he had the opportunity to meet many attractive women. Peter's wife began to suspect that he was becoming interested in some girl. Things came to a head when she somehow learned that Peter and the girl were spending the night at a local hotel. She got the police to go with her to find him and they came upon Peter in a hotel room with the girl. Although there was no direct evidence of any illicit relationship, Peter explaining that he had met the girl in connection with his promotional activities, he nevertheless revealed his guilt by jumping out of the hotel window to avoid arrest. In this attempt he broke his ankle and had to go to a hospital for several weeks. During this time he had a chance to think things over and apparently decided that the game was not worth the candle. After his recovery he secured work on the W.P.A. for about a year and supplementary relief from welfare agencies. Peter did not return to his promotional work, because his wife felt that the influences surrounding this were detrimental. Toward the end of the five-year period he succeeded in getting work in a photographic studio where he has been an assistant photographer earning as much as $25 a week. He has resumed his normal family life and there has been no further evidence of straying from the path.

In his early years *William* committed larcenies and this misconduct persisted throughout the first five-year period, during which time he went from the east to the middle west, where he was employed in a woodworking plant earning an average of $40 a week. Shortly after a year's commitment to a house of correction for petty larceny, William married a fellow employee with whom he had been keeping company for a year and a half, and settled down with her in a small shack owned by her parents in a factory district. She continued to work for a year after their marriage but gave up her job at her husband's request.

Soon a child was born to the couple and William's wife says that he was not only "a good man but a perfect father." William and his wife were very fond of one another. The family recreation consisted of occasional attendance at a neighborhood movie and sitting on a bench in front of their little house during the evenings. Until the end of the fourth year of the second follow-up period his work was steady. At that time, however, the company for which he had worked for a number of years moved away and William lost his job. Although the family had $140 in savings, this small amount was quickly used up. Since then William has had to resort to odds and ends of work—as an extra hand in the meat market, labor in other factories, and the like, but nothing steady—and for several years the family have had to accept relief from public and private agencies.

A year and a half after the beginning of the third follow-up span, when William was thirty-six years old, he was arrested for committing a robbery with two fellow employees whom he knew only casually. William's wife explains that following his lay-off he became despondent over his inability to pay rent to her mother who was herself in dire need at the time. Assistance from welfare agencies covered only the food needs of the family. His wife thinks that William "fell in" with the idea of robbing a milkman because of his discouragement about securing a job. In view of the fact that William is mentally deficient, it is possible that the two men took the initiative and influenced him to join in the hold-up from which a total of $27 was netted. At any rate, William was sent to prison on a sentence of from one to twenty years but was paroled in a year and three months. Since then he has been working in a factory earning just enough to make ends meet, and his conduct during a long period of parole from the prison has been excellent.

When *George* was sixteen, he was sentenced to the Reformatory for assault to rob. He has had no other criminal record either before or since. The story of this arrest would indicate that it was not much more than a boyish prank and that he was never an habitual criminal. Ever since his parole from the Reformatory at the age of seventeen he has behaved well, working largely in factories and living with his family until his marriage just before the end of the parole period.

George settled down with his wife, first in the home of her parents and then in their own small house in the country not far from a big city where he was working as a weaver. During the first five-year period one child was born to the couple and in the second period another. Both George and his wife have been very devoted to the children.

George earned on the average $35 a week. At the beginning of the second five-year period he had to have a little assistance from public welfare agencies when the mill in which he was working moved south and he was left without a job. But in a few months he was again steadily employed as a weaver.

He spent most of his leisure time with his family, except for hunting and trapping expeditions in the fall, which he greatly enjoyed. Occasionally he would play cards with his cronies in a pool-room in the rear of a store.

Toward the end of the second follow-up period the industrial depression began to have its effect on George's life. By now he was thirty-two years old. Soon he was laid off from a job which he had held for some time, because work was slack. At about this time George's older child, a boy to whom both he and his wife were dearly devoted, became ill and died of acute leukemia and bronchial pneumonia. George was so deeply distressed over this that he could not do his work properly and was discharged for irregular attendance. Meanwhile his income had dropped to $28 a week and he again had to apply for a little help from the agencies, something he very much resented having to do. He looked around for another job as a weaver, but without success. With no savings and very little insurance, no prospects for steady work and some debts, he was faced with the necessity of applying for work relief.

For three months after the death of his boy and his discharge from the mill George says that he walked around "in a trance." Then he accepted a job for a "bookie" selling lottery tickets. "What would you do under such circumstances? Out of a job, badly in need of money, and someone comes to you and offers you a good paying job." George says he made as much as $25 a week and continued to work for the bookie for one and a half years, at which time his employer gave up the "business." It is evident that George's indulgence in the illicit occupation of selling lottery tickets was of a temporary and fortuitous character. He did not seek to continue this illegal employment further but went to work on the W.P.A. where he is at present, receiving $14 for four days a week. He likes weaving and hopes to get a steady job as soon as business conditions improve. Upon the urgency of his friends, he had been thinking about opening a pool-room. When questioned about earning his living in such a doubtful enterprise, he commented, "What's the difference? Don't the rich financiers steal from their clients?"

*Edward* has a long record for larceny and burglary, but from the time he was thirty-two until he was forty, all evidence of criminal conduct had disappeared, so that by the beginning of the second follow-up period he was nicely settled and living in a comfortable two-family house in a fairly decent residential neighborhood, and running a trucking business of his own. He was managing to support his family (wife and three children) without assistance. He remained in the trucking business until well into the third five-year period, when he finally had to give it up following a long illness with pneumonia. Unable to attend to it during this time, and because of the general industrial decline, he lost his business. He could no longer make payments still due on a fairly new truck and this indispensable equipment of his occupation was taken away from him. He believes that if he had had a little more reserve capital, he would have weathered the combination of adverse circumstances. He had enjoyed the trucking business a great deal because it was outdoor work.

After Edward's recovery from pneumonia he was left in such a weakened condition that he took a drink now and then as a "bracer." He began to indulge a little too heavily and finally, following an assault on his wife while under the influence of liquor for which offense he was placed on probation, his wife arranged for his commitment to a state hospital for treatment, hoping he would be cured of his newly acquired habit of drinking. He was very shortly discharged and continued to drink a little for the next year and a half but then stopped entirely. Meanwhile he was placed on the W.P.A. as a laborer and was receiving $14 a week and some assistance from private social agencies.

Edward hopes that when the depression is over he will be able to return to his trucking work. He had done a good deal of trucking for one concern who had used him continually over a period of twelve years and always found his work very satisfactory. A business associate speaks of Edward in the highest terms as always a dependable, honest, straightforward, and industrious fellow. Edward's wife says that she can readily see a connection between his drinking and his physical condition. His wife is very thrifty and the family manages to get along even on his small earnings. He does not like to be on W.P.A. or accept anything from public relief.

## Comment

It is evident from the cases of *Henry, Philip, Joseph, Peter, William, George,* and *Edward* that the nature of relapse into antisocial behavior after years of law-abiding conduct largely involves submission to mental tensions engendered by the burden of economic stress rather than any deliberate and calculated return to criminalism. Of the 21 men who recidivated temporarily the nature of their relapses may be briefly summarized as follows: one man lapsed into petty larceny, one into robbery, one embezzled a small sum of money from an employer but promptly made restitution, one committed adultery, one neglected to support his wife and children, two resorted briefly to the gambling racket, one committed assault and battery on his wife, and thirteen drank heavily for a brief time.

Of the 21 men, two were under twenty when they had presumably reformed and were between thirty-five and forty years old when they relapsed into delinquent conduct. Of 11 men who were between twenty and twenty-five when they apparently reformed, one was between twenty-five and thirty at relapse, three between thirty and thirty-five, six between thirty-five and forty and one was between forty and forty-five. Of six men who were twenty-five to thirty years of age when they apparently reformed, three were between thirty and thirty-five at relapse and three were between thirty-five and forty. One man who was between thirty and thirty-five when he reformed was between forty and forty-five when he relapsed; and one man who was between thirty-five and forty at reformation was between forty and forty-five at the time of relapse. It will be seen that the span of time between the age of presumably permanent reformation and relapse was, on the whole, considerable.

Part I of this work is now completed. We have described the changes in the behavior of our group of Reformatory graduates over a fifteen-year span following the expiration of their Reformatory sentences and have then compared the characteristics of those who reformed at one time or another during this span with those who have continued to recidivate. We have further compared the characteristics of those who continued to be serious offenders during the fifteen-year span with those who became minor offenders and, finally, we have studied the characteristics of those in the group who, although they apparently settled into law-abidingness and remained non-criminal for some years, relapsed into criminal conduct for a brief time during the third five-year follow-up period.

We are now ready to turn our attention to Part II of this work which deals with the responses of the offenders to the various forms of peno-correctional treatment to which they have been subjected from the onset of their delinquent careers to the end of (and in some cases beyond) the fifteen-year follow-up span.

# PART II

## RESPONSE OF OFFENDERS TO PENO-CORRECTIONAL TREATMENT

## IX

## BEHAVIOR DURING PENO-CORRECTIONAL
## TREATMENT

W E now come to the second portion of this work which has to do with the behavior of our men during the various peno-correctional treatments to which they have been subjected from the onset of their delinquent careers until the present. As these men were on the average of 14.8 years old at the time of their first arrest and now, at the end of the fifteen-year span following the completion of their sentences to the Reformatory, they are on the average of 40.15 years, a considerable period is covered in the following analysis of their behavior during peno-correctional treatment.

In a previous work, *Juvenile Delinquents Grown Up*,[1] which deals with a different series of offenders (those who passed through the hands of a juvenile court) whom we have followed for a span of fifteen years after the end of their contact with the court and its associated agencies, we also studied the behavior of offenders while under treatment. This first attempt at analysis of the conduct of offenders *during* treatment was precipitated by our observations over the years that not all offenders react poorly or well to any particular form of treatment; that some respond more satisfactorily to intramural control than to extramural oversight and vice versa; that some, though behaving well on probation, do not respond satisfactorily to parole; that others, who do not respond favorably to any form of peno-correctional treatment, nevertheless behave reasonably well under the strict discipline and planned régime of the Army and Navy, and so on. The great importance of this finding to sentencing and releasing authorities is obvious. It seems well worth the effort, therefore, to analyze the responses of the present group of offenders to the various forms of peno-correctional treatment to which they have been subjected in the course of their criminal careers.

This was done by setting down in chronological order every "treatment experience" which an offender had had and then determining through an examination of records what his conduct had been thereunder. The reader is invited to consult Chapter XIII of *Juvenile Delinquents Grown Up* for details of how such data are gathered. It should here be stressed, however, that because a description of the offender's behavior during treatment was made so many years after the event, it was not possible to state in any detail the nuances of his conduct. Reliance had to be placed on the purely objective record of be-

---

[1] New York, The Commonwealth Fund, 1940.

havior as gathered from police, courts, fingerprint files, and institutional reports.

Since *Juvenile Delinquents Grown Up* was a pioneer attempt to study behavior during peno-correctional treatment on an extensive basis, it was in many respects crude. We did not make any effort to differentiate behavior during treatment at various age levels, beyond separating out conduct under various forms of treatment during the first, second, and third follow-up periods, which of course roughly indicated the changes which took place with advancing years. In the analysis of behavior during treatment we confined ourselves very largely to a comparison of the characteristics of those who succeeded and failed during extramural and during intramural treatment, the former including "straight probation,"[2] probation under suspended sentence, and parole; the latter covering terms served in industrial and truant schools, reformatories, prisons and jails. We were able to establish the following four general *"treatment types,"* the characteristics of which we proceeded to analyze:

1. Those who succeeded during some, though not necessarily all, intramural and extramural treatments;
2. Those who failed during all intramural and extramural treatments;
3. Those who succeeded during intramural but failed during extramural treatments;
4. Those who failed during intramural but succeeded during extramural treatments.

Our series of comparisons of the characteristics of these various treatment types led to certain general conclusions about the reasons for the success and failure of the men comprising them and served to point the way to more detailed studies; so that in the present work, in addition to a comparison of the characteristics of those who succeeded and those who failed during *extramural* and during *intramural* treatments, we have broken these down into the following more specific forms of treatment: straight probation, probation under suspended sentence, parole, correctional schools, reformatories, prisons, jails, and also Army or Navy, and have compared the characteristics of the successes and failures under each of these peno-correctional treatments. And we have taken still a further step beyond the prior research, by determining their response to these various forms of peno-correctional treatment at different age levels.

The purpose of the remainder of our research is therefore threefold: first, to describe the conduct of this group of ex-inmates of the Reformatory during various forms of peno-correctional treatment and at different age levels; secondly, to compare the characteristics of those who succeeded and failed under

[2] Unaccompanied by a suspended sentence to an institution.

each specific type of peno-correctional treatment; and thirdly, to construct a further series of illustrative prediction tables of a kind which judges and others concerned in the treatment of offenders can in the future (when these and similar tables have been properly validated by checking them on other series of cases) utilize in determining the treatment needs of a *particular class of offenders at a particular age level.*

The first two of these general purposes are developed in Part II of the present work, while Part III concerns itself with the illustrative and as yet only experimental prediction tables that have resulted from this detailed analysis.

### Definition of "Success" and "Failure"

Before proceeding with an analysis of the behavior of the offenders during the various forms of peno-correctional treatment and at different age levels, it is necessary to indicate the distinction between *"success"* and *"failure"* during treatment. As in the previous work, *Juvenile Delinquents Grown Up,* this is essentially the difference between criminality and non-criminality, and no attempt is made to separate failures into minor and serious. The information available is too sketchy to furnish a safe basis for this finer differentiation.

As in *Juvenile Delinquents Grown Up,* the definition of failure during a period of *extramural* treatment (ordinary probation, probation under suspended sentence, parole) was based upon actual arrests during the period of such treatment; or more than occasional violations of the conditions of probation or parole; or the offender's commitment by surrender to an institution for violating probation under suspended sentence or parole; or the known or recorded commission of offenses (such as stealing, sex offenses, drinking, etc.) for which the offender might well have been arrested but somehow escaped arrest. An occasional minor infringement of the rules of probation or parole (such as neglect to report on time, or changing jobs without permission, or arrest for traffic violations) was not regarded as indicative of failure.

Failure during a period of *intramural* treatment (correctional school, reformatory, prison, jail) was determined from the conduct reports kept by the institutional authorities. If such records revealed that an inmate was a constant disciplinary problem, frequently running away from the institution or stealing or inciting others to misbehavior, encouraging others in the commission of sex offenses, or otherwise generally disturbing the good order of the institution, he was regarded as a failure. Sometimes no such specific information was available, but it was found that a youth had been punished by being placed in solitary confinement; and this was sufficient evidence that he had not been getting on well. An offender who was reported as being entirely or usually amenable to the institutional routine and only very occasionally violating the rules was classified as a success during the relevant period of intramural treatment.

Although service in the Army or Navy is of course not a peno-correctional treatment, we have gathered information on the behavior of our men during such periods of service, because the routine and discipline of military life require a certain degree of adaptability and submission to authority not wholly unlike that in peno-correctional institutions. Failure in the Army or Navy was determined entirely from the official reports of Army or Navy authorities. Dishonorable discharge or desertion, or imprisonment by the military or naval authorities, was the test of failure; success in the Army or Navy was for our purposes determined by honorable discharge.

## Summary of Behavior

As preliminary to a detailed description by age groups of the behavior of the offenders during various peno-correctional treatments, it will be helpful to consider, first, their behavior during extra- and intramural peno-correctional treatment as a whole and, secondly, their behavior during each specific type of extra- and intramural treatment. In Table 4 is a comparison of the behavior

TABLE 4. COMPARISON OF BEHAVIOR DURING EXTRA- AND INTRA-
MURAL PENO-CORRECTIONAL TREATMENT*

|  | Extramural treatment | | Intramural treatment | |
| --- | --- | --- | --- | --- |
|  | Number | Per cent | Number | Per cent |
| Always succeeds ......... | 64 | 13.4 | 133 | 26.6 |
| Always fails ............ | 291 | 61.0 | 184 | 36.8 |
| Succeeds at first, later fails | 10 | 2.1 | 36 | 7.2 |
| Fails at first, later succeeds | 85 | 17.8 | 97 | 19.4 |
| Erratic as to success and failure ................. | 27 | 5.7 | 50 | 10.0 |
| Total ............. | 477 | 100.0 | 500 | 100.0 |

* Compare *Juvenile Delinquents Grown Up*, pp. 156–158.

of our men during extra- and intramural treatment from which it becomes evident that a considerably higher proportion of offenders behaved satisfactorily during various forms of intramural treatment than during extramural, and conversely a much higher proportion misbehaved during extramural than during intramural treatment. The obvious general conclusion is that the greater restraint of life within the four walls of an institution tends to reduce the opportunity for antisocial behavior;[3] but this generalization is of little value with-

---

[3] Misbehavior within an institution is, however, more readily detected than extramural misconduct.

out a more detailed analysis of the responses of the offenders to the various types of extra- and intramural treatment.

In Table 5, therefore, is presented a comparison of the behavior of our men

TABLE 5. COMPARISON OF BEHAVIOR DURING VARIOUS FORMS OF
EXTRAMURAL PENO-CORRECTIONAL TREATMENT

| | Straight probation | | Probation under suspended sentence | | Parole | |
|---|---|---|---|---|---|---|
| | Number | Per cent | Number | Per cent | Number | Per cent |
| Always succeeds .......... | 6 | 2.4 | 4 | 2.8 | 105 | 22.6 |
| Always fails .............. | 230 | 92.4 | 129 | 91.5 | 296 | 63.7 |
| Succeeds at first, later fails ... | 2 | .8 | 0 | 0.0 | 4 | .9 |
| Fails at first, later succeeds ... | 10 | 4.0 | 6 | 4.3 | 55 | 11.8 |
| Erratic as to success and failure | 1 | .4 | 2 | 1.4 | 5 | 1.0 |
| *Total* .............. | *249* | *100.0* | *141* | *100.0* | *465* | *100.0* |

during ordinary probation, probation under suspended sentence (that is, under threat of commitment to an institution should the rules of probation be violated), and parole. From this we see that a considerably lower proportion of offenders misbehaved on parole than under "straight probation" or probation under suspended sentence. As probation usually occurs prior to a commitment to an institution, while parole follows imprisonment, it would seem reasonable to conclude that the stark realities of a stay in a penal institution have contributed to good behavior on parole. Certainly an offender who has already experienced an institutional commitment would take special care not to be returned to confinement.[4]

In regard to behavior within institutions and in the Army and Navy, Table 6 reveals that a higher proportion of offenders got alone satisfactorily in prisons and jails, and even in the Army and Navy, than in correctional schools and reformatories. This is accounted for by the fact that by the time offenders are committed to the former institutions they are more mature and more experienced in making adaptations. Perhaps, also, the less complex régime of prisons and jails makes adaptation easier.

### Behavior at Different Age Levels

We now turn to an analysis of the conduct of the offenders under treatment at various *age levels*.[5] Our purpose in such an analysis is twofold: first, to see whether within any specific age span there is any marked difference in be-

---

[4] It should be stressed that inasmuch as our search for the criminal records of probationers and parolees was equally intensive, the above differences are reliable findings and not due to some extraneous influence, such as inequality in the check-up of behavior on probation and on parole.

[5] This has to our knowledge never before been done in the history of criminology.

TABLE 6. COMPARISON OF BEHAVIOR DURING VARIOUS FORMS OF INTRAMURAL PENO-
CORRECTIONAL TREATMENT AND IN THE ARMY AND NAVY

| | Correctional school | | Reforma- tories | | Prisons | | Jails | | Army and Navy | |
|---|---|---|---|---|---|---|---|---|---|---|
| | Num- ber | Per cent | Num- ber | Per cent | Num- ber | Per cent | Num- ber | Per cent | Num- ber | Per cent |
| Always succeeds | 43 | 33.9 | 153 | 30.9 | 66 | 52.8 | 100 | 61.7 | 67 | 47.2 |
| Always fails ... | 73 | 57.5 | 298 | 60.2 | 32 | 25.6 | 43 | 26.6 | 57 | 40.1 |
| Succeeds at first, later fails ... | 6 | 4.7 | 11 | 2.2 | 3 | 2.4 | 5 | 3.1 | 15 | 10.6 |
| Fails at first, later succeeds | 4 | 3.2 | 32 | 6.5 | 21 | 16.8 | 10 | 6.2 | 2 | 1.4 |
| Erratic as to suc- cess and failure | 1 | .7 | 1 | .2 | 3 | 2.4 | 4 | 2.4 | 1 | .7 |
| Total .... | 127 | 100.0 | 495 | 100.0 | 125 | 100.0 | 162 | 100.0 | 142 | 100.0 |

havior under various forms of treatment; and secondly, to determine what changes occur in reactions to a specific form of treatment with advancing years.

*Behavior under 17 years.* Since the average age at first arrest of this group was 14.8 years, they had already had a considerable number of peno-correctional experiences before they reached their seventeenth year. At least 80 of the group had been on straight probation, 24 had experienced probation under suspended sentence, at least 111 had been in correctional schools, and at least 84 had been on parole.[6]

Table 7 indicates the behavior of the youths during the particular treatments to which they were subjected when under seventeen years of age. It should be remembered that those who are described as successes are those who are known to have behaved satisfactorily during the specific forms of treatment which they experienced during this particular age span.

From this table it is seen that on the whole the behavior of our youths during various forms of extramural treatment (straight probation, probation under suspended sentence, parole) was equally poor. This assumes a special significance when it is related to the fact revealed in Table 5 that considering behavior on parole as a whole, as compared with behavior during the two forms of probation, a far higher proportion of offenders succeeded on parole throughout their criminal careers (regardless of age) than did so under the other forms of extramural treatment. This was obviously not so of the 84 youths paroled during the early years of their criminal careers, when adaptation to any form of

---

[6] These figures do not necessarily represent the entire number who had experienced such peno-correctional treatments, because cases in which information was unknown or in which there were not sufficient data to make an accurate estimate of success and failure during a particular form of treatment have been excluded from consideration.

TABLE 7. PERCENTAGE OF SUCCESSES DURING VARIOUS FORMS OF PENO-CORRECTIONAL TREATMENT AT DIFFERENT AGE LEVELS

| | Percentage of successes | | | | | | |
|---|---|---|---|---|---|---|---|
| | Under 17 | 17–21 | 22–26 | 27–31 | 32–36 | 37–41 | 42 and older |
| *Extramural* | | | | | | | |
| Probation | 6.3 (80) | 3.6 (112) | 0.0 (36) | 13.3 (45) | 12.5 (24) | 9.1 (22) | 11.1 (18) |
| Probation with suspended sentence | 0.0 (24) | 0.0 (50) | 6.7 (30) | 0.0 (40) | 14.3 (42) | 15.4 (26) | 5.0 (20) |
| Parole | 2.4 (84) | 18.3 (257) | 31.2 (253) | 19.5 (123) | 27.5 (69) | 26.5 (34) | 5.9 (17) |
| *Intramural* | | | | | | | |
| Correctional schools | 39.6 (111) | 23.8 (42) | – | – | – | – | – |
| Reformatories | – | 25.6 (356) | 37.9 (214) | 55.9 (68) | 68.4 (19) | – | 50.0 (2) |
| Prisons | – | 43.8 (16) | 54.2 (48) | 61.1 (54) | 69.0 (42) | 75.8 (33) | 92.3 (13) |
| Jails | – | 50.0 (30) | 61.3 (62) | 55.6 (63) | 76.9 (52) | 92.5 (40) | 79.3 (29) |
| Army and Navy | – | 39.7 (58) | 61.3 (75) | 66.7 (24) | 42.9 (7) | 50.0 (2) | 100.0 (1) |

extramural oversight was apparently very difficult. On the other hand, over a third of the youths who were sent to correctional schools while still under seventeen, responded satisfactorily to such treatment. Apparently, therefore, during the early years of criminality a much better response is to be expected from institutional treatment than from extramural treatment.

*Behavior at 17–21 years.* Continuing now into their later adolescent years, when our youths experienced not only the type of treatments they had already had when under seventeen but also commitments to reformatories, prisons, and jails and service in the Army or Navy, we note some significant differences as revealed in Table 7.

Here we see that response to straight probation and probation under suspended sentence remains about the same as it was in the prior age span, but that a larger proportion of the youths behaved well during parole than was the case among younger parolees. On the whole, also, behavior in this age span is better during intramural treatment than during extramural; but it is to be noted that not so high a proportion of our youths conducted themselves satisfactorily in correctional schools during the 17–21 age level as was true of those committed when under seventeen. This can be explained by the fact that the youths who continued to serve in correctional schools beyond the seventeenth year were the worst offenders, that is, those returned for violation of parole; a selection had occurred which left institutional authorities to cope with the residue of more serious offenders.

The behavior of these youths in the 17–21 age span is little better in reformatories than in correctional schools, probably for the same reason. However, it is to be noted that conduct in prison and jail is, at 17–21, considerably better than conduct in correctional schools and reformatories. That this cannot be due to the more rigid discipline in the first type of institution is evident from the fact that behavior is even better in jails, where discipline is generally much more lax, than it is in prisons. It may be, however, that those who were sent to prisons and jails at so early an age span were youths whose experiences had led them to "know the ropes" and therefore to adapt more acceptably in institutions for adults, where standards demanded of inmates can more easily be met.[7] It is to be noted also that almost as high a proportion of offenders be-

---

[7] To some extent, the analyses in this chapter are affected by differences in the standards of acceptable conduct in the various types of treatment involved. In certain jails and prisons, for example, acceptable behavior may consist in the inmate's docile adherence to the institution's rules. While this is not always a true indication of the offender's reform and may, in fact, not be socially desirable in the long run, from the standpoint of the prison administrator an inmate who does not violate institutional rules and goes about his duties without causing trouble is deemed a "success"; and such a performance in the institution is given great weight by parole boards in determining which prisoners to release on parole and when to release them.

haved well under the rigid discipline of the Army or Navy as did so in prisons or jails.

*Behavior at 22–26 years.* Turning now to the next age span, which may be regarded as the early post-adolescent period (although we know that not a few offenders continue to be adolescent well beyond the outside limit of this span), we find little change in behavior during ordinary probation or probation under suspended sentence, but a growing adaptability to parole supervision. In this age span there are of course no commitments to correctional schools; the increase in satisfactory adjustments pertains to life in reformatories, prisons, jails, and in the Army or Navy.

Further examination of Table 7 reveals that in the 22–26 year age span, behavior during intramural treatment is better than extramural behavior to an even greater degree than was the case in the preceding age span.

*Behavior at 27–31 years.* Table 7 shows that within the age span of 27–31 the trend toward improvement in behavior during peno-correctional treatment continues except as regards behavior on parole, under which form of control not so high a proportion of offenders succeeded as in the preceding age span. It is particularly to be noted that a considerably higher proportion did well on straight probation at the 27–31 year level than in prior age spans; but there was no marked change in behavior during probation under suspended sentence. However, behavior in reformatories and prisons and in the Army or Navy was slightly better at the 27–31 year level than it was in the prior age spans, while the incidence of acceptable conduct in jails dropped.

*Behavior at 32–36 years.* At the age level of 32–36, we see from Table 7 that there occurs a considerable improvement in behavior on probation with suspended sentence; conduct on parole is better than in the previous age span; conduct on probation maintains the improved level attained during the 27–31 year span; conduct in the reformatory is better even than in the previous period, as is also conduct in prisons or jails; but there is a falling off in good behavior in the Army or Navy.

*Behavior at 37–41 years.* Table 7 shows that in the age span 37–41 the proportion of successes in extramural treatments remains about the same as during the previous age span, but behavior during intramural treatment (reformatory, prisons, and jails) continues to improve.

*Behavior at 42 and older.* Coming now to the highest age span involved in our study, Table 7 shows a drop in the proportion of adjustments during extramural and intramural treatment, with the exception of conduct in prisons.

It is evident from the above analysis, first, that throughout the criminal careers of our group, behavior during intramural treatment is always better than it is during extramural. The obvious reason is that there is less opportunity for misbehaving inside walls than outside, and greater ease in meeting the adaptive demands of simplified and supervised environments. Secondly, it is evident that with advancing years behavior on the whole improves to approximately forty years when some drop becomes evident. Those who are still criminals by the time this age has been reached are already beginning to deteriorate physically and mentally. They are of course the worst offenders, so that their poorer behavior in and out of institutions explains the decreasing proportion of successes beyond forty.

So much for success or failure at different age levels. To indicate more significantly the changes in behavior that have occurred during peno-correctional treatment with advancing years, we now turn to an analysis of *conduct changes in response to each form of treatment at various age levels* in order to see at what age span the sharpest differentiations in behavior have occurred under each type of peno-correctional treatment.

### Conduct Changes during Treatment at Various Age Levels

*Behavior on probation at various age levels.* Table 7 presents a comparison of successes on *straight probation* under 17 years, 17–21 years, 22–26 years, 27–31, 32–36, 37–41, and 42 years or older. It discloses that behavior on straight probation continued to be very poor until roughly the twenty-seventh year; so that for all practical purposes it can be considered that up to that age the likelihood is very slight of good adjustment to probation for offenders of the type described in this work. From the twenty-seventh year behavior on probation improves and remains at about the same level throughout the later years.[8]

*Behavior on probation under suspended sentence at various age levels.* Turning now to behavior on probation with suspended sentence (that is, with threat of commitment to an institution if the conditions of probation are violated), Table 7 reveals a sharp differentiation in the behavior of this group, at roughly the thirty-two year level. From the onset of their delinquent careers until approximately thirty-two years of age, the offenders do not respond at all well to probation under suspended sentence; but from thirty-two to forty-two years there is a marked improvement, and thereafter a slump. In general, however, it may be said that the differentiation in behavior on probation with suspended sentence occurs roughly at under and over thirty-two years.[9]

[8] It will be seen in Part III of this book, in which tentative prediction tables indicate likelihood of success and failure on probation, that the above facts are taken into account in constructing the prediction tables. Instead of preparing seven different tables to cover each age level, we have prepared only two, one covering the age span *under 27,* and the other the age span *27 and older.*

[9] In building up tentative prediction tables for behavior under this form of treatment, two

*Behavior on parole at various age levels.* Turning now to changes in behavior on parole, an examination of Table 7 reveals that the highest proportion of parole successes occurred at the age span twenty-two to twenty-six, followed by a sharp decline in good adaptation to parole oversight at the twenty-seven to thirty-one year level; a rise occurred thereafter, from thirty-two to forty-one, though not to the peak achieved at twenty-two to twenty-six, followed by a sharp decline beyond forty-one. The improvement in conduct on parole after the juvenile court age may be partially attributable to a better superficial adaptation of delinquents to this form of treatment with their growing experience. The poorer adjustment to parole in the later years may be due partly to the mental and physical deterioration of certain types of offenders who find it more and more difficult to get along under any form of extramural supervision in which adaptive capacity plays a considerable role. The reason for the appreciable drop in parole success at the twenty-seven to thirty-one year level, though more obscure, may possibly be that at that age level offenders who are on parole are of a more serious kind, men who in their youth had been given longer prison sentences and are now serving the latter part of them on parole. Such offenders are more likely to find adaptation to a life of supervised freedom in the community difficult. At this same age level, it will be recalled, there was not a single success on probation under suspended sentence, a form of treatment closely resembling parole in involving the threat of commitment or re-commitment to prison.[10]

*Behavior in correctional schools at various age levels.* Turning now to a consideration of the conduct of our offenders during intramural treatment, we come first to a comparison of their behavior in correctional schools under 17, and at 17–21 years. (Youths are not committed to correctional schools beyond this time.) This comparison, made in Table 7, indicates that the proportion of youths behaving well in correctional schools decreases with advancing years. As has already been suggested, this can be explained by the fact that the youths who are returned to correctional schools because of misbehavior during parole, and who largely appear in the 17–21 year group, are the more serious offenders and therefore do not adapt themselves quite so readily to the routine of such institutions.[11]

tables have been prepared (see Part III, p. 242), one covering the span *under thirty-two* and the other *thirty-two and over.*

[10] For the purposes of building up tentative prediction tables we have made a differentiation between the age levels *under twenty-two years, twenty-two to twenty-six years,* and *twenty-seven years and older.* Such a division has furnished, as will be seen in Part III, p. 248, sufficiently effective prediction tables for behavior on parole during various age spans.

[11] For predictive purposes we have therefore prepared two tables (see Part III, p. 259), one covering the age span *under 17* and the other *17–21* years.

*Behavior in reformatories at various age levels.* Considering, now, the behavior at various age levels of our offenders while incarcerated in reformatories, we note in Table 7 a consistent increase with age, in acceptable adjustment to such institutions. This is partly explainable by a growing facility in meeting institutional demands, and partly by the more settled make-up of the older men.[12]

*Behavior in prisons at various age levels.* As in adaptation to life in reformatories so to the régime of prisons, there is a consistent improvement with age. An examination of Table 7 reveals that the sharpest differentiations, considering the number of cases involved, occur in the age spans *under 27, 27–31, 32–36* and *37 and over.*[13]

*Behavior in jails at various age levels.* In contrast to behavior in prisons, which are long-term institutions for serious offenders and where continuous improvement in behavior occurred from the earliest to the latest years involved in this research, Table 7 reveals that the behavior of the offenders who were subjected to jail sentences at various age spans improved consistently until roughly the forty-second year and then deteriorated. This can be explained by the fact that those committed to jails are largely offenders against the public welfare, drunkards, and vagrants; and as their drinking habits increase, they tend to deteriorate and therefore cannot make as good an adaptation even to the comparatively lax régime of jails as they were able to make in earlier years.[14]

*Behavior in Army or Navy at various age levels.* Coming, finally, to behavior in the Army or Navy, which has been included because it represents a kind of discipline resembling certain aspects of treatment in peno-correctional institutions, we see from Table 7 that there is a consistent improvement in behavior under this type of régime from the seventeenth to roughly the thirty-second year and thereafter the response is not quite so good. However, in view of the small number of men who were in the Army or Navy from age thirty-two, no conclusions can be drawn about their behavior under this form of supervision.[15]

---

[12] Taking account of smallness of numbers involved in the age span thirty-seven and older, we have for purposes of prediction built up three tables, one covering the age span *17–21,* the second *22–26,* and the third *27 and older,* which the reader can consult in Part III, pp. 264 and 266.

[13] Therefore prediction tables have been prepared for these four age levels (see Part III, pp. 268 and 270).

[14] For purposes of prediction tables, considering the number of cases involved, we have made a differentiation between behavior under thirty-seven and behavior at thirty-seven and older. The marked difference in the incidence of favorable response shows that, had there been a greater number of cases, it would have been desirable to treat the age span thirty-seven to forty-one separately from the age span forty-two and over (see Part III, pp. 273, 274, 276).

[15] For purposes of prediction tables, we have made a differentiation between the age span *17–21* and *22 and older* (see Part III, p. 279).

*Comment*

From the analysis in this chapter we have seen that there is some association between behavior during various forms of peno-correctional treatment and the age of the offenders subjected to them. This finding shows that the factor of age must be taken into account in preparing prediction tables indicating what the response of particular offenders is likely to be to various forms of peno-correctional treatment (see Part III of this work).

# X

## SUCCESSES AND FAILURES DURING EXTRAMURAL AND INTRAMURAL TREATMENT

IT is the purpose of this chapter to compare the traits and characteristics of the offenders who succeeded and those who failed during various forms of peno-correctional treatment, in the belief that from such an analysis may emerge useful clues to the *reasons for differentiation in the response of offenders to various forms of treatment*. In *Juvenile Delinquents Grown Up* the characteristics of extramural and of intramural successes and failures were analyzed, but no attempt was made to go beyond these general comparisons to the characteristics of offenders who succeeded and failed during *specific forms of treatment* (straight probation, probation under suspended sentence, parole, correctional school, reformatory, prison, jail). In the present work an effort at such comparison will be made wherever possible. It seems best, however, to begin this presentation with a more general analysis of the resemblances and differences in the characteristics (a) of those who succeeded and those who failed during extramural treatment, and (b) those who succeeded and those who failed in intramural treatment, even though the analysis made in the previous chapter indicates that with advancing years changes occur in the responses of offenders to the various forms of intra- and extramural treatment.

To avoid a too complicated and possibly meaningless analysis of the resemblances and differences between successes and failures, we are for present purposes not including those offenders who did not behave well under oversight in the earlier portions of their criminal careers and adapted themselves well later; or those who responded satisfactorily to treatment in the earlier stages and later misbehaved; or those who succeeded at times and failed at other times during treatment and in whose conduct there was therefore no definite trend either toward improvement or deterioration. Our comparison of characteristics of successes and failures is clearly confined to those offenders who throughout their delinquent careers behaved *satisfactorily* during *all* treatments to which they happened to have been subjected and to those who *seriously misbehaved* during *all* treatments to which they were subjected from the onset of their delinquent careers until the present time. This span covers both the stage prior to commitment of our men to the Reformatory and thereafter, comprising, roughly, a period of twenty-five years (average age at first arrest was 14.8 years and average age at end of third five-year period was forty years).

Before analyzing the resemblances and differences between successes and failures, it will be helpful to list the twenty-seven factors which have been included in this comparison and in all those in succeeding chapters (as well as in Chapters VII and VIII).

FACTORS OF COMPARISON AND THEIR SUB-CATEGORIES

Nativity of the delinquents
  Native born
  Foreign born
Nativity of delinquents as related to nativity of the parents
  One or both foreign, son native
  All native
  All foreign
Size of family
  Only child
  Two, three children
  Four, five, six children
  Seven or more children
Rank of offender among siblings
  Only child
  First child
  Second or later in rank
Delinquency in the family
  Yes
  No
Economic condition of family in offender's youth
  Dependent
  Marginal
  Comfortable
Conjugal relations of parents
  Good
  Fair
  Poor
Broken and inadequate homes
  Broken homes
  Homes not broken but otherwise inadequate
  Homes not broken or inadequate
Education of parents
  No education
  One or both at least common school
Occupation of mother in offender's youth
  Housewife
  Worked out
Skill of father in offender's youth
  Semi-skilled or skilled
  Unskilled

Social services rendered to family in offender's youth
  None
  One or more
Grade attained in school
  No schooling
  Less than sixth
  Sixth, seventh, eighth
  Entered but did not complete high school
  Completed high school
Retardation in school
  Normal or advanced
  Retarded one year
  Retarded two or more years
Misconduct in school
  Truancy
  Other maladjustment
  None
Age began work
  Under fifteen
  Fifteen and over
Skill of offender in youth
  Skilled
  Semi-skilled
  Unskilled
Work habits of offender in youth
  Good
  Fair
  Poor
Economic responsibility of offender in youth
  Good
  Fair
  Poor
Age first left home
  Under fourteen
  Fourteen and over
Family relationships of offender in youth
  Good
  Fair
  Poor
Age at first known delinquency
  (See p. 162)

| | |
|---|---|
| Age at first known delinquency | Intelligence of offender |
|   Under eleven |   Normal |
|   Eleven to thirteen |   Dull |
|   Fourteen to sixteen |   Borderline |
|   Seventeen and over |   Feebleminded |
| Leisure, use of, by offender in youth | Mental condition of offender in youth |
|   Constructive |   Normal |
|   Negative |   Abnormal |
|   Harmful | Physical condition of offender in youth |
| Habits in youth |   Good |
|   Bad habits |   Fair |
|   No bad habits |   Poor |

The foregoing twenty-seven factors have each been related in turn to success and failure not only during extra- and intramural treatment in general, but to each particular form of peno-correctional treatment.[1]

## EXTRAMURAL TREATMENT

It should be mentioned that there were at least 64 offenders who had always behaved well during all forms of extramural treatment to which they have been subjected throughout their criminal careers, while at least 291 offenders failed in their conduct during extramural treatment. Although there actually were more extramural successes and failures than these figures indicate, where information about their conduct was incomplete the cases could not be included for analysis.[2]

### Resemblances between Extramural Successes and Failures

There are only two factors of *resemblance* between the offenders who always succeeded and those who always failed during periods of extramural treatment; namely, the age at which they first began to work and the occupational skill of their fathers. These being neutral factors, they cannot be the ones that have contributed to the varying responses of our men to extramural treatment. We are justified, therefore, in laying them aside in our search for the reasons for the differences in behavior of the two groups of men while under supervision outside of institutions.

[1] The interested reader is invited to consult *Later Criminal Careers* (Appendix B: Definition of Terms, pp. 231 *et seq.*), in which the definitions of most of the factors listed above can be found in alphabetical order.

[2] In comparing the characteristics of these successes and failures, it is, of course, further necessary to omit those cases in which it was unknown in what particular sub-category of a factor an offender should be placed. For example, although at least 64 men always behaved well during extramural treatment, the occupational skill of their fathers was known in only 54; while of at least 291 men who always misbehaved during extramural treatment, the occupational skill of their fathers was known in 265 cases. However, unless the number of unknown characteristics of a factor were so great as to affect the comparison, no mention of this is made in the text.

## Differences between Extramural Successes and Failures

We come now to those factors in which differences of 4 per cent or more are found to exist between extramural successes and failures. Although obviously no single factor can be given any significance in itself, taken together, these differences tend to show the trend of divergence between the characteristics of those who succeeded and those who failed during extramural peno-correctional treatment. As the analysis which follows shows, the differences, presented in Table 8, are all in favor of the extramural successes.

TABLE 8. PRE-REFORMATORY DIFFERENCES IN FAMILY AND PERSONAL BACKGROUND OF EXTRAMURAL SUCCESSES (64)* AND FAILURES (291)*

| Factors of difference† | Percentage of extramural successes | Percentage of extramural failures |
|---|---|---|
| Offenders foreign born ............................. | 28.1 (64)‡ | 16.2 (290) |
| Offenders not exposed to culture conflict (nativity of parents and sons the same) ............................. | 56.4 (62) | 48.4 (281) |
| No other members of family delinquent ................ | 46.8 (47) | 21.4 (248) |
| Parents had at least common school education .......... | 26.2 (61) | 14.5 (276) |
| Parents not economically dependent ................... | 98.1 (52) | 80.2 (263) |
| Families were not clients of social agencies ............ | 64.6 (48) | 38.1 (231) |
| Mothers did not work outside home .................. | 84.9 (53) | 71.4 (266) |
| Parents harmonious ................................. | 75.4 (57) | 58.6 (249) |
| Offenders not reared in broken or inadequate homes ...... | 32.8 (61) | 16.5 (285) |
| Offenders were not first-born children ................ | 75.4 (61) | 70.3 (283) |
| Offenders of normal intelligence ..................... | 41.8 (55) | 28.3 (269) |
| Offenders had more than eighth grade schooling ........ | 15.0 (60) | 10.4 (289) |
| Offenders were not retarded in school ................ | 31.2 (48) | 22.3 (229) |
| Offenders showed no evidence of mental pathology ....... | 90.9 (44) | 55.0 (229) |
| Offenders were in good health ....................... | 95.2 (62) | 88.6 (281) |
| Offenders were first delinquent at fourteen or over ........ | 88.8 (63) | 53.3 (287) |
| Offenders were not school truants§ .................... | 86.7 (15) | 44.8 (105) |
| Offenders first left home at fourteen or older ........... | 77.1 (48) | 54.1 (246) |
| Offenders did not use leisure time harmfully ............ | 11.1 (63) | 1.7 (287) |
| Offenders did not have bad habits .................... | 11.5 (61) | 3.2 (280) |
| Offenders were semi-skilled or skilled workers ......... | 59.7 (62) | 11.3 (289) |
| Offenders had good work habits ..................... | 48.8 (43) | 12.7 (221) |
| Offenders met economic responsibilities toward their families | 44.4 (45) | 11.7 (230) |
| Offenders had ties of affection to parents and siblings ..... | 52.6 (57) | 25.4 (248) |

* Maximum number of cases on which observations were possible.
† The factors of difference are presented in the order of their discussion in the text.
‡ As to the significance of the percentage differences, see note 2, p. 127.
§ See note, Table 1, re truancy figures.

First, a higher proportion of those who reacted satisfactorily to all extramural treatments had been born in foreign countries than of those who always failed. In this connection it should be remembered that respect for authority is deeply rooted in certain foreign countries. Further, a lower proportion of those who always behaved well during extramural treatment were exposed to the hazards of culture conflict for they were not to so great an extent the native-born sons of one or two foreign-born parents.

The extramural successes were, further, better circumstanced in that a considerably lower proportion come from families, other members of whom are also delinquents or criminals. So also, there is a higher educational achievement among their parents.

As further indication of the better general background of the extramural successes, it is to be noted that a higher proportion of those who always behaved well while under oversight in the community came from families who were not economically dependent than of those who always misbehaved during extramural treatment. The generally greater adequacy of the background of the youths who succeeded during extramural treatment is further reflected in the fact that a far lower proportion of their families were dealt with by the social agencies of the community during the offender's youth, than of the families of the men who misbehaved during extramural treatment. Their greater adequacy is further borne out by the finding that a lower proportion of the mothers of the youths who behaved acceptably during extramural treatment found it necessary to work outside the home in order to supplement the family income, than of the mothers of the youths who always failed during extramural treatment.

Even as regards the conjugal relationships of the parents of our youths, we find that a far higher proportion of the parents of the successes lived happily together than of the parents of the failures; and a far higher proportion of those who succeeded during extramural treatment came from homes which were neither broken by death, separation, desertion, or divorce of parents or were in other ways unsuited to the rearing of children.

The evidence as to family background, therefore, clearly points to the conclusion that the offenders who always responded well to extramural treatment (probation and parole) were more favorably endowed and circumstanced in childhood and youth than were those who always failed.

Turning now to differences in the characteristics of the youths themselves, we find that they were somewhat less likely to be spoiled children than were the extramural failures because they were not to so great an extent first-born children. We find also, very significantly, that a far higher percentage of those who behaved well during extramural treatment were of normal intelligence than of those who failed. This explains why a higher proportion of them advanced beyond the eighth grade in school and were not behind grade for their age.

In regard to mental health, a far higher percentage of those who always behaved well during extramural treatment were free of mental disease or distortion and could therefore be considered in good or "normal" mental health. In addition to this, they were also in slightly better physical condition in youth than were the extramural failures.

As to age at onset of delinquency, a far higher proportion of those who always behaved well during extramural treatment began their delinquencies in later childhood (fourteen years or over) than of those who always failed; the delinquencies of those who behaved satisfactorily during extramural treatment were not as deeply rooted as were the delinquencies of the extramural failures. The antisociality of the extramural failures is more closely related to their biologic make-up and early conditioning than is the original delinquency of the extramural successes.

In regard to school truancy, despite the small number of cases on which information was available, it seems entirely in accord with other differences between extramural successes and failures that a lower proportion of those who behaved well during extramural treatment had been school truants than of those who failed; and logically following this is the fact that a far lower proportion of those who behaved well during extramural treatment had left their parental homes when under fourteen years of age than of those who always failed during extramural treatment. These findings are all consistent with the fact that those who responded well to extramural treatment did not use their leisure time as harmfully in youth as the extramural failures; nor did they have bad habits to the extent of the extramural failures.

In regard to industrial skill, work habits, and assumption of economic and family responsibilities in youth, we find that a considerably higher proportion of those who got along satisfactorily during extramural supervision than of those who failed were semi-skilled or skilled workers in their youth. So also, a far higher proportion of the successes than of the failures were reliable, industrious workers and assets to their employers.

A much higher percentage of the successes than of the failures met their economic responsibilities toward their parents and siblings. Finally, it is to be noted that a considerably higher proportion of the extramural successes than of the failures manifested ties of affection to their families.[3]

---

[3] Failure to show ties of affection is reflected in the fact that if they lived at home during their youth they remained there only because they were in need of help of one sort or another, or if they lived away from home they kept in touch with their parents or closest relatives only because they were in financial need.

## INTRAMURAL TREATMENT

We now turn our attention to a comparison of the characteristics of those offenders who behaved well during all the *intramural* treatments (correctional schools, reformatories, prisons, jails) to which they were subjected in the course of their delinquent careers with those who did not respond satisfactorily to any such forms of imprisonment.[4]

It is from a sharp differentiation between those who always behaved satisfactorily during intramural peno-correctional treatment and those who did not that we can most clearly see the resemblances and the trend of differences between successes and failures under intramural control.

There were in our group of 510 men at least 133 who always behaved acceptably during intramural treatment and at least 184 who always misbehaved.[5]

### Resemblances between Intramural Successes and Failures

There are several factors in which intramural successes and failures resemble each other, which means that in these factors or characteristics are not to be found explanations for the differences in the response of the offenders to institutional treatment.

In the first place, the two groups of offenders came from families of like size, that is, they had the same number of brothers and sisters. Both groups were of the same order of birth among their living siblings. Both came from homes of like economic background; which is further reflected in the finding that a like proportion of mothers of the intramural successes and failures found it necessary to supplement the family income by part or full-time work during the boyhood of the offenders. The two groups were further of like background in that their fathers were in similar proportions unskilled workers.

As for the youths themselves, there are five ways in which the successes and failures are alike. First, their physical condition in youth was the same; secondly, they were to the same extent burdened with mental disease or distortion; third, they had bad habits to a like extent; fourth, they were of approxi-

---

[4] As in the comparison of extramural successes and failures, we are not taking into consideration the offenders who did not behave well during earlier incarcerations but did adapt themselves later on to one or another kind of institutional control; nor have we included those offenders who made a good adjustment during the earlier part of their criminal careers to life in institutions but did not do so later; or those who sometimes succeeded and sometimes failed, but who did not show any trend either toward improvement or deterioration in conduct.

[5] The reader is reminded that for the purposes of this analysis only those cases could be included in which information on all intramural peno-correctional treatments was available; so that, although there may have been more men in the group who succeeded or failed throughout intramural treatment, sufficient data were not available to make accurate estimates of their conduct.

mately the same age when they first began to work; and finally, their affectional ties to their parents and brothers and sisters were equally weak.

None of the above resemblances can explain the reasons for their different responses to intramural peno-correctional treatment.

### Differences between Intramural Successes and Failures

Most of the differences between the intramural successes and failures, as is evident in Table 9, are to be found in the characteristics of the youths themselves, but several reflect their family background.

TABLE 9. PRE-REFORMATORY DIFFERENCES IN FAMILY AND PERSONAL BACKGROUND OF INTRAMURAL SUCCESSES (133)* AND FAILURES (184)*

| Factors of difference† | Percentage of intramural successes | Percentage of intramural failures |
|---|---|---|
| Offenders not exposed to culture conflict (parents and offenders native born) ......................... | 34.4 (128)‡ | 20.1 (179) |
| Offenders native born ......................... | 83.5 (133) | 77.2 (184) |
| No other member of family delinquent ............. | 38.9 (108) | 29.0 (145) |
| Parents harmonious ........................... | 67.8 (118) | 63.8 (163) |
| Offenders not reared in broken or inadequate homes ... | 27.2 (129) | 22.2 (180) |
| Parents had at least common school education ........ | 20.9 (129) | 12.1 (174) |
| Families were not clients of social agencies .......... | 62.9 (108) | 40.1 (142) |
| Offenders of normal intelligence .................. | 45.8 (120) | 28.7 (157) |
| Offenders were not retarded in school more than one year | 34.9 (106) | 21.3 (146) |
| Offenders had more than eighth grade schooling ....... | 20.9 (129) | 8.3 (181) |
| Offenders did not misbehave in school§ ............. | 37.5 (32) | 14.9 (67) |
| Offenders were not school truants§ .................. | 75.0 (32) | 50.7 (67) |
| Offenders were first delinquent at seventeen or older .... | 42.8 (131) | 15.4 (181) |
| Offenders first left home at fourteen or older .......... | 75.5 (90) | 60.0 (150) |
| Offenders did not use leisure time harmfully .......... | 7.6 (132) | 2.2 (184) |
| Offenders were semi-skilled or skilled workers ........ | 55.2 (132) | 47.0 (183) |
| Offenders had good or fair work habits .............. | 65.6 (99) | 37.6 (133) |
| Offenders met their economic responsibilities .......... | 29.0 (100) | 16.1 (137) |

* Maximum number of cases on which observations were possible.
† The factors of difference are presented in the order of their discussion in the text.
‡ As to the significance of the percentage differences, see note 2, p. 127.
§ See note, Table 1, re truancy figures.

First of all, the intramural successes were not to so great an extent as the failures exposed to the hazards of a conflict of standards and customs between themselves and their parents, because a higher proportion of them than of the intramural failures were native-born sons of native-born parents; and a higher proportion of the intramural successes were themselves native-born than is true of the intramural failures. The intramural successes have a better family background as reflected in a slightly lower proportion coming from families in which other members were delinquent or criminal. Further, the group who succeeded during intramural treatment were to a somewhat greater extent than the failures the sons of parents who were harmonious in their relationships; and to a greater extent they were reared in homes which were neither broken by death, desertion, separation, or divorce, or in other ways inadequate to the wholesome rearing of children. Further, the intramural successes were to a somewhat greater extent than the failures the sons of parents with some education. And a far greater percentage of the successes than of the failures came from families who, despite hardships, had been able to manage their own affairs, as reflected in the proportion who had not been dealt with by social welfare agencies.

Turning now to the youths themselves, we find that a markedly higher percentage of those who behaved well during intramural control are of normal intelligence than of those who did not respond satisfactorily to such treatment. This is consistent with the finding that the former were not to as great an extent retarded in school as were the intramural failures. In view of their higher intelligence, it is not surprising to discover that they had more schooling than the failures. Moreover, as to conduct in school, despite the small number of cases on which observations were based, it seems consistent with the other findings that the intramural successes were better behaved in school and a lower proportion of them had been school truants, than the intramural failures.[6]

Further, a far higher proportion of those who responded satisfactorily to intramural treatment than of the failures had not begun their delinquencies until over sixteen years of age rather than earlier in life. This indicates, as it did among the *extramural* successes, that those who make a poorer adjustment to correctional treatment are youths whose delinquencies are deep-rooted, and seemingly, therefore, have more of a biologic than an environmental basis.

Because the intramural successes became delinquent in the later rather than the earlier years of childhood, we would expect to find that they did not leave home at as early an age as the intramural failures. Consistent with this is the fact that those who responded well to life in peno-correctional institutions did not use their leisure time quite as harmfully as the intramural failures.

Even in industrial status, they are more advantaged than the intramural failures. Those who behaved well in institutions were to a greater extent semi-

[6] The reader has no doubt observed that in all the tables in which truancy has been recorded (Tables 1, 3, 8, and 9) the trend or direction of difference is the same despite the small number of cases on which observations were made, i.e., those who reformed (Tables 1 and 3) or responded successfully to extra- or intramural treatment (Tables 8 and 9) had not been school truants to as great an extent as the failures.

skilled or skilled workers than were the intramural failures. In regard to work habits, a far lower proportion of those who adapted satisfactorily to imprisonment were poor workers.[7] And finally, as might be expected from these findings, a greater proportion of those who responded satisfactorily to intramural treatment met their economic responsibilities to their families during their youth than of the intramural failures.

## COMPARISON OF EXTRAMURAL AND INTRAMURAL SUCCESSES AND FAILURES

This comparison of the characteristics of those who responded well to life in institutions and those who did not shows clearly that, like the successes under extramural treatment, they were decidedly advantaged over the failures. The fact that there is a difference not only in the characteristics of extramural successes and failures but of intramural successes and failures suggests that it should be possible to determine in advance of treatment which offenders are likely to respond better to one type of treatment than to another.

It might be profitable at this point to summarize the resemblances and differences between the extramural successes and failures, on the one hand, and the intramural successes and failures, on the other.

By and large, such differences as do exist, though not necessarily equally marked, are to a considerable extent in the same general direction and reveal on the whole that those who respond well to extramural peno-correctional treatment and to intramural peno-correctional treatment are better endowed and circumstanced than those who do not react satisfactorily to either form of treatment. This holds true of intelligence level, both groups of successes having better intelligence than both groups of failures; of age when delinquency first manifested itself, both groups of successes being older than both groups of failures when they first became delinquent; of school truancy, a markedly lower proportion of both groups of successes having been school truants than of both groups of failures. In regard to work habits, also, both groups of successes were to a greater extent assets to their employers than both groups of failures. Also, those who responded well to extramural and intramural treatment are both characterized by a greater assumption of their economic responsibilities to their families than is true of both groups of failures. Finally, both groups of successes came from families who were better able to manage their own affairs than the families of the youths who did not respond well to either extramural or intramural peno-correctional treatment.

Capacity to adapt satisfactorily, whether to institutional life or during over-

[7] This means that they had been lazy or loafed a great deal, permitted their work to be interrupted by drunkenness, and were altogether a liability to their employers.

sight in the community, is apparently distinguished by certain advantages of mentality and early conditioning. It is nevertheless true, on the whole, that the degree of difference in the characteristics of those who succeeded and those who failed during *intramural* treatment is less than between the extramural successes and failures. This is reflected in the factors in which *extramural* successes and failures differ from each other markedly or slightly,[8] while intramural successes and failures either resemble each other or differ much less extensively from each other. This is true of the factors of broken homes, conjugal relations of parents, educational achievement of parents, size of the family, their economic dependency, the extent to which the mothers of the youths had to work outside the home, delinquency among members of the family, the industrial skill of the youths themselves, their affectional relations to their families, bad habits among the youths, their physical condition in boyhood, and the presence of mental abnormalities apart from intellectual deficiency. In all these characteristics the extramural successes are more advantaged than the extramural failures, while the intramural successes are either less so or not at all.

This would indicate that adaptation to the routine of institutional life is much easier than adaptation to extramural oversight. In an institution the economic needs of the offender are provided, more intensive supervision can be given, the activities are of a more routine nature than are possible under supervision in the community, and the standard of acceptable response can be more easily met.

The only way in which the intramural successes appear to differ from the extramural is the fact that more of the extramural successes than of the failures are foreign-born youths of foreign-born parents, while more of the intramural successes than the intramural failures are native-born of native parentage. Evidently the foreign-born, with their greater tradition of law-abidingness, do not require as close extramural oversight as the native-born, but find it more difficult to rub shoulders with their fellow inmates behind walls.

## COMMENT

Even if the slight differences in the characteristics of extramural successes and failures be entirely disregarded (and their cumulative significance all points in the same direction as do the greater differences), it is clear beyond doubt that the offenders who always responded satisfactorily to extramural treatment were of a distinctly better type than those who responded poorly.

---

[8] As a rough differentiation between slight and marked differences, they are considered slight if they are no less than 4 per cent and under 10 per cent; and marked if they are 10 per cent or more.

Not only were they more favorably circumstanced in the economic and psychologic aspects of their childhood homes, but they were persons of more satisfactory innate and early acquired equipment, as is shown both in their much better intellectual and emotional-volitional make-up, and (as partial expressions of these), in their more satisfactory school records, much better industrial equipment, and, even more significant, in their embarkation upon delinquent careers at a later stage of development.

For those offenders who are likely to fail under absolute restraint, but can make a reasonably good adaptation to extramural supervision, probation or early release on parole is desirable. For those who are likely to fail under any form of intramural or extramural treatment, obviously little can be done with existing facilities. But their very definition as a class should tend to a more intensive examination of their constitution and background, with a view to the setting up of therapeutic experiments to which they might respond. Year in and year out sentences are imposed, without detailed check-ups of the result. Such procedures belong to the ox-cart era of penal treatment. They have no place in an age that is beginning to recognize that the best insurance to society against the criminal is a system that will understand him rationally and treat him therapeutically.

Were the facts presented in this chapter available in usable form to judges and parole boards, two social values of prime importance would be achieved. In the first place, many of the offenders who are favorably circumstanced and endowed might be treated entirely in the community or released earlier on parole; and thereby much loss of time in imprisonment would be avoided and much expense of incarceration saved. Secondly, many of the less favorably endowed offenders who are now released into the community on probation or parole as a "shot in the dark," would not be subjected to treatments under which they are likely to fail.

How differences in the make-up and circumstances of offenders can be utilized in selecting the form of peno-correctional treatment most suitable to the particular type of offender involved is illustrated in Chapters XIV, XV, and XVI.

## XI

# SUCCESSES AND FAILURES DURING VARIOUS FORMS OF EXTRAMURAL TREATMENT

## PROBATION

Having compared the characteristics of extramural successes and failures and of intramural successes and failures, we are now ready to analyze the field more specifically, and to consider the characteristics of those who responded well to the various forms of extra- or intramural peno-correctional treatment and those who did not. Such an analysis should throw further light on the practical implications of the work done by sentencing judges.

We shall begin with a comparison of the characteristics of those who succeeded and those who failed on *straight probation,* and consider later in this chapter those who behaved well during probation under suspended sentence and those who did not. The reader will recall that there is a difference between these two forms of probation, the former being applied usually to early or mild offenders and the latter to those whom a judge considers to be more serious criminals, requiring the threat of commitment to an institution in the event of non-compliance with the conditions of probation. Not only is there some difference in the characteristics of those to whom these two different kinds of probation ought to be applied in the first place, but also in the responses of various types of offenders to the freedom implied in straight probation and to the restraint in probation under suspended sentence; for certain types of people undoubtedly are held in check by threat of commitment.

### Resemblances between Probation Successes and Failures

There are no fewer than eleven factors in which those offenders who always behaved well on probation *resemble* those who seriously violated the conditions of their probation in one way or another. First, they are to a like extent sons of native or of foreign-born parents, and they are both to the same extent native-born sons of foreign-born parents. They come in like measure from families who had to turn to the social welfare agencies of their communities for assistance of one kind or another. They are, moreover, to a similar extent products of homes that were broken by death, separation, desertion, or divorce of their parents or were in other ways unsuitable to the wholesome rearing of the children; and, further, the probation successes and failures were to an equal degree reared in households in which the conjugal relations of the parents were poor. They came in like proportion from families in which the mothers had to work outside the home to supplement the family income. The industrial skill of their fathers was similar.

Turning now to the offenders themselves, the probation successes and failures had bad habits in youth in similar measure, and they utilized their leisure time in equally harmful ways. The probation successes were retarded in school to the same extent as the probation failures. And, finally, they were of roughly the same age when they first began to work.

In none of these factors of similarity can we find any explanation of their difference in response to oversight on probation.

### Differences between Probation Successes and Failures

Turning now to the differences between the probation successes and failures, we see from Table 10 that *unfortunately the number of cases of probation suc-*

TABLE IO. PRE-REFORMATORY DIFFERENCES IN FAMILY AND PERSONAL BACKGROUND OF PROBATION SUCCESSES (6)* AND FAILURES (230)*

| Factors of difference† | Percentage of probation successes | Percentage of probation failures |
|---|---|---|
| No other members of family delinquent .............. | 50.0 (6)‡ | 26.8 (198) |
| Parents economically comfortable ................... | 50.0 (6) | 22.2 (216) |
| Offenders came from families of less than four children .. | 50.0 (6) | 33.8 (228) |
| Offender was only child ........................... | 16.7 (6) | 6.7 (225) |
| Parents had at least common school education ......... | 50.0 (6) | 13.8 (217) |
| Offenders did not show evidence of mental pathology .... | 75.0 (4) | 56.7 (180) |
| Offenders were in good health ...................... | 100.0 (6) | 88.7 (222) |
| Offenders first left home at fourteen and over ......... | 66.7 (3) | 55.2 (174) |
| Offenders were first delinquent at fourteen years or older | 66.6 (6) | 53.1 (228) |
| Offenders had more than sixth grade schooling ......... | 83.3 (6) | 63.0 (227) |
| Offenders were not school truants ................... | 100.0 (4) | 45.6 (90) |
| Offenders had affectional ties to parents and siblings ..... | 83.3 (6) | 31.5 (200) |
| Offenders had good work habits .................... | 25.0 (4) | 15.5 (181) |
| Offenders were skilled workers ..................... | 16.7 (6) | 5.7 (229) |
| Offenders met their economic responsibilities .......... | 25.0 (4) | 14.9 (187) |

  * Maximum number of cases on which observations were possible.
  † The factors of difference are presented in the order of their discussion in the text.
  ‡ As to the significance of the percentage differences, see note 2, p. 127.

*cesses is much smaller than of probation failures. It is probable, therefore, that the comparisons are attended by some degree of error. However, while the element of chance may play a considerable part in any single one of the following comparisons, it is hardly likely that the consistency and rationality of the differences as a whole can be entirely attributed to chance. There is a definite pattern of differentiation, which is obviously not fortuitous. This is especially so in view of similar rational differences shown to exist among the successes and failures under other forms of treatment.*

From Table 10 we see, first, that those who responded satisfactorily to probation came from families in which there was a lower incidence of delinquency or criminality among other members. Further, a higher proportion of those who behaved well on probation came from homes of comfortable economic circumstances than is true of those who always failed. Possibly their better economic background is in turn due to the fact that the probation successes came from smaller families. The probation successes had another advantage over the failures in that a greater proportion of their parents had had at least common school education than of the parents of probation failures.

In regard to the youths themselves, a higher proportion of the probation successes than of the failures were free of mental disease or distortion of one sort or another. Further, they were in better health in youth than those who always failed on probation. More of them than of the probation failures first left home when they were older (fourteen years or more) which means that they had the protection of their families for a longer time. Those who behaved well on probation were also older at onset of their first delinquency than those who failed on probation (fourteen years or more), a fact that would seem to indicate that the delinquencies of probation successes were not quite as deep-seated as those of probation failures.

Like their parents, the probation successes had more schooling than the failures, for four-fifths of the successes had progressed beyond the sixth grade in school, compared to two-thirds of the failures. None of the probation successes had actually been school truants, while half the failures had truanted. A higher proportion of probation successes had shown attachment to their families in youth than is true of probation failures. Evidently family interest and aid played some role in probation success, at least in the early years.

As for their industrial status, the more favored position of the probation successes is further evidenced in better work habits and greater industrial skill. And, finally, they met their economic responsibilities to their families to a greater extent than did the probation failures.

### Resemblances between Successes and Failures on Probation under Suspended Sentence

Having compared the characteristics of those who behaved well and those who did not under straight probation, we now turn to a comparison of those who responded well to *probation under suspended sentence,* and those who did not.

Probation under suspended sentence differs of course from straight probation in that the former carries with it a threat of commitment to an institution in the event that the conditions of probation are violated. That psychologically at least such threat is bound to have some effect upon the probationer goes without saying; and we would expect to find that those who respond well to this form of treatment differ from those who behave well under straight probation. What these differences are we shall see by comparing the background and traits of those who behaved well under suspended sentence with those who did not.

First of all, the two groups resemble each other in that, to an equal extent, their families had to turn to social welfare agencies in the community for assistance of one sort or another. This is consistent with the second finding that the two groups of parents were in similar economic circumstances during the childhood of the offenders. Thirdly, they resemble each other in the equally limited educational achievement of their parents.

The offenders themselves are alike in that their physical condition in youth was about the same, and both groups were of the same rank in birth among their living siblings.[1]

### Differences between Successes and Failures on Probation under Suspended Sentence

Table 11 reveals the differences between those who always responded well under probation with threat of commitment to an institution and those who did not. *The reader is reminded that there are only four in our group of offenders who always behaved well on probation under suspended sentence. This is to be expected because we have been studying a group of offenders who were committed to a reformatory. Obviously, therefore, very few of them responded well to suspended sentences, or they would not have been sentenced to this or to other peno-correctional institutions. To find four offenders, therefore, in such a group who responded well to this particular form of treatment whenever they were subjected to it is almost tantamount to finding four cured cases of cancer, let us say; and therefore a comparison of any number of offenders who did not respond well to this form of peno-correctional treatment with four offenders who did, has some significance, particularly when, as the reader will see from the following analysis, the findings have a strong internal consistency.[2]*

---

[1] Because of the small number of known cases of school truancy and of family delinquency among those who succeeded on probation under suspended sentence, it is not possible to determine whether the successes and failures resemble each other or differ from one another on these two factors.

[2] In future researches particularly designed for comparisons of the characteristics of treatment successes and failures, a large and, if possible, equal number of cases in each group would be

TABLE II. PRE-REFORMATORY DIFFERENCES IN FAMILY AND PERSONAL BACKGROUND
OF PROBATION-UNDER-SUSPENDED-SENTENCE SUCCESSES (4)* AND FAILURES (129)*

| Factors of difference† | Percentage of successes on probation under suspended sentence | Percentage of failures on probation under suspended sentence |
|---|---|---|
| Offenders mentally defective ......................... | 100.0 (4)‡ | 16.8 (125) |
| Offenders were retarded two or more years in school ..... | 100.0 (4) | 77.1 (109) |
| Offenders left school before sixth grade ............... | 75.0 (4) | 37.2 (129) |
| Offenders showed evidence of mental pathology ........ | 0.0 (4) | 55.9 (102) |
| Parents and sons foreign born ...................... | 25.0 (4) | 8.6 (128) |
| Offenders not exposed to culture conflict (parents and offenders of like nativity) ......................... | 50.0 (4) | 37.5 (128) |
| Fathers unskilled workers .......................... | 100.0 (4) | 39.3 (122) |
| Mothers did not work outside home ................:.. | 100.0 (4) | 75.6 (123) |
| Offenders one of four or fewer children .............. | 50.0 (4) | 25.6 (129) |
| Offenders not reared in broken homes ............... | 75.0 (4) | 21.1 (128) |
| Parents harmonious .............................. | 75.0 (4) | 61.9 (113) |
| Offenders were first delinquent at fourteen and older .... | 75.0 (4) | 55.8 (129) |
| Offenders first left home at fourteen years and older ..... | 66.7 (3) | 51.1 (90) |
| Offenders did not use leisure time harmfully .......... | 25.0 (4) | 2.3 (129) |
| Offenders did not have bad habits in youth ........... | 25.0 (4) | 4.0 (126) |
| Offenders under fifteen when began to work .......... | 66.7 (3) | 42.4 (125) |
| Offenders were unskilled workers ................... | 75.0 (4) | 59.7 (129) |
| Offenders had poor work habits .................... | 100.0 (3) | 55.6 (99) |
| Offenders did not meet their economic responsibilities ... | 100.0 (3) | 88.5 (104) |
| Offenders had affectional ties to families .............. | 50.0 (4) | 32.2 (118) |

\* Maximum number of cases on which observations were possible.
† The factors of difference are presented in the order of their discussion in the text.
‡ As to the significance of the percentage differences, see note 2, p. 127.

The fact that all four successes are mental defectives as compared with less than a fifth of those who did not respond well to this form of extramural supervision would seem to indicate not only that offenders of low mentality are more likely to be impressed with threats than those of higher intelligence but, indirectly, that their hereditary equipment is poorer.

Flowing logically from the fact that the successes are all mental defectives is the finding that all of the former had been two or more years retarded in school, as compared to four-fifths of the failures; and, further, proportionately twice the number of the successes as of failures had not progressed beyond the fifth grade in school. However, none of the successes had any mental disease

selected for study. In this particular research we are necessarily limited to those cases which happened to have had a particular form of treatment and whose response to that treatment was known. Although our findings can for this reason be deemed only tentative, the general direction in which they point is clear.

or any other distortions, while almost half of those who did not behave well on probation under suspended sentence were found to have mental abnormalities of a kind noted by psychiatrists. Clearly, emotional instability is a handicap to success under this form of treatment.

In regard to the nativity of the youths and their parents, it is significant that a higher proportion of those who responded satisfactorily to probation with suspended sentence than of those who did not are foreign-born youths of foreign-born parents. There was also less opportunity for culture conflict among those who succeeded under this form of treatment than among those who did not, for more of the successes were of like nativity as their parents than were the failures. But the fact that a greater proportion of the parents of the successes were foreign-born may account for the higher proportion of unskilled workers among the fathers of the successes than among the fathers of the failures. And this may also be related to the finding that none of the mothers of the youths who succeeded under probation with suspended sentence had been gainfully employed during the childhood of the offenders as compared with a fourth of the other mothers; for there is more prejudice among the foreign-born against mothers working outside the home than among the native-born.

In regard to the size of the families, it should be mentioned that the youths who behaved well on probation with suspended sentence came from smaller families than those who did not respond well to this form of supervision. And while three of the four successes came from integrated homes (those not broken by death, desertion, separation or divorce of the parents or in other ways inadequate to the rearing of children), only a fifth of the failures did. The better home background of the former is further reflected in the finding that the parents of those who responded well to probation under suspended sentence were on the whole more harmonious in their conjugal relationships than were the parents of those who did not react satisfactorily to this form of treatment.

Although the youths who behaved well on probation under suspended sentence were of lower intelligence than the failures, a higher proportion of them first became delinquent later in childhood (when they were fourteen or older). This would seem to indicate that their delinquencies were not as deep-seated as those of the youths who did not behave well under this form of supervision and that possibly they were manifestations of the first difficulties of adaptation encountered during the adolescent period of instability when the mentally defective is required to get along without oversight in a growingly complex environment. So also a somewhat higher proportion of the youths who behaved well on probation under suspended sentence than of the failures remained under the parental roof until they were at least fourteen years old. Only one of the four successes had not utilized his leisure time harmfully in youth but even this proportion is better than among the failures. So also a lower proportion of the successes than of the failures had had bad habits in youth.

However, a greater proportion of the youths who responded well to probation with suspended sentence had begun to work early in life (when under fifteen years of age) than of those who did not respond satisfactorily. This may be accounted for by the fact that the successes are of low intelligence and had left school earlier than the failures, which in turn may be related to the next significant difference between the successes and failures on probation under suspended sentence; namely, that a higher proportion of those who behaved well were unskilled workers than were those who failed. It may also have bearing on the fact that the work habits of the successes were poorer than those of the youths who did not respond well to this form of treatment. All of the youths who behaved well on probation under suspended sentence had been industrial liabilities, as compared with half the failures. And flowing from this finding is the one that while none of the youths who got along satisfactorily on probation under suspended sentence had previously met his economic responsibilities to the family, an eighth of the group of the failures had done so. However, a higher proportion of those who responded satisfactorily to probation under suspended sentence than of the failures had been attached to their families in young manhood.

### Comparison of Straight Probationers with Those under Suspended Sentence

It will be interesting at this point to draw distinctions between the "straight" probation cases, in which there was no threat of commitment to an institution for failure to comply with the requirements of this form of treatment, and those who were under probation with threat of sentence to an institution.

First in regard to the economic status of their early homes, although the successes on ordinary probation came to a markedly greater extent than the failures from homes in which the economic conditions were not too unfavorable, the suspended-sentence successes and failures resembled each other in the economic status of their early homes. However, the mothers of those who responded well to straight probation did not work outside the home any more than did the mothers of those who did not respond well to this form of treatment, which is in contrast to the suspended-sentence cases, among whom a lower proportion of the mothers of successes than of failures worked outside the home. But each group of successes resembles each group of failures in the extent to which their families had to turn to social welfare agencies for assistance of one sort or another.

As to the occupational skill of their fathers, there is no difference between the straight probation successes and failures; but the fathers of those who behaved well under suspended sentence were to a markedly greater extent unskilled workers than the fathers of those who did not respond well to this form of supervision.

Considering now the educational background of their families, we find that the parents of those who behaved well on straight probation had more schooling than the parents of those who did not respond well to this form of treatment; while there was no difference in the amount of schooling among parents of suspended-sentence successes and failures.

Although the successes on ordinary probation came to as great an extent as the failures from homes which had been broken by the death, desertion, separation, or divorce of parents, among suspended-sentence successes and failures the successes are to a lesser extent the products of broken homes than the failures. Consistent with this is the finding that as high a proportion of the straight probation successes as of the failures had parents whose conjugal relationships were poor, while among the suspended-sentence cases a greater proportion of the parents of the successes lived compatibly together than the parents of the failures.

Turning now to the youths themselves, we find that in considering the differences in their nativity as compared with that of their parents, no greater opportunities for culture conflict existed among the straight probation successes than among the failures, for they were of like nativity in relation to that of their parents; but among those who were under suspended sentence there is a difference in this regard. A lower proportion of the successes under this form of supervision were native-born sons with one or both foreign-born parents than among the failures. Again, in regard to the nativity of the youths themselves, there is no difference between probation successes and failures; but those who responded well to probation under suspended sentence were to a greater extent foreign-born than the failures.

Turning now to the size of the families, we find that the probation successes came from somewhat larger families than probation failures, while those who behaved well under suspended sentence came from somewhat smaller families than the failures. In regard to the rank of the youths among their siblings, those who behaved well on probation were to a greater extent only children or first-born children than were the probation failures, while there was no difference in this regard between the suspended-sentence successes and failures.

As to intelligence, none of those who behaved well on straight probation (which is the freest kind of extramural supervision) was feebleminded; while all of those who responded well to probation with threat of commitment to an institution in case of violation of the conditions were of very low intelligence.

As to the differences between both groups of successes and failures in regard to the presence of mental distortions of the kind that concern psychiatrists, both groups of successes were freer than both groups of failures from such conditions, the successes on probation under suspended sentence being, as a matter of fact, entirely free of mental disease or distortion. Those who behaved well on straight probation were in slightly better physical condition as youths than those who did not, but there was no difference between the suspended-sentence successes and failures in this regard.

Considering, now, the differences in their educational background, the straight probation successes had more schooling than the failures, while those who behaved well on probation with suspended sentence had had less schooling than the failures. Although the ordinary probation successes and failures resembled each other in the extent to which they were behind grade in school for their age, those who responded well to oversight under suspended sentence were somewhat more retarded in school than were the failures. A further resemblance between the probationers and those under suspended sentence lies in the fact that a greater proportion of each success group did not become delinquent until they were fourteen years or older (rather than younger) than is true of each group of failures. Likewise, each group of successes had, to a greater extent than the respective failures, first left the parental roof when they were fourteen or older rather than in earlier years.

In regard to bad habits, however, the straight probation successes and failures resembled each other while those who behaved well under suspended sentence did not have bad habits to as great an extent as those who failed under this form of supervision. This is likewise true of use of leisure time.

Considering now their industrial history, the probation successes and failures were about the same age when they first began to work; but the successes under suspended sentence were on the whole younger when they first began to work than the failures. As to their industrial skill, those who behaved well on ordinary probation and those who responded satisfactorily to probation under suspended sentence had less skill than that possessed by the failures in either group. But those who successfully met the conditions of ordinary probation had only slightly better work habits than those who did not, while those who responded well to supervision under suspended sentence had markedly poorer work habits than those who did not. The probation successes had met their economic responsibilities to their families in youth better than the probation failures; but those who responded well to supervision under

suspended sentence had not fulfilled their economic obligations as well as the
failures under this form of treatment.

Finally, both the ordinary probation successes and those who responded
well to probation under suspended sentence were markedly more attached to
their families than were those who did not react satisfactorily to either form
of treatment.

### Comment

Despite the smallness of numbers among the probation successes, these
comparisons of the characteristics (a) of those who succeeded and those who
failed under straight probation, (b) of those who responded well to supervision on probation under suspended sentence and those who did not and (c)
of straight probation successes and failures with suspended-sentence probation
successes and failures, tend to reveal, by and large, that *those who succeeded
were on the whole more advantaged than those who failed;* and this by virtue
of better parentage on the one hand and of better stuff in the make-up of the
offenders themselves on the other.

It is to be particularly noted that the most highly differentiating characteristic between those who responded well to probation under suspended sentence
as compared with those who did not, is low intelligence. But this intellectual
defect was unaccompanied by abnormalities in the emotional-volitional realm,
as evidenced by the absence of any mental disease or distortion among the
successes and the high incidence of such distortions among the failures. This
reveals how much more important for the purpose of adjustment to the demands of the penal code is a sound temperamental equipment than good intelligence.

As we indicated at the outset, the foregoing comparisons are affected by the
small numbers of successes on probation and probation under suspended sentence. For this reason we do not wish to emphasize the meaning of any single
difference in the characteristics of successes and failures. At the same time it
cannot be overlooked that, taken as a whole, the comparisons show a consistent
and rational pattern of differentiation. Because differences exist between offenders who respond satisfactorily to straight probation and those who behave well on probation under suspended sentence (i.e., with threat of commitment to an institution if the conditions of probation are not met), a judge
in considering which form of probation to apply would be greatly aided by
prediction tables (if constructed on a substantial number of cases) that would
take these differences into account. In Chapter XV we illustrate a method of
selecting out for ordinary probation or probation with suspended sentence the
respective offenders who are most likely to make satisfactory responses to each

of these forms of treatment. Although these particular tables are necessarily based on a limited number of cases, they nevertheless illustrate at least for the group of offenders under study, what the possibilities are of selecting for treatment those offenders who are most likely to respond to a particular form of peno-correctional supervision.

## PAROLE

It must be remembered that in contrast with probation or probation under suspended sentence (treatments which are entirely independent of and precede imprisonment), parole *follows* commitment to an institution. Therefore, one would expect to find some differences in the characteristics of those who react satisfactorily to probation or probation under suspended sentence and those who respond well to parole supervision. Certainly the influence of institutional life must make itself felt in the conduct of parolees, while no such influence would occur on the behavior of probationers except in the instances where probation takes place after institutional commitments.

### Resemblances between Parole Successes and Failures

In six factors, those who responded well to parole supervision and those who failed *resemble* each other: They come from families of equal size and occupy the same birth rank among their brothers and sisters. Their fathers had the same degree of industrial skill. The youths themselves had the same amount of schooling, were of approximately the same age when they first began to work, and in childhood had used their leisure time with equal harmfulness.

### Differences between Parole Successes and Failures

Turning now to the differences between those who responded well to parole supervision and those who did not, we find, first, from Table 12, that those who behaved well on parole were not potentially at least exposed to as great an extent to the conflicting of cultures between themselves and their parents as were the parole failures, for more of them were of the same nativity as their parents than is true of those who failed. Further a higher proportion of the parole successes were of foreign birth than of the parole failures. Their respect for authority is traditional.

The moral atmosphere of their homes was better, in that a lower percentage of them than of parole failures came from families among whom there were other delinquent members. They were more advantaged, also, in the fact that a greater proportion of them were the products of homes neither broken by the death, desertion, separation, or divorce of their parents nor in other ways unsuitable to the wholesome rearing of children. The force of circumstance was further in their favor because the relationship of their parents to each other was more harmonious than that of the offenders who did not respond well to parole supervision.

Additional evidence of the better family background of the parole successes is the finding that a lower proportion of their families had been dealt with by various kinds of social welfare agencies during the youth of the offenders. Their superior status is further reflected in the finding that a considerably lower percentage of their families had been economically dependent. Their better financial status may have resulted from the fact that the parents of the parole successes had had more schooling than those of the parole failures. Certainly a lower proportion of the mothers of parole successes had had to go to work to supplement the family income than of the mothers of parole failures.

TABLE 12. PRE-REFORMATORY DIFFERENCES IN FAMILY AND PERSONAL BACKGROUND OF PAROLE SUCCESSES (105)* AND FAILURES (296)*

| *Factors of difference†* | *Percentage of parole successes* | *Percentage of parole failures* |
|---|---|---|
| Offenders were not exposed to culture conflict (parents and sons of like nativity) | 52.0 (102)‡ | 46.2 (286) |
| Offenders were foreign born | 23.8 (105) | 16.7 (294) |
| No other members of family delinquent | 45.6 (79) | 19.5 (251) |
| Offenders not reared in broken homes | 27.7 (101) | 15.8 (290) |
| Parents harmonious | 72.0 (93) | 59.1 (254) |
| Families were not clients of social agencies | 59.8 (82) | 38.0 (234) |
| Parents not economically dependent | 95.6 (91) | 79.9 (268) |
| Parents had at least common school education | 22.0 (100) | 13.2 (280) |
| Mothers did not work outside the home | 82.2 (90) | 71.3 (232) |
| Offenders of normal intelligence | 42.4 (92) | 27.8 (273) |
| Offenders were not retarded more than one year in school | 27.6 (80) | 22.5 (235) |
| Offenders did not show evidence of mental pathology | 83.6 (73) | 55.4 (231) |
| Offenders were in good health | 95.0 (95) | 88.4 (252) |
| Offenders were first delinquent at fourteen or older | 84.1 (101) | 53.7 (294) |
| Offenders were not school truants§ | 76.9 (26) | 41.4 (111) |
| Offenders first left home at fourteen or older | 75.0 (72) | 53.6 (248) |
| Offenders did not use their leisure harmfully | 7.8 (103) | 2.0 (293) |
| Offenders were semi-skilled or skilled workers | 57.3 (103) | 40.1 (294) |
| Offenders had good work habits | 42.9 (77) | 12.9 (225) |
| Offenders met their economic responsibilities | 37.5 (80) | 12.1 (232) |
| Offenders had affectional ties to their families | 45.7 (92) | 27.1 (251) |

* Maximum number of cases on which observations were possible.
† The factors of difference are presented in the order of their discussion in the text.
‡ As to the significance of the percentage differences, see note 2, p. 127.
§ See note, Table 1, re truancy figures.

Turning now to the differences in the youths themselves, we find that a markedly higher proportion of parole successes than of the failures are of normal intelligence. This is reflected in the finding that the parole successes were not as retarded in school as the parole failures. In their favor, also, is the fact that a much higher proportion of them are free of mental disease or distortion of one sort or another, and that they were in better physical health in youth than the parole failures.

Another significant finding is that a markedly higher proportion of those who behaved well on parole than of the parole failures had not become delinquent until they were at least fourteen years old. This would again indicate that those who respond well to a particular form of oversight are less of the type whose difficulties of adaptation, expressed in delinquency, are close to biologic roots; for we have seen that among the successes antisocial behavior began during the adolescent years and not in the earlier stages of childhood.[3]

Turning now to their behavior in school, we find that a lower proportion of parole successes than of failures had been school truants. Despite the smallness of numbers on which the comparison is based, it bears out the finding of previous chapters that those who adjusted more readily to treatment were not truant to as great an extent as those who failed. And closely related to this finding is one indicating that a substantially higher proportion of parole successes than of failures remained in the protective atmosphere of their homes until they were fourteen or older. This probably explains the fact that a lower percentage of the parole successes than of the failures had in childhood used their leisure time harmfully.

Turning now to their industrial history, we find first of all that a substantially higher proportion of parole successes than of failures were either semi-skilled or skilled workers in youth. And, furthermore, a far higher percentage of them had good work habits in youth. Also, a considerably higher proportion of the parole successes than of the failures had met their economic obligations to their families in youth.

Finally, a greater percentage of those who responded well to parole supervision had some affectional ties to their families than was true of the parole failures.

[3] This significant phenomenon has been noted in all our analyses, including that of the successes and failures on probation with suspended sentence. In that group, it will be recalled, the successes were, as a class, below par intellectually; but they were normal so far as emotional-volitional aspects of mental life are concerned. The "biologic roots" of which we have spoken pertain more to the instinctual, emotional-inhibitory mechanisms than to defect in intelligence. Even the feebleminded, provided they are not too far below par intellectually, are able to make satisfactory adjustments to the demands of the penal code if properly supervised. It is only those mental defectives who are also deficient in their emotional controls, who find adaptation difficult or impossible.

*Comment*

The reasons why some offenders succeed on parole and others do not have to some extent been revealed by this analysis. The former are obviously better endowed by Nature and more privileged by Nurture than the latter. Distinguishing characteristics clearly exist that permit of the construction of prediction tables which, though not ready for use without validation against another series of cases, at least serve to illustrate to paroling authorities how it can be determined in advance of parole which prisoners are likely to respond well to this form of oversight and which are likely not to do so.

In this form of treatment, however, a complication exists of an administrative nature. The theory of parole is that most prisoners reach a point in their incarceration when it is better for society, as well as for themselves, that they be released into the community under supervision. There are others who clearly do not reach this point for many years, if at all. On the one hand, social protection requires that these be kept behind walls as long as possible; on the other hand, since our existing sentence legislation requires that the vast majority of prisoners *must* be released at the expiration of the maximum statutory limit of the sentence, the question arises whether, despite the prediction of failure on parole, they should not be released anyway before the expiration of their sentences, in order to give them some supervision during the most troublesome period of adjustment between prison life and unrestrained freedom in the community. Were sentences wholly indeterminate, permitting, where necessary, even life-long incarceration, many of these prisoners would not be returned to society at all, or they would be released only experimentally, at different age levels in accordance with an age constituent of prediction tables (see Chapter XV).

## XII

## SUCCESSES AND FAILURES DURING VARIOUS FORMS
## OF INTRAMURAL TREATMENT

HAVING made an analysis of the resemblances and differences in the back-ground of extramural successes and failures, and then more specifically of probation successes and failures, suspended-sentence successes and failures, and parole successes and failures, we now turn to a series of comparisons of those among our offenders who succeeded and failed under various forms of *intramural* peno-correctional treatment.

### CORRECTIONAL SCHOOLS

*Resemblances between Correctional School Successes and Failures*

Correctional school successes and failures *resemble* each other in nativity, and in the extent to which they are exposed to the hazards of culture conflict. They come from families of equal size, and are, to a like extent, the products of homes broken by separation, divorce, or death of parents. Their parents have an equally limited educational background; and a like percentage of both groups of families had to turn to social welfare agencies for assistance of one kind or another.

In regard to the offenders themselves, the correctional school successes were in about the same state of physical health in youth as the failures. The two groups had the same amount of schooling. They had bad habits in like proportion, used their leisure time in equally harmful ways, and their bonds of affection for their families were the same.

In none of these factors, therefore, can we seek any explanations of the reasons for the differences in the responses of the two groups of offenders to the régime of correctional schools.

*Differences between Correctional School Successes and Failures*

It becomes evident from the trend of differences between the correctional school successes and failures, as revealed in Table 13, that those who adjusted themselves well to the régime of such schools have only in some respects a better background than those who did not. Considering their advantages over the correctional school failures, we see first, that their parents lived together more harmoniously than did the mothers and fathers of the offenders who did not respond satisfactorily to this form of treatment. Secondly, more of them had the position of first-born children, on whom more attention and affection is often showered than on those who are later in rank.

Further to their advantage is the fact that a substantially greater proportion of correctional school successes than of failures are of normal intelligence. This explains why they were not retarded in school to as great an extent as the correctional school failures.

TABLE 13. PRE-REFORMATORY DIFFERENCES IN FAMILY AND PERSONAL BACKGROUND OF CORRECTIONAL SCHOOL SUCCESSES (43)* AND FAILURES (73)*

| Factors of difference† | Percentage of correctional school successes | Percentage of correctional school failures |
|---|---|---|
| Parents were harmonious ......................... | 65.8 (38)‡ | 60.3 (63) |
| Offenders were first-born children .................. | 30.0 (40) | 18.6 (70) |
| Offenders were of normal intelligence .............. | 38.1 (42) | 22.1 (68) |
| Offenders were not retarded in school .............. | 11.8 (34) | 6.8 (59) |
| Offenders did not show evidence of mental pathology ... | 96.9 (32) | 78.7 (61) |
| Offenders were first delinquent at fourteen or older ..... | 32.5 (43) | 26.3 (72) |
| Offenders did not misbehave in school .............. | 17.4 (23)§ | 9.6 (42) |
| Offenders first left home at fourteen and older ........ | 46.5 (43) | 32.4 (71) |
| Offenders under fifteen when began to work .......... | 48.8 (41) | 21.4 (70) |
| Offenders were unskilled workers ................... | 67.5 (43) | 61.1 (72) |
| Offenders had good work habits .................... | 11.4 (35) | 4.3 (46) |
| Offenders met their economic responsibilities ......... | 11.8 (34) | 5.9 (51) |
| Parents were economically marginal or dependent ...... | 82.5 (40) | 70.4 (71) |
| Fathers were unskilled workers ..................... | 41.0 (39) | 33.8 (65) |
| Mothers worked out ............................. | 36.6 (41) | 28.1 (64) |
| Other members of family delinquent ............... | 84.2 (38) | 74.1 (66) |

* Maximum number of cases on which observations were possible.
† The factors of difference are presented in the order of their discussion in the text.
‡ As to the significance of the percentage differences, see note 2, p. 127.
§ See note, Table 1, re truancy figures.

As regards mental disease or distortions, it is significant that a higher proportion among those who adjusted themselves to life in correctional schools did not suffer from such handicaps to the extent that were found among those who misbehaved in such institutions. This may in turn explain the fact that correctional school successes first showed signs of antisocial conduct when they were somewhat older than the correctional school failures; and it probably also explains the reason why they did not truant from or otherwise misbehave in school to the extent of the failures.[1] A markedly higher proportion of the correctional school

[1] The reader is again reminded that despite the small number of cases on which this particular comparison is based, the trend of difference continues in the same direction as in previous tables. See note §, Table 1, p. 127; and note 2, p. 127.

successes than of the failures did not leave home until they were fourteen years or over.

Not all the advantages, however, are on the side of the correctional school successes. For instance, a far greater percentage of the correctional school successes than of the failures began to work when they were under fifteen rather than later, a move necessitated, no doubt, by the poorer economic status of their parents. Despite this, they had better work habits and met their economic responsibilities more effectively than did those who did not respond well to correctional school régimes even though they embarked upon gainful employment with fewer industrial skills than the failures.

The earlier entry of the correctional school successes into employment may be accounted for by the fact that a higher proportion of the parents of the successes than of the failures were in marginal or dependent economic circumstances. And this in turn explains two slight differences between correctional school successes and failures. First, the fathers of those who behaved well in correctional schools were unskilled workers to a slightly greater extent than the fathers of the failures. Secondly, a somewhat higher proportion of the mothers of the correctional school successes than of the failures had had to work outside the home to supplement the family income. Whether the lower economic status of the families of the correctional school successes is in turn related to the fact that a greater proportion of their families had delinquent members is difficult to say; we are dealing with a vicious circle whose beginning is obscure, except in certain individual cases.

### Comment

The marked differences between those who responded well to correctional school régimes and those who did not, have to do partly with the better native endowment of the former as reflected in higher mentality and greater freedom from mental disease and distortion; but also with less secure economic status as reflected in the following findings: that those who behaved well in correctional schools came from homes of less comfortable economic circumstances than those who did not respond satisfactorily to life in such institutions; their fathers were less skilled industrially; more of the mothers of the industrial school successes were gainfully employed; the youths themselves had entered industrial life earlier than the failures and were less skilled workers. In addition there was slightly more delinquency among members of their families than in the families of correctional school failures.

It may reasonably be concluded, therefore, that the economic security of life in a correctional school holds a special appeal for youngsters who have been bred in an atmosphere of financial stress, but who, nevertheless, have a mental equipment with which they can face the shock of being, by reason of commitment, deprived of the sheltering arm of home and parents.

Certainly factors of differentiation between correctional school successes and failures can be utilized in determining which offenders are more likely than others to respond well to this form of peno-correctional treatment (see illustrative prediction tables in Chapter XVI).

## REFORMATORIES

Now we turn to a comparison of offenders who behaved satisfactorily in reformatories and those who did not adapt themselves to this type of régime. The reformatory is designed for young-adult offenders while the correctional schools are for juveniles.[2] There is, however, a certain amount of overlapping in the age span, because in the correctional schools of Massachusetts, with which institutions we are largely concerned, boys are initially admitted up to the age of seventeen but may be returned to these institutions from parole until they are twenty-one; but offenders are generally sentenced to reformatories when they are already well over the juvenile court age.

### Resemblances between Reformatory Successes and Failures

In four respects the families of reformatory successes and failures *resemble* each other: in their limited schooling, in their economic status, in the extent to which their mothers worked to add to the family income, and in the occupational skill of their fathers.

As to the youths themselves, there are a number of ways in which those who behaved well in reformatories and those who did not, resemble each other: they are of like nativity; they occupy the same birth rank among their brothers and sisters; they were in like physical health during boyhood and were to the same extent characterized by mental disease or distortion. Further, the reformatory successes and failures resemble each other in the harmful ways in which they used their leisure time and in the extent of their bad habits in childhood. And, finally, both groups began to work at an equally early age.

### Differences between Reformatory Successes and Failures

Turning next to the differences between reformatory successes and failures as listed in Table 14, we find that those who behaved well in reformatories came from smaller families than did the reformatory failures and that their parents were more self-reliant than were the families of reformatory failures, as reflected in the finding that they did not have to turn for assistance to various

---

[2] For a description of the régime of the Reformatory at the time our men were inmates of that institution, see *500 Criminal Careers*, Chap. III.

TABLE 14. PRE-REFORMATORY DIFFERENCES IN FAMILY AND PERSONAL BACKGROUND
OF REFORMATORY SUCCESSES (153)\* AND FAILURES (298)\*

| Factors of difference† | Percentage of reformatory successes | Percentage of reformatory failures |
|---|---|---|
| Offender was one of four or fewer children .......... | 38.4 (151)‡ | 30.8 (295) |
| Families were not clients of social agencies ........... | 60.0 (125) | 36.9 (236) |
| No other members of family were delinquent ........ | 35.9 (128) | 24.7 (243) |
| Parents harmonious ............................. | 67.6 (136) | 61.5 (260) |
| Offenders not reared in broken or inadequate homes ... | 28.3 (148) | 17.9 (291) |
| Offenders were not exposed to culture conflict (nativity of offenders and parents same) ................... | 52.4 (147) | 45.7 (289) |
| Offenders were of normal intelligence ............... | 45.9 (137) | 27.2 (268) |
| Offenders had more than eighth grade schooling ....... | 21.6 (148) | 13.3 (196) |
| Offenders were not retarded in school more than one year | 34.8 (121) | 20.9 (240) |
| Offenders were not school truants§ ................. | 65.0 (40) | 41.6 (125) |
| Offenders were first delinquent at seventeen or older ... | 40.4 (151) | 14.8 (296) |
| Offenders first left home at fourteen or older .......... | 69.5 (105) | 55.7 (253) |
| Offenders had affectional ties to their families ......... | 38.9 (136) | 30.2 (245) |
| Offenders were semi-skilled or skilled workers ........ | 52.7 (150) | 42.4 (297) |
| Offenders had good work habits ................... | 31.3 (112) | 13.8 (225) |
| Offenders met their economic responsibilities ......... | 27.0 (115) | 14.2 (232) |

\* Maximum number of cases on which observations were possible.
† The factors of difference are presented in the order of their discussion in the text.
‡ As to the significance of the percentage differences, see note 2, p. 127.
§ See note, Table 1, re truancy figures.

social welfare agencies to nearly the extent that is true of the families of reformatory failures. Another advantage of the successes over the failures is the fact that the former came to a lesser extent than the latter from families containing other members who are delinquent or criminal. Reformatory successes were further advantaged by the fact that they were reared in homes in which parents were more harmonious in their relationship to one another than the parents of the reformatory failures; and secondly, by the fact that they were not reared to as great an extent as the reformatory failures in homes broken by the death, desertion, separation, or divorce of their parents or in other ways unwholesome to the rearing of children; and thirdly, by the fact that they were not exposed to the problem of conflicting cultural backgrounds between themselves and their parents, a greater proportion of them being of the same nativity as their parents than of the reformatory failures.

In regard to the youths themselves, it is notable that a far higher percentage of those who behaved satisfactorily in reformatories were of normal intelligence than of those who did not. This finding largely accounts for the fact that a somewhat higher proportion of the reformatory successes than of the failures have more than eighth grade schooling. Further, those who behaved well in reformatories were not as behind grade in school for their age as were the reformatory failures. As foreshadowing later adaptive capacity, a far lower proportion of the reformatory successes had been school truants than is the case among reformatory failures.[3]

As has already been made evident from previous analyses, those who succeeded under a particular form of treatment (in this case the reformatory régime) were older on the average when they began to show signs of delinquency than were those who failed. This would seem to indicate, as it has already among failures under other types of treatment, that the delinquencies of those who did not adjust themselves well to life in reformatories were more nearly related to the biologic make-up of the offenders than were the delinquencies of those who did make satisfactory adaptations to treatment. That the organic factor is probably more significant than the early conditioning is suggested by the fact that under some forms of treatment the successes had had a rather bad environmental background in early childhood accompanied, however, by an advantage in intelligence or in emotional-volitional aspects of mental constitution.

Related to the foregoing finding is the fact that those who did well in reformatories were not quite so young when they first left home as were those who did not respond satisfactorily. Perhaps this in turn is due to the fact that they had greater affectional ties to their families than did the reformatory failures.

In regard to industrial skill and work habits, it should be pointed out that a higher proportion of the reformatory successes than of the failures had been semi-skilled or skilled workers prior to commitment, and a far greater percentage of the former had had good work habits. And finally, a major difference between the two groups lies in the fact that a higher percentage of the reformatory successes than of the failures had met their economic obligations to their families prior to commitment.

From this analysis it is again evident that those who behaved satisfactorily in institutions came on the whole from a better background and had a better original equipment than those who did not respond well.

### Comparison of Correctional School and Reformatory Successes and Failures

In view of the fact that sentence to reformatories occurs after commitment to correctional schools and offenders are necessarily somewhat older when committed to reformatories, it would be well before leaving this chapter to see whether there is sufficient differentiation in their characteristics to have made

---

[3] Once again despite the smallness of numbers it is evident that those who adjusted to treatment have not been school truants to as great an extent as the failures.

it possible to ascertain in advance of treatment whether a particular kind of offender was more likely to respond better to one form of treatment than to another.

Although by and large the trends of difference between correctional school and reformatory successes and failures are both in the same direction and more favorable to the successes, nevertheless there are some differences between the two groups which are significant. Such differences are apparent in thirteen of the twenty-seven factors. First of all in the matter of resort to assistance from social agencies, the families of the youths who responded well to reformatory treatment did not have to ask the aid of social welfare agencies to as great an extent as the families of reformatory failures, but in this regard the correctional school successes and failures resemble each other. As to the adequacy of their environment, those who behaved well in reformatories had been brought up in homes better suited to the rearing of children than is true of the reformatory failures, but in this regard also the correctional school successes and failures resemble each other.

There is a resemblance between reformatory successes and failures in the extent to which the mothers of these youths had to work outside the home to help supplement the family income; but a somewhat higher proportion of the mothers of correctional school successes than of failures had worked outside the home.

In the case of reformatory successes and failures the fathers of both groups of youths were of equal industrial skill; but the fathers of correctional school successes were less skilled industrially than those of correctional school failures.

The youths who behaved well in reformatories came from slightly smaller families than the reformatory failures, while the correctional school successes and failures came from families of equal size.

Those who behaved well in reformatories had slightly more schooling than the reformatory failures, but correctional school successes and failures resemble each other in amount of schooling. As to parent-child nativity the reformatory successes were to a lesser extent than the failures exposed to culture conflict between themselves and their parents; correctional school successes and failures, however, resemble each other in the relation of the nativity of the youths themselves to that of their parents, indicating that there was no greater amount of culture conflict in the one group than the other. The reformatory successes and failures resemble each other in the economic status of their parents; but the correctional school successes come from homes of slightly lower economic status than the failures.

A somewhat higher proportion of those who behaved well in reformatories had been attached to their families in youth than of the failures; but there is no difference in the affectional ties of correctional school successes and failures. In regard to the age at which the youths began to work, the reformatory successes and failures did not differ from one another; but those who behaved well in correctional schools were as a group younger when they first began to earn their living than the correctional school failures. In regard to presence of mental conditions, reformatory successes and failures resembled each other, but a lower proportion of those who behaved well in correctional schools had psychiatric conditions than of those who failed. Finally as to the family background of delinquency and criminality, among the reformatory successes there were proportionately more youths whose families did not have other delinquent members than among the failures; but slightly more of the correctional school successes came from families containing other delinquent or criminal members than is true among the failures.

Clearly, there are differentiating criteria between reformatory successes and failures and correctional school successes and failures.

*Comment*

Once again we see that it is not mere accident which determines the behavior of offenders under a specific form of treatment. First of all, it is evident both from the slight and substantial differences between the reformatory successes and failures that those who responded well to life in reformatories were on the whole more advantaged than the failures; for they included among their numbers more youths from families who showed ability to manage their own affairs without constant propping up by social agencies; they came from less criminalistic families; they were themselves of higher intellect; they were not so retarded in school as the reformatory failures; nor had they been school truants to as great an extent. Delinquent behavior did not manifest itself as early in their lives as among the failures, which means that the tendency to maladaptation probably did not have as deep biological roots. The reformatory successes did not leave their parental homes as early as the failures. They were more skilled industrially and had better work habits, and they had already shown more tendency to meet their economic obligations to their families than the failures.

From the comparison which has been made of the reformatory successes and failures, on the one hand, and correctional school successes and failures, on the other, it would appear that, since the reformatory group was necessarily older than the correctional school successes and failures at the time of commitment, the passage of a few years brings about a much sharper differentiation in response to treatment.

Because distinguishing marks do exist between treatment successes and failures, their varying characteristics should provide a basis for tentative prediction tables by which those offenders who are likely to respond satisfactorily to a particular form of treatment can be selected in advance (see illustration, Chapter XVI).

## PRISONS AND JAILS

In this section we consider the characteristics of those who did and those who did not respond well to life in prisons and jails. Prisons are, of course, institutions for long-term offenders and generally they house felons and more hardened criminals; while jails and houses of correction usually receive misdemeanants and less serious though habitual offenders, such as chronic drunkards, vagrants, drug addicts, and non-supporters. Prison régimes generally provide a stricter supervision of inmates than do jails, and in prisons inmates are often engaged in industries and some of their time is absorbed in other ways; while in jails, in which the régime is freer and sentences usually shorter, little or no constructive utilization of time is provided for. We would expect, therefore, to find marked differences between prison successes and failures on the one hand and jail successes and failures on the other.

### Resemblances between Prison Successes and Failures

Turning first to the background of prison successes and failures, we find nine factors in which they resemble each other. The incidence of delinquency among other members of their families was the same among the successes as the failures. Their parents had to rely to an equal extent upon aid of one sort or another from social welfare agencies.

As to the youths themselves, they were of like age when they first left the parental roof. They had undesirable childhood habits in similar proportion; they made equally poor use of their leisure time. Likewise, both groups began to work at the same age and similar proportions were unskilled workers in their youth. Further, they were equally neglectful of their economic responsibilities; and, finally, their affectional ties to their families were equally weak in youth.

### Differences between Prison Successes and Failures

Turning now to the differences in the background of those who got along satisfactorily in prisons and those who did not, as reflected in Table 15, there are eighteen factors in which such differences are evident. First, there is a considerably higher proportion among the prison successes of native-born youths of native-born parents, which means that they were not exposed to as great an extent to the danger of a conflict of cultures between themselves and their par-

TABLE 15. PRE-REFORMATORY DIFFERENCES IN FAMILY AND PERSONAL BACKGROUND
OF PRISON SUCCESSES (66)\* AND FAILURES (32)\*

| *Factors of difference†* | *Percentage of prison successes* | *Percentage of prison failures* |
|---|---|---|
| Offenders not exposed to culture conflict (parents and offenders native born) .......................... | 30.8 (65)‡ | 23.3 (30) |
| Offenders native born ........................... | 90.9 (66) | 81.3 (32) |
| Offender is the first-born child .................... | 38.4 (65) | 20.0 (30) |
| Offenders had seven or more brothers and sisters ...... | 29.3 (65) | 15.6 (32) |
| Parents had at least common school education ........ | 21.5 (65) | 6.9 (29) |
| Parents not economically dependent ................ | 85.0 (60) | 76.0 (25) |
| Fathers skilled or semi-skilled workers .............. | 80.3 (61) | 72.0 (25) |
| Offenders reared in broken or inadequate homes ....... | 81.6 (65) | 74.2 (31) |
| Parents inharmonious (as reflected in separation or divorce) ........................................ | 27.2 (59) | 7.1 (28) |
| Mothers worked outside home ..................... | 30.0 (60) | 14.8 (27) |
| Offenders mentally defective ...................... | 18.3 (60) | 35.4 (31) |
| Offenders did not show evidence of mental pathology ... | 55.8 (52) | 50.0 (24) |
| Offenders were in good health ..................... | 88.7 (62) | 83.9 (31) |
| Offenders had good or fair work habits ............. | 41.3 (46) | 34.7 (23) |
| Offenders had more than eighth grade schooling ....... | 20.9 (67) | 9.7 (31) |
| Offenders were not retarded in school ............... | 19.6 (51) | 0.0 (22) |
| Offenders did not misbehave in school§ .............. | 30.0 (20) | 9.1 (11) |
| Offenders were first delinquent at seventeen and older .. | 12.2 (65) | 3.1 (32) |

\* Maximum number of cases on which observations were possible.
† The factors of difference are presented in the order of their discussion in the text.
‡ As to the significance of the percentage differences, see note 2, p. 127.
§ See note, Table 1, re truancy figures.

ents as were the failures. More of those who behaved well in prisons are themselves native-born (regardless of the nativity of their parents) than those who did not adapt themselves to life in prison. Further, a much higher proportion of those who got along well in prisons were first-born children and therefore, presumably, had received more attention and affection from their parents than the other children, particularly as we see that they come from larger families than the prison failures.

Those who adjusted themselves well to life in prison are to a much greater extent than the latter sons of parents with at least a common school education; and they come from homes of slightly better economic circumstances than the prison failures. This finding is associated with the fact that a somewhat higher proportion of the fathers of prison successes than of the failures were skilled or semi-skilled workers.

Despite these seeming advantages, a slightly higher proportion of those who got on well in prisons than of those who failed came from homes that were broken or inadequate, and the conjugal relationships of their parents were poorer. So also, a higher proportion of mothers of the successes had had to work outside the home during the offenders' youth. Some inference may legitimately be drawn from this group of findings to the effect that possibly some early insecurity in the home life of the prison successes has contributed to their good adjustment in prison, where they experienced a sense of protection and care previously absent in their lives.

However, the prison successes had better native intelligence than the prison failures, as evidenced by the fact that there are only half as many feebleminded among them as among the failures. Not only were the prison successes of higher intelligence but they did not show evidence of mental pathology to as great an extent as the prison failures. And further they were in better general health, and had better work habits.

Following logically upon the finding of their better mental make-up is the fact that the prison successes had more schooling that the prison failures; and they had not been as retarded in school (two or more years behind grade for their age) as the prison failures. Further, fewer of them had manifested behavior problems in school.[4] This may in turn be related to the finding that they did not become delinquent at as early an age as those who did not respond well to life in prisons. The greater difficulty of adaptation of the latter group seems to be related to the deeper roots of their delinquency which in turn seems to be associated with their sub-standard biologic make-up, judging by their inferiority both temperamentally and intellectually.

In view of the fact that prisons generally house older men than those received either in correctional schools or reformatories, no comparison will be attempted between prison successes and failures and reformatory successes and failures; but after analyzing jail successes and failures, a comparison will be undertaken between prison and jail successes and failures.

### Resemblances between Jail Successes and Failures

Turning now to behavior in jails, a comparison of successes and failures indicates that there are seven factors in which the two groups *resemble* each other. They showed like evidence of emotional-volitional disturbances; they were in equally good physical condition in youth; they had bad habits in youth to the same extent; they used their leisure time equally harmfully; they were of the same average age when they first left home; they misbehaved in school to an equal extent; and, finally, the jail successes and failures had, as young men, to a like extent neglected to meet their economic responsibilities toward their families.

---

[4] Again as in previous comparisons of treatment successes and failures, the difference is in the same direction—less school misconduct among those who adjusted to treatment.

*Differences between Jail Successes and Failures*

There are differences between those who responded well to life in jail and those who did not, in respect to a number of factors in their background, as will be seen in Table 16. First, there was less opportunity for culture conflict

TABLE 16. PRE-REFORMATORY DIFFERENCES IN FAMILY AND PERSONAL BACKGROUND
OF JAIL SUCCESSES (100)* AND FAILURES (43)*

| Factors of difference† | Percentage of jail successes | Percentage of jail failures |
|---|---|---|
| Offenders exposed to culture conflict (native born with one or two foreign born parents) ................... | 44.3 (97)‡ | 60.0 (40) |
| Offenders are foreign born .......................... | 18.0 (100) | 9.8 (41) |
| Offenders reared in broken homes ................... | 48.5 (97) | 54.8 (42) |
| Families were not clients of social agencies ............ | 46.5 (86) | 27.6 (29) |
| Parents inharmonious (separated or divorced) .......... | 23.4 (81) | 11.1 (36) |
| Offender is one of six or fewer children .............. | 77.8 (99) | 65.0 (40) |
| Offenders are first-born children .................... | 30.6 (98) | 44.7 (38) |
| Parents economically comfortable .................... | 27.7 (94) | 44.4 (36) |
| Mothers worked outside the home .................... | 34.7 (95) | 23.5 (34) |
| Other members of family delinquent .................. | 82.0 (89) | 74.3 (35) |
| Parents had at least common school education .......... | 20.8 (96) | 13.9 (36) |
| Fathers unskilled workers .......................... | 37.6 (93) | 29.4 (34) |
| Offenders have normal intelligence ................... | 30.2 (96) | 20.0 (40) |
| Offenders had more than eighth grade schooling ........ | 10.8 (100) | 21.4 (42) |
| Offenders not retarded in school .................... | 11.1 (81) | 6.9 (29) |
| Offenders were first delinquent at seventeen or older ..... | 22.2 (99) | 4.9 (41) |
| Offenders under fifteen when began to work ........... | 48.9 (94) | 25.6 (39) |
| Offenders were semi-skilled or skilled workers ......... | 49.0 (100) | 35.7 (42) |
| Offenders had good or fair work habits ............... | 41.8 (79) | 32.4 (34) |
| Offenders had affectional ties to parents and siblings ..... | 29.7 (91) | 18.2 (33) |

* Maximum number of cases on which observations were possible.
† The factors of difference are presented in the order of their discussion in the text.
‡ As to the significance of the percentage differences, see note 2, p. 127.

in the homes of those who conducted themselves satisfactorily in jail than among those who did not, as fewer jail successes than failures are native-born sons with one or both foreign-born parents. Further, those who responded well to the free and easy life of jails are to a greater extent foreign-born than are the jail failures.

Reflecting the differences in the family background of the two groups is the fact that a lower proportion of the successes than of the failures were reared in broken or inadequate homes, and that the families of a considerably lower percentage of those who got along acceptably in jails than of the failures had turned to social welfare agencies for aid of one sort or another during the offenders' youth, which would imply that the former were more self-sufficient than the families of the jail failures. However, the offenders who behaved well in jails were to a much greater extent than those who did not, sons of parents who had separated or were divorced during the offenders' youth. But the jail successes came from smaller families than those who did not behave well in jails; and fewer of them were first-born children. Further, a much lower proportion of the former than of the latter came from families in comfortable economic circumstances. It is not surprising, therefore, that during the youth of these inmates, a higher proportion of the mothers of jail successes were gainfully employed to help supplement the family income than of the mothers of jail failures.

A slightly higher proportion of those who responded satisfactorily to the easy régime of short-term jail sentences than of those who did not, came from families containing other delinquents or criminals. Slightly more of the former were sons of parents with at least common school education; but somewhat more of them were sons of fathers who were unskilled workers.

As for the offenders themselves, a higher proportion of those who responded acceptably to jail routine were of normal intelligence than of those who did not. In view of this, it is surprising to find that a *lower* proportion of jail successes had gone beyond the eighth grade in school than of the jail failures, and that a slightly higher percentage of successes than of failures had been retarded in school.

Again, as in all the previous comparisons of treatment successes and failures, those who responded satisfactorily to the jail régime were older than the failures when they first showed signs of delinquent conduct.

In regard to industrial history, the jail successes began to work earlier than the jail failures. This is, of course, associated with a previous finding that their families had been subjected to greater economic stress.

A higher proportion of the jail successes than of the failures were semiskilled or skilled workers in youth; and they had better work habits than the jail failures. And, finally, more of the former had affectional ties to their families than the jail failures.

It would seem, therefore, that although there is a thread of greater advantages running through the background and characteristics of the jail failures (as reflected in less exposure to culture conflict; being to a lesser extent products of broken homes; families being more self-sufficient; the youths themselves coming from smaller families; more education among their parents; better intellectual endowment; less school retardation; their delinquencies less deeply rooted; better industrial skills and work habits and closer bonds of affection to their parents and siblings), nevertheless they are more *disadvantaged* than we have found other treatment successes to be. Although, on the whole, they came from more adequate homes, a higher proportion of their parents were separated or divorced; they were in more dire economic circumstances; more of their mothers were gainfully employed outside the home; more of their families had other delinquent members; their fathers had less industrial skill; the youths themselves had less schooling; they were younger when they entered gainful employment, which fact is of course related to the lower economic status of their families. Perhaps it is because of these disadvantages and insecurities of their early upbringing that they found warmth and congeniality in the free and easy routine of jails, and responded successfully to it. The fact is, as we have seen in Chapter IX, that a very high proportion of *all* offenders do meet satisfactorily the low standards demanded by life in jails, and it is therefore not surprising to find among them those with both favorable and unfavorable backgrounds and characteristics.

## Comparison of Prison and Jail Successes and Failures

It is evident that there are marked differences in the characteristics of prison successes and failures, on the one hand, and jail successes and failures, on the other, and that the differences between them are often in opposite directions.

In regard to family background, although no difference was found between prison successes and failures in the extent to which they came from delinquent or criminalistic families, the men who got along satisfactorily in jails were members of such families to a slightly greater extent than those who did not.

While the men who did well in prisons came from families in somewhat better economic circumstances than those who did not respond satisfactorily, those who adapted successfully to the jail régime came to a much greater extent than the jail failures from families in poor economic circumstances. However, both a higher percentage of those who behaved well in prisons and those who got along acceptably in jails, than of their respective failures, were sons of mothers who had to work outside the home. But while proportionately more of the fathers of prison successes than of prison failures were semi-skilled or skilled workers, the reverse is true of jail successes and failures.

As to the education of the parents, a much greater percentage of the parents of the men who got along satisfactorily, whether in prison or in jail, had had at least common school education, than of the parents of either prison or jail failures.

Although there is no difference in the degree to which families of prison successes and failures had to turn to social welfare agencies for aid of one kind or another, the men who behaved well in jails were to a greater extent than the jail failures the sons of families who did not have to resort to such assistance.

The men who responded satisfactorily to life in prisons came to a greater extent from broken or inadequate homes than the men who did not, but those who behaved acceptably in jails came to a lesser extent from such abnormal homes.

In regard to the conjugal relationships of the parents, both the prison successes and the jail successes were to a greater extent than their respective failures sons of parents whose conjugal relationships had been poor.

Although among prison successes and failures there was no evidence of conflicting culture between the youths and their parents (they were in equal proportion native-born sons with one or two foreign-born parents), among the jail failures a considerably higher percentage than among jail successes were native-born youths with one or both parents foreign-born. Although a higher proportion of prison successes than of failures were native-born, a lower percentage of jail successes than of failures were native-born. The native-born seemingly adapt more satisfactorily to prison life while the foreign-born make a better adjustment to jail régimes; however, as the differences between each group of successes and failures are slight, nothing conclusive can be derived from this finding.

In regard to the size of the families, the men who did well in prisons came from substantially larger families than those who did not; while just the opposite is true of jail inmates. As to the rank of offenders among their brothers and sisters, a higher proportion of those who got along satisfactorily in prisons were either only sons or first-born children; while a substantially lower proportion of the jail successes were so classifiable.

Concerning physical condition, a slightly higher percentage of the prison successes than of the failures were in good physical health; but this factor did not differentiate the behavior of offenders in jail, for the successes and failures under that régime had a like health status in youth.

Turning now to the intelligence and other mental conditions of the two groups of offenders, a considerably lower proportion of the prison successes than of the failures had been found to be feebleminded; while among jail successes and failures, there is an equal proportion of mental defect. Since the routine of these latter institutions is so much freer, and the terms of incarceration much shorter, this finding is not surprising. In regard to the presence of mental abnormalities other than intellectual defect, there is a lower proportion among prison successes of youths with mental deviations but like percentages among jail successes and failures.

Turning now to the schooling of prison and jail inmates, a higher proportion of the prison successes than of the failures had gone beyond the eighth grade; while the opposite is true among jail successes and failures. As to retardation in school, a considerably lower percentage of those who did well in prison than of those who failed to adjust satisfactorily, were two or more years behind grade for their age, while there was very little difference in this regard between jail successes and failures.

As to conduct in school, those who behaved well in prisons had been, to a lesser extent than the failures, conduct problems in school, but jail successes and failures resembled each other in this regard.

As to their habits and use of leisure time, there is no difference either between prison successes and failures, on the one hand, or jail successes and failures on the other; both had bad habits to a like extent and used their leisure time equally harmfully.

As to age at which the offenders first became delinquent, each success group was older than its corresponding failure group when first showing signs of delinquency. But both prison successes and failures and jail successes and failures had left the protection of their parental roofs at approximately the same age.

Turning now to their industrial history, although the offenders who behaved well in prisons and those who did not had begun to work at approximately the same age, those who got along satisfactorily in jails were younger when they began to work than the jail failures. Each success group had slightly better work habits than the failures. However, while prison successes and failures did not differ in their early industrial skill, those who behaved well in jails were to a greater extent than the failures semi-skilled or skilled workers in youth. In regard to assumption of economic responsibilities in youth, both groups of successes resembled both groups of failures.

Finally, although those who got on well in prisons did not manifest any greater attachment to their families than those who did not, the men who responded satisfactorily to life in jails had had greater attachment to their families in youth than those whose conduct was unsatisfactory.

From this comparison it becomes evident that in some respects those who responded well to the free and easy jail routine were *less* advantaged than those who did not behave well in jails. They came from larger families, and of lower economic status than the jail failures; their fathers had less industrial skill; the men themselves had less schooling, were more retarded in school, were of lower intelligence. They would undoubtedly have found it very difficult to adapt to the demands of life in freedom, without protective assistance, or even to the demands of life under the more strict routine of a prison. They were able, however, without much effort to adjust themselves to the loose régime of a jail, where food and shelter and more comfort than they are normally accustomed to, are provided. It is in this regard that jail successes appear to differ from prison successes, for prison successes are certainly more advantaged than prison failures.

## Comment

Once again we see that despite certain similarities between the prison and jail successes and failures, certain characteristics do differentiate them. On the whole the prison successes were of sounder background than the prison failures. Their parents had better education, they were themselves of higher intelligence, had had more schooling, and had been less retarded in school.

Those who behaved well in jails were in some ways also advantaged over the jail failures, but they were in many respects in *worse* circumstances than the failures. We have already indicated that despite these disadvantages they have been able to adapt themselves to the easy routine of jails, because so much less was demanded of them there than in a prison.

So once again we see that there are enough marked differences in the traits and backgrounds of prison and jail successes and failures to provide a basis for the construction of prediction tables which if validated against another series of cases could be used by judges in imposing sentence (see Chapter XVI).

### ARMY AND NAVY

The reason why a study of the behavior of our group of offenders in the Army or Navy has been made is because a considerable number of them served terms of enlistment, and we were interested to find out whether, despite their criminalistic background, they were able to make adjustments to the kind of life and discipline which is characteristic of Army and Navy régimes and which is in some ways not so different from the discipline of certain forms of peno-correctional treatment. There are at least 67 men in our group who always behaved well in the Army or Navy (as evidenced by honorable discharge) and 57 who always misbehaved (as evidenced by dishonorable discharge).[5]

### Resemblances between Army or Navy Successes and Failures

There are six factors of *resemblance* between those who behaved well in the Army or Navy and those who did not. The two groups resemble each other in the extent to which they came from families of which other members besides themselves were delinquent or criminal. Likewise, they came from families which, to an equal extent, depended on social welfare agencies for assistance

[5] In view of the current war emergency, the data contained in this section may prove at least suggestive, if not of practical use, to the military authorities.

of one sort or another. The Army or Navy successes and failures were to a similar extent the sons of mothers who had to work outside the home to supplement the family income.

As to the men themselves, they were in equally good physical condition in youth. The two groups indulged in bad habits to an equal extent, and both utilized their leisure time harmfully.

## Differences between Army or Navy Successes and Failures

In twenty factors we find differences in the background of the Army or Navy successes and failures, as will be seen in Table 17. First, a greater proportion of those who responded well to life in the Army or Navy than of the others were foreign-born sons of foreign-born parents. Army and Navy successes were to a lesser extent the traditionally spoiled "only children," and came from slightly larger families than the failures. The parents of Army-Navy successes had less schooling than the parents of those who did not be-

TABLE 17. PRE-REFORMATORY DIFFERENCES IN FAMILY AND PERSONAL BACKGROUND OF ARMY OR NAVY SUCCESSES (67)* AND FAILURES (57)*

| Factors of difference† | Percentage of Army or Navy successes | Percentage of Army or Navy failures |
|---|---|---|
| Parents and offenders all foreign born ............... | 24.6 (65)‡ | 14.5 (55) |
| Offenders foreign born ........................... | 24.2 (66) | 14.1 (57) |
| Offender is not an only child ...................... | 92.4 (66) | 85.2 (54) |
| Offender one of four or more children ............... | 68.2 (66) | 61.4 (57) |
| Parents had some common school education .......... | 4.5 (66) | 17.9 (56) |
| Parents economically marginal or dependent ......... | 77.1 (61) | 70.6 (51) |
| Fathers unskilled workers .......................... | 46.6 (58) | 30.9 (55) |
| Offenders reared in broken homes .................. | 58.7 (63) | 53.6 (56) |
| Parents separated or divorced ..................... | 32.8 (61) | 24.0 (54) |
| Offenders are of normal intelligence ................ | 39.7 (63) | 22.6 (53) |
| Offenders not retarded in school more than one year .... | 22.8 (57) | 17.8 (45) |
| Offenders showed no evidence of mental pathology ..... | 71.7 (53) | 58.7 (46) |
| Offenders were first delinquent at seventeen or older .... | 29.3 (65) | 10.7 (56) |
| Offenders did not misbehave in school§ .............. | 21.1 (19) | 3.5 (29) |
| Offenders first left home at fourteen or older ......... | 58.3 (48) | 41.7 (48) |
| Offenders under fifteen when began to work .......... | 54.7 (64) | 35.2 (54) |
| Offenders were semi-skilled or skilled workers ........ | 55.4 (65) | 29.8 (57) |
| Offenders had good work habits ................... | 23.9 (46) | 9.1 (44) |
| Offenders met their economic responsibilities ........ | 18.4 (49) | 8.5 (47) |
| Offenders had affectional ties to parents and siblings .... | 35.1 (57) | 18.8 (48) |

* Maximum number of cases on which observations were possible.
† The factors of difference are presented in the order of their discussion in the text.
‡ As to the significance of the percentage differences, see note 2, p. 127.
§ See note, Table 1, re truancy figures.

have acceptably in the armed services. Furthermore, a higher proportion of the successes came from homes in which there was economic insecurity than is true of the Army or Navy failures, and their fathers were less skilled workers. This may, in turn, be due to the fact that a greater percentage of their parents were foreign-born.

That there was less security in the homes of those who responded well to life in the Army or Navy is further reflected in the finding that a higher proportion of the successes had been reared in broken homes; and, further, that a greater proportion of the successes came from homes in which the conjugal relationships of the parents were poor, that is, in which an open breach had occurred between the mother and father, resulting in separation, desertion, or divorce. This bears out the previous finding that the general domestic background of the offenders who adjusted themselves well to life in the Army or Navy was *not as good* as that of the Army failures.

Turning from the family background to the youths themselves, it becomes evident that those who got along satisfactorily in the Army or Navy were, in their own constitution and make-up, more favorably circumstanced than those who did not respond well to military life. First, those who succeeded in the Army or Navy were of normal intelligence to a markedly greater extent than the failures. Their better intelligence explains the finding that they were not retarded in school to as great an extent as the Army or Navy failures. They were also to a greater extent than the failures free of mental disease or distortion. Furthermore, they were on the whole older at the onset of their first delinquencies than were the Army or Navy failures, from which it seems reasonable to conclude that failure of adjustment in the Army or Navy, like failure of adjustment to various forms of peno-correctional treatment, is probably essentially attributable to certain defects in biologic make-up.

In regard to their conduct in school, a much higher proportion of the Army-Navy successes than of the failures had manifested no behavior difficulties in school.[6] Their markedly superior adaptability to the demands of school life probably also reflects their sounder innate biologic equipment.

Although those who behaved well in the Army or Navy remained for a longer time under the parental roof than those who failed, they began to work at an earlier age than the failures. The need for assisting in the support of their parents is evident in the fact already mentioned, that the economic condition of their families was *worse* than of the youths who did not respond well to Army or Navy discipline. Although the Army-Navy successes entered gainful

---

[6] Despite the smallness of numbers on which the finding is based, the reader will see that the differences in school conduct between successes and failures remains throughout in the same direction, the successes having always been better behaved in school than the failures.

employment earlier, they had greater industrial skill than the failures, and they were more reliable and efficient workers; and they assumed their economic responsibilities to their families more readily than did the Army and Navy failures.

And, finally, a markedly greater proportion of those who behaved well in the Army or Navy than of those who did not, had close affectional ties to their families.

### Comment

It is evident from this analysis that, although there was greater underprivilege in the family background of the youths who adjusted themselves well to life in the Army or Navy, the youths themselves had better native intelligence and were freer of emotional-volitional disturbances than the failures; and their delinquencies were not as deep-seated.

How the differences in the background and characteristics of Army-Navy successes and failures might be utilized in selecting for military service those with criminal records, is illustrated in the tentative prediction tables which appear in Chapter XVI.

## XIII

## SUMMARY OF DIFFERENCES BETWEEN
## SUCCESSES AND FAILURES

Having compared the characteristics of the offenders who succeeded and of those who failed during each specific form of peno-correctional treatment, it might be helpful now to summarize the trends of difference between each group of treatment successes and failures as compared with every other group of treatment successes and failures. The reader would perhaps like to know whether the differences between each group of successes and failures (probation, probation under suspended sentence, parole, correctional school, reformatory, prison, jail) are essentially in the same direction or not.

### Socio-Economic Background of Offenders

Considering first a group of factors which reflect the socio-economic level from which our offenders come, we find that in regard to the *size* of their families, there is no difference between parole successes and failures, correctional school successes and failures, and prison successes and failures, the same proportion of successes and failures under each one of these forms of treatment coming from families in which there were four or more siblings. However, straight probation successes, those who succeeded on probation under suspended sentence, those who behaved well in reformatories and those who got along satisfactorily in jails all came from smaller families than did those who did not respond well to each one of these particular forms of treatment. Some of these differences between the successes and failures were only slight, others marked. However, for the purpose of the present summary, the nature rather than the amount of difference is important.

In regard to *family history of criminality* or delinquency, prison successes and failures resemble each other; but of those who succeeded on probation or parole or in reformatories a greater proportion came from families in which there was no criminality or delinquency among other members of the family group. Just the opposite is true of those who behaved well in correctional schools or in jails; for among them those who succeeded were to a greater extent than the failures sons of families having other members who were delinquent.[1]

Further reflecting the differences in the socio-economic status of treatment successes and failures is the factor of *education of their parents*. There is no difference in the educational achievement of the parents of those who re-

[1] See p. 175, note 1.

sponded well to probation under suspended sentence and those who failed, or between correctional school successes and failures, or between reformatory successes and failures; but those who behaved well on ordinary probation, or parole, or in prisons or jails were all to a greater extent than the respective failures the sons of parents one or both of whom had had at least a common school education.

As regards the *skill of the fathers,* there is no difference between probation successes and failures, or between parole successes and failures, or between those who responded well to treatment in reformatories and those who did not; but those who succeeded on probation under suspended sentence, in correctional schools or in jails were, to a greater extent than the failures, sons of industrially unskilled fathers. The opposite is true of the inmates of prisons, for those who responded satisfactorily to this form of treatment were, to a greater extent than the prison failures, sons of occupationally skilled fathers.

Turning now to the *economic status of the families* of the youths, there is no difference in the economic condition of families of offenders who responded well to probation under suspended sentence and those who did not; nor is there any difference in this regard between reformatory successes and failures. However, probation successes, parole successes and those who behaved well in prisons were, to a greater extent than the respective failures, sons of parents who were in favorable economic circumstances. The opposite is true of those who responded well to treatment in correctional schools and in jails, these men having come from families who were in less secure circumstances.

There is no difference in the extent to which the *mothers of the youths worked out of the home,* between ordinary probation successes and failures, or between reformatory successes and failures; but those who responded well to probation under suspended sentence or to parole differed from those who failed under each of these forms of treatment in that a lower proportion of the mothers of the successes had worked outside the home during the youth of the offenders. The opposite is true of those who got along satisfactorily in correctional schools, prisons, or jails, among whom a greater proportion of those who behaved well under each form of treatment had mothers who had worked outside the home during the boyhood of the offenders.

There is no difference in the extent to which the families of treatment successes and failures had to resort to *assistance from social welfare agencies* among those who responded well to straight probation and those who did not, or among those who behaved well on probation under suspended sentence and those who did not, or among correctional school or prison successes and failures; but those who got along satisfactorily while on parole, or in reformatories or jails came to a greater extent than the respective failures from families who were independent of aid from social agencies.

### Rank, Nativity, and Culture Conflict of Offenders

Much has been written about the influence of *birth rank* among siblings in relation to misconduct. It has been particularly believed that only children, or first-born children, are, because of their preferred position in a family group, the most "spoiled" of a family and therefore more likely than other children to get into serious difficulties. Our comparison of treatment successes and failures reveals that those who behaved well on probation with suspended sentence do not occupy any different birth rank in the family group than do the probation failures. This is likewise true of parole successes and failures and of reformatory successes and failures. However, it is a curious fact that those who behaved well on straight probation or in correctional schools or prisons were either only children or first-born children to a greater extent than those who did not respond well to these forms of supervision, while the opposite is true of those who got along acceptably under the free and easy routine of jails.

Turning now to the *nativity* of the offenders, we find that there is no difference between probation successes and failures, or between correctional school successes and failures, or between those who behaved well in reformatories and those who did not. But a greater proportion of those who responded satisfactorily to probation under suspended sentence, to parole, or to the routine of jails were foreign-born than is true of those who failed under any of these forms of treatment. However, the opposite was found to be true of those who responded well to life in prisons, among whom a greater proportion were native-born than of the prison failures.

In regard to the presence of *culture conflict* between the offenders and their parents as suggested by a difference in nativity, we find that there is no distinction on this score between probation successes and failures and correctional school successes and failures; but among those who got along well on probation under suspended sentence, on parole, in reformatories, in prisons, or in jails there was less culture conflict than among those who did not respond satisfactorily to any of these particular treatments; in these groups a lower proportion of the successes were native-born sons with one or both parents of foreign birth than was true of the failures.

### Home Life of Offenders

Turning, next, to the trend of differences between treatment successes and failures in regard to the *adequacy of their early homes* for the wholesome rearing of children, in the conjugal relationships of their parents, in the affectional ties of the youths to their families, and the age at which they first left the parental roof, we find, first, that in the extent to which they were the products of homes broken by death, desertion, separation, or divorce of parents there is no difference between parole successes and failures, between correctional school successes and failures, between reformatory successes and failures, or between prison successes and failures; but those who behaved well on probation came to a greater extent than the failures from broken homes. However, the opposite is true of those who got along satisfactorily on probation under suspended sentence or in jails, among whom a lower proportion came from broken homes than of those who failed under either of these forms of supervision.

As to the *conjugal relationships* of the parents there was no essential difference between probation successes and failures; but the parents of those who behaved well on probation under suspended sentence, on parole, in correctional schools or in reformatories, had been more compatible in their marital life than were the parents of those who did not succeed under any of these forms of treatment. The opposite is true of those who behaved well in prisons and jails.

In regard to the *early affectional ties* of the offenders to their families there is no difference between correctional school successes and failures, or between prison successes and failures. However, those who behaved well on probation, on probation under suspended sentence, on parole, in reformatories or in jails were more closely bound to their families in youth than those who did not respond well to these forms of treatment.

Although *leaving home early in life* appears to have no effect on behavior in prisons, or jails, which, it must be remembered, are institutions for adult offenders, the effect is obvious on treatments that are usually applied to younger offenders; namely, probation, probation under suspended sentence, correctional schools, reformatories, and parole, in which a greater proportion of the successes than of the failures were well along in youth when they first left home.

### Physical and Mental Condition of Offenders

Turning now to the physical and mental health and intelligence of treatment successes and failures, we find, first, that there is no difference in the childhood *physical condition* of those who behaved well on probation under suspended sentence and of those who did not, or between correctional school successes and failures, reformatory successes and failures, or jail successes and failures. However, the health of probation successes, parole successes, and prison successes was better than the health of those who failed under each of these forms of treatment.

In regard to the presence of *mental pathology* (disease or distortion) there is no difference between reformatory successes and failures and jail successes and failures. Those who behaved well on probation, on probation under suspended sentence, on parole, or in correctional schools and prisons had been noted by psychiatrists to be freer of mental pathology than were those who did not respond satisfactorily to these particular forms of treatment.

In regard to the *intelligence* of the treatment successes and failures, there were among the youths who responded well to probation and among those who did not an equal proportion with normal intelligence; and among those who behaved well on probation under suspended sentence there was a lower percentage with normal intelligence than among the failures. But among those who responded well to parole, to life in correctional schools, in reformatories, in prisons or in jails a greater proportion were of normal intelligence than of those who did not succeed under any of these forms of treatment.

### School History of Offenders

In regard to the amount of *schooling,* there is no difference between those who behaved well on parole and those who did not, nor between correctional school successes and failures. However, those who behaved well on probation and in reformatories and prisons had more schooling than those who did not respond satisfactorily to these forms of treatment. The opposite is true of those who got along satisfactorily on probation under suspended sentence or in jails, for they had less schooling than did those who did not do well.

As for *retardation in school* (that is, being two or more years behind grade for their age) there is no difference between probation successes and failures; but those who behaved well on probation under suspended sentence had been more retarded in school than those who did not. However, those who were successful on parole, in correctional schools, in reformatories, in prisons or in jails were less retarded in school than were those who failed.

There was less *school misconduct* (mostly truancy) among the youths who responded well to probation, to parole, to the régime of correctional schools, reformatories, and prisons than among those who failed under each of these forms of treatment.[2] However, among jail successes and failures, a like proportion had misbehaved in school.

### Industrial History of Offenders

Turning now to the industrial efficiency of the men, we find in regard to *occupational skill* that similar proportions of prison successes and failures were unskilled workers, but that a greater percentage of ordinary probation successes, of those who behaved well on probation with suspended sentence, and

[2] See p. 175, footnote 1.

of correctional school successes were unskilled workers than of those who failed under any of these forms of treatment. But the opposite is true of the men who responded well to parole supervision, to life in reformatories and in jails, among whom there were more semi-skilled or skilled workers than among the failures.

As to *work habits,* those who behaved well on probation under suspended sentence were to a greater extent industrial liabilities than were the probation failures; but under every other form of treatment proportionately more of the successes than the failures were either fair or good workers, by which is meant that they were at least not liabilities to their employers.

In regard to the *age at which the offenders first began to work,* there is no difference between probation successes and failures, or parole, reformatory, or prison successes and failures; but among those who responded well to probation under suspended sentence, to life in correctional schools or to jails, a greater proportion were very young when they first began to work than is true of those who failed under these forms of treatment.

The extent to which *assumption of economic responsibilities* reflects the probable behavior of offenders under peno-correctional treatment is indicated by the fact that there is no difference in this regard between prison successes and failures and jail successes and failures. However, those who got along satisfactorily on probation, parole, in correctional schools or in reformatories met their economic responsibilities to their families more effectively than those who did not respond satisfactorily to these forms of treatment. The opposite is true of those who were successes on probation under suspended sentence.

### Leisure and Habits of Offenders

In regard to their *use of leisure* during youth, there is no difference between probation successes and failures, correctional school successes and failures, reformatory, prison, or jail successes or failures. But a greater proportion of those who responded well to probation under suspended sentence, or to parole, than of those who failed thereunder, had not used their leisure time harmfully in youth.

In regard to *vicious habits,* there is no difference between those who succeeded and those who failed under each form of treatment except that among those on probation under suspended sentence a greater proportion of successes were free of harmful habits than is true of the failures.

### Age at First Delinquency

Perhaps the most significant finding of this portion of our research is the one about to be presented: *age at first delinquency.* A greater proportion of those who responded well to *each* form of peno-correctional treatment were *further along in years when they first became delinquent* than of those who did not respond satisfactorily to treatment; among the latter, delinquent trends became evident very early in childhood. It is to be stressed that this is the *only factor in respect to which all the treatment failures were consistently and uniformly inferior to the successes. This finding would seem to suggest that inability to adapt to peno-correctional treatment is somehow related to a biologic difference between successes and failures.*

*Comment*

It should be clear from the above analysis that resemblances and differences between various treatment successes and failures are not always in the same direction and that an offender who responds well to one form of treatment does not necessarily respond well to another. How effectively these differences in the characteristics of treatment successes and failures can be utilized in the construction of prediction tables indicating probable behavior during various forms of peno-correctional treatment is illustrated in Chapters XV and XVI. The reader should remember, however, that for the purpose of differentiating treatment successes and failures only those offenders were included in the comparisons in Chapters X through XIII who clearly *always behaved well* under a particular form of treatment and those who *always misbehaved*. But in the preparation of tentative prediction tables we had, in addition, to take into account those offenders who did not react favorably to early treatments but who adjusted themselves later to some particular type of treatment, as well as those who responded well in earlier years but deteriorated in their conduct later, and those who were erratic in their conduct, which means that they behaved well at times and poorly at others with no consistent trend toward improvement.

# PART III

# CRIMINAL CAREERS IN PROSPECT

## XIV

# PREDICTING BEHAVIOR DURING FIFTEEN-YEAR SPAN FOLLOWING REFORMATORY TREATMENT

FREQUENT references have been made throughout the previous portions of this work to the possibility of utilizing the fact that there are differences in the characteristics (a) of offenders who reform and those who recidivate and (b) of those who respond well to a particular type of peno-correctional treatment and those who do not, as a basis for prognostic instruments by means of which it would be possible to select in advance the offenders most likely to respond best to any particular form of treatment.

In Part I of this book, comparisons were made of the characteristics of the men who reformed and those who continued to recidivate during a fifteen-year span following the expiration of sentence to a reformatory. In Part II comparisons were made of the characteristics of those who responded well to extramural treatment (probation, probation with suspended sentence, parole), and those who did not; and comparisons were also made between the men who got along satisfactorily during intramural treatment (correctional schools, reformatories, prisons and jails) and those who did not. And then, more specifically, comparisons were made of the characteristics of those who did and those who did not respond well to each special form of peno-correctional treatment (probation, probation with suspended sentence, parole, correctional schools, reformatories, prisons, and jails). Because a number of the offenders had had experience in the Army or Navy, a comparison was also made of the characteristics of those who adapted satisfactorily to military life and those who did not.

From all these comparisons it became evident that differences do exist in the background and make-up of offenders who adjust themselves well to a particular form of peno-correctional treatment and those who do not. It should certainly be possible, therefore, to utilize such information in determining whether or not a new offender for whom treatment is under consideration has a reasonable chance of responding well to a particular form of treatment; and in determining what course his criminal career is likely to take. This can be done by means of prediction tables. It will be recalled, however, that for the purpose of differentiating successes and failures under treatment only those offenders were included in the comparisons who clearly *always behaved well* under a particular form of treatment and whose who *always misbehaved*. In the preparation of prediction tables, it is useful, in addition, to take into account the offenders who did not react favorably to early treatment but adjusted themselves later to some particular type of control or supervision, as well as those who responded well in earlier years but deteriorated in their conduct later, and those who were erratic in their conduct, i.e., behaving well at times and poorly at others with no consistent trend toward improvement. The differences in the characteristics of complete and continuous treatment successes and failures, as described in prior chapters, are not the bases for the particular prediction tables about to be presented. The value of the comparisons themselves lies in revealing the significant *fact* of difference, and the general *trends* of difference between the successes and failures. The differences establish a basically important finding: *that neither chance nor the various treatment régimes are primarily responsible for variations in behavior, but rather certain characteristics in the make-up and background of the different types of offenders.*[1] It is this finding which justifies the development of prognostic devices.

The theory behind such prediction tables is that which underlies any kind of actuarial work. It merely represents objectified and tabulated experience in numerous cases. Insurance companies have built up actuarial tables out of the thousands of cases which they have handled or studied, from which they can determine what are the chances of longevity for persons of various ages and different physical conditions. On the basis of such tables they are able to determine whether or not a person is a good insurance risk. The theory is sound and has worked satisfactorily in the field of insurance. It is as yet very new in the practice of administering criminal justice, but sufficient analysis of the methods involved and some test of their operation have demonstrated their feasibility in the field of parole, and suggest their practicability in the imposition of sentence.[2]

---

[1] It is apparent, of course, that in any research of this kind only a part of all possibly relevant factors can be included. The factors embraced in this study are (a) of a kind referred to in criminological studies as possibly significant, and (b) available for analysis. In a new research we are engaged in, many other factors are included.

[2] Our method of constructing prognostic tables was first described in 1930 in *500 Criminal Careers*, a study begun in 1925. The reader who is interested to acquaint himself with other methods is referred to the following publications: Warner, S. B., "Factors Determining Parole from the Massachusetts Reformatory," 14 *J. Crim. Law and Crimin.* (1923), 172–207; Hart, H., "Predicting Parole Success," 14 *J. Crim. Law and Crimin.* (1924), 405–413; Bruce, Harno, and Burgess, *Parole and the Indeterminate Sentence*, Illinois Parole Board, 1928; Burgess, E. W., "Factors Determining Success or Failure on Parole," 21 *J. Crim. Law and Crimin.* (1928), 241–271; Tibbits, Clark, "Success or Failure on Parole Can Be Predicted," 22 *J. Crim. Law and Crimin.* (1931), 11–50; Vold, George B., *Prediction Methods and Parole*, Hanover, N. H., Sociological Press, 1931; Monachesi, Elio D., *Prediction Factors in Probation*, Hanover, N. H., Sociological Press, 1932; Lanne, W. F., "Parole Prediction as Science," 26 *J. Crim. Law and Crimin.* (1935), 377–400; Laune, Ferris F., *Predicting Criminality*, Chicago, Northwestern University Studies in Social Sci-

In the prognostic instruments about to be presented in this and the two succeeding chapters, the age factor has been taken into account,[3] both in the tables covering the probable behavior of offenders within a fifteen-year span *following* the original reformatory treatment and those predicting behavior while undergoing various types of peno-correctional treatment. Given an offender of certain characteristics who falls within a certain age span, the probability of his satisfactory adjustment to various forms of peno-correctional treatment is now more specifically determined than was possible in the tables presented in *Juvenile Delinquents Grown Up.*

ence, No. 1, 1936; Vold, G. B., "Prediction Methods Applied to Problems of Classification within Institutions," 26 *J. Crim. Law and Crimin.* (1936), 202–209; Argow, W. W., "A Criminal Liability Index for Predicting Possibility of Rehabilitation," 26 *J. Crim. Law and Crimin.* (1936), 561–577; Horst, Paul, *The Prediction of Personality Adjustment,* New York, Social Science Research Council Bulletin 48 (1941).

[8] The reader who is familiar with our previous researches will perhaps recall that we have already done considerable work in the field of prediction. The first attempt was made in *500 Criminal Careers* (New York, Knopf, 1930, Chap. XVIII), in which was presented a table indicating the probable behavior of offenders during a five-year span following the end of treatment in a reformatory. We have continued to apply to other series of cases the method of constructing prediction tables evolved in that research, and have extended it to cover predictions of behavior not only *following* certain specific forms of treatment but also *during* various treatments. In *Five Hundred Delinquent Women* (New York, Knopf, 1934, Chap. XVII), we presented a prediction table covering the probable behavior of women offenders during a five-year period following expiration of sentence to a reformatory. And in *One Thousand Juvenile Delinquents* (Cambridge, Harvard University Press, 1934, Chap. XI), we published a table indicating the probable behavior of different types of offenders within a five-year period following control by a juvenile court. In these three basic researches, each of which represents the first follow-up study of each one of the three series of cases, we did not attempt to go beyond the preparation of prediction tables covering behavior during a five-year span following the particular treatment involved. But in the further follow-up studies of the groups originally described in *500 Criminal Careers* and in *One Thousand Juvenile Delinquents* (a second follow-up study has not been made of *Five Hundred Delinquent Women*), we developed the prognostic tables further. Thus in *Later Criminal Careers,* which covers the second five-year follow-up period for the group originally described in *500 Criminal Careers,* a prediction table was constructed covering the probable behavior of offenders during a *ten*-year span after completion of treatment in a reformatory. In *Juvenile Delinquents Grown Up* (a further follow-up of *One Thousand Juvenile Delinquents* embracing three five-year follow-up periods) we presented a prediction table covering the probable behavior of offenders during a *fifteen*-year span *following* the end of the stewardship of a juvenile court, as well as prediction tables indicating the probable behavior of offenders *during* various forms of peno-correctional treatment (on probation, on probation under suspended sentence, on parole, in correctional schools, in reformatories, in jails, in prisons). By studying the behavior of offenders throughout as long a span as fifteen years following contact with a juvenile court, it was also possible to construct tables showing, more specifically, the probable *age* at which a given offender is likely to reform altogether, or to change from the commission of serious to the commission of minor offenses (see *Juvenile Delinquents Grown Up,* Chaps. XII and XIX). Apart from these tables predicting ultimate reform within a certain age span, the other prediction tables—those constructed for forecasting the behavior of offenders while *under* treatment—did not take the age factor into account. This gap has been filled in the present work.

*Validation of Prediction Tables*

Before a prediction table can be adopted for actual use by courts and parole agencies it should be validated. In the previous pages, whenever we mentioned the possibility of developing prediction tables out of the materials of this particular research, we cautioned that such tables are of an illustrative, tentative, and experimental character based as they are on but one series of cases, and because the number of cases involved in some tables is necessarily small.[4]

It should be borne in mind that the construction of prediction tables was not the original or primary purpose of this or of any of our previous researches. Prognostic devices are rather a by-product of these investigations. Therefore, the number of cases on which some of the tables are based is limited and may, for this reason, not stand the test of validation against other series of cases. However, they do apply to the particular series from which they have been derived and are therefore suitable at least as illustrations of the applicability of such tables by courts and other peno-correctional authorities.[5] Were it our primary purpose to construct prediction tables, we would not only utilize larger series of cases, but would select equal numbers of offenders who responded to and those who failed to respond to each particular form of peno-correctional treatment.

The tables about to be presented are therefore not being offered for immediate adoption by courts and parole boards. They must each first stand the test of validation against at least one other series of cases.[6]

Regarding validation of prognostic tables, the preferable and obvious way is of course to apply them to a sufficiently large new group of similar current cases to see if, in fact, the prognoses made at the time of sentence or parole prove accurate by the actual demonstration that they foretold the "shape of things to come."[7]

---

[4] Such as Tables 34 and 45.

[5] In discussing with Professor Edwin B. Wilson of the Harvard School of Public Health the question of whether or not to present the tables based on small numbers of cases, he suggested that we do so, "because it enables persons who have tables about the same things to accumulate the numbers. . . . It is entirely possible that sooner than you might now think there would be tables based on other cases which could be combined with yours so that even when yours weren't significant but were merely corroborative of a general situation, they might become significant when augmented. This, I take it, is really the chief reason for printing numbers rather than percentages or in addition to percentages when numbers are small and the results aren't of themselves significant."

[6] We are now in the process of testing out all the prediction tables which were developed in connection with *Juvenile Delinquents Grown Up.*

[7] Professor George B. Vold, in his work, *Prediction Methods and Parole, op. cit.,* applied the Burgess prediction method (which utilizes all unweighted factors instead of a few of the highest weighted factors) in constructing a prediction table based on 542 cases paroled from the Minnesota State Prison. Applying its predictions to a series of 282 new cases paroled from that institu-

A second method of validation—which we might call artificial validation—occurred to us from the very beginning of our work. We could see from the nature of the materials and the orderly distribution of incidences of success and failure on the basis of the differentiating factors involved, that it would be possible to divide the whole series of cases used in the actual construction of the prognostic tables, into two groups, placing every other case in each of the groups. The prediction tables could then have been constructed on the basis of only the first group, and then applied to "predict" the probable outcomes in the second group. The chances of the predictions being high would be good, especially in the larger series of a thousand cases used in *Juvenile Delinquents Grown Up.*

Such a method of artificial validation was in fact employed by Professor George B. Vold in his work, *Prediction Methods and Parole.*[8] He divided his total of 1,192 cases of men paroled during a five-year period (July 1, 1922 to June 30, 1927) from two peno-correctional institutions for male adults in Minnesota (reformatory and prison, 650 cases and 542 cases, respectively) into "two randomly selected halves in order that the results from one half (the 'operating group') might be used to predict the outcome in the other ('control group') and in the group as a whole. These predicted values may then be compared with the actual distributions obtained."[9] Using the Burgess method of scoring,[10] he compared the outcomes, and found a high rate of similarity in behavior.[11]

tion, he found a high incidence of correct predictions and concluded that "parole prediction seems to have worked within the limits of about a 2 per cent error."

"Using the experience table for the 1922–27 group (on the 282 cases released after 1927), it is possible to predict 57 violators in the group of 282 cases—an error of 13 cases. Out of the total group of 282 cases this represents a 4.6 per cent error. The actual experience violation rate, however, in the 1927–29 group of 282 cases is 22.3 per cent (or 63 cases) and not 24.7 per cent. The difference between 63, the number actually violating, and the 57, the number expected to violate, is 6, or a 2.1 per cent error." Vold, *op. cit.,* pp. 134–135.

[8] Hanover, N. H., Sociological Press, 1931.    [9] Vold, *op. cit.,* p. 86.

[10] Prof. E. W. Burgess, in his "Factors Determining Success or Failure on Parole," in Bruce, Harno and Burgess, *Parole and the Indeterminate Sentence,* Illinois Parole Board, 1928, pp. 205–269, utilized all available factors without weighting them, while our method consists of a selection of a few weighted factors (see below, Method of Constructing Prediction Tables).

"The Glueck method of scoring was not used extensively because it involves considerably more work than the Burgess method, and besides, was found to give substantially the same result when applied to the Prison and Reformatory 'operating' group." Vold, *op. cit.,* p. 88. It should be pointed out that the extra work involved in the Glueck method pertains only to the original construction of the tables. Once the highest predictive factors have been determined and the proper ones chosen for the tables, the Glueck method involves far less work than the Burgess, because only the few predictive items need be gathered for each new case upon which predictions are to be made.

[11] Comparing the "experience and expectancy rate of parole violation" on the 597 cases in the "operating group" with the 595 cases in the "control group," the following figures emerged:
Those with from 15 to 17 factors having violation rates *lower than the average rate* for the

The evidence from studies other than our own, therefore, tends to confirm the probability of the practical value of prognostic instruments in the administration of criminal justice. The experience we have ourselves already had with our prediction tables has convinced us that at least some of them will more than justify their eventual employment by judges, parole officials and, perhaps also, institutional administrators. However, we cannot recommend for use the specific tables about to be presented, until they have been checked against other series of cases, as we are now doing with all the prediction tables reported in *Juvenile Delinquents Grown Up*.

### Method of Constructing Prediction Tables

In regard to our method of constructing prediction tables, the reader is again reminded that the factors which enter into them are derived from among those traits and characteristics in the family and personal background of the offenders which happen to have been included in this particular research. There are probably other factors of higher predictive value but their discovery remains to future researches.[12]

The first step in the construction of a prediction table is to correlate each factor with the behavior of the offenders during or following the particular form of treatment for which a table is to be made. After these correlations have been made, those factors are selected for *possible* use in a prediction table which have been found to bear the highest relationship to behavior during or following a particular form of treatment, as the case may be.[13] We have found it ade-

---

institution comprised 2.5 per cent in the operating group and 2.6 per cent in the control; those with 13 to 14 such factors constituted 2.7 per cent in the first group, none in the second; those with 11–12 such factors, 10.2 per cent in the first group, 10.1 per cent in the second; those with 9–10 such factors, 14.8 per cent in the first group, 18.5 per cent in the second; those with 7–8 such factors, 27.4 per cent in the first group, 30.1 per cent in the second; those with 5–6 such factors, 39.4 per cent in the first group, 42.1 per cent in the second; those with 2–4 such factors, 52.4 per cent in the first group, 66 per cent in the second. Vold, *op. cit.*, pp. 92 and 108.

Separate treatment of the prison operating group (272 cases) and the prison control group (270 cases), as well as the reformatory operating group (325 cases) and the reformatory control group (325 cases) also showed similarities; however, the control group of the reformatory cases showed an appreciably higher incidence of parole violators among the men with but few factors having violation rates lower than the average rate for the institution, than did the operating group of the reformatory cases. *Ibid.*, pp. 109, 112.

It should be pointed out that the Vold study deals only with the behavior of the men while on parole.

12 We are now engaged in a research in which well over two hundred factors in the background and make-up of offenders are being considered. From among these we will undoubtedly discover more significant predictive factors than those already established.

13 Prof. Vold, *op. cit.*, found the substantial coefficient of correlation (r) of .92 between the Burgess method, which utilizes all available factors, unweighted, and our method. In 1932, Professor Elio Monachesi, reporting on *Prediction Factors in Probation*, The Sociological Press, ap-

quate, for effective prognostic instruments, to select five out of the total group of factors which bear a considerable relationship to the particular treatment or post-treatment behavior under study. In our numerous researches, experience has shown that for the purpose of prediction it is not necessary to utilize the five factors which bear the very highest relationship to behavior.[14] It is only necessary that the group of factors selected bear a sufficiently high association with behavior during or following a particular form of treatment, as the case may be, to assure a workable prognostic instrument.

For practical purposes there are several other considerations which enter into the actual selection of the predictive factors. Naturally, out of any series of possible factors which might be included among the five on which a prediction table is to be constructed, those should be chosen about which accurate information is available in the greatest number of cases in the series from which the table is derived; too many "unknowns" would seriously reduce their statistical validity. In constructing the original table it is necessary to look ahead to its practical applications. Another practical consideration, therefore, has to do with the ease with which courts and other institutions or agencies would, in practice, be able to obtain the needed data about any particular offender on the five factors. If there is a sufficiently wide choice of factors of essentially equal prognostic power on which to base the table, it is wise to eliminate those factors on which it would be difficult for courts and other agencies to secure information. For example, if *Mental condition* happens to be a factor that is highly related to *Behavior following or during a particular form of treatment,* this factor should, as a rule, not be utilized in the construction of the prediction table if there is another factor, equally or almost as highly related to outcome, which a court or parole board could more readily secure about a given offender, such as, for example, *Birthplace of father.* For most courts and parole boards are as yet unequipped with psychiatric clinics; standard intelligence tests are, however, more widely used. However, it is only the technician in this field who needs to be particularly concerned with these and similar considerations.[15]

plied our prediction method (as originally developed in *500 Criminal Careers*) and the Burgess all-factor, unweighted method to 403 juvenile probation cases of Ramsey County, Minnesota. He reported a coefficient of correlation (r) of .865 (p. 108).

[14] Selection of factors is determined either by inspection or, in doubtful cases, through computation of a coefficient of mean square contingency.

[15] The writers are fully cognizant of the technique of selecting prediction factors from among those that are not intercorrelated. But in view of the limitations of our data, and the greater practical importance of other considerations (described above) in the selection of the factors, this technique has not been applied except in so far as our understanding of the meanings of the factors has determined a choice of those that are less, rather than more, interrelated, all other considerations being equal. The writers think, too, that there might be wisdom in deliberately using five partially interrelated factors rather than, say, three purely independent ones; because in consider-

For most readers, it is perhaps sufficient to have a general idea of what the theory is that underlies the tables and some knowledge of how they are constructed.

Once the factors to be utilized in a prediction table have been determined upon, the next step is to set down the percentage incidence of failure found among offenders who are classifiable within each particular sub-category of a factor. For example, suppose that it has been determined by correlating the factor *Age at first delinquency* with *Behavior during fifteen-year span following completion of sentence to the Reformatory* that of those offenders who were *under fourteen* when they first became delinquent 36.3 per cent continued to be delinquent during this fifteen-year span; while of those who were *fourteen or older* when they first became delinquent 24.7 per cent continued to be delinquent. Such a finding shows at once that the age at which an offender first became delinquent somehow bears a relationship to his behavior during a fifteen-year period following completion of his reformatory sentence; and since this is so, *Age at first delinquency* has prognostic value and can be included in a predictive table. Each of the five factors selected for inclusion in the

ing the practical application of the tables, an error of classification on the part of those who would be charged with the gathering of information for determining an individual offender's prediction score would not have the serious result that would ensue if the prediction tables were based on only three wholly independent factors.

At the suggestion of Professor Edwin B. Wilson and Professor Lowell J. Reed, with whom we consulted about this matter, the correlations between the five predicting variables (Number of Children in Family, Economic Status of Parents, Skill of Father, Intelligence of Offender, Age of Offender at First Delinquency) utilized as the basis of Table 18 (Behavior During Fifteen Years Following Expiration of Reformatory Sentence) were worked out, by way of a test. These correlations resulted in ten tables as follows:

Number of children in family related to skill of father ($r = .062$).
Number of children in family related to intelligence of offender ($r = -.024$).
Number of children in family related to age at first known delinquency ($r = -.0176$).
Number of children in family related to economic status of parents ($r = -.045$).
Economic status of parents related to skill of father ($r = .20$).
Economic status of parents related to intelligence of offender ($r = .011$).
Economic status of parents related to age at first delinquency ($r = .082$).
Skill of father related to intelligence of offender ($r = -.109$).
Skill of father related to age at first delinquency ($r = .0047$).
Intelligence of offender related to first known delinquency ($r = .012$).

Professor Edwin B. Wilson, to whom these correlations were sent for examination, was good enough to work out the *average* value of all ten correlation coefficients, which he found to be .016; and "the value of the determinant of all the correlation coefficients when one puts unity in the main diagonal appears to be .95." It would seem to be apparent, therefore, that the intercorrelation between the five variables is extremely small.

We have not worked out the intercorrelations between the variables utilized in our other prediction tables but the reader is reminded that wherever possible we tried to select factors having less rather than more interrelationship.

table is analyzed in the same way. These percentages represent the likely "failure score" (recidivism) of a particular offender.

By adding the percentage incidence of the lowest possible failure scores, on the one hand, and of the highest possible failure scores, on the other, on the five factors to be included in the table, the two extremes of a *"total failure score"* are derived within which zone all the offenders must fall. This zone is next divided into score classes.[16] A tabulation is then made of all the offenders included in the particular research, taking into account, on the one hand, the score class in which each particular offender belongs and, on the other, his actual criminal or non-criminal conduct during a particular follow-up span or his success or failure during a particular form of treatment. From the resulting correlation table it is possible to forecast the probable behavior of *other* offenders with similar characteristics.

An abbreviated description of the construction of the particular prediction table which is the basis of this chapter should clarify the method. For greater detail the interested reader is referred to Chapter XII of *Juvenile Delinquents Grown Up.*

### Factors for Predicting Behavior over a Fifteen-Year Span

A correlation of twenty-seven factors[17] in the family and personal history of our Reformatory graduates with their behavior during the fifteen years following the expiration of their sentences to the Reformatory reveals that the following five factors are sufficiently related to the behavior outcomes of the group of cases to be included in the prognostic table (Table 18). In eliminating certain factors as the basis of the table and utilizing others, the practical considerations mentioned above were applied.

Once the five factors were determined upon, the next step was to ascertain the lowest and the highest possible failure scores in order to derive the score zone, which in this instance is 132.7–201.1. The cases were then individually scored and each placed in its particular score class on the one hand and behavior class on the other. It should be pointed out that, naturally, only those cases could be utilized in constructing the prediction table in which information on all five factors was available, as well as information on the conduct of the men

---

[16] The particular score classes that result in the sharpest predictive instrument vary from table to table. The first tabulation of cases is made into detailed score classes (10-point intervals). The resulting table is then studied in order to see what combination of score classes provides the sharpest differentiation between the cases. It is for this reason that the score classes in the prediction tables in this and the two succeeding chapters vary.

[17] These twenty-seven factors are listed on p. 161.

FACTORS PREDICTIVE OF BEHAVIOR DURING FIFTEEN-YEAR SPAN FOLLOWING
COMPLETION OF SENTENCE TO REFORMATORY

| *Prediction factors and sub-categories** | *Percentage incidence of criminality†* |
|---|---|
| Number of children in family | |
|    Seven or more children | 26.7 (101) |
|    Two to six children | 33.2 (287) |
|    One child | 48.1 (27) |
| Economic status of parents | |
|    Dependent or marginal | 27.5 (274) |
|    Comfortable | 39.8 (108) |
| Skill of father | |
|    Unskilled | 23.3 (131) |
|    Semi-skilled or skilled | 36.1 (244) |
| Intelligence of offender | |
|    Not feebleminded | 30.5 (311) |
|    Feebleminded | 40.8 (76) |
| Age at first delinquency | |
|    Fourteen and older | 24.7 (251) |
|    Under fourteen | 36.3 (168) |

\* Whatever contractions have been made of the original, more detailed, sub-categories of the factors are based on an inspection of the raw tables, from which it could readily be determined which sub-categories to combine.

† The parenthesized figures represent the number of cases from which the particular percentage is derived.

TABLE 18. BEHAVIOR DURING FIFTEEN YEARS FOLLOWING EXPIRATION OF
REFORMATORY SENTENCE (323 CASES)

| *Failure score* | *Remains serious offender* | *Becomes minor offender* | *Reforms entirely* | *Temporary lapse into criminality after reform* | *Number of cases** |
|---|---|---|---|---|---|
| Under 150 | 22.1 | 28.6 | 41.6 | 7.7 | 77 |
| 150–160 | 28.0 | 37.0 | 34.0 | 1.0 | 100 |
| 160–170 | 36.0 | 22.0 | 35.0 | 7.0 | 100 |
| 170–180 | 45.0 | 25.0 | 30.0 | 0.0 | 40 |
| 180 and over | 66.6 | 16.7 | 16.7 | 0.0 | 6 |

$$C = .26†$$

\* In this and corresponding tables, the figures in the right-hand column represent the number of cases on which the percentages (or chances out of 100 of a particular kind of behavior) are based.

† "C," the Pearsonian "mean square contingency coefficient," "is . . . only unity if the number of classes be infinitely great; for any finite number of classes the limiting value of C is the smaller the smaller the number of cases." Thus, in a twofold table, C cannot exceed .71; in a threefold, .82; in a fourfold, .87, etc. See Yule, G. Udny, *An Introduction to the Theory of Statistics*, 1922, pp. 65, 66. Therefore, the degree of association between failure score and behavior is higher than the raw figure of .26 would seem to imply. Computation of the probable error of C is highly complicated and time-consuming; and experience has taught that knowledge of the raw materials involved is sufficient check-up on the validity of any association indicated by C.

throughout the fifteen-year span. The scoring which was done in each case is illustrated by Case X below:

CASE X. BEHAVIOR DURING FIFTEEN-YEAR SPAN

(Remained serious offender)

| Prediction factors | Failure score |
|---|---|
| Number of children in family: *Seven or more* | 26.7 |
| Economic status of parents: *Dependent* | 27.5 |
| Skill of father: *Unskilled* | 23.3 |
| Intelligence of offender: *Not feebleminded* | 30.5 |
| Age at first delinquency: *Fourteen and older* | 24.7 |
| Total failure score | *132.7* |

## Prediction Table

The next step in the procedure was to divide the general score zone (as illustrated above, 132.7–201.1) into units of ten. It is always well to make the first distribution of the cases into such narrower score classes and after studying the results to make broader classifications which more sharply distinguish the successes from the failures. For an illustration of this, the reader is referred to Chapter XII of *Juvenile Delinquents Grown Up,* pages 141–142.

For the purposes of the present research the cases were grouped into those who (a) remained serious offenders throughout the fifteen-year span, (b) became minor offenders, (c) reformed entirely, (d) reformed for as long as five years but relapsed temporarily into criminal conduct.

Table 18 resulted after the uncontracted table (not included herein) had been carefully examined. From this table the probable behavior over a fifteen-year span following the expiration of their sentences to a reformatory, of offenders about to be sentenced, can be determined.

Although the summation of the lowest failure score of the sub-categories within each factor at one end of the scale, and the highest at the other, established the score classes as ranging between 132.7 and 201.1, inspection of the tabulated results suggested the most effective limits to be those indicated in the table. From this table it can be seen, for example, that if an offender scores under 150 he has two chances in ten (22 out of 100) of continuing to be a serious offender during a fifteen-year period following expiration of a reformatory sentence, almost three chances in ten of becoming a minor offender; four in ten of reforming entirely and less than one in ten of relapsing into criminality after a long period of good behavior (Case X falls into this group). But if an offender scores 180 or more he has almost seven chances in ten of remaining a serious offender, less than two in ten of becoming a minor offender or of reforming entirely.

As a number of case illustrations will be given at the end of this chapter, there is no need to explain further the meaning of this table or its possible use.

*Predicting Age at Change from Serious to Minor Delinquency and Age at Reformation*

As in *Juvenile Delinquents Grown Up* (Chapter XII), so in the present work, we have attempted to make the table predicting behavior during a fifteen-year span following reformatory treatment more useful by indicating also (a) the age at which the group of offenders under study actually did become minor offenders and (b) the age at which they reformed entirely. By relating the age incidence to the actual failure score in each case and distributing the cases accordingly, it is possible to present Table 19, indicating the probable age at change from serious to minor delinquency. Case X, it will be recalled, scoring 132.7, falls within the group who have three chances in ten of becoming minor offenders (see Table 18). If for any reason, in planning a program of treatment for this particular offender, it would be helpful to know roughly at what age he is likely to become a minor delinquent, consultation of Table 19

TABLE 19. PROBABLE AGE AT CHANGE FROM SERIOUS TO MINOR DELINQUENCY (92 CASES)

| Failure score | Under 27 | 27 and older | Number of cases |
|---|---|---|---|
| Under 150 ... | 36.4 | 63.6 | 22 |
| 150–160 ..... | 51.4 | 48.6 | 37 |
| 160–170 ..... | 22.7 | 77.3 | 22 |
| 170–180 ..... | 30.0 | 70.0 | 10 |
| 180 and over | 0.0 | 100.0 | 1 |

C = .25

TABLE 20. PROBABLE AGE AT REFORMATION (114 CASES)

| Failure score | Under 27 | 27 and older | Number of cases |
|---|---|---|---|
| Under 150 ... | 34.4 | 65.6 | 32 |
| 150–160 ..... | 55.9 | 44.1 | 34 |
| 160–170 ..... | 22.9 | 77.1 | 35 |
| 170–180 ..... | 66.7 | 33.3 | 12 |
| 180 and over | 0.0 | 100.0 | 1 |

C = .32

might prove illuminating; for this indicates that he has about four chances in ten of becoming a minor offender while under 27 years of age, and six chances in ten of becoming a minor offender when twenty-seven or older.

By the same method as was used to determine the age at change from serious to minor delinquency, Table 20 has been constructed for determining the probable age at reformation during the fifteen-year span following the expiration of reformatory treatment. Utilizing, again as an illustration, Case X who, it will be remembered, scores 132.7 on the five predictive factors and who has four in ten chances of reforming entirely during the fifteen-year follow-up span, he is shown to have, according to Table 20, three and a half chances in ten of reforming while under twenty-seven years old and six and a half in ten of abandoning criminal behavior at twenty-seven or older. This information would obviously have been helpful to a judge or probation officer in planning the long-time treatment of this particular offender.

## Some Illustrative Cases

Illustrations of the use of these tables from the nine cases presented in Chapter II will be helpful at this point. Even though these tables have not yet been validated against another series of cases, they nevertheless apply to this particular group from which they have been derived.

The reader will recall that in Chapter II we raised the question *whether it would have been possible at the time of their commitment to the Reformatory to predict the subsequent careers of Frank, John, Armand, Robert, Arthur, Dennis, Jack, Peter, and Antonio.* We know from our study of them over the years what has actually happened to them. We may now illustrate the use of the prediction tables by indicating the failure score in each case and interpreting the meaning of this in terms of the prediction tables presented in this chapter. The reader is reminded that the cases of these nine offenders were not particularly chosen because they effectively illustrate the validity of the prediction tables. More striking predictions could have been obtained from many other cases. When in 1930, the authors were writing *500 Criminal Careers* and chose these particular nine offenders as illustrating types of criminal careers for a chapter entitled "A Sheaf of Lives," they had been followed for only five years after expiration of their Reformatory sentences and the prediction tables now developed after a fifteen-year follow-up span had not even been thought of. The cases had not been chosen to illustrate prediction methods. Now, more than ten years later (1942), their stories are continued because it seemed to us that it would be more interesting to readers of the first work to know what has happened to these particular offenders, than to describe in detail the doings of another group of offenders among the original five hundred and ten.

Bearing this in mind, we turn to *Frank* who, it will be remembered, developed a chronic *Wanderlust* and was often arrested on suspicion of burglary. He spent a good deal of time in mental hospitals where he was diagnosed variously as a psychopath, a defective delinquent, a chronic vagrant. At several points in his career, Frank was discharged from incarceration of one kind or another even though the authorities recognized that he needed further care. In the discussion of this case we pointed out that the most serious of these discharges was from a hospital for the criminal insane by reason of expiration of sentence even though the authorities realized that his condition was not improved, and from the Reformatory by expiration of sentence despite the fact that the psychiatrist believed that Frank required permanent segregation. Cer-

tainly the need for long-term treatment in this case under a wholly indeterminate sentence is obvious.

How might consultation of a prediction table in Frank's case when he was
committed to the Reformatory at the age of twenty-five on the particular sentence which furnishes the point of departure for our follow-up investigation,
have prevented the wasteful and dangerous procedures which were actually
followed? On the five factors included in the table predicting behavior during
the fifteen-year span, Frank scored 161.1. Consultation of Table 18 indicates
that at the time of sentence he had three and one-half chances in ten of remaining a serious offender, two in ten of becoming a minor delinquent, three and
one-half chances in ten of reforming entirely and less than one chance in ten
of temporary relapse into delinquency after at least five years of good conduct. It would have been apparent, therefore, that Frank's chances of remaining a serious offender were greater than his chances of becoming a minor
delinquent, and that his chances of remaining a criminal (whether his offenses were of a serious or minor character) were considerably higher than his
chances of reformation. A judge, probation officer, or institutional authority,
knowing this, could hardly have permitted Frank to go back into the community, at least without intensive supervision, provided the statutes permitted
his further retention. *This case illustrates the fact that for maximum effectiveness prediction tables have to be supplemented by legislation providing for
either a completely indeterminate sentence (permitting, where necessary, life-
long incarceration) or wide-zone indeterminate sentences.*

Consultation of Table 19 indicates that with Frank's failure score of 161.1,
his chances of becoming a minor offender are considerably greater when he
is twenty-seven or older than when under twenty-seven years of age. This
should have indicated to treatment authorities that Frank needed particularly
close supervision until roughly the age of twenty-seven, especially in view of
the fact that he is mentally defective. It will be seen from Table 20 that his likelihood of complete reformation was also much greater at twenty-seven and
older than when under twenty-seven; so that taking into account all of the
findings revealed from the prediction tables it becomes evident that at least to
about the twenty-seventh year Frank needed extremely close supervision under an adequate indeterminate sentence which would not have permitted the
many loopholes that actually did frequently return him to unsupervised freedom and crime in the community.

Turning now to *John,* who throughout his career was a burglar and hold-up
man, who had spent many years in prison and who finally lost his life at the
age of thirty-seven by shooting in a brawl with police, his failure score on the

five factors included in the table predicting behavior during a fifteen-year span following expiration of sentence from the Reformatory (John was twenty when committed) is 162.3, which places him in the same general category as Frank. This means that his chance of reformation was only three and one-half in ten. (See Table 18.) Actually, he remained a serious criminal to the end of his life, cut off at the premature age of thirty-seven. John, like Frank, should have been under a wholly indeterminate sentence and under very close supervision. His prediction scores indicate that if he did not actually become a minor offender, or did not reform by the time he was twenty-seven or thereabouts, he was hardly likely to do so thereafter (see Tables 19 and 20).

Turning now to the brothers *Armand* and *Robert,* both of whom it will be recalled settled down to law-abiding behavior, although one did so very much earlier than the other, a comparison of their prediction scores and the implications of these are worth noting. Armand and Robert were each nineteen when committed to the Reformatory. Armand settled down by the time he was twenty-six, shortly after marriage, while Robert's career of delinquency (he was a burglar and sex offender) persisted until he was about thirty-seven years old. Armand's failure score is 157.1 and Robert's 167.4. Consulting Table 18, we find that Robert's chances of reformation were just as great as Armand's (three and one half in ten) but that his chances of continuing to be a serious offender were greater than Armand's. This might have indicated to a judge or probation officer or anyone planning the peno-correctional treatment of the two brothers that Robert needed considerably more supervision than Armand. In regard to the age at which the brothers were likely to reform (it should again be recalled that Armand settled down when he was about twenty-six and Robert not until he was thirty-seven), consultation of Table 20 indicates that Armand's chances of reform, with a failure score of 157.1, were greater when under twenty-seven years of age than when twenty-seven or older; and this is exactly what happened. Robert, with a failure score of 167.4, had only two chances in ten of reforming when under twenty-seven, but almost eight chances out of ten when twenty-seven or older. Here again the prediction table would have shed light on the future; for Robert actually settled down at about the age of thirty-seven.

*Arthur,* who was sentenced to the Reformatory at the age of twenty, has a prediction score of 149.5. It should be recalled that during the first five-year follow-up period Arthur, who was a mental defective, behaved well under the careful supervision of his parents. During the second five-year period since the expiration of his Reformatory sentence, however, Arthur got into difficulty by burglarizing the home of a friend from which he took several small articles. He continued to receive careful supervision from his family; and, after he married, his wife carried on the oversight that his family had always given him. During the third follow-up period, however, Arthur's wife left him because of financial difficulties and a sexual maladjustment between them. Then Arthur began to drift around from pillar to post, supported by public agencies. Except for the fact that he is considered "queer" he cannot in any way be regarded as a delinquent. He is, however, a mental defective and in need of constant guidance. From Arthur's failure score, it would appear that he had reasonably high chances of reformation, four in ten. Except for the one episode of breaking into the home of a friend, Arthur has had no criminal career since his release from the Reformatory. It would appear that in view of his mental defect extremely close supervision was indicated in his case and that, had this been applied throughout his career, he would hardly have gotten even into the slight difficulties in which he was involved. Consultation of Tables 19 and 20 indicate that, with a failure score of 149.5, Arthur's chances of becoming a minor offender or settling down altogether were considerably greater at twenty-seven or older than at an earlier age. Actually he settled down reasonably well for a time at about the age of twenty-three but reverted to criminality briefly some years later; so he would have borne close watching at least to the age of twenty-seven.

*Dennis,* it will be recalled, was a bootlegger and a drug addict. However, he was extremely devoted to his family and particularly to the children of his dead sister, whom he helped to rear. He drank occasionally through the years, but never permitted himself to get into a drunken state in the presence of his nieces and nephews. It will be recalled that Dennis occasionally picked pockets in order to secure money for "dope." It is obvious that Dennis' difficulties were due to his drug habit and that if not for this he could not be considered a criminal. For the last five years he has been in a mental hospital suffering from a psychosis due to drugs. He is now fifty-one years of age. Dennis, who was sent to the Reformatory at the age of twenty-four, scores 139.2 on the five factors which have entered into the construction of the prediction table indicating probable behavior during the fifteen-year span following the end of reformatory treatment. This means (see Table 18) that Dennis had only two chances in ten of remaining a serious offender; in other words, that his joint chances either of total reform or of development into a minor offender were far greater (eight in ten) than his likelihood of remaining a serious criminal. As long as drug addiction, with its attendant evils, is considered in the realm of criminality rather than as a medical condition requiring commitment and hospital treatment, Dennis had to be called a criminal (and a serious one, because he subsequently committed larcenies to get money for drugs); but from a more fundamental point of view, he is not. Had he early been committed to a mental hospital or narcotics farm for treatment of his drug addiction and kept there for a long period of time, it is reasonably probable that he would not now be confined in a mental hospital for a psychotic condition. Apparently Dennis had within himself the capacity to integrate sufficiently to abandon criminalistic ways. But the overpowering habit of drug addiction caused him to use every means to secure the drug even if this meant stealing. Underlying all this, however, are very acceptable qualities in Dennis' personality, and except for the drug habit it cannot be said that he presented too great a social problem.

*Jack* settled down soon after his release from the Reformatory, where he had been diagnosed as a "moron and addicted to drink." He returned to his wife and children and determined to keep away from alcohol, which he certainly succeeded in doing throughout the first five-year span. During the second follow-up period, however, bad industrial conditions had added pressure to the lives of Jack and his family. Loss of jobs and discouragements resulted in his succumbing again to drink, and despite the affection and attention of his family, he has continued in his alcoholic habits with, however, brief periods of abstinence. He is a responsible earner when sober. It is probable that without the devotion of his wife and children he would long ago have become a vagrant. Jack was not committed to the Reformatory until the age of thirty-one. His prediction score is 161.1, which indicates a three and one-half in ten chance of remaining a serious offender in the fifteen-year span following the expiration of his Reformatory sentence, two chances in ten of becoming a minor offender and three and one-half chances in ten of reforming entirely. From the prediction, it would appear that his chances of developing in either one of two directions were almost equal; and this should have indicated to a judge that the deciding factor in the outcome would be close supervision and provision for a secure livelihood.

Unfortunately, it is not possible to give the prediction score in the case of *Peter* because information was not available on all the five factors which make up the score. Naturally, in current cases, there is no reason why a court about to impose sentence should not be able to secure all the data necessary to make a prediction of the offender's behavior.

We turn, finally, to the case of *Antonio* who was committed to the Reformatory at the age of twenty-one and who, it will be remembered, learned there the trade of photo engraving and subsequently made a career out of this. He settled down very promptly and has shown no behavior difficulties since the expiration of this sentence. His failure score is 147.8. By consulting Table 18 we see that his chances of reforming entirely were four in ten, which is considerably higher than his chances of remaining a serious offender or even of becoming a minor delinquent. A judge having this information available to him would have seen that Antonio was a reasonably good risk for life in freedom. In regard to the age at which he was most likely to reform, consultation of Table 20 indicates that he had three and one-half chances of reforming when under twenty-seven and six and one-half of reforming when twenty-seven or older. Actually he was twenty-six years old when he showed the first signs of really settling down.

### Comment

It should be evident from the presentation of these few cases that the utilization of prediction tables affords a more effective basis for planning the treatment of offenders than the present more haphazard administration of criminal justice provides, particularly if the information derived is considered in relation to the opportunities that the environment of the offender furnishes for adequate supervision outside of institutions. Of course, the utilization of prediction tables is of but limited value without some such administrative device as that offered by the statutory provision of wholly indeterminate or at least broad-zone sentences.

It should also be pointed out that the use of predictive instruments presupposes a causal attitude toward crime and a correctional philosophy rather than a vindictive-punitive one, or even one narrowly concerned with prevention or deterrence through threats and the appeal to fear. The former recognizes that human behavior is determined by biologic and social causes and can therefore be modified only by modification of those causes. The latter proceeds upon a grossly oversimplified conception of human nature. It presumes that there is little more to crime-causation than intentional wrong-doing through exercise of a wholly "free will"; and that punitive repression will alone produce the socially desirable result of turning offenders from further crime. That pain-inflicting punishment, as such, fails to bring about this result is amply demonstrated by any available compilation of prison statistics, which invariably shows that a major proportion of prison inmates have been punished before, only to repeat their crimes.

If the administration of criminal justice and criminal legislation themselves express an attitude of dogged and blind reliance upon the efficacy of suffering through punishment, the great majority of offenders will continue to recidivate. If, on the other hand, there is a belief in the operation of multiple and complex causes in the bringing about of delinquency and in its evolution into persistent criminality, then some device which will systematically relate the traits and background of offenders to their behavior becomes indispensable to an effective administration of criminal justice.

A chief aim of the older approach is the same as that of the newer: the prevention of the repetition of crime on the part of wrong-doers. The question is, which system is more likely to achieve that aim? Is it a system already shown to be inadequate based as it is upon an oversimplification of human nature? Or is it a system which can be demonstrated to be founded on the realities of the situation, that is, the make-up and background of offenders? If it be the latter, then judges, exercising discretion as to the type and length of sentence to impose, can profit greatly from the careful consideration of the make-up and background of the particular defendant at the bar in the light of many hundreds of others with essentially similar make-up and background. This is "individualization" in the true sense of the term. Individualization based on unsystematic consideration of only the particular defendant's constitution and social situation is, to be sure, a step in advance of the mechanical application of the same sentence to all persons committing a crime of the same definition. But individualization based on predictive instruments is two steps in advance of the old system. Implemented with a sufficiently flexible sentencing law and applied by a specially qualified tribunal representing the cooperation of all relevant disciplines, it should more effectively than any practice heretofore tried, bring about the social desideratum of preventing recidivism.

## XV

## PREDICTING BEHAVIOR DURING VARIOUS FORMS
## OF EXTRAMURAL TREATMENT

A MAJOR purpose of this research has been to determine the behavior of the 510 men originally reported upon in 500 *Criminal Careers,* during the various forms of peno-correctional treatment to which they have been subjected from the onset of their delinquencies throughout the fifteen years that followed the expiration of their sentences to the Massachusetts Reformatory. On the average, this covers some twenty-five years in their criminal careers. Some readers may recall that in another research, *Juvenile Delinquents Grown Up,* the behavior of the offenders originally described in *One Thousand Juvenile Delinquents* was likewise followed during the various peno-correctional treatments to which the youths were subjected from the onset of their delinquencies until they reached an average age of twenty-nine. In Chapter XIII of that work prediction tables[1] covering the behavior of these offenders during probation, probation under suspended sentence, parole, in correctional schools, prisons, and jails were presented. These tables did not, however, take into account the factor of the age of the offenders at the time the youths were subjected to each particular form of treatment. In the present research we have constructed tables not only to cover a particular form of peno-correctional treatment regardless of the age of the offenders, but also[2] the age spans at which differentiation in responses to various forms of treatment typically occurs.

Since a brief résumé of the method of constructing prediction tables has been made in the previous chapter, there is no need to repeat this in the present or succeeding chapters, which deal with prediction tables covering the probable responses of offenders to various forms of extramural and intramural treatment.

### Predicting Behavior during Extramural Peno-Correctional Treatment

Before presenting the illustrative tables dealing with behavior during specific forms of peno-correctional treatment, we may consider one covering *extramural treatment in general.* In the next chapter a similar table is presented covering responses to *intramural* treatment. Obviously, such all-inclusive tables

[1] These are being validated in a new series of cases as part of a research in which the authors are now engaged.

[2] As has already been indicated in Chapter IX.

would be helpful in quickly narrowing down the search for the probable form of treatment most suitable to a particular offender, by indicating, first of all, whether he is better suited to extramural or intramural supervision. Once this primary question has been answered, consideration can be given to the specific form of either extramural or intramural treatment to which a particular offender is best suited.[3]

The five factors which entered into the construction of a table from which probable behavior of offenders during extramural treatment may be derived are shown in list A.

### A. FACTORS PREDICTIVE OF BEHAVIOR DURING EXTRAMURAL TREATMENT

| *Prediction factors and sub-categories** | *Percentage incidence of failure†* |
|---|---|
| Number of children in family | |
| Two or more ......................................... | 59.8 (438) |
| Only child ............................................ | 76.5 (34) |
| Broken or inadequate homes | |
| Homes not broken or inadequate ......................... | 50.0 (220) |
| Homes broken or inadequate ............................. | 63.9 (246) |
| Age at first delinquency | |
| Fourteen and older ..................................... | 54.4 (281) |
| Under fourteen ........................................ | 70.9 (189) |
| Grade attained in school | |
| Beyond eighth grade .................................... | 51.7 (58) |
| Eighth grade or lower .................................. | 62.8 (412) |
| Industrial skill | |
| Semi-skilled or skilled .................................. | 52.3 (444) |
| Unskilled ............................................. | 68.5 (29) |

* Whatever contractions have been made of the original, more detailed, sub-categories of the factors are based on an inspection of the raw tables, from which it could readily be determined which sub-categories to combine.

† The parenthesized figures represent the number of cases on which the particular percentage is based.

One illustration of the possible use of Table 21, which has been constructed from these five factors, may be helpful at this point. The reader will remember *Frank,* who was described in Chapter II and mentioned again in Chapter XIV in connection with a prediction of his behavior during the fifteen-year period

[3] The reader is reminded that although in Part II of this work differences were revealed between those who always responded well to a particular form of peno-correctional treatment and those who did not, no account was taken in those comparisons of the offenders whose responses to a particular form of extra- or intramural treatment changed from better to worse, or vice versa, or whose course of conduct was not consistently toward improvement or deterioration. In constructing prediction tables, all types of responses to treatment have to be considered, since all cases have to be provided for in such tables. Therefore, the differences in the characteristics of those who always responded well to some form of peno-correctional treatment and those who always failed do not furnish the basis for the prediction tables presented in this part of the book.

TABLE 2I. BEHAVIOR DURING EXTRAMURAL PENO-CORRECTIONAL
TREATMENT (473 CASES)

| Failure score | Always succeeds | Always fails | Early success, later failure | Early failure, later success | Erratic | Number of cases |
|---|---|---|---|---|---|---|
| Under 300 ....... | 20.7 | 47.9 | 2.7 | 21.8 | 6.9 | *188* |
| 300–320 ......... | 9.2 | 65.0 | 1.8 | 17.8 | 6.2 | *163* |
| 320 and over ..... | 1.0 | 81.8 | 1.0 | 12.1 | 4.1 | *122* |

$$C = .28$$

following expiration of his sentence from the Reformatory (see page 227). Frank developed a chronic *Wanderlust* and behaved so peculiarly that he was sent in and out of mental hospitals where he was variously diagnosed as a psychopath, a defective delinquent, and a chronic vagrant. During the course of his criminal career he failed under every extramural treatment to which he was subjected. What could a judge have ascertained about Frank's chances of responding well to extramural supervision had he been able to consult Table 21? On the five factors listed above, Frank scores 312.0, which immediately makes it evident that he had less than one chance in ten of succeeding under extramural treatment. His chances of complete failure were so high (six and one-half in ten) that any judge, without knowing anything more about Frank, would have hesitated to place him under any form of extramural oversight.

In the next chapter, in which appears a prediction table for probable behavior during *intramural* treatment, the likelihood of Frank, John, Armand, Robert, Arthur, Dennis, Jack, Peter, and Antonio responding better to the one or the other general type of control will be presented, in order that the reader may see how such information, obtained at the time the youths were arrested, convicted and committed to the Reformatory, might have been utilized by the judge in a more efficient determination of the proper sentence to impose.

### Predicting Behavior during Probation

Turning now to behavior during specific forms of extramural treatment, we begin with a consideration of probable behavior during straight probation, first, regardless of the age factor, and then including a consideration of the age of the offender at the time of sentence.

On the basis of correlations of twenty-seven factors in the background of the offenders (see Chapter X) with their behavior on probation, the five factors shown in list B have been utilized in constructing Table 22. From Table 22 it becomes evident that anyone of our offenders scoring under 440 has ten in ten chances of responding well to probation, while one scoring 440 or over

B. FACTORS PREDICTIVE OF BEHAVIOR DURING STRAIGHT PROBATION

| Prediction factors and sub-categories* | Percentage incidence of failure† |
|---|---|
| Family relationships | |
| Fair | 86.3 (73) |
| Poor | 94.5 (145) |
| Education of parents | |
| One or both parents common school | 85.7 (35) |
| Both parents without formal education | 93.0 (201) |
| Church attendance | |
| Regular | 84.2 (19) |
| Irregular | 93.1 (218) |
| Age at first delinquency | |
| Under eleven | 86.2 (29) |
| Eleven to sixteen | 91.9 (174) |
| Over sixteen | 97.7 (44) |
| Number of children in family | |
| Seven or more | 84.6 (65) |
| Less than seven | 95.0 (182) |

\* Whatever contractions have been made of the original, more detailed, sub-categories of the factors are based on an inspection of the raw tables, from which it could readily be determined which sub-categories to combine.

† The parenthesized figures represent the number of cases on which the particular percentage is based.

has less than one chance in ten of responding well to this type of extramural supervision.

Unfortunately, we do not have the data from which to derive Frank's chances of good behavior on probation. Let us, therefore, turn to the case of *Robert* who, it will be remembered from Chapter II and from the previous chapter, was one of two delinquent brothers. Robert persisted in a career of sex delinquency and burglary until he was about thirty-seven years of age, by which time he had gradually settled down into conventional ways of life. How would consultation of this prediction table at the time of Robert's first arrest at the age of seventeen have been of help to the judge in determining whether or not to place him on probation rather than to utilize some other form of treatment? Robert's score on the five factors included in this table is 457.1.

TABLE 22. BEHAVIOR DURING PROBATION (201 CASES)

| Failure score | Always succeeds | Always fails | Early success, later failure | Early failure, later success | Erratic | Number of cases |
|---|---|---|---|---|---|---|
| Under 440 | 100.0 | 0.0 | 0.0 | 0.0 | 0.0 | 4 |
| 440 and over | 2.0 | 92.0 | 1.0 | 4.5 | .5 | 197 |

$$C = .41$$

From this it becomes immediately evident that his chances of responding well to probation supervision are less than one in ten. Therefore, certainly this particular form of treatment should not have been applied in his case. Actually, however, Robert was placed on probation several times in the course of his criminal career and failed miserably on each occasion.

## Predicting Behavior during Probation at Various Age Levels

Turning now to the prediction of behavior on probation at various age levels, the reader is invited to consult page 153 of Chapter IX in which the conduct of our group of offenders at different age levels is presented. It will be seen that there was a very close resemblance in response to probation treatment in the groups who were under seventeen, those seventeen to twenty-one, and those twenty-two to twenty-six, on the one hand; and among those who were twenty-seven to thirty-one years old, thirty-two to thirty-six, thirty-seven to forty-one, and forty-two years and older, on the other. Therefore, in any prediction tables to be constructed from these findings the major differentiation has to be made in behavior on probation under twenty-seven years of age on the one hand, and at twenty-seven or older on the other. Hence, two prediction tables were constructed. The five factors entering into the table dealing with probation under twenty-seven years of age are shown in list C.

C. FACTORS PREDICTIVE OF BEHAVIOR DURING PROBATION UNDER 27 YEARS

| Prediction factors and sub-categories* | Percentage incidence of failure† |
|---|---|
| Age at first known delinquency | |
| Under eleven | 92.0 (25) |
| Eleven to sixteen | 96.0 (150) |
| Seventeen and over | 100.0 (27) |
| Bad habits in childhood | |
| No bad habits | 85.7 (7) |
| Bad habits | 96.4 (192) |
| Church attendance | |
| Regular | 88.2 (17) |
| Irregular | 96.6 (179) |
| Family relationships | |
| Fair | 89.8 (59) |
| Poor | 98.3 (120) |
| Industrial skill (before twenty-one years) | |
| Skilled | 90.9 (10) |
| Semi-skilled or unskilled | 96.3 (185) |

\* Whatever contractions have been made of the original, more detailed, sub-categories of the factors are based on an inspection of the raw tables, from which it could readily be determined which sub-categories to combine.

† The parenthesized figures represent the number of cases on which the particular percentage is based.

TABLE 23. PROBABLE BEHAVIOR DURING
PROBATION UNDER 27 YEARS (165 CASES)

| Failure score | Success | Failure | Number of cases |
|---|---|---|---|
| Under 460 ... | 100.0 | 0.0 | *1* |
| 460 and over | 4.3 | 95.7 | *164* |
| | C = .32 | | |

TABLE 24. PROBABLE BEHAVIOR DURING
PROBATION AT 27 YEARS AND
OLDER (67 CASES)

| Failure score | Success | Failure | Number of cases |
|---|---|---|---|
| Under 410 ... | 75.0 | 25.0 | *4* |
| 410–420 ..... | 23.1 | 76.9 | *13* |
| 420 and over | 4.0 | 96.0 | *50* |
| | C = .47 | | |

On the basis of these five factors, Table 23 was constructed. From this it becomes evident that an offender whose prediction score is under 460 has ten chances in ten of succeeding on probation, but if he scores 460 and over he has nine and one-half chances in ten of failing on probation when under twenty-seven years of age. Unfortunately, it was not possible to derive the prediction score for Robert when under twenty-seven years of age, but we do have all the data necessary to obtain his score for behavior on probation at twenty-seven and older.

Into the construction of the prediction table dealing with behavior at twenty-seven or older the factors shown in list D have entered. From these factors Table 24 has been derived. On them Robert scored 425.1. From a consultation

D. FACTORS PREDICTIVE OF BEHAVIOR DURING PROBATION AT 27 YEARS OR OLDER

| Prediction factors and sub-categories* | Percentage incidence of failure† |
|---|---|
| Number of children in family | |
|     Seven or more children | 78.3 (23) |
|     Four, five, six children | 84.2 (38) |
|     Two, three children | 95.8 (24) |
|     Only child | 100.0 (6) |
| Economic status of parents | |
|     Marginal | 80.0 (55) |
|     Dependent or comfortable | 100.0 (3) |
| Broken or inadequate homes | |
|     Home not broken or inadequate | 78.6 (14) |
|     Home broken or inadequate | 88.1 (76) |
| Age at first delinquency | |
|     Under eleven years | 69.2 (13) |
|     Eleven and older | 86.2 (78) |
| Mental disease or distortion | |
|     None | 81.3 (32) |
|     Mental disease or distortion | 92.5 (40) |

\* Whatever contractions have been made of the original, more detailed, sub-categories of the factors are based on an inspection of the raw tables, from which it could readily be determined which sub-categories to combine.

† The parenthesized figures represent the number of cases on which the particular percentage is based.

of Table 24 it becomes evident that he has nine and one-half chances in ten of not responding well to oversight on probation at the age of twenty-seven or more. Actually Robert did appear before a judge exactly at the age of twenty-seven for burglary; he was placed on probation for a two-year period and he failed thereunder, committing several offenses during this time.

Many other illustrations could be given of the practical value of prediction tables of this kind.

## Predicting Behavior on Probation with Suspended Sentence

It was unfortunately not possible to construct an overall table for behavior on probation under suspended sentence because in none of the cases of offenders who succeeded under this form of treatment were all the five factors in list E known. As the predictive factors themselves have already been determined (list E), it should be possible at some later time to construct the predictive table from another series of cases.

### E. FACTORS PREDICTIVE OF BEHAVIOR ON PROBATION WITH SUSPENDED SENTENCE

| Prediction factors and sub-categories* | Percentage incidence of failure† |
|---|---|
| Nativity | 78.7 (14) |
|     Foreign born | 92.9 (127) |
|     Native born | |
| Intelligence | 84.0 (25) |
|     Feebleminded | 94.0 (110) |
|     Not feebleminded | |
| Grade attained in school | 87.7 (55) |
|     Less than sixth grade | 94.0 (67) |
|     Sixth, seventh, eighth grade | 100.0 (18) |
|     Beyond eighth grade | |
| Age at first delinquency | 89.5 (124) |
|     Eleven and older | 100.0 (17) |
|     Under eleven years | |
| Industrial skill | 61.1 (18) |
|     Skilled worker | 95.9 (123) |
|     Semi-skilled or unskilled worker | |

\* Whatever contractions have been made of the original, more detailed, sub-categories of the factors are based on an inspection of the raw tables, from which it could readily be determined which sub-categories to combine.

† The parenthesized figures represent the number of cases on which the particular percentage is based.

## Predicting Behavior on Probation with Suspended Sentence at Various Age Levels

From Chapter IX, page 153, it will be recalled that those under thirty-two years of age could be distinguished in their response to probation under suspended sentence from those who were thirty-two or older; for within the age spans included in each of these two groups, the offenders most closely resembled each other in their response to probation under suspended sentence. This finding was, therefore, used as the basis for constructing two prediction tables for which, fortunately, there were a sufficient number of known cases on the particular factors involved to make the resulting prediction tables useful at least for illustrative purposes. First, we present list F of the five factors entering into the construction of the table predicting behavior during probation with suspended sentence when offenders being considered for this form of treatment are under thirty-two years of age.

### F. FACTORS PREDICTIVE OF BEHAVIOR DURING PROBATION WITH SUSPENDED SENTENCE UNDER 32 YEARS

| Prediction factors and sub-categories* | Percentage incidence of failure† |
|---|---|
| Nativity of offender | |
| Foreign born | 90.0 (10) |
| Native born | 99.0 (101) |
| Age at first delinquency | |
| Seventeen and over | 92.9 (14) |
| Fourteen to sixteen | 97.9 (47) |
| Under fifteen | 100.0 (50) |
| Intelligence of offender | |
| Feebleminded | 89.5 (19) |
| Not feebleminded | 100.0 (87) |
| Mobility | |
| Yes | 93.5 (31) |
| No | 100.0 (78) |
| Use of leisure | |
| Negative | 50.0 (2) |
| Harmful | 99.1 (109) |

* Whatever contractions have been made of the original, more detailed, sub-categories of the factors are based on an inspection of the raw tables, from which it could readily be determined which sub-categories to combine.

† The parenthesized figures represent the number of cases on which the particular percentage is based.

These factors are the basis of Table 25, from which it will be seen that a person scoring under 440 has a ten in ten chance of responding well to probation under suspended sentence, while one scoring 440 and over has practically certain likelihood of failure. We can illustrate the possible use of such a table in the case of *Robert,* who, on the five factors which enter into this particular prediction chart, scores 487.6. From this it is evident that he has practically no chance of behaving well during this particular form of treatment when under thirty-two years of age. In fact, Robert had been placed on probation under suspended sentence for a six-month period when he was seventeen years old, and

TABLE 25. BEHAVIOR DURING PROBATION UNDER SUSPENDED SENTENCE UNDER 32 YEARS (102 CASES)

| Failure score | Success | Failure | Number of cases |
|---|---|---|---|
| Under 440 ... | 100.0 | 0.0 | 1 |
| 440 and over | 1.0 | 99.0 | 101 |

C = .57

TABLE 26. BEHAVIOR DURING PROBATION UNDER SUSPENDED SENTENCE AT 32 YEARS AND OLDER (63 CASES)

| Failure score | Success | Failure | Number of cases |
|---|---|---|---|
| Under 410 ... | 38.5 | 61.5 | 13 |
| 410–440 ..... | 9.1 | 90.9 | 44 |
| 440 and over | 0.0 | 100.0 | 6 |

C = .35

during this time he failed, committing burglary for which he was sent to a reformatory.

Now let us proceed to the prediction table covering behavior on probation with suspended sentence at the age level of thirty-two years or over. The five factors entering into this table are shown in list G.

G. FACTORS PREDICTIVE OF BEHAVIOR DURING PROBATION WITH SUSPENDED SENTENCE AT 32 YEARS AND OLDER

| Prediction factors and sub-categories* | Percentage incidence of failure† |
|---|---|
| Number of children in family | |
| Seven or more children | 76.5 (17) |
| Four, five, six children | 82.1 (28) |
| Two, three children | 94.4 (18) |
| Only child | 100.0 (1) |
| Economic status of parents | |
| Dependent | 76.9 (13) |
| Marginal | 83.3 (30) |
| Comfortable | 90.5 (21) |
| Intelligence of offender | |
| Below normal | 81.8 (44) |
| Normal | 94.4 (18) |
| Age at first delinquency | |
| Eleven and older | 83.3 (60) |
| Under eleven | 100.0 (4) |
| Industrial skill | |
| Semi-skilled or unskilled | 83.6 (61) |
| Skilled | 100.0 (3) |

* Whatever contractions have been made of the original, more detailed, sub-categories of the factors are based on an inspection of the raw tables, from which it could readily be determined which sub-categories to combine.

† The parenthesized figures represent the number of cases on which the particular percentage is based.

On these five factors Robert scores 450; and Table 26 indicates that, as in the previous age span, he had no chance of succeeding under this form of treatment even when applied at the time he was thirty-two or over. Actually, Robert was not placed under this form of treatment in this particular age span, but it seems likely, in view of his previous record of behavior on probation under suspended sentence, that he would not have behaved well. We might use as an illustration, however, the case of *Dennis* who, it will be recalled, was a bootlegger and drug addict and who occasionally picked pockets in order to secure money for the drug. It will be remembered that he was finally admitted to a mental hospital suffering from a psychosis due to drugs, and that he is still there. Dennis scores 439 on the five factors entering into the prediction of behavior on probation under suspended sentence (see Table 26) at thirty-two or older. This places him in the group having nine chances in ten of not responding well to this form of treatment. Actually, he was placed on probation under suspended sentence at the age of thirty-three for attempted larceny from the person and failed, being arrested during this time for possessing morphine and for violating the liquor law.

## Predicting Behavior on Parole

We now come to the construction of tables from which behavior during parole can be derived; first the general table and then the more specific ones indicating probable behavior on parole at various age levels. Here, of course, is involved the discretion of a parole board in determining which prisoners to release on parole and when to release them, rather than that of a court in deciding upon the type of sentence to impose and at what age. The five factors entering into the construction of the table predicting behavior during *parole regardless of age* have been listed (H). On the basis of these five factors Table 27 was evolved.

TABLE 27. BEHAVIOR DURING PAROLE (390 CASES)

| Failure score | Always succeeds | Always fails | Early success, later failure | Early failure, later success | Erratic | Number of cases |
|---|---|---|---|---|---|---|
| Under 290 ....... | 50.0 | 0.0 | 0.0 | 50.0 | 0.0 | 2 |
| 290–310 ......... | 30.6 | 49.0 | 3.1 | 16.3 | 1.0 | 98 |
| 310–330 ......... | 22.9 | 62.7 | 0.0 | 13.3 | 1.1 | 166 |
| 330–340 ......... | 11.3 | 78.3 | .9 | 7.8 | 1.7 | 115 |
| 340 and over ..... | 0.0 | 100.0 | 0.0 | 0.0 | 0.0 | 9 |

$$C = .30$$

In view of the fact that most of the offenders served time on parole following release from the Reformatory, the reader will no doubt be interested at this point to know what the parole scores were of the nine offenders described in Chapter II, and how the prediction of their conduct on parole checks with what actually happened to them.

H. FACTORS PREDICTIVE OF BEHAVIOR DURING PAROLE

| Prediction factors and sub-categories* | Percentage incidence of failure† |
|---|---|
| Education of parents | |
| One or both common school | 52.9 (70) |
| Both without formal schooling | 65.5 (371) |
| Number of children in family | |
| Two or more | 62.5 (430) |
| One | 80.0 (30) |
| Broken or inadequate homes | |
| Not broken or inadequate | 50.0 (92) |
| Broken or inadequate | 67.1 (362) |
| Intelligence | |
| Normal | 55.9 (136) |
| Dull | 61.3 (111) |
| Borderline or feebleminded | 72.0 (179) |
| Grade attained in school | |
| Beyond eighth grade | 56.3 (58) |
| Eighth grade or less | 65.2 (388) |
| No schooling | 75.0 (12) |

* Whatever contractions have been made of the original, more detailed, sub-categories of the factors are based on an inspection of the raw tables, from which it could readily be determined which sub-categories to combine.

† The parenthesized figures represent the number of cases on which the particular percentage is based.

*Frank* scored 315.2 on the five factors entering into the prediction of behavior on parole. Consultation of Table 27 indicates that his chances of not responding well to parole supervision are six in ten and that his likelihood of always behaving well on parole is expressed by the low odds of two in ten. Actually, during his parole period he not only was a deserter from the Army but also received a dishonorable discharge from the Navy and, further, while on furlough from the Navy, he was sentenced to a penitentiary in a southern state. It is evident, therefore, that the authorities would have been justified, from Frank's prediction score, to hold him in custody for a longer time, or in the event of deciding to release him on parole even in the face of his low chance of responding satisfactorily to this form of treatment, to provide very close supervision for him.

The parole score of *John* is 315.2. As in the case of Frank, this places him in the group whose likelihood of failure on parole is six in ten. In fact, during his parole period John robbed his employer, taking about $300 worth of jewelry. He then left a note for his parents saying he was going to Texas and was for some time a fugitive from justice. Finally, he was trailed to Chicago and shortly thereafter was arrested by police of his home town and was given a new sentence to the Reformatory. His parole officer characterized him as a "highway man."

*Armand* (brother of Robert) scores 332.3, which places him in the class of offenders whose chances of failing on parole are eight in ten, and of always succeeding on parole only one in ten. Armand was committed to the Reformatory at the age of twenty and was paroled a year later. Although we do not know whether during the early part of this period Armand got into serious difficulty or not (he made occasional trips away from home to New York, Pennsylvania, and Maine presumably seeking employment but not holding any of his jobs for long), later during his parole period he was accused of larceny of a watch from a fellow-employee; and when the watch was discovered in a pawn shop he was arrested. The case was dismissed, but his permit to be at liberty on parole was revoked and Armand was returned to the Reformatory.

Armand's brother, *Robert,* also scores 332.3. As in the case of Armand, this places him in the group whose chances of good behavior during parole are only one in ten. It is difficult to gauge his conduct during his parole period, because he immediately enlisted in the Army and remained there beyond the end of his sentence. Certainly, up to the end of the parole period he apparently behaved satisfactorily, because he was given an honorable discharge; apparently the combination of being on parole and being under Army control at the same time held him in check. That this inference is valid is shown by the indication of what his behavior would have been had he not joined the Army; for on a previous parole from the Reformatory Robert had committed burglaries and was then given the particular sentence upon which we happen to be focusing our attention.

*Arthur* also scores 332.3 for probable behavior on parole, so that he, like Armand and Robert, had only a single chance out of ten of behaving well during parole; and we know that during his parole period he actually committed burglary and was thereupon placed on probation under suspended sentence for two years. It is evident, from a study of his parole history, that when Arthur was very closely supervised by the family and by the minister of his church, he behaved well; and for three years of a four-year parole period he did not get into any difficulty. But whether the supervision broke down or he was faced with an irresistible temptation, he committed burglary.

*Dennis,* who scores 316.2, has only two chances in ten of always responding well to this form of treatment, six in ten of always failing when under parole supervision and about one and one-half of failing in the earlier years but subsequently adapting satisfactorily. Actually, Dennis was placed on parole from the Reformatory at the age of twenty-five, and during that time he committed larceny. He was again placed on parole at the age of twenty-seven and again committed larceny while under this form of supervision. For a third time he was paroled at the age of twenty-eight, and for a third time he committed larceny. However, when he was placed on parole for a fourth time, at the age of thirty-one, Dennis completed a parole period of seventeen months without committing any offenses.

*Jack,* too, scores 332.3, which places him in the group who have eight in ten chances of not responding well to parole supervision. On the particular Reformatory sentence and parole with which we happen to be concerned, Jack was at large for only seven months, when he was returned to the Reformatory on a charge of non-support. Following his second parole from the Reformatory, he worked very irregularly and occasionally lapsed into periods of drunkenness.

*Peter* also scores 332.3, which places him, too, in the group whose chances of not responding well to parole are as high as eight in ten. During his parole period he was arrested for larceny, his permit to be at liberty was revoked, and he was returned to the Reformatory from which he was again paroled after four months. A few months after this second parole, Peter was again arrested for larceny and his permit to be at liberty was once more revoked. He was in such bad physical shape from the use of drugs that he had to be hospitalized, but after eleven months he was again paroled. After a month of parole, however, his permit to be at liberty was revoked because he failed to report to the parole officer, had done no work, had been loafing, and had made false reports. He was, however, not returned to the Reformatory because he had absconded. Several years later, however, it was discovered that he had been peddling drugs up to the time of the end of his parole period.

*Antonio* scores 286.5. This places him in the group whose chances of always failing on parole are five in ten; in other words, Antonio had an equal chance of always responding well to parole supervision either immediately on release from the Reformatory or later. Antonio was committed to the Reformatory at the age of twenty-one for burglary, on the particular commitment which is the point of departure for this study. He was on parole for three years and throughout this time his behavior was excellent. He lived with his parents, worked fairly steadily and was always on the lookout for an opportunity as an engraver. It will be recalled that he learned how to do this work in the Reformatory and had shown deep interest in it. He finally found work as an engraver and told the parole officer that "as long as I can be busy I'll never get into trouble. . . . I am very glad to have learned the engraving trade at the Reformatory . . . now that I have found a job that I like, I am going to stick to it."

It should be mentioned, however, that on parole from the Reformatory on a sentence previous to this one (at which time Antonio was nineteen) he did not behave well. He committed burglary and was given a new sentence to the institution. This bears out the forecast of his prediction score than Antonio was the kind of risk that could be turned either to success or failure, and that if his vocational interests had been discovered earlier than they were, his return to law-abiding conduct would probably have occurred sooner than it did. Certainly in a case where there is a fifty-fifty chance of good adjustment during a particular form of treatment special effort has to be made to find the means for bringing this about.

Many other case illustrations out of this research might be given, for a very large proportion of the 510 men included in this study were actually placed on parole following a stay of a few months to several years in the Reformatory. But those given should be sufficient to indicate that the utilization of prediction tables as a guide to the parole authorities, together of course with a consideration of the environmental conditions to which a particular parolee returns upon his release from prison, should result in more scientific parole treatment than has hitherto been possible.

### Predicting Behavior on Parole at Various Age Levels

Turning now to the prediction of behavior on parole at different age levels, consultation of Chapter IX, page 153, indicates that there are three age spans which are sufficiently differentiated from each other in the behavior of our men during parole to form the basis for the construction of three tables pre-

I. FACTORS PREDICTIVE OF BEHAVIOR DURING PAROLE UNDER 22 YEARS

| Prediction factors and sub-categories* | Percentage incidence of failure† |
|---|---|
| Delinquency in family | |
| No | 67.9 (56) |
| Yes | 87.0 (192) |
| Age at first delinquency | |
| Seventeen and over | 65.4 (26) |
| Fourteen to sixteen | 74.1 (108) |
| Under fourteen | 91.8 (147) |
| Bad habits | |
| No | 52.6 (19) |
| Yes | 84.6 (254) |
| Industrial skill | |
| Semi-skilled or skilled | 77.8 (122) |
| Unskilled | 86.7 (158) |
| Physical condition | |
| Good or fair | 81.0 (264) |
| Poor | 100.0 (9) |

* Whatever contractions have been made of the original, more detailed, sub-categories of the factors are based on an inspection of the raw tables, from which it could readily be determined which sub-categories to combine.

† The parenthesized figures represent the number of cases on which the particular percentage is based.

dicting probable behavior (a) when under twenty-two years of age, (b) at twenty-two to twenty-six, (c) at twenty-seven or older.

Into the construction of the table indicating behavior of offenders on parole when under twenty-two years of age, five factors have entered, as shown in list I. From these factors Table 28 has been derived. We do not have Dennis' score for behavior on parole in this age span, but will return to the case of *Robert* for an illustration. Robert's score on the basis of the five factors entering into the table predicting behavior on parole when the parolee is under twenty-two is 457.1. This would have indicated to a parole board that Robert had no chance of responding well to this form of supervision when under twenty-two years of age. Actually he was placed on parole at the age of eight-

TABLE 28. BEHAVIOR DURING PAROLE
UNDER 22 YEARS (230 CASES)

| Failure score | Success | Failure | Number of cases |
|---|---|---|---|
| Under 390 ................. | 54.8 | 45.2 | *31* |
| 390–400 ................. | 38.5 | 61.5 | *13* |
| 400–410 ................. | 17.1 | 82.9 | *35* |
| 410–440 ................. | 7.4 | 92.6 | *149* |
| 440 and over .............. | 0.0 | 100.0 | *2* |

$$C = .41$$

J. FACTORS PREDICTIVE OF BEHAVIOR DURING PAROLE AT 22–26 YEARS

| Prediction factors and sub-categories* | Percentage incidence of failure† |
|---|---|
| Delinquency in family | |
| No ..................................................... | 54.2 (59) |
| Yes ..................................................... | 75.7 (148) |
| Economic status of parents | |
| Marginal or comfortable ................................ | 65.2 (190) |
| Dependent ............................................. | 92.3 (39) |
| Broken or inadequate homes | |
| No ..................................................... | 52.8 (53) |
| Yes ..................................................... | 73.3 (195) |
| Work habits | |
| Good ................................................... | 47.2 (40) |
| Fair or poor ............................................ | 75.6 (148) |
| Economic responsibility | |
| Fair ................................................... | 47.5 (40) |
| Poor ................................................... | 74.8 (155) |

* Whatever contractions have been made of the original, more detailed, sub-categories of the factors are based on an inspection of the raw tables, from which it could readily be determined which sub-categories to combine.

† The parenthesized figures represent the number of cases on which the particular percentage is based.

een and during this time was arrested for burglary and committed to the Reformatory.

As to behavior on parole between the ages of twenty-two and twenty-six years, the five factors which entered into the construction of the prognostic table are shown in list J. Returning now to the case of Dennis, who scores 343.1, it is evident from Table 29 that he has four chances in ten of responding well to parole if placed under such extramural oversight when between twenty-two and twenty-six years of age, and six chances in ten of not behaving well. As a matter of fact, Dennis was placed on parole at the age of twenty-five and during this period committed larceny for which he was sent to jail.

| TABLE 29. BEHAVIOR DURING PAROLE AT 22–26 YEARS (150 CASES) | | | |
|---|---|---|---|
| *Failure score* | *Success* | *Failure* | *Number of cases* |
| Under 300 ... | 71.4 | 28.6 | *14* |
| 300–340 ..... | 45.8 | 54.2 | *24* |
| 340–360 ..... | 39.1 | 60.9 | *23* |
| 360–370 ..... | 23.7 | 76.3 | *59* |
| 370 and over | 3.3 | 96.7 | *30* |
| | C = .39 | | |

| TABLE 30. BEHAVIOR DURING PAROLE AT 27 YEARS AND OLDER (161 CASES) | | | |
|---|---|---|---|
| *Failure score* | *Success* | *Failure* | *Number of cases* |
| Under 340 ... | 46.2 | 53.8 | *13* |
| 340–360 ..... | 39.6 | 60.4 | *48* |
| 360–380 ..... | 25.3 | 74.7 | *99* |
| 380 and over | 0.0 | 100.0 | *1* |
| | C = .17 | | |

K. FACTORS PREDICTIVE OF BEHAVIOR DURING PAROLE AT 27 YEARS AND OLDER

| *Prediction factors and sub-categories** | *Percentage incidence of failure†* |
|---|---|
| Nativity | |
| Foreign | 59.4 (32) |
| Native born | 75.2 (153) |
| Rank of offender among siblings | |
| Second or later in rank | 69.0 (129) |
| First child | 75.6 (41) |
| Only child | 84.6 (13) |
| Age at first delinquency | |
| Seventeen and over | 63.6 (55) |
| Under seventeen | 75.1 (129) |
| Use of leisure | |
| Negative | 50.0 (4) |
| Harmful | 73.1 (182) |
| Physical condition | |
| Good | 69.7 (152) |
| Fair | 78.9 (19) |
| Poor | 87.5 (8) |

* Whatever contractions have been made of the original, more detailed, sub-categories of the factors are based on an inspection of the raw tables, from which it could readily be determined which sub-categories to combine.

† The parenthesized figures represent the number of cases on which the particular percentage is based.

Into the construction of the table covering behavior on parole at twenty-seven years and over, the five factors shown in list K have entered. Unfortunately, we do not have a score for behavior on parole at twenty-seven and older on any one of the cases which were described in Chapter II, but it is evident from Table 30 that a judge could determine, for example, that if an offender had a score of 360 to 380 he would have only two and one-half in ten chances of behaving well on parole when twenty-seven or older and seven and one-half chances in ten of not responding well to this form of supervision when twenty-seven or older.

### Comment

The feasibility of using prediction tables in administering criminal justice is further supported by the data presented in this chapter. Nowadays, there are few informed students who would urge a return to the Gilbert and Sullivan ideal of "making the punishment fit the crime." If the punishment is to fit the criminal, however, judges must be given ample discretion in determining upon the particular type of sentence to impose. And this, in turn, means that judges must have the instruments for exercising sound discretion. In the historic swings of the pendulum between adherence to legislatively prescribed rules and exercise of judicial discretion, a chief reason for abandonment of discretion has been that it is so easily abused. To avoid inefficiency or worse, some device is needed for the disciplining of free discretion. This is provided in the use of prognostic tables.

It has been demonstrated, moreover, that it is possible so to construct prediction tables as to take account of the effect of age on response to various forms of peno-correctional treatment. Age, in this connection, is of course only an index of maturity. Individuals differ in the degree of maturity achieved at different ages. But the use of prediction tables based on cases differentiated as to age, realistically narrows the field for the judge and parole board. As we have pointed out in prior publications, it is not proposed that they blindly follow the signs to which a prediction table leads. It is merely suggested that prognostic instruments can aid the officials in narrowing down the search for the peno-correctional treatment that experience has shown is most suited to an individual of a particular class.

In considering the use of prediction tables by parole boards, it must be borne in mind that such boards are constantly faced with a dilemma arising from the fact that existing legislation does not provide for a *wholly indeterminate sentence* for felons. Consequently, even though a prediction score in an individual case may show that the probability of good conduct on parole is extremely low, the members of a parole board may still decide to release the offender. They must often face the issue of whether it is preferable, despite the fact that the prisoner is a poor parole risk, to release him for at least a brief fraction of his sentence. This would make possible supervision during the dangerous transitional period from imprisonment to complete freedom.

A completely indeterminate, or broad-zone-sentence statute would make the entire parole procedure more rational and would at the same time protect society more effectively.

Analysis of response of offenders to the several types of extramural treatment has further suggested a basic weakness in existing practices. On the one hand, the two forms of probation are administered by courts; on the other, parole is administered by an outside body known as a parole board. There is no valid reason, except historical accident, why the one type of extramural oversight should be administered by the courts and the other by a separate body. This practice only results in dividing the offender's destiny among several independent agencies. It would seem more rational that the same authority which imposes sentence should supervise both probation and parole. Recent projects are taking this advisability into account.[4]

---

[4] See The Draft Bill for a Youth Correction Authority Act, prepared by a committee of the American Law Institute, and Glueck, S., "Indeterminate Sentence and Parole in the Federal System," 21 *B.U. Law Rev.* (1941), 20–32; 5 *Fed. Probation* (1941), 17–23.

## XVI

## PREDICTING BEHAVIOR DURING VARIOUS FORMS OF INTRAMURAL TREATMENT

A s in the case of extramural treatment, so in intramural, we have prepared both a general table from which can be derived the chances of good and poor behavior during institutional control in general, and tables which indicate the chances of adjustment to the various forms of intramural treatment: correctional schools, reformatories, prisons, and jails. In addition, we present tables predicting behavior during these various forms of treatment at different age levels.

### Predicting Behavior during Intramural Peno-Correctional Treatment

The five factors on which Table 31 is based, and from which may be derived the chances of success or failure during intramural treatment *in general,* are found in list A. From Table 31 it can be determined, for example, that an offender scoring under 160 on the five included factors has almost nine in ten chances of responding satisfactorily to any form of intramural treatment,

A. FACTORS PREDICTIVE OF BEHAVIOR DURING INTRAMURAL TREATMENT

| *Prediction factors and sub-categories** | *Percentage incidence of failure†* |
|---|---|
| Nativity of parents and offender | |
| All native born | 27.1 (133) |
| One or both parents foreign born, son native | 39.5 (256) |
| All foreign born | 44.2 (95) |
| Education of parents | |
| One or both parents common school | 28.0 (75) |
| Both parents without formal schooling | 38.3 (400) |
| Number of children in family | |
| Seven or more | 31.7 (120) |
| Two to six children | 38.0 (342) |
| Only child | 41.2 (34) |
| Grade attained in school | |
| Beyond eighth grade | 23.8 (63) |
| Eighth grade or less | 38.7 (428) |
| Age at first delinquency | |
| Seventeen and over | 25.5 (110) |
| Under fourteen | 36.4 (192) |
| Fourteen to sixteen | 43.7 (190) |

* Whatever contractions have been made of the original, more detailed, sub-categories of the factors are based on an inspection of the raw tables, from which it could readily be determined which sub-categories to combine.

† The parenthesized figures represent the number of cases on which the particular percentage is based.

while if he scores 190 or over he has less than two chances in ten of satisfactory adjustment to intramural treatment.

Let us again see what actually happened to the nine offenders described in Chapter II in the light of what their prediction scores on intramural treatment indicate. It will be recalled that *Frank*, the chronic wanderer who was fre-

TABLE 31. BEHAVIOR DURING INTRAMURAL TREATMENT (457 CASES)

| Failure score | Always succeeds | Always fails | Early success, later failure | Early failure, later success | Erratic | Number of cases |
|---|---|---|---|---|---|---|
| Under 160 ....... | 87.4 | 0.0 | 6.3 | 6.3 | 0.0 | *16* |
| 160–170 ......... | 41.3 | 28.3 | 0.0 | 17.4 | 13.0 | *46* |
| 170–190 ......... | 26.7 | 32.3 | 6.9 | 23.7 | 10.4 | *232* |
| 190 and over ..... | 17.2 | 48.5 | 9.8 | 15.3 | 9.2 | *163* |

$$C = .35$$

quently released from mental hospitals, had very little chance of doing well under *extramural* oversight (see page 236). His prediction score for behavior during intramural treatment is 190.9, which means that he has less than two chances in ten of always responding satisfactorily to institutional treatment, one chance in ten of making a good adaptation at first but failing under later commitments, one and one-half chances in ten of not responding well to earlier incarcerations but making a satisfactory later adjustment in institutions, one chance in ten of sometimes succeeding and sometimes failing but with no clear-cut trend in one or the other direction, and five chances in ten of always failing. If his chances of success during extramural treatment had been contrasted with his chances of success during intramural, it would have become immediately obvious to a judge having to make disposition of his case that certainly incarceration was indicated, because intramural treatment was far safer for him than extramural. Which particular form of institutional treatment to have placed him under would of course have depended upon where was his best chance of good adjustment (see pages 261 et seq.). It might be said in passing that throughout his career Frank did not behave well in reformatories and prisons but did adjust satisfactorily to the less stringent régime of jails and houses of correction.

It might be well to present at this time further contrasts in the likelihood of good behavior during extramural and intramural treatment of the offenders described in Chapter II. It is on the basis of such preliminary information derived from prediction tables that a judge could solve his basic problem in the exercise of discretion, that is, whether he should resort to extramural penocorrectional treatment for the particular offender before him or to intramural control.

Turning to the case of *John*, his score for extramural treatment is 295.5 and for intramural, 198.2. Consultation of Table 21 in Chapter XV reveals that with a score of 295.5 John falls in the class who have a fifty-fifty chance of not responding well to oversight outside of institutions. However, for intramural treatment, John, who scores 198.2 likewise has a fifty-fifty chance of not adjusting well under imprisonment. With such information at his disposal, a judge would be justified, first, to resort to strict extramural control, and if that failed, to imprisonment. Given a prediction score that permits of placement of the offender on probation, there are many good reasons for resort to this form of treatment. It prevents the break-up of the offender's normal family and occupational ties; it avoids his being subjected to the routinizing and mechanizing influences of prison life and to the possibility of further moral contamination through intimate contact with more hardened offenders. It is much cheaper to the state. For all these reasons, probation is preferable to imprisonment, provided such type of correctional treatment is indicated in the particular case. In cases like John's, where the chances of success or failure are equal, a judge can legitimately experiment with the preferable form of extramural oversight, resorting to imprisonment if the probationer fails to respond satisfactorily.

In fact, however, this was not done in John's case. His criminal record indicates that on the occasion of his first arrest at seventeen for burglary, he was immediately committed to a correctional school where, it will be recalled from Chapter II, he claimed to have been severely maltreated by frequent whippings. As a result of this experience, John became very much embittered and he was of the conviction that his subsequent lack of adaptation to any form of penocorrectional experience was due to resentment against authorities engendered by this particular unfortunate experience.

*Armand* scores 309.7 on extramural treatment and 189.3 on intramural. Consultation of Tables 21 and 31 would have indicated to a judge at the time of Armand's first arrest that his likelihood of not responding well to extramural treatment was six and one-half in ten, while his chances of not responding well to intramural treatment were only three in ten. Obviously, in this case commitment to an institution was indicated, rather than extramural treatment. Actually, at the age of seventeen, following Armand's first arrest for larceny, he was placed on probation, a treatment also resorted to after two succeeding arrests; and only then was Armand finally committed to an institution.

*Robert's* score for extramural treatment is 325.9, and for intramural 184.6. This places him in the group whose chances of not behaving well under extramural treatment are eight in ten, and during imprisonment three in ten; here again, therefore, as in the case of his brother Armand, Robert rather than being placed on probation under suspended sentence following his first arrest at seventeen should have been committed to an institution. He shortly violated his probation and was only then sent to a reformatory.

*Arthur* scores 309.4 on extramural treatment and 167.6 on intramural. Therefore, he has six and one-half chances in ten of not reacting satisfactorily to oversight in the community and less than three out of ten of not responding satisfactorily to imprisonment. Again in his case, therefore, institutional commitment following the first arrest was indicated. Instead, Arthur was placed on probation after his first arrest at the age of nineteen for burglary; and during this time he committed larcenies for which he finally had to be sent to an institution.

*Dennis* scores 293.2 on extramural treatment and 198.2 on intramural. This indicates that he had more than a fifty-fifty chance of responding well to extramural treatment, although he was likely not to do well on the earlier treatments but should have made an adaptation eventually. His chances of responding well to intramural treatment were also fifty-fifty, although this five in ten hazard is evenly divided between his likelihood of immediately adjusting himself and of adjusting well later. In the face of such information, a judge would have been justified in first attempting extramural treatment in the case of Dennis. The fact is that Dennis was placed on probation following his first arrest at the age of twenty. Unfortunately, we do not know how he behaved during oversight in the community; we do know that he responded satisfactorily to almost all the intramural treatments to which he was subjected later on in his delinquent career but did not make a good record on most of the extramural treatments. Particularly in the latter part of his career, when Dennis had become a drug addict, extramural treatment was of course not wise, because he could thereby readily continue to obtain the drug and would steal to do so.

*Jack*, who developed into a "drunk" and non-supporter, scores 325.9 on extramural treatment and 195.6 on intramural. Consultation of Tables 21 and 31 indicates that his chances of not responding well to extramural treatment are eight in ten while the odds of his not responding well to intramural treatment are five in ten. Obviously, intramural treatment was indicated in his case. The facts are that at twenty-nine he was first arrested for non-support, again six months later, and once more a year later. On all three occasions he was committed to jail, but only for very brief periods; and unfortunately we do not know how he behaved in jail. But we do know that during every *extramural* peno-correctional treatment to which he was subjected (probation, probation with suspended sentence, and parole) throughout his criminal career, from the time of his first extramural experience at the age of thirty until he was fifty (which is the period for which we have information), he on no occasion responded satisfactorily to extramural oversight. Despite this fact, Jack was repeatedly placed on straight probation or probation under suspended sentence and released on parole from reformatories and jails. His conduct during the institutional treatments for which we do have information, particularly that in jails, has been satisfactory.

*Peter* scores 309.4 on extramural treatment and 191.9 on intramural. This places him among the offenders whose chances of not doing well under extramural oversight are six and one-half in ten, but whose chances of behaving well during intramural peno-correctional treatment are five in ten. Therefore, immediate commitment of Peter to a peno-correctional institution following his first arrest at the age of eighteen would have been desirable. Instead, he was placed on probation with suspended sentence and during this time committed larceny for which he was sent to a reformatory. Throughout his career, Peter, like Jack, was placed on probation under suspended sentence and on parole several times and each time failed to respond satisfactorily; but it is worth noting that although during his early imprisonments he did not behave any too well, later in his criminal career he did make excellent adjustments to the demands of institutional life.

Finally, *Antonio* scores 295.5 on extramural peno-correctional treatment and 181.6 on intramural. Consultation of Tables 21 and 31 reveals that his chances of getting along satisfactorily under extramural supervision are almost five in ten and the probabilities of his not responding well to intramural treatment are three in ten. In view of the fact that he has about a fifty-fifty chance of doing well during extramural treatment, a judge would have been more than justified in placing him on probation following his first arrest. Instead, however, he was committed to a correctional school. Although he behaved very well while there, it is to be noted that on two or three subsequent paroles he did not respond satisfactorily; and the question naturally arises whether if the indicated extramural treatment had been tried preceding incarceration, Antonio might not have responded satisfactorily at less expense to the state and less moral hazard to himself. In this connection, when Antonio, at eighteen, was committed to a reformatory, the institution examiner ascribed the youth's downward drift to poolroom and bowling alley associates, "plus a pleasure-loving disposition and the *additional influence of his correctional school associates*" (italics ours).

## Predicting Behavior in Correctional Schools

Turning, now, to *specific* forms of intramural treatment, we are concerned first with behavior in correctional schools, to which offenders are usually committed before the age of seventeen and under whose supervision they are sometimes held until the age of twenty-one. The five factors entering into the construction of Table 32 are shown in list B. From Table 32 it becomes evident

### TABLE 32. BEHAVIOR IN CORRECTIONAL SCHOOLS (97 CASES)

| Failure score | Always succeeds | Always fails | Early success, later failure | Early failure, later success | Erratic | Number of cases |
|---|---|---|---|---|---|---|
| Under 290 ....... | 50.0 | 38.0 | 6.0 | 4.0 | 2.0 | 50 |
| 290–330 ......... | 18.2 | 75.0 | 4.5 | 2.3 | 0.0 | 44 |
| 330 and over ..... | 0.0 | 100.0 | 0.0 | 0.0 | 0.0 | 3 |

$$C = .37$$

#### B. FACTORS PREDICTIVE OF BEHAVIOR IN CORRECTIONAL SCHOOLS

| Prediction factors and sub-categories* | Percentage incidence of failure† |
|---|---|
| Criminality or delinquency in family | |
|     Yes ...................................................... | 53.3 (92) |
|     No ...................................................... | 73.9 (23) |
| Usual economic status of parents | |
|     Dependent or marginal .................................. | 53.7 (93) |
|     Comfortable ............................................ | 72.4 (29) |
| Intelligence | |
|     Normal or superior ..................................... | 46.9 (32) |
|     Borderline or feebleminded ............................. | 54.3 (57) |
|     Dull ................................................... | 68.8 (32) |
| Age began work | |
|     Under fifteen .......................................... | 36.6 (41) |
|     Fifteen and over ....................................... | 68.8 (80) |
| Age at leaving home | |
|     Fourteen and over ...................................... | 47.9 (48) |
|     Under fourteen ......................................... | 63.2 (76) |

\* Whatever contractions have been made of the original, more detailed, sub-categories of the factors are based on an inspection of the raw tables, from which it could readily be determined which sub-categories to combine.

† The parenthesized figures represent the number of cases on which the particular percentage is based.

that a youth scoring under 290 has almost four chances in ten of not adjusting himself satisfactorily to the kind of régime offered in correctional schools; but if he scores 330 and over the chances of his adapting satisfactorily to the régime in such institutions are nil.

The reader will recall *John*, the offender who finally lost his life at the age of thirty-six in a brawl with police after serving a long term in prison. His prediction score for intramural treatment is 198.2. By consulting Table 31 it will be seen that he had five chances in ten of not responding well to life in institutions, which of course means also that he had a fifty-fifty chance of adjusting himself at one time or another; in other words, that he really had capacity for adaptation to institutional life. His score for correctional school treatment, the specific form of intramural control which now concerns us, is 245.8. This indicates (Table 32) that he had almost four chances in ten of not doing well in correctional schools, six out of ten of making a satisfactory adaptation to this kind of régime. As the reader will recall, his life history shows that at the age of seventeen John was sent to a correctional school and made a very poor showing while there. If the correctional school authorities had had at their disposal the information that John had pretty good odds of responding satisfactorily to this type of régime, greater effort might have been made to assist him to make this adjustment. Instead, John revealed that they made any sort of adjustment impossible for him, for he was whipped there so often that he left this institution with a feeling of intense hatred against society, to which attitude he largely ascribes the continuance of his criminal career.

## Predicting Behavior in Correctional Schools at Various Age Levels

In regard to the more detailed prediction tables based on age of the offenders at the time of commitment, it is evident from Chapter IX, page 153, that two tables are feasible, one of probable behavior in correctional schools when under seventeen and another when seventeen to twenty-one years of age.

The five factors entering into the construction of the first of these two tables

#### C. FACTORS PREDICTIVE OF BEHAVIOR IN CORRECTIONAL SCHOOLS
#### UNDER 17 YEARS

| *Prediction factors and sub-categories** | *Percentage incidence of failure†* |
|---|---|
| Family relationships | |
|     Fair | 27.8 (18) |
|     Poor | 64.9 (77) |
| Age at first delinquency | |
|     Eleven and older | 57.3 (89) |
|     Under eleven | 80.0 (20) |
| School retardation | |
|     None | 33.3 (6) |
|     Retarded one or more years | 64.2 (84) |
| Age at leaving home | |
|     Fourteen and older | 42.1 (38) |
|     Under fourteen | 69.9 (73) |
| Age began work | |
|     Under fifteen | 37.8 (37) |
|     Fifteen and older | 72.5 (69) |

* Whatever contractions have been made of the original, more detailed, sub-categories of the factors are based on an inspection of the raw tables, from which it could readily be determined which sub-categories to combine.
† The parenthesized figures represent the number of cases on which the particular percentage is based.

| TABLE 33. BEHAVIOR IN CORRECTIONAL SCHOOLS UNDER 17 YEARS (74 CASES) | | | |
| --- | --- | --- | --- |
| *Failure score* | *Success* | *Failure* | *Number of cases* |
| Under 290 ... | 80.0 | 20.0 | 20 |
| 290 and over | 27.8 | 72.2 | 54 |
| | C = .42 | | |

| TABLE 34. BEHAVIOR IN CORRECTIONAL SCHOOLS AT 17–21 YEARS (24 CASES) | | | |
| --- | --- | --- | --- |
| *Failure score* | *Success* | *Failure* | *Number of cases* |
| Under 380 ... | 38.5 | 61.5 | 13 |
| 380 and over | 0.0 | 100.0 | 11 |
| | C = .42 | | |

are presented in list C. Consultation of Table 33 would readily indicate that an offender under seventeen who scores less than 290 on these five factors has eight in ten chances of making a good adjustment to the correctional school régime, but if he scores 290 or over he has less than three chances out of ten.

Turning now to the table indicating probable behavior in correctional schools between the ages of seventeen and twenty-one, the five factors entering into the construction of Table 34 are shown in list D. From Table 34 it is

### D. FACTORS PREDICTIVE OF BEHAVIOR IN CORRECTIONAL SCHOOLS AT 17–21 YEARS

| *Prediction factors and sub-categories** | *Percentage incidence of failure†* |
| --- | --- |
| Nativity of parents and offender | |
| One or both parents foreign, son native | 68.0 (25) |
| All native | 90.9 (11) |
| All foreign | 100.0 (5) |
| Economic status of parents | |
| Dependent | 60.0 (10) |
| Marginal | 79.2 (24) |
| Comfortable | 87.5 (8) |
| Family relationships | |
| Poor | 69.2 (26) |
| Fair | 90.0 (10) |
| Economic responsibility of offender | |
| Fair | 50.0 (2) |
| Poor | 78.6 (28) |
| School retardation | |
| None | 50.0 (4) |
| One or more years | 77.4 (31) |

* Whatever contractions have been made of the original, more detailed, sub-categories of the factors are based on an inspection of the raw tables, from which it could readily be determined which sub-categories to combine.

† The parenthesized figures represent the number of cases on which the particular percentage is based.

evident that a youth of seventeen to twenty-one scoring under 380 has four in ten chances of behaving well in correctional schools, but if he scores 380 and over he is very likely to fail under this treatment.

## Predicting Behavior in Reformatories

Turning now to conduct in institutions for young adult offenders, the five factors entering into Table 35, predicting behavior in reformatories, are shown in list E.

E. FACTORS PREDICTIVE OF BEHAVIOR IN REFORMATORIES

| Prediction factors and sub-categories* | Percentage incidence of failure† |
|---|---|
| Nativity of parents and offender | |
| All native born | 53.5 (129) |
| One or more foreign born | 62.8 (350) |
| Education of parents | |
| One or both common school | 49.4 (77) |
| Neither with formal schooling | 62.3 (392) |
| Broken or inadequate homes | |
| Not broken or inadequate | 51.5 (101) |
| Broken or inadequate homes | 62.5 (382) |
| Age at first delinquency | |
| Seventeen and older | 38.9 (113) |
| Fourteen to sixteen years | 61.5 (187) |
| Under fourteen | 72.1 (190) |
| Industrial skill | |
| Skilled | 42.9 (28) |
| Semi-skilled | 59.4 (192) |
| Unskilled | 63.1 (271) |

\* Whatever contractions have been made of the original, more detailed, sub-categories of the factors are based on an inspection of the raw tables, from which it could readily be determined which sub-categories to combine.

† The parenthesized figures represent the number of cases on which the particular percentage is based.

In view of the fact that all the men included in this work had at least one commitment to a reformatory, it might be of special interest to the reader if we present the prediction scores for reformatory treatment of the nine men included in Chapter II and relate these to how the men actually did behave during the particular reformatory commitment which was the point of departure for *500 Criminal Careers, Later Criminal Careers,* and the present volume.

TABLE 35. BEHAVIOR IN REFORMATORIES (448 CASES)

| Failure score | Always succeeds | Always fails | Early success, later failure | Early failure, later success | Erratic | Number of cases |
|---|---|---|---|---|---|---|
| Under 270 | 70.8 | 16.7 | 4.2 | 8.3 | 0.0 | 24 |
| 270–290 | 48.5 | 45.4 | 2.1 | 3.1 | .9 | 97 |
| 290–310 | 30.0 | 61.8 | 1.8 | 6.4 | 0.0 | 170 |
| 310 and over | 14.0 | 74.5 | 3.2 | 8.3 | 0.0 | 157 |

$$C = .35$$

First as to *Frank,* who scores 311.8 on the five factors which enter into the table predicting behavior in a reformatory, from Table 35 it becomes evident that with this score his chances of not responding well to reformatory treatment are seven and one-half in ten. This prognosis is borne out by the facts. Frank was committed to the Reformatory at the age of twenty-five for larceny on the particular sentence with which we happen to be concerned, remained there for two and one-half years and was altogether a failure during this time. He was extremely difficult to manage throughout his stay and several times feigned attempts at suicide. His excuse for these actions was that "there is no use in living," and similar infantile expressions. He stated he would kill the person responsible for his serving in the Reformatory if he ever got a chance. The psychiatrist at the Reformatory commented that Frank should be permanently segregated.

"Hard-boiled *John*" was committed to the Reformatory at the age of twenty for assault with a revolver. He scores 301.2, which places him in the group of offenders whose chances of not responding well to life in such an institution are six in ten. In view of his high failure expectancy, it does not surprise us to find that John did not prove amenable to the institution régime. He violated rules on an average of once in two and two-thirds months, which is much more frequently than the mean for the men in the institution.[1] His offenses usually consisted in outbreaks of violence, assaulting inmates, and frequent fighting with officials and inmates.

*Armand,* brother of Robert, was committed to the Reformatory at the age of nineteen for burglary. He scores 319.1, which, as in the case of Frank, places him in the group whose likelihood of not adjusting well to life in a reformatory is seven and one-half in ten. He too did not in fact behave well in the institution. He did not, however, prove to be too serious an offender. He committed offenses on the average of once every four months and these were of a relatively minor character, such as talking and "fooling." In connection with this prediction the reader will recall that no differentiation was made in our prediction tables between the commission of serious and the commission of minor offenses in an institution or for that matter during any form of extramural treatment. So fine a distinction in behavior was not possible, in view of the difficulties of reconstructing the behavior history of offenders so many years after the event.[2]

Turning now to Armand's brother, *Robert,* he too was committed to the Re-

---

[1] See *500 Criminal Careers,* page 159.

[2] In a research now under way it will be possible to distinguish between the commission of serious and the commission of minor offenses in institutions, as this is a study of behavior during treatment which is *contemporaneously* recorded. On the basis of this we should be able to prepare

formatory at the age of nineteen for burglary. He scores 322.8 which also places him in the group whose chances of not adjusting well to reformatory life are seven and one-half out of ten; and, as a matter of fact, he too did not behave satisfactorily, although he violated institutional rules only occasionally (on the average of once in seven months). His offenses were gross carelessness, being out of place, malicious mischief, talking, causing disturbance in school, and similar violations of the rules. It will be seen that Robert, like his brother Armand, was really only a minor offender in the institution, however.

*Arthur,* the defective delinquent who during his earlier years was given close supervision by his step-parents but who in later life, particularly following separation from his wife, was left pretty much to his own resources, did not continue in serious criminality; but he did become a burden upon social welfare agencies. He scored 280.3 on the five factors entering into the prediction of behavior in a reformatory. Consultation of Table 35 indicates that Arthur had a fifty-fifty chance of responding well to reformatory treatment. He remained in the Reformatory for sixteen months. He was given some training in the plumbing class and worked in the dining-room. The dining-room official stated that he did not consider "Arthur mentally responsible, but that he does make an honest effort to do the work as well as it should be done. . . . His principal difficulty has been his insistent talking, which it seems impossible for him to stop, and no warnings or repeated reports for this offense seem to have any effect on him." From the plumbing instructor essentially the same size-up of Arthur was made. He considered him a "fair worker with very limited capacity." It is evident from Arthur's entire career that he needed a great deal of supervision and propping. This is naturally more effectively provided in an institutional régime than on the outside. There seems no question that he would get along in a correctional establishment without causing any more difficulty than is likely with his limited mentality and high suggestibility.

*Dennis,* the drug addict, who it will be recalled is in a mental hospital suffering from a drug psychosis, was committed to the Reformatory at the age of twenty-four for breaking and entering. He scores 308.5, which places him in the group who have six chances in ten of not responding well to reformatory control. The record shows that in fact Dennis behaved extremely well in the institution. It should be remembered that but for the fact that he is a drug addict, Dennis cannot really be considered a criminal. Whatever stealing he did was in order to get drugs to feed the habit of which he had become a victim.

prediction tables indicating to a judge and to institution authorities whether a particular delinquent is likely to prove a serious disturbance to the régime or will merely make a minor nuisance of himself. Naturally, "serious" and "minor" misconduct during treatment will have to be carefully defined.

The reader may wish to review the discussion of this case in Chapter II on pages 47 et seq.

Now to the case of *Jack,* who it will be remembered developed into a chronic "drunk" and non-supporter. He was committed to the Reformatory at the age of thirty-one for assault with intent to rob. He scores 322.8, which places him in the group who have seven and one-half chances in ten of not responding well to reformatory life. As could have been forecast, Jack did poorly in the institution. He proved extremely troublesome in the Reformatory school; he committed offenses as often as once in three months, among them being talking, disobedience of orders, and fighting. Although he became more amenable as he grew accustomed to the routine, he attempted to escape shortly before he was to be paroled, was captured, and had his parole postponed.

*Peter* was committed to the Reformatory at the age of eighteen for larceny. He scores 312.2, which likewise places him in the group whose chances of not responding well to life in a reformatory are seven and one-half in ten. He committed offenses there as frequently as once every five weeks, smoking, not keeping his room clean, fighting, talking persistently, causing disturbances, refusing to obey orders, being disorderly, and quarreling.

Finally we come to *Antonio,* the youth who made an excellent adjustment following his release from a second commitment to the Reformatory, where he had learned the trade of an engraver. On the sentence in which we are interested, Antonio was committed at the age of twenty-one for burglary. He scores 288.3, which places him in the group with a fifty-fifty chance of responding well to a reformatory régime; and, as a matter of fact, he did behave satisfactorily in the Reformatory. He proved very industrious and interested in trade training and it was said of him that "he possesses skill and judgment in the work and is capable of making a good engraver." His conduct record in the Reformatory was practically perfect, but it is doubtful whether such would have been the result had Antonio's special ability not been discovered and his energies harnessed to his strong interest in engraving.

## Predicting Behavior in Reformatories at Various Age Levels

Turning, now, to the prediction of the behavior of offenders in reformatories at various age levels, reference to Chapter IX, page 153, will indicate that in adaptation to life in reformatories, the greatest age differentiation occurs (a) under twenty-two years, (b) at twenty-two through twenty-six years, (c) at twenty-seven and older. On the basis of these findings, three tables were therefore constructed, indicating the probable behavior of offenders in reformatories at these separate age levels. Into the first of these, the factors shown in list F have entered.

F. FACTORS PREDICTIVE OF BEHAVIOR IN REFORMATORIES AT 17–21 YEARS

| Prediction factors and sub-categories* | Percentage incidence of failure† |
|---|---|
| Intelligence of offender | |
| Normal | 66.7 (102) |
| Below normal | 77.9 (222) |
| Age at first delinquency | |
| Seventeen and older | 52.8 (53) |
| Fourteen to sixteen | 71.7 (138) |
| Under fourteen | 84.6 (156) |
| Grade attained in school | |
| More than eighth | 53.4 (43) |
| Eighth or less | 77.5 (307) |
| Family relationships | |
| Fair | 63.3 (98) |
| Poor | 77.1 (205) |
| Industrial skill | |
| Skilled | 47.4 (19) |
| Semi-skilled or unskilled | 76.6 (333) |

* Whatever contractions have been made of the original, more detailed, sub-categories of the factors are based on an inspection of the raw tables, from which it could readily be determined which sub-categories to combine.

† The parenthesized figures represent the number of cases on which the particular percentage is based.

Comparing the prognostic picture with what actually occurred in the case of *Arthur*, it is evident from Table 36 that Arthur, whose prediction score for

TABLE 36. BEHAVIOR IN REFORMATORIES AT 17–21 YEARS (262 CASES)

| Failure score | Success | Failure | Number of cases |
|---|---|---|---|
| Under 330 ... | 100.0 | 0.0 | 7 |
| 330–350 ..... | 57.1 | 42.9 | 28 |
| 350–370 ..... | 32.1 | 67.9 | 84 |
| 370–380 ..... | 23.8 | 76.2 | 21 |
| 380 and over | 13.9 | 86.1 | 122 |

C = .37

TABLE 37. BEHAVIOR IN REFORMATORIES AT 22–26 YEARS (145 CASES)

| Failure score | Success | Failure | Number of cases |
|---|---|---|---|
| Under 280 ... | 88.9 | 11.1 | 9 |
| 280–300 ..... | 52.2 | 47.8 | 23 |
| 300–330 ..... | 34.4 | 65.6 | 61 |
| 330 and over | 26.9 | 73.1 | 52 |

C = .30

behavior in a reformatory at this age level is 348.1, had almost six chances in ten of responding well to a reformatory régime at this age. It so happens that Arthur's reformatory experience described above is the one which occurred in the age span seventeen to twenty-one. It was seen that on the whole he did behave quite well in the Reformatory.

Into Table 37, from which can be derived the probable behavior of offenders in a reformatory at twenty-two to twenty-six years of age, the five factors presented in list G have entered. From Table 37 it can be determined that an of-

G. FACTORS PREDICTIVE OF BEHAVIOR IN REFORMATORIES AT 22–26 YEARS

| Prediction factors and<br>sub-categories* | Percentage incidence<br>of failure† |
|---|---|
| Delinquency in family | |
| No | 50.0 (42) |
| Yes | 66.1 (127) |
| Broken or inadequate homes | |
| No | 46.7 (45) |
| Yes | 66.2 (63) |
| Occupation of mother | |
| Housewife | 62.6 (147) |
| Worked out | 80.5 (41) |
| Age of offender at first delinquency | |
| Seventeen and older | 44.4 (54) |
| Fourteen to sixteen | 60.5 (81) |
| Under fourteen | 76.0 (75) |
| Intelligence of offender | |
| Normal | 46.2 (52) |
| Below normal | 69.6 (141) |

* Whatever contractions have been made of the original, more detailed, sub-categories of the factors are based on an inspection of the raw tables, from which it could readily be determined which sub-categories to combine.

† The parenthesized figures represent the number of cases on which the particular percentage is based.

fender scoring under 280 has about nine in ten chances of responding well to a reformatory régime during this particular age span; but if he scores 330 and over he has over seven in ten chances of failing. *Dennis,* the drug addict, at present confined in a mental hospital suffering from a psychosis due to drugs, was committed to the Reformatory at the age of twenty-four. His prediction score is 285.5. Consultation of Table 37 indicates a slightly higher than fifty-fifty chance of his adjusting well to a reformatory régime. Actually Dennis did behave satisfactorily during the entire year that he was confined in the Reformatory. He was again committed at the age of twenty-seven and again his behavior was excellent.

The factors entering into the table predicting behavior in a reformatory at the age of twenty-seven or more are shown in list H. From Table 38 it is evident that a person scoring under 160 is very likely to respond successfully to a reformatory régime, while one scoring 160 and over has four in ten chances of not behaving well in reformatories. Let us revert to the case of *Dennis,* whose score for behavior in a reformatory at this particular age span is 221.4. This gives him a six in ten chance of responding well to a reformatory régime; and actually Dennis, who was again committed to a reformatory at the age of twenty-eight, and once more at the age of thirty, behaved exceedingly well on both these occasions.

H. FACTORS PREDICTIVE OF BEHAVIOR IN REFORMATORIES
AT 27 YEARS AND OLDER

| Prediction factors and sub-categories* | Percentage incidence of failure† |
|---|---|
| Education of parents | |
| One or both parents attended common school .................. | 15.4 (13) |
| Both parents without formal education ....................... | 42.5 (66) |
| Economic status of parents | |
| Comfortable ............................................... | 30.0 (30) |
| Dependent or marginal .................................... | 46.9 (49) |
| Work habits | |
| Good .................................................... | 25.0 (16) |
| Fair or poor ............................................. | 44.2 (52) |
| Economic responsibility | |
| Fair .................................................... | 26.7 (15) |
| Poor .................................................... | 46.4 (56) |
| Use of leisure | |
| Negative ............................................... | 0.0 (3) |
| Harmful ............................................... | 41.5 (82) |

* Whatever contractions have been made of the original, more detailed, sub-categories of the factors are based on an inspection of the raw tables, from which it could readily be determined which sub-categories to combine.

† The parenthesized figures represent the number of cases on which the particular percentage is based.

TABLE 38. BEHAVIOR IN REFORMATORIES
AT 27 YEARS AND OLDER (58 CASES)

| Failure score | Success | Failure | Number of cases |
|---|---|---|---|
| Under 160 ........... | 100.0 | 0.0 | 4 |
| 160 and over ......... | 59.3 | 40.7 | 54 |

C = .20

## Predicting Behavior in Prisons

The five factors on the basis of which a prediction table has been constructed indicating probable behavior in prisons have been listed (I). From Table 39

TABLE 39. BEHAVIOR IN PRISONS (108 CASES)

| Failure score | Always succeeds | Always fails | Early success, later failure | Early failure, later success | Erratic | Number of cases |
|---|---|---|---|---|---|---|
| Under 110 ........ | 84.6 | 7.7 | 0.0 | 7.7 | 0.0 | 13 |
| 110–130 ......... | 61.2 | 14.3 | 2.0 | 20.5 | 2.0 | 49 |
| 130–150 ......... | 43.6 | 35.9 | 5.1 | 15.4 | 0.0 | 39 |
| 150 and over ..... | 0.0 | 71.4 | 0.0 | 28.6 | 0.0 | 7 |

C = .42

I. FACTORS PREDICTIVE OF BEHAVIOR IN PRISONS

| Prediction factors and sub-categories* | Percentage incidence of failure† |
|---|---|
| Nativity of parents and offender | |
| All native | 19.5 (36) |
| One or both parents foreign, son native | 25.4 (67) |
| All foreign | 35.3 (17) |
| Education of parents | |
| One or both parents common school | 11.1 (18) |
| Both parents without formal education | 26.7 (101) |
| Broken or inadequate homes | |
| Homes broken or inadequate | 23.2 (99) |
| Homes not broken or inadequate | 34.8 (23) |
| Intelligence | |
| Normal or dull | 18.8 (69) |
| Borderline or feebleminded | 36.7 (49) |
| Age at first delinquency | |
| Seventeen and over | 9.1 (11) |
| Under seventeen | 27.6 (112) |

* Whatever contractions have been made of the original, more detailed, sub-categories of the factors are based on an inspection of the raw tables, from which it could readily be determined which sub-categories to combine.

† The parenthesized figures represent the number of cases on which the particular percentage is based.

it would be evident to a judge that an offender scoring under 110 has eight and one-half in ten chances of behaving well in prisons; while if he scores 150 and over his chances of not getting along acceptably in prisons is seven in ten. "Hard-boiled *John*" scores 151.2 for behavior in prisons, which places him in the latter group. Actually, he did have a very bad record in prison. He himself admitted that "I have one of the worst 'reps' in here." He made frequent attempts to escape and actually spent five out of ten years in prison in solitary confinement because of his recalcitrance.

## Predicting Behavior in Prisons at Various Age Levels

As to the age factor in tables indicating behavior in prison, the reader, by consulting Chapter IX, page 153, will see that the most clear-cut differentiation in behavior in prison occurs at the age levels (a) under twenty-seven, (b) at twenty-seven to thirty-one, (c) at thirty-two to thirty-six, (d) at thirty-seven and over.

The five factors entering into the table indicating the behavior of offenders in prison under twenty-seven years of age have been listed (J). From Table 40 it will be seen that *John,* for example, whose chances of always failing in prison were seven in ten, shows with a score of 280.3 almost eight and one-half chances in ten of not responding well to a prison régime when under twenty-

J. FACTORS PREDICTIVE OF BEHAVIOR IN PRISONS UNDER 27 YEARS

| *Prediction factors and sub-categories** | *Percentage incidence of failure†* |
|---|---|
| Education of parents | |
| One or both parents attended common school ................. | 25.0 (12) |
| Both parents without formal education ...................... | 56.3 (48) |
| Intelligence of offender | |
| Normal or dull ......................................... | 44.1 (34) |
| Borderline or feebleminded .............................. | 58.3 (24) |
| Broken or inadequate homes | |
| Broken or inadequate ................................... | 44.0 (50) |
| Not broken or inadequate ............................... | 72.7 (11) |
| Age at first delinquency | |
| Eleven and older ....................................... | 46.4 (56) |
| Under eleven .......................................... | 66.7 (6) |
| Industrial skill | |
| Skilled ............................................... | 0.0 (2) |
| Semi-skilled or unskilled ................................ | 46.6 (60) |

\* Whatever contractions have been made of the original, more detailed, sub-categories of the factors are based on an inspection of the raw tables, from which it could readily be determined which sub-categories to combine.

† The parenthesized figures represent the number of cases on which the particular percentage is based.

seven. Actually, he was committed to prison at the age of twenty-four and his conduct was consistently poor.

The five factors entering into the construction of the table predicting behavior in prison in the age span twenty-seven to thirty-one are shown in list K.

TABLE 40. BEHAVIOR IN PRISONS UNDER 27 YEARS (57 CASES)

| *Failure score* | *Success* | *Failure* | *Number of cases* |
|---|---|---|---|
| Under 220 ... | 100.0 | 0.0 | 4 |
| 220–230 ..... | 80.0 | 20.0 | 5 |
| 230–270 ..... | 47.5 | 52.5 | 40 |
| 270–290 ..... | 16.7 | 83.3 | 6 |
| 290 and over | 0.0 | 100.0 | 2 |
| | | C = .39 | |

TABLE 41. BEHAVIOR IN PRISONS AT 27–31 YEARS (44 CASES)

| *Failure score* | *Success* | *Failure* | *Number of cases* |
|---|---|---|---|
| Under 200 ... | 83.3 | 16.7 | 12 |
| 200 and over | 43.8 | 56.2 | 32 |
| | | C = .33 | |

Again using the case of *John* as an illustration, his chances of good behavior in prison during this age span, as indicated in Table 41, were greater than in the previous age span (his score is 232.4). John was in prison from the age of twenty-four to thirty-five. Actually he got along quite well until his twenty-ninth year and then made several attempts to escape.

Turning now to the table predicting behavior in prison at the age span thirty-two to thirty-six, the five factors entering into the construction of this table are shown in list L. From Table 42 it is evident that an offender scoring

### K. FACTORS PREDICTIVE OF BEHAVIOR IN PRISONS AT 27–31 YEARS

| Prediction factors and sub-categories* | Percentage incidence of failure† |
|---|---|
| Nativity of parents and offender | |
| All native | 33.3 (18) |
| One or both parents foreign, son native | 42.3 (26) |
| All foreign born | 57.1 (7) |
| Education of parents | |
| At least common school | 11.1 (9) |
| No schooling | 46.5 (43) |
| Conjugal relations of parents | |
| Poor | 20.0 (10) |
| Good or fair | 46.1 (39) |
| Number of siblings | |
| Only child | 16.7 (6) |
| One or more siblings | 42.5 (47) |
| Intelligence of offender | |
| Normal or dull | 32.2 (31) |
| Borderline or feebleminded | 55.0 (20) |

\* Whatever contractions have been made of the original, more detailed, sub-categories of the factors are based on an inspection of the raw tables, from which it could readily be determined which sub-categories to combine.

† The parenthesized figures represent the number of cases on which the particular percentage is based.

### L. FACTORS PREDICTIVE OF BEHAVIOR IN PRISONS AT 32–36 YEARS

| Prediction factors and sub-categories* | Percentage incidence of failure† |
|---|---|
| Number of siblings | |
| None | 0.0 (4) |
| One or more siblings | 33.3 (36) |
| Intelligence of offender | |
| Normal or dull | 12.0 (25) |
| Borderline or feebleminded | 58.0 (17) |
| Grade attained in school | |
| Beyond eighth grade | 0.0 (10) |
| Sixth, seventh, eighth grade | 31.6 (19) |
| Less than sixth grade | 50.0 (12) |
| Conjugal relations of parents | |
| Poor | 0.0 (8) |
| Good or fair | 40.6 (32) |
| Broken or inadequate homes in childhood | |
| Yes | 22.5 (17) |
| No | 50.0 (22) |

\* Whatever contractions have been made of the original, more detailed, sub-categories of the factors are based on an inspection of the raw tables, from which it could readily be determined which sub-categories to combine.

† The parenthesized figures represent the number of cases on which the particular percentage is based.

| TABLE 42. BEHAVIOR IN PRISONS AT 32–36 YEARS (35 CASES) | | | |
|---|---|---|---|
| Failure score | Success | Failure | Number of cases |
| Under 180 ... | 90.0 | 10.0 | 22 |
| 180–210 ..... | 44.5 | 55.5 | 9 |
| 210 and over | 0.0 | 100.0 | 4 |
| | C = .57 | | |

| TABLE 43. BEHAVIOR IN PRISONS AT 37 YEARS AND OLDER (39 CASES) | | | |
|---|---|---|---|
| Failure score | Success | Failure | Number of cases |
| Under 120 ... | 92.6 | 7.4 | 27 |
| 120–140 ..... | 54.5 | 45.5 | 11 |
| 140 and over | 0.0 | 100.0 | 1 |
| | C = .47 | | |

under 180 has nine in ten chances of responding well to the prison régime in this age span, while if he scores 210 and over there is every likelihood that he will not respond well. The score of *John* for behavior in prison at this age is 231.9, and this indicates that his likelihood of failure was very great. He was in prison during these years and we know that he made numerous attempts to escape and had to be placed in solitary confinement.

Finally, the factors entering into the prediction of behavior in prison at thirty-seven and older have been listed (M). From Table 43 it is evident that

#### M. FACTORS PREDICTIVE OF BEHAVIOR IN PRISONS AT 37 YEARS AND OLDER

| Prediction factors and sub-categories* | Percentage incidence of failure† |
|---|---|
| Rank of offender among siblings | |
| Only child ............................................... | 0.0 (3) |
| First child ............................................... | 12.5 (8) |
| Second or later in rank .................................. | 27.6 (29) |
| Intelligence of offender | |
| Normal or dull ......................................... | 12.0 (25) |
| Borderline or feebleminded ............................. | 40.0 (15) |
| Grade attained in school | |
| Ninth or higher ........................................ | 0.0 (6) |
| Less than ninth grade .................................. | 24.2 (33) |
| Age at first delinquency | |
| Seventeen and older .................................... | 0.0 (4) |
| Under seventeen ....................................... | 25.7 (35) |
| Industrial skill | |
| Semi-skilled or unskilled ................................ | 18.9 (37) |
| Skilled ................................................. | 66.7 (3) |

* Whatever contractions have been made of the original, more detailed, sub-categories of the factors are based on an inspection of the raw tables, from which it could readily be determined which sub-categories to combine.

† The parenthesized figures represent the number of cases on which the particular percentage is based.

an offender scoring under 120 has nine in ten chances of responding well to life in prison while the chances of failure for an offender scoring 140 and over are extremely high.

## Predicting Behavior in Jails

Jails and houses of correction are institutions for short-term offenders and their régimes are generally more lax than those provided in correctional schools, reformatories, or prisons. Often little supervision or training of any kind is given to inmates. It is a fact that certain types of offenders get along more satisfactorily under this lack of restraint within walls than under a régime which subjects them to a strict routine. Into Table 44, predicting behavior in jails, *regardless of age,* the five factors listed (N) have entered.

### N. FACTORS PREDICTIVE OF BEHAVIOR IN JAILS

| Prediction factors and sub-categories* | Percentage incidence of failure† |
|---|---|
| Nativity of parents and offender | |
| Son foreign, both parents foreign | 18.5 (27) |
| Son native, both parents native | 22.5 (49) |
| One or both parents foreign, son native | 30.8 (78) |
| Usual economic status of parents | |
| Dependent or marginal | 19.4 (103) |
| Comfortable | 35.6 (45) |
| Rank of offender | |
| Second or higher in rank | 20.2 (104) |
| Only child or first child | 33.3 (51) |
| Grade attained in school | |
| Eighth grade or lower | 23.5 (141) |
| Beyond eighth grade | 50.0 (20) |
| Age began work | |
| Under fifteen | 15.6 (64) |
| Fifteen and over | 29.9 (97) |

\* Whatever contractions have been made of the original, more detailed, sub-categories of the factors are based on an inspection of the raw tables, from which it could readily be determined which sub-categories to combine.

† The parenthesized figures represent the number of cases on which the particular percentage is based.

### TABLE 44. BEHAVIOR IN JAILS (134 CASES)

| Failure score | Always succeeds | Always fails | Early success, later failure | Early failure, later success | Erratic | Number of cases |
|---|---|---|---|---|---|---|
| Under 120 | 75.0 | 12.5 | 7.1 | 3.6 | 1.8 | 56 |
| 120–140 | 66.0 | 22.6 | 1.9 | 3.8 | 5.7 | 53 |
| 140 and over | 36.0 | 52.0 | 0.0 | 12.0 | 0.0 | 25 |

$$C = .39$$

*Frank,* for example, scores 136.9 on these five factors. From Table 44 it is evident that this score places him in the group of offenders whose chances of responding well to the régime of jails is six and one-half in ten; and actually, during five jail sentences which he experienced and about which we have any information, Frank did behave well. These commitments occurred at the ages of twenty-three, twenty-four, forty-three, forty-four, and forty-five.

### Predicting Behavior in Jails at Various Age Levels

Turning now to tables predicting behavior in jails at various *age levels,* consultation of Chapter IX, page 153, indicates that the greatest differentiation in response to jail régimes occurs at less than twenty-two years, at twenty-two to twenty-six years, at twenty-seven to thirty-one, at thirty-two to thirty-six, and at thirty-seven or older. On the basis of this finding, a series of tables have been constructed indicating probable behavior in jails at these various age levels. The five factors on which the first is based, behavior when under twenty-two years of age, are given in list O.

O. FACTORS PREDICTIVE OF BEHAVIOR IN JAILS UNDER 22 YEARS

| Prediction factors and sub-categories* | Percentage incidence of failure† |
|---|---|
| Number of siblings | |
| More than two siblings | 42.8 (21) |
| One or two siblings | 57.1 (7) |
| None | 100.0 (2) |
| Broken or inadequate homes | |
| No | 40.0 (5) |
| Yes | 54.1 (24) |
| Grade attained in school | |
| Less than sixth grade | 36.3 (11) |
| Sixth, seventh, eighth grade | 53.8 (13) |
| Beyond eighth grade | 66.6 (6) |
| Age at first delinquency | |
| Under fourteen | 40.0 (15) |
| Fourteen and older | 60.0 (15) |
| Age at leaving home | |
| Fourteen and over | 44.4 (18) |
| Under fourteen | 63.6 (11) |

* Whatever contractions have been made of the original, more detailed, sub-categories of the factors are based on an inspection of the raw tables, from which it could readily be determined which sub-categories to combine.

† The parenthesized figures represent the number of cases on which the particular percentage is based.

From Table 45 it becomes evident that an offender scoring under 240 has six in ten chances of responding well to life in jails, but if he scores 270 and over his chances of good adjustment are practically nil.

Into the table indicating probable behavior of offenders in jail during the age span twenty-two to twenty-six years, the five factors listed in P have entered. From Table 46 it will be seen that an offender scoring under 180 has

TABLE 45. BEHAVIOR IN JAILS UNDER
22 YEARS (26 CASES)

| Failure score | Success | Failure | Number of cases |
|---|---|---|---|
| Under 240 .......... | 60.0 | 40.0 | 10 |
| 240–270 ............. | 46.2 | 53.8 | 13 |
| 270 and over .......... | 0.0 | 100.0 | 3 |

C = .33

P. FACTORS PREDICTIVE OF BEHAVIOR IN JAILS AT 22–26 YEARS

| Prediction factors and sub-categories* | Percentage incidence of failure† |
|---|---|
| Number of siblings | |
| None ..................................................... | 0.0 (2) |
| One or more ............................................. | 35.7 (56) |
| Economic condition in childhood | |
| Dependent .............................................. | 21.0 (14) |
| Marginal ............................................... | 31.0 (29) |
| Comfortable ............................................ | 50.0 (12) |
| Mobility | |
| Not excessive .......................................... | 31.6 (38) |
| Excessive .............................................. | 55.0 (20) |
| Age began work | |
| Under fifteen .......................................... | 17.4 (23) |
| Fifteen and over ....................................... | 47.2 (36) |
| Industrial skill | |
| Skilled ................................................ | 0.0 (2) |
| Semi-skilled ........................................... | 26.3 (19) |
| Unskilled .............................................. | 45.0 (40) |

* Whatever contractions have been made of the original, more detailed, sub-categories of the factors are based on an inspection of the raw tables, from which it could readily be determined which sub-categories to combine.

† The parenthesized figures represent the number of cases on which the particular percentage is based.

nine and one-half chances in ten of responding well to the régime of jails in the age span twenty-two to twenty-six; but if he scores 180 and over his likelihood of good adjustment is only four and one-half out of ten.

The five factors which have entered into a table predicting the behavior of offenders in jails during the age span twenty-seven to thirty-one have been listed (Q).

An illustration of the value of the prediction table may be given from one of the cases described in Chapter II, that of *Robert* who, it will be remembered, eventually reformed at the age of thirty-seven. Robert's prediction score for behavior in jail during the age span twenty-seven to thirty-one is 229.8. Con-

Q. FACTORS PREDICTIVE OF BEHAVIOR IN JAILS AT 27–31 YEARS

| Prediction factors and sub-categories* | Percentage incidence of failure† |
|---|---|
| Number of siblings | |
| None | 0.0 (1) |
| One or more | 45.7 (59) |
| Intelligence of offender | |
| Normal | 23.5 (17) |
| Below normal | 54.4 (44) |
| Economic status of childhood home | |
| Dependent or marginal | 40.8 (44) |
| Comfortable | 58.8 (17) |
| Age began work | |
| Under fifteen | 33.3 (30) |
| Fifteen and over | 58.1 (31) |
| Industrial skill | |
| Skilled | 0.0 (3) |
| Semi-skilled | 33.3 (24) |
| Unskilled | 55.6 (36) |

* Whatever contractions have been made of the original, more detailed, sub-categories of the factors are based on an inspection of the raw tables, from which it could readily be determined which sub-categories to combine.

† The parenthesized figures represent the number of cases on which the particular percentage is based.

sultation of Table 47 places Robert in the group who have five and one-half chances in ten of responding satisfactorily to the régime of jails in this age span. Actually Robert was committed to jail at the age of twenty-seven and again at the age of twenty-eight. In both instances his behavior was good, and this despite the fact that, as has already been revealed through his other prediction scores, he did not respond well to life in reformatories nor under any types of extramural treatment.

Turning next to a table indicating the probable behavior of offenders in jail in the age span thirty-two to thirty-six, the five factors in list R have entered into the construction of such a table. From Table 48 it would be evident to a judge that an offender scoring under 130 on these five factors has every likelihood of behaving well in jails, while if he scores 150 and over his chances of not re-

TABLE 46. BEHAVIOR IN JAILS AT 22–26 YEARS (52 CASES)

| Failure score | Success | Failure | Number of cases |
|---|---|---|---|
| Under 180 ... | 95.8 | 4.2 | 24 |
| 180 and over | 46.4 | 53.6 | 28 |

C = .47

TABLE 47. BEHAVIOR IN JAILS AT 27–31 YEARS (48 CASES)

| Failure score | Success | Failure | Number of cases |
|---|---|---|---|
| Under 200 ... | 100.0 | 0.0 | 10 |
| 200–230 ..... | 54.2 | 45.8 | 24 |
| 230 and over | 33.3 | 66.7 | 14 |

C = .41

### R. FACTORS PREDICTIVE OF BEHAVIOR IN JAILS AT 32–36 YEARS

| Prediction factors and sub-categories* | Percentage incidence of failure† |
|---|---|
| **Conjugal relations of parents** | |
| Fair or poor | 0.0 (18) |
| Good | 39.3 (28) |
| **Broken or inadequate homes** | |
| Broken homes | 15.4 (26) |
| Not broken but otherwise inadequate | 25.0 (16) |
| Neither | 44.4 (9) |
| **School misconduct** | |
| Yes | 26.3 (19) |
| No | 66.7 (3) |
| **Industrial skill** | |
| Skilled | 0.0 (1) |
| Semi-skilled | 11.8 (17) |
| Unskilled | 29.4 (34) |
| **Mental disease or distortion** | |
| No | 13.3 (15) |
| Yes | 33.3 (27) |

* Whatever contractions have been made of the original, more detailed, sub-categories of the factors are based on an inspection of the raw tables, from which it could readily be determined which sub-categories to combine.

† The parenthesized figures represent the number of cases on which the particular percentage is based.

### S. FACTORS PREDICTIVE OF BEHAVIOR IN JAILS OVER 36 YEARS

| Prediction factors and sub-categories* | Percentage incidence of failure† |
|---|---|
| **Intelligence** | |
| Normal | 6.3 (16) |
| Below normal | 17.0 (41) |
| **Age at first delinquency** | |
| Under eleven | 0.0 (5) |
| Eleven and older | 12.9 (54) |
| **School retardation** | |
| None | 0.0 (4) |
| Retarded year or more | 17.7 (45) |
| **School misconduct** | |
| None | 0.0 (3) |
| Truancy or other misconduct | 10.0 (20) |
| **Mobility** | |
| None | 6.1 (33) |
| Yes | 22.2 (27) |

* Whatever contractions have been made of the original, more detailed, sub-categories of the factors are based on an inspection of the raw tables, from which it could readily be determined which sub-categories to combine.

† The parenthesized figures represent the number of cases on which the particular percentage is based.

| TABLE 48. BEHAVIOR IN JAILS AT 32–36 YEARS (16 CASES) | | | |
|---|---|---|---|
| Failure score | Success | Failure | Number of cases |
| Under 130 ... | 100.0 | 0.0 | 9 |
| 130–150 ..... | 33.3 | 66.7 | 3 |
| 150 and over | 25.0 | 75.0 | 4 |
| | C = .61 | | |

| TABLE 49. BEHAVIOR IN JAILS AT 37 YEARS AND OLDER (21 CASES) | | | |
|---|---|---|---|
| Failure score | Success | Failure | Number of cases |
| Under 60 ... | 100.0 | 0.0 | 7 |
| 60–70 ....... | 90.0 | 10.0 | 10 |
| 70 and over .. | 75.0 | 25.0 | 4 |
| | C = .28 | | |

sponding well to a jail régime are seven and one-half in ten. Unfortunately no one of our nine offenders was in jail in the 32–36 year span and we therefore cannot illustrate the use of this table.

Finally, a table indicating probable behavior of offenders in jail at the age of over thirty-six has been constructed from the five factors listed (S).

An illustration of the use of Table 49 can be given from the case of *Frank,* whose jail score for the age span of thirty-six or over is 66.9. This places him in the group who have nine in ten chances of responding satisfactorily to life in jails. Actually Frank, who it will be remembered was sent in and out of mental hospitals and did not respond to any of the treatment to which he was subjected except the free and easy routine of jails, was committed to jail at the age of forty-three and again at the ages of forty-four and forty-five, and in each instance responded satisfactorily.

## Predicting Behavior in the Army and Navy

It will be recalled that in *Juvenile Delinquents Grown Up,* in which a series of prediction tables was presented indicating the behavior of offenders during various forms of peno-correctional treatment without regard to age, a table was also set out which showed their probable behavior in the Army or Navy. Response of offenders to service in the Army or Navy has been included in our works because we have noted in these researches that certain offenders who did not get along well during various peno-correctional régimes nevertheless responded very satisfactorily to the Army or Navy régime. This finding aroused our curiosity, and we determined to study the response of offenders to this type of routine somewhat more closely, because it is possible that from this we may eventually learn something about needed modifications in peno-correctional régimes in order to meet the requirements of certain types of delinquents. We have not deliberately sought this opportunity to study the behavior of offenders in the Army or Navy, but in view of the fact that a considerable number of our men have been in the armed services at one time or another, and we have been able to secure authoritative information about their behavior during these periods, we could not let the opportunity pass to construct prediction tables.

The five factors entering into the prediction of behavior in the Army or Navy *regardless of age* are shown in list T. From Table 50 it is evident, for

#### T. FACTORS PREDICTIVE OF BEHAVIOR IN ARMY AND NAVY

| Prediction factors and sub-categories* | Percentage incidence of failure† |
|---|---|
| Education of parents | |
| Both without formal education ............................ | 37.1 (124) |
| One or both had at least common school education .............. | 66.7 (15) |
| Intelligence of offender | |
| Normal or superior ...................................... | 29.3 (41) |
| Dull, borderline, or feebleminded ......................... | 44.0 (93) |
| Age at first delinquency | |
| Seventeen and older ..................................... | 21.4 (28) |
| Eleven through sixteen .................................. | 41.3 (92) |
| Under eleven .......................................... | 66.7 (18) |
| Age began work | |
| Under fifteen .......................................... | 31.1 (61) |
| Fifteen and over ....................................... | 47.3 (74) |
| Industrial skill | |
| Skilled ............................................... | 0.0 (9) |
| Semi-skilled .......................................... | 34.0 (50) |
| Unskilled ............................................. | 49.4 (81) |

* Whatever contractions have been made of the original, more detailed, sub-categories of the factors are based on an inspection of the raw tables, from which it could readily be determined which sub-categories to combine.
† The parenthesized figures represent the number of cases on which the particular percentage is based.

example, that an offender scoring under 180 has eight in ten chances of always responding well to life in the Army or Navy, while if he scores 220 and over his likelihood of not doing well under such a régime is very high. Let us turn to the case of *Robert* for an illustration of the application of Table 50. For behavior in the Army or Navy, Robert's score is 202.9, which places him in the group of offenders with three and one-half chances of always behaving

#### TABLE 50. BEHAVIOR IN ARMY OR NAVY (131 CASES)

| Failure score | Always succeeds | Always fails | Early success, later failure | Early failure, later success | Erratic | Number of cases |
|---|---|---|---|---|---|---|
| Under 180 ....... | 82.6 | 8.6 | 4.4 | 0.0 | 4.4 | 23 |
| 180–190 ......... | 57.7 | 26.9 | 11.5 | 3.9 | 0.0 | 26 |
| 190–220 ......... | 37.1 | 46.8 | 14.5 | 1.6 | 0.0 | 62 |
| 220 and over ..... | 30.0 | 60.0 | 10.0 | 0.0 | 0.0 | 20 |

$$C = .47$$

well in the Army or Navy, one and one-half of succeeding at first and later failing, and four and one-half of not responding well at all to Army or Navy life. Before proceeding further to the analysis of what actually happened to him, let us consider the prediction tables indicating probable behavior of offenders in the Army or Navy at various age spans.

### Predicting Behavior in the Army and Navy at Various Age Levels

It will be recalled (Chapter IX, page 153) that the greatest differentiation in response to the Army or Navy régime occurs at the age span under twenty-two and twenty-two or over. On the basis of this finding tables were constructed; the five factors in list X entered into Table 51 indicating behavior of offenders in the Army or Navy when under twenty-two.

X. FACTORS PREDICTIVE OF BEHAVIOR IN ARMY AND NAVY UNDER 22 YEARS

| Prediction factors and sub-categories* | Percentage incidence of failure† |
|---|---|
| Economic status of parents | |
| Dependent or marginal | 52.3 (42) |
| Comfortable | 77.8 (9) |
| Conjugal relations of parents | |
| Good | 48.4 (31) |
| Fair or poor | 66.6 (21) |
| Number of siblings | |
| One or more | 52.2 (46) |
| None | 90.0 (10) |
| Grade attained in school | |
| Eighth grade or less | 56.8 (51) |
| Beyond eighth grade | 100.0 (5) |
| Industrial skill | |
| Skilled | 0.0 (1) |
| Semi-skilled | 50.0 (20) |
| Unskilled | 69.4 (36) |

* Whatever contractions have been made of the original, more detailed, sub-categories of the factors are based on an inspection of the raw tables, from which it could readily be determined which sub-categories to combine.

† The parenthesized figures represent the number of cases on which the particular percentage is based.

From Table 51 it is evident that an offender scoring under 270 on these five factors has eight in ten chances of getting on satisfactorily in the Army or Navy, while one scoring 280 and over has eight in ten chances of not responding well. *Robert's* score for behavior in the Army or Navy in this age span is 307.3, which indicates eight in ten chances of failure. Again, before commenting further about Robert's behavior in the Army, let us proceed with the table showing probable behavior of offenders at twenty-two or over.

The five factors entering into the construction of Table 52 are presented in

<table>
<tr><td colspan="4">TABLE 51. BEHAVIOR IN ARMY OR NAVY UNDER 22 YEARS (50 CASES)</td></tr>
</table>

| Failure score | Success | Failure | Number of cases |
|---|---|---|---|
| Under 270 ... | 81.8 | 18.2 | 11 |
| 270–280 ..... | 63.6 | 36.4 | 11 |
| 280 and over | 21.4 | 78.6 | 28 |

C = .47

TABLE 52. BEHAVIOR IN ARMY OR NAVY AT 22 YEARS AND OLDER (73 CASES)

| Failure score | Success | Failure | Number of cases |
|---|---|---|---|
| Under 170 ... | 100.0 | 0.0 | 2 |
| 170–200 ..... | 74.1 | 25.9 | 27 |
| 200–230 ..... | 48.6 | 51.4 | 25 |
| 230 and over | 22.2 | 77.8 | 9 |

C = .35

list Y. From Table 52 it will be seen that an offender scoring under 170 is very likely to respond well to life in the Army or Navy, while if he scores 230 and over his chances are eight in ten of failure. For behavior in the Army or Navy in the age span of twenty-two or older, *Robert* scores 221.3. This places him in the group which has a slightly higher chance of failure than of success.

Y. FACTORS PREDICTIVE OF BEHAVIOR IN ARMY AND NAVY OVER 22 YEARS

| Prediction factors and sub-categories* | Percentage incidence of failure† |
|---|---|
| Nativity | |
| Foreign born | 18.2 (11) |
| Native born | 44.6 (74) |
| Economic status of parents | |
| Dependent | 33.3 (18) |
| Marginal or comfortable | 43.5 (62) |
| Conjugal relations of parents | |
| Poor | 24.0 (25) |
| Good or fair | 50.9 (53) |
| Broken or inadequate homes | |
| Broken homes | 36.5 (52) |
| Homes not broken but otherwise inadequate | 43.8 (16) |
| Homes not broken or inadequate | 60.0 (15) |
| Industrial skill | |
| Skilled | 16.7 (6) |
| Semi-skilled | 38.7 (31) |
| Unskilled | 45.8 (48) |

* Whatever contractions have been made of the original, more detailed, sub-categories of the factors are based on an inspection of the raw tables, from which it could readily be determined which sub-categories to combine.

† The parenthesized figures represent the number of cases on which the particular percentage is based.

Consider now what actually happened in Robert's case. He went into the Army at the age of twenty-one, a month after his parole from the Reformatory, spent this entire parole period in the Army, and was honorably discharged. It will be recalled from Table 51 (his score for behavior in the Army or Navy in the age span of under twenty-two was 307.3) that Robert's chances of behaving well in the Army in this age span were only two in ten. Actually, however, he did get along satisfactorily, but this is probably due to the fact that he was on parole at this time and failure to live up to parole conditions might have resulted in return to the Reformatory. Evidently Robert preferred the Army to return to a peno-correctional institution. However, in the next age span Robert, who re-entered the Army at the age of twenty-three and served for two years, scored 221.3, which places him in the group having a fifty-fifty chance of failure (Table 52). On this occasion he was not on parole from any institution and he did not behave well in the Army, for he received a dishonorable discharge. It will be recalled from Table 50 that Robert's overall chances of responding well to life in the Army (with a score of 202.9) were only three and one-half in ten of always succeeding. Actually, he did succeed on the first enlistment (while on parole) and failed during the second while not on parole. (For Robert's behavior on parole, see p. 245.)

*Prediction Method in Action*

Now that we have presented in these three chapters all the tentative prediction tables that have resulted from this particular research and have given illustrations along the way of the application of almost every table, it might be well to indicate with one illustration the reasoning that would be used by a judge availing himself of prognostic aids in determining what disposition to make of a particular case. Let us turn for such an illustration to the case of *Robert* who has already been mentioned on several occasions throughout these three chapters. Robert was first arrested at the age of seventeen for larceny. The question before the judge at this stage would be, "What disposition shall I make of Robert? What treatment is likely to prove the most effective in his case?" He would then reason, "First of all I want to know what his chances are for reformation altogether." To answer this query he would ask his probation officer to secure the necessary information and compute the score on the five factors entering into the construction of Table 18. On these Robert would be found to score 167.4, which places him in the group who have three and one-half in ten chances of remaining serious offenders, two chances in ten of becoming law violators, three and one-half chances in ten of reforming entirely and one chance in ten of lapsing temporarily into criminality after a long period of non-delinquency.

The next question which the judge would ask himself is this: "If Robert should become a minor offender or should reform entirely, at what age is this likely to occur?" Consultation of Tables 19 and 20 would indicate that a youth scoring 167.4 has eight in ten chances of becoming a minor offender at the age of twenty-seven or older, and a similar chance should he reform, of doing so in this age span rather than when younger. Since Robert is only seventeen as he stands before the judge, this means that for roughly ten years he will certainly require close supervision.

The next question which the judge would ask himself is, whether, in view of these facts, extramural peno-correctional treatment should be applied (probation or probation under suspended sentence), or some form of intramural peno-correctional control. He would therefore ask his probation officer to secure information on the five factors necessary for determining Robert's score with respect to behavior during extramural peno-correctional treatment (the factors entering into the construction of Table 21), as well as the factors reflecting the score for behavior during intramural peno-correctional treatment (those on which Table 31 is based). Robert's score for behavior during extramural treatment is 325.9, which places him in the group whose chances of always behaving well while under supervision outside of institutions are practically nil while his chances of always failing during such extramural treatment are as much as eight in ten. But Robert's score for *intramural* treatment, which is 184.6, places him in the group who have two and one-half chances in ten of always behaving well thereunder, three chances in ten of always failing, and two and one-half chances in ten of not doing well at first but adjusting eventually (see Table 31). The judge would now have a means of comparing Robert's probable behavior during extramural treatment with his expected behavior during intramural treatment and he would clearly see that institutional control is indicated for Robert, because the youth has only three chances in ten of always failing during intramural treatment but eight in ten of always failing during extramural. Therefore, the judge's search for a form of treatment most suitable for Robert would now be narrowed down to intramural peno-correctional treatment.

The judge would next be concerned with selecting the specific kind of institution best suited to offenders of the type represented by Robert. Since Robert is seventeen, he is clearly too old for a correctional school and too young for a prison or jail. Therefore, the judge would have no choice, within the present limitations of institutional treatment, except to place him in a reformatory. He would, however, bear in mind the fact that Robert's chances of good behavior during extramural treatment, including *parole,* are low. In the light of such information, he would impose a longer, rather than a shorter, sentence on Robert, remembering also that his chances of becoming a minor offender or reforming when under twenty-seven are only two in ten.

The reader will be interested to know that instead of being committed to an institution following his first arrest, Robert was placed on probation under suspended sentence and, as might have been expected, he seriously misbehaved, committing burglaries during this time.

*Comment*

In the illustrations given in this and the two prior chapters we have assumed that various statutory limitations upon the exercise of judicial discretion would not tie the hands of the judge in applying prediction tables. Statutes in the different states vary regarding length of different indeterminate sentences, age limitations placed on commitments to various institutions, limitation of certain penal or correctional institutions to persons committing specified crimes, limitation of the right of probation to persons committing certain crimes, and the like. *For a sentencing judge to do effective work, the scope of his discretion must not be too greatly circumscribed.* Given a fair opportunity of choice among alternative forms of peno-correctional treatments and length of such treatments, the modern judge might derive great aid from a reliable system of prediction tables of the kind illustrated.

Without such tables, discretion readily deteriorates into mechanical and superficial practices. For example, the cases of Armand, Robert, and Arthur in Chapter II show how judges fall into the routine of "granting probation" as a "lenient disposition" to first or second offenders, when, in many instances, placing them on probation is not only not justified by the kind of evidence presented above, but constitutes a positive danger to society. Scientific individualization of sentences would not proceed upon any such mechanical rules, but would be based on a careful study of individual cases in the light of the responses to different forms of peno-correctional treatment of hundreds of similar cases in the past. Of course, other facts, in addition to those which enter into prediction scores, have to be taken into account in determining treatment in any individual case, particularly where the alternative treatments indicated by the tables involve the same probabilities of success or failure. However, even if the disposition of offenders were based on the application of the prediction tables alone, the results, from the point of view of protecting society as well as aiding the offender, would in the long run be far better than they are under existing practices.

Let it also be said that the proposed system, whether applied by sentencing judges or parole boards or some new administrative sentencing and paroling body, would not be "treating human beings like numbers." Such a superficial criticism can only be based upon a failure to understand thoroughly the implications of the proposed method. Prognostic tables will not take the place of mature judgment. The scalpel without the trained surgeon may do more harm than good. Prediction tables are suggested as merely one additional aid to those who must exercise discretion in administering criminal justice. Without such a means of bringing to bear on the individual case the systematized experience derived from hundreds of similar cases, even the wisest judge or parole board member must make many mistakes that could be avoided if his judgment were illuminated and supported by the relevant data of experience.

As for criminology generally, the intensive development of prognostic tables would help to make it a more scientific discipline. A well-known criterion of a science is its ability to predict "the shape of things to come" by organized knowledge of the shape of things as they are. If criminologists were to develop further the processes of gathering and verifying relevant information regarding the make-up and background of different kinds of offenders, and to relate such information to accurate check-ups on the behavior of these offenders under different forms of treatment and thereafter, they might some day be justified in dignifying this loose discipline with the name of Science.

# XVII

## SOME IMPLICATIONS OF THE FINDINGS

WE have spanned the careers of five hundred criminals from childhood to middle age, and have had an opportunity to observe the major changes that occurred in their behavior under various kinds of punitive and corrective treatment and with the passing of time. Since this is the second series of offenders who have been traced over so many years,[1] some of the conclusions which follow can now be considered as more than tentative.

Probably the most significant conclusion of this work is, essentially, that it is neither accident, nor the traditionally stressed factors and forces in the criminal law and its administration, that determine the ultimate response of offenders to peno-correctional treatment.

It is no mere accident that some of our youths have settled into a law-abiding life. It is not mere chance that some of them have become minor offenders while others have persisted in serious and aggressive criminalism; or that some reformed permanently while others relapsed into crime. It is not an accident that determined which offenders would respond well to probation under suspended sentence but poorly to "straight" probation. Nor is it chance that dictates whether offenders get along well in jails but not in reformatories; or respond successfully to probation and parole but not to incarceration. Neither can it be contended that accident accounts for the better response of some offenders to peno-correctional treatment in one age span rather than in another.

Nor is it, primarily, the treatment these men received at the hands of the law, specifically the threat of punishment or the kind of sentence that happened to have been imposed under existing practices, that chiefly accounts for either successful response to one form of treatment or another at one age or another, or to ultimate reform or recidivism. Comparison of the characteristics of the reformed and unreformed and of the serious and minor offenders leads to the legitimate inference that the threat of punishment—upon which legislators and judges chiefly rely—apparently plays only a secondary role in bringing about desirable changes in the behavior of criminals. All our offenders were at one time or another during the fifteen-year follow-up period subjected to a more or less equal threat of punishment. Yet the evidence shows that some of them continued, undeterred, upon their aggressive antisocial careers; others

---

[1] The first is reported upon in *Juvenile Delinquents Grown Up*, Commonwealth Fund, New York, 1940, and embraced a series of 1,000 boy delinquents grown to manhood.

settled down to a law-abiding life; still others became minor offenders, such as drunkards, vagrants, non-supporters.

*We are thus led to the conclusion that it is not primarily or fundamentally either chance or the fear of punishment, but rather the presence or absence of certain traits and characteristics in the constitution and early environment of the different offenders, which determines their respective responses to the different forms of treatment and determines, also, what such offenders will ultimately become and what will become of them.* Those who behaved well, either during or after treatment, were, as a class, more favorably endowed by Nature and circumstanced by Nurture than were those who did not respond well.[2]

In view of these findings, it becomes clear that the sentencing process must be transformed into a systematic and informed fitting of offenders to treatment. The different classes of offenders for whom the various existing kinds of social control and peno-correctional treatment are seemingly best suited have been described in detail in the preceding chapters. The prediction tables, as well as illustrative analyses of their possible use have demonstrated that Justice need not be blind in an undesirable sense.

This new approach has great possibilities for experimental penology. It has been shown that in some instances the chances of successful response of an offender to one or another type of treatment are about equally balanced. It is particularly in such cases that the well-informed probation officer, institution worker, or parole agent can exercise his greatest ingenuity in helping the offender across the line into law-abidingness. We have seen, further, that there are certain types of offenders who evidently do not respond satisfactorily to any of the existing forms of treatment. Here again the ingenuity of the penologist[3] has broad scope in developing new kinds of character therapy.

It is well at this point to remind the reader of our cautions in this and other works that these *prediction tables are to be regarded as only illustrative and experimental*. They are not to be put into effect immediately as a basis for general sentencing and parole practices. At the most, they can apply only to groups of offenders that closely resemble ours.[4] The experimental use of our tables

---

[2] We are fortified in these conclusions not only by the two preceding studies of these same men (in *500 Criminal Careers* and *Later Criminal Careers*), but by our two studies of a thousand boy delinquents (*One Thousand Juvenile Delinquents* and *Juvenile Delinquents Grown Up*).

There may, of course, be still other factors than those embraced in this study which were operative in the lives of these men. In a research upon which we are now at work we are investigating more than a hundred possibly influential factors.

[3] Poverty of language induces us to continue to use this word. The official envisaged is really a character therapist.

[4] In *500 Criminal Careers*, p. 286, we said: "In presenting the above illustration of a possible prognostic device to aid the courts, it should be added that we do not propose the immediate adop-

is therefore limited.[5] However, even on a purely illustrative basis they amply justify the conclusion that both the response of different types of offenders to any of the existing kinds of punitive or corrective treatment at any age span, and their ultimate reform or failure to reform within a reasonable time, can be predicted with sufficient accuracy to justify a fundamental change in existing sentencing and releasing procedures.

Books on criminology are full of discussions of "individualization" of punishment.[6] At present this consists largely of a compound of hunches and "experience" of judges and members of parole boards. No doubt, experience in imposing sentence and in releasing offenders has given many a judge and parole official a shrewd insight into the motivations of wrong-doing. However, prediction tables, based as they are on an analysis of the results of treatment, would induce judges and members of parole boards[7] to individualize in terms of *objectified and systematically organized experience*.

Some psychiatrists and social workers, as well as judges and parole board members, strenuously oppose the use of predictive devices on the ground that such instruments would destroy individualization of justice. This objection arises from a not too profound conception of the place and role of such devices. The question is whether it is better for clinical criminologists, judges, and parole board members to rely exclusively on that vague something called

tion of the rates of failure and success given above. It is the idea and the method of prognosis in this field that concerns us, rather than the construction of a failure-rate prognostic table which might be used in the courts of Massachusetts or elsewhere tomorrow."

We are of opinion, however, that our prognostic tables based on a thousand boy delinquents who had appeared in the Boston Juvenile Court are adapted to experimental validation. We are in fact now engaged in the prediction of the future careers of 500 delinquent boys, employing the tables published in *Juvenile Delinquents Grown Up*. On pp. 270–271 of that volume we said: "The construction of predictive tables has advanced to a stage where their careful experimental use in juvenile and adult courts and by parole boards would disclose their practical value in the administration of justice. If every second case appearing before a juvenile court were disposed of with the aid of prognostic tables, and a comparison of follow-up results were made between the offenders dealt with under existing methods and those whose disposal rested essentially on prognostication, a great step forward would be taken in the all-too-slow progress of correctional technique. The prediction tables contained in Chapters XII and XIX might serve as the basis for such an experiment, because they have several unique advantages. In the first place, they are based on a large number of former juvenile delinquents; second, they cover a considerable segment in the life cycle; third, they differentiate outcomes under various types of treatment as well as after the close of treatment."

[5] On the typicality of this group in relation to other reformatory graduates, see *500 Criminal Careers*, pp. 8–11.

[6] The chief impetus to individualization of justice seems to have come from two important pioneer contributions—that of R. Saleilles, *The Individualization of Punishment*, Modern Criminal Science Series No. 4, trans. by R. S. Jastrow (Boston, Little, Brown, 1911), and William Healy, *The Individual Delinquent* (Boston, Little, Brown, 1914).

[7] The Illinois Parole Board employs prognostic tables.

"expert knowledge," or to objectify, organize, and reflect upon their experience so that they can bring it to bear intelligently upon the problem of disposing of the individual case.

By the proper use of such devices, those who are charged with the disposition and treatment of offenders can determine, first, in what manner and to what extent an individual offender resembles hundreds of others who have come and gone before him; secondly, what the results have been in treating such offenders with one kind of correctional instrument or another; thirdly, what remaining, more subtle characteristics, not taken into account in prediction tables, seem to distinguish the individual under consideration from the hundreds of others whom he resembles in other respects; finally, in the light of these data, what form of treatment is indicated in the instant case.

There need be no concern that by such a procedure courts and parole boards would become mere "rubber stamps," or "slot machines," for it is not proposed that judges or members of administrative boards should dispose of their cases by the mere mechanical and routine following of the treatment suggested by prediction tables. Individual differences would still have to be taken into account.[8] But a much more intelligent individualization of correctional treatment should result if the process of distinguishing one offender and one form of treatment from another is grounded in objectified and systematized experience with hundreds of similar cases.

*We have proposed a fundamental change in sentencing and releasing procedures. This change has as its theoretical basis an emphasis upon the corrective aim of the criminal law.* Is this justified by available evidence?

What is the theoretical foundation of existing modes of punishment? Several theories (or rationalizations) of punishment are operative in varying degrees, both in the legislative provision of sentences supposedly appropriate to different kinds and grades of crime and in the imposition of sentences by judges and the enforcement of release procedures by parole boards. Commentators have found it very difficult to work out a rationale of these more or less conflicting theories of retribution, deterrence, prevention, and correction or reformation; or to decide upon the order of their importance in the administration of criminal justice.

The *retributive-expiative* theory still too often dictates the sentence. The old argument that punishment is necessary as a "just retribution" or requital of "wickedness" is considerably weakened by the evidence that the causes of

---

[8] In fact, if certain significant individual differences turned up frequently enough, they would naturally lead to the modification of the tables. The prognostic devices are not to be set up once and for all. Periodically, they would have to be re-examined with a view to finer discriminations and improvement of predictive power.

criminality are numerous and complex rather than that wrong-doing is "caused" by the calculated exercise of a completely "free will." Official social institutions—the criminal law and its peno-correctional instruments—ought in this day no longer to be founded essentially upon a theory of sublimated social vengeance or that "expiative theory" which is the reverse of the shield of retribution. Vengeance is a destructive and short-sighted emotional basis for coping with the biological and social problem of crime. Not only is it the expression of an infantile way of solving problems, but unjust and destructive of the very purpose of protecting society. The official social institutions of criminal law and penal treatment should not be occupied with the futile quest of making the criminal "expiate" his "sins." That is properly the domain of religion. Society's legal institutions are concerned with the utilitarian possibilities of a correctional régime—possibilities founded upon the social purpose of the apparatus of justice; namely, the maintenance of the general security, with as little interference with the individual's rights as a human being as may be necessary for the achievement of that social purpose.

It is sometimes argued that it is "natural" and thus "right and proper" that we "hate the criminal" and show our hatred. But much of our hate-reaction to criminals has been conditioned by education. Men used to hate the insane, and punished them accordingly. To employ as a fundamental basis of a policy of social protection against crime the hatred of those who commit such acts is both uneconomical and unjust. It is uneconomical because, far from the vengeful attitude producing socially desirable results, it has failed throughout to stem the tide of recidivism.[9] It is unjust because every human being in a civilized polity has the right to be considered as such, with his hereditary and acquired weaknesses, as well as his strengths. This is to some extent feasible with modern scientific and quasi-scientific instrumentalities and techniques; but no device yet developed can dive into the heart and mind of an individual offender and come up with that exact apportionment of blame and blamelessness which even a rationalized vengeance, called "solemn justice," demands as a prerequisite to castigation.[10]

[9] Our various researches have amply revealed the high incidence of recidivism. Further, it is a well-known phenomenon that when punishment becomes so severe as to suggest the revenge motif rather than a deterrent aim or the idea of social protection, juries are loath to convict and the law tends to defeat its own purpose, a fact indicated by the ineffective administration of various "fourth offender" statutes.

[10] The attitude we are discussing may also be conceived of as a rationalization of something which is psychologically more profound. To one unfamiliar with the data of psychoanalytic psychology the following analysis of this attitude will doubtless be a surprise, but there is not a little truth in the statement of the late dean of American psychiatrists:

"The criminal [says Dr. William A. White] becomes the handy scapegoat upon which he [the ordinary citizen] can transfer his feeling of his own tendency to sinfulness and thus by punishing

Reformers of the administration of criminal justice must, however, be realistic. Public opinion is not yet ready to abandon the retributive-expiative theory as one of the bases of penal policy. Certain revolting crimes give rise spontaneously to the demand for vengeance. The retributive-expiative attitude is deeply rooted in primitive emotions of fear and anger; and the best that can be hoped for is to place this constituent of the theoretical foundation of criminal justice in a minor place.

The motive of *deterrence* plays an important role in legislation and judicial practice. It is difficult to measure the effectiveness of the fear of punishment on prospective wrongdoers. Clearly, however, this is an appeal to but one constituent of the personality—the fear instinct. Since the motives for abstention from crime are many and varied, and their interplay intricate, crime has flourished throughout the ages despite the threat of punishment. Moreover, reflection upon the history of penology hardly justifies a conclusion that the harsher the punishment, the lesser the incidence of crime. A case might even be made out for the opposite conclusion.

*Prevention of recidivism* as the chief aim of punishment has, under existing methods and régimes, miserably failed; as witness the high proportions of recidivism on the part of those already punished one or more times. The present study has demonstrated that, as with first offenders so also with ex-prisoners, the motives for abstention from criminality are numerous and complex. They are most assuredly not confined to the fear of new punishment.

There remains the theory of *correction or reformation* as the chief goal in the hierarchy of aims of the criminal law. This, too, has not shown satisfactory results in practice. The reason is plain, yet almost universally ignored. Punishment, in the sense of the infliction of pain, does not sufficiently affect human personality and character to bring about "reform." Its unfavorable reactions may even exceed the favorable. Indeed, psychoanalysis has made us familiar with the phenomenon of the deliberate seeking out of punishment by some individuals as an expression of a deep-seated personality need. If the correctional aim is to succeed, it must be predicated upon a less naive causal conception than the view that men commit crimes solely or primarily because they are wicked, and refrain from committing them solely or primarily because

the criminal he deludes himself into a feeling of righteous indignation, thus bolstering up his own self-respect and serving in this roundabout way, both to restrain himself from like indulgences and to keep himself upon the path of cultural progress. The legal punishment of the criminal today is, in its psychology, a dramatic tragic action by which society pushes off its criminal impulses upon a substitute. The principle is the same as that by which an emotion such as anger is discharged upon an inoffensive lifeless object." White, W. A., *Insanity and the Criminal Law*, New York, Macmillan, 1923, pp. 13–14. See also Alexander, F., and Staub, H., *The Criminal, the Judge and the Public*, trans. by G. Zilboorg, New York, Macmillan, 1931.

they are afraid. It must rather be founded upon a *completely causal attitude;* and since the causes are numerous and varied, so must the corrective devices be many, varied, and experimental.

The correctional aim, nevertheless, furnishes the best basis of the desirable objectives of the State in exercising social control through criminal law. It can be modernized into a theory based on the view that crime and recidivism are caused by a complex interplay of forces and factors inside and outside the offender; and that just as the physician aims to remove symptoms by getting at root causes, so the modern administrator of criminal justice should probe for causes and remove them if possible. Surely, the preceding analysis of the numerous factors that determine the fate of different types of offenders both under treatment and thereafter, should carry conviction on this score.

It would, however, be unrealistic to insist that such a modernized correctional theory should be the *sole* basis for determining sentence and treatment. The law in the books lives through the law in action. The other theories would still have to play a role, albeit a minor one. We have said that to bar the retributive motive from the criminal code would be very civilized; but a provision of that nature could hardly be enacted into law, and even if it could be it would be eliminated upon the commission of the very first shockingly heinous crime. Consequently, the vindictive element, the cloven hoof of Man's baser nature, must be retained. But its employment ought to be strictly limited to the very occasional and unusual case which has particularly aroused public rage and fear. Clearly, the vindictive element is inconsistent with the correctional aim; but in the vast majority of instances, fortunately, the correctional-therapeutic goal can predominate both in the imposition of sentence and in the determination of release on parole.

The deterrent element, too, would still play a part in an improved system. Those who condemn the correctional theory on the ground that it would weaken deterrence, are in error. The wholly indeterminate sentence or broad-zone sentence provision called for by an effective correctional system should prove just as deterrent as the fixed-sentence or narrow-zone sentence now prevailing, if not more so. The possibility of incarceration or extramural control during a long period of time, for crimes at present punished with brief sentences, would add a powerful deterrent element to the correctional approach.

The preventive theory would of course not be eliminated under the proposal to make the modernized correctional theory predominate. The deliberate putting of the correctional motive into the forefront of the proposed practice will more effectively implement the preventive theory of punishment than is the case at present. Instead of the miserable failure it has proved to be when its chief reliance was upon the infliction of pain and the appeal to fear, it gives promise of really preventing recidivism through a fundamental attack upon the deep-lying causal factors in the individual offender's constitution and background.

But in order to make our suggested *causal-correctional* theory effective in practice, it is indispensable that judges and parole boards avail themselves of such prognostic devices as have been illustrated in the preceding pages and in our other researches.[11] If the chief aim be to correct and rehabilitate by striking at causes, then the make-up and background of each offender become basically relevant. But, as has been indicated, the full significance of such data for purposes of correction and rehabilitation does not become apparent until the particular offender is placed in a class of offenders with similar characteristics, whose past response to the available kinds of treatment has already been ascertained.

The proposed approach does not necessarily involve either an expansion or a narrowing of judicial or parole-board discretion. It provides merely for a means of more intelligent exercise of discretion. The illustrative case-history summaries in Chapter II demonstrate the ease with which judges and parole officials fall into superficial routine practices in exercising discretion. Not only is this bad for the prisoner at the bar, but it endangers society in allowing offenders to remain at large when they belong to a type who will almost certainly recidivate under extramural treatment at certain age spans. (See the predictions applied to the different cases in Chapter XIV, especially that of John.)

Individualization of justice merely on the basis of the crime committed, or of the offender's prior criminal record, will certainly not reflect a sound exercise of discretion, considering correction as the chief aim of modern criminal justice. Even disposition of the case on a probation officer's investigation report will not necessarily mean effective individualization of justice with a corrective aim. Our case illustrations show that judges will slip into superficial and mechanical routine practices—such as releasing all first offenders on probation —or that they will make bad mistakes in drawing inferences from the single case history before them.

Prediction tables which take into account relevant factors of differentiation between successes and failures under each of the possible forms of sentence, as well as at different age spans, afford a sound way of putting into effect the aims of corrective penology.

It has been shown in the last few chapters, particularly toward the end of Chapter XVI, just how a judge would use such prognostic devices in actual

---

[11] In a new research, we are making prognoses of the behavior of juvenile delinquents on the basis of the prediction tables reported in "Juvenile Delinquents Grown Up," and putting these aside for a check-up of actualities several years hence.

practice. It has been indicated how he would distinguish between the offender's chances of success and failure under each of the existing kinds of treatment, and how he would take the age of the offender into account in such process of analysis. Even under existing sentencing provisions the use of carefully validated prediction tables would render the sentencing practices of our courts much more effective than they are today. To function still more effectively, however, judges and parole boards would need to have at their disposal at least a broad-zone indeterminate sentence law, if not a statute fixing no upper limits whatsoever to the length of sentence. Under existing statutes judges and parole officials are often compelled to release dangerous prisoners, when all concerned realize that such men will promptly renew their criminal careers. Our researches—the present work and preceding ones—have shown that certain types of these prisoners can safely be released when they have reached a certain stage in their development.

As we pointed out in *Juvenile Delinquents Grown Up*:

with the passage of the years, a differentiation seems to occur between the offenders whose delinquency and criminality is due more to adverse environmental and educational influences than to any deep-seated organismal weaknesses, and those whose inability to conform to the demands of a complex society is more nearly related to innate (and, partly, early-conditioned) abnormalities of the kind that set limits to the achievement of a socially adequate degree of maturity. The former, sooner or later, acquire the requisite amount of integration of intelligence, impulse and behavior. The latter never achieve a stage of maturity needed for lawful social adaptation. Despite their arrival at a high chronologic age they continue to be criminalistic until physically and mentally "burned out." Misbehavior due to *un*integration gives way to misbehavior due to *dis*integration until the organism runs down and finally stops.

In discussing "maturation" we should not ignore this slowing down process which begins to manifest itself after the organism has reached its peak of maturity. Organismal changes, to which all flesh is heir, occur regardless of the rate of maturation of the particular individual. With the passage of time, the human being loses some of his energy and aggressiveness; he tends to slow down and to become less venturesome. Just as individuals differ in the rate at which they climb to the maximum maturity of which they are capable, so they may differ in the rate at which they descend the hill. But whether the two sets of influences are definitely related or not, some of our offenders doubtless abandoned criminalistic ways largely as the result of the settling and disintegrative influences which were operative, regardless of the tempo of their maturation or of the maximum stage of maturity they were finally able to reach.[12]

[12] *Op. cit.*, pp. 268–269.

Differences in the pace of personality integration or maturation, as well as in the deteriorative process, have been illustrated in Chapter II, particularly in the cases of Robert, Armand, Antonio, and Arthur. A practical implication of this finding is that reform of sentence-legislation is required, calling for either a wholly indeterminate sentence law, at least for felons and persistent misdemeanants, or for a broad-zone indeterminate sentence law. (See the cases of Frank and John in Chapter II.)

Correct use of adequate prediction tables as an aid in sentencing and releasing procedures should do much to improve the general situation. However, *if the sentencing, correcting, and releasing functions were turned over to a specially qualified body, representing all relevant disciplines, we could reasonably expect still more effective implementation of the·causal-correctional theory.* When a causal approach to the problems of that form of maladaptation, designated crime, takes the place of the simplistic notions of intentional, wicked wrongdoing, the doors are thrown open to various fields of learning and experimentation that may well have some bearing on the pro-social reconstruction of behavior. Psychiatry, psychoanalysis, psychology, endocrinology, education, social work, and other disciplines must all be enlisted. The search for causes may lead into heretofore unsuspected areas. This means that the traditional attitude of the law-trained judge may not only be inadequate to the task in hand but may, on occasion, even be a handicap. Simple punishment on the basis of moral and legal "guilt" should be replaced by causal therapy. Another practical conclusion is, therefore, that the traditional imposition of sentences by judges must be replaced, or supplemented, by the doctor, the social worker, the research scientist. The sentencing, correctional, and releasing functions of tomorrow should be in the hands of specially qualified, therapeutically-minded persons.

The actual process of peno-correctional treatment is so superficial that all existing techniques appear to have little effect on the reorientation of attitudes, the reconditioning of habits, the improved management of impulses, the redefinition of ethical ideals, and the basic reformation of·character. There are, of course, significant exceptions. But it is a challenging fact that the opinions, standards, mores, and activities of fellow prisoners frequently exert a much more profound influence upon the future behavior of offenders than do the efforts of judges, wardens, chaplains, probation and parole officers.

In such a state of affairs, the make-up of the offender and his early conditioning are much more decisive of his behavior under one form of treatment or another, and of his later recidivism or reform, than are the punitive or corrective "medicines" given him by society and its agents.

In this connection, it has been shown that different types of offenders, at various age spans, get along more satisfactorily under one form of existing treatment than another. Therefore, especially under existing forms of imprisonment and extramural supervision, it is the part of wisdom to fit the individual offender, as nearly as possible, to that form of treatment to which experience has demonstrated offenders of his particular biosociologic class are most likely to respond satisfactorily.

But the fundamental task remains of redesigning and reshaping all existing forms of treatment in such a way as to permit them to exert a more discriminating and penetrating influence upon offenders of different types than most of them do at present; and the further fundamental task remains of devising new forms of corrective therapy.

The correction and rehabilitation of criminals will make but little headway unless and until these two tasks are made the goals of imaginative endeavor on the part of psychiatrists, psychologists, educators, vocational guidance experts, religious leaders, and others whose métier it is to probe into human motivation and to teach men how to live happily and successfully without resort to unethical and illegal conduct.

What we said in *Juvenile Delinquents Grown Up* bears repeating here:

The fact should be stressed that the best of systems must fail if those who do the work are not adequately equipped in attitude and training. If the business of criminal justice is to be a scientific work of segregating the incurable and, as early as possible, reforming and rehabilitating those offenders who are capable of entering legitimately upon life in society, the attitude of those who carry on the affairs of justice must be that of scientists, not of persons who see the criminal simply in terms of "leniency" and "severity" of punishment. And a "scientific attitude" without requisite equipment in the biologic and social sciences is of little value. If criminal justice is to be more than the dealing out of sentences on principles neither consistent nor effective, judges, probation officers, administrators of correctional institutions, and parole officers must have specialized training, and criminology must be recognized as a profession that is striving to replace guesswork and prejudice with facts and legitimate inferences.[13]

[13] P. 273.

# APPENDICES

# DEFINITION OF TERMS

In view of the fact that in Appendix B of *Later Criminal Careers* an exhaustive set of definitions was arranged in alphabetical order and covered the materials included in both *500 Criminal Careers* and *Later Criminal Careers,* it seems unnecessary to repeat them all here. However, for the purposes of the present work, the definitions of factors used in the third five-year follow-up period are presented here in alphabetical order and table numbers are given in each case so that ready reference can be made to Appendices B, C, and D in which the tables are presented; also the number of the page on which the tables are discussed.

AGE AT CHANGE FROM SERIOUS TO MINOR DELINQUENCY SINCE SENTENCE TO REFORMA-
TORY

B, 3–68 (p. 122)

AGE AT DEATH

B, 3–79b (p. 73)

AGE AT END OF PERIOD

B, 3–2 (p. 3)
That is, at end of third five-year period. If dead, age at time of death.

AGE AT REFORMATION

B, 3–67 (p. 122)

ALIASES

C, 52; D, 44 (p. 114)
The purpose of this is to indicate not what aliases were used, but whether any were used.

ASSOCIATES IN CRIME

B, 3–57a; C, 53 (p. 114)

ATTITUDE OF OFFENDER TO MARITAL RESPONSIBILITY

C, 12a (p. 86)
If more than one marriage occurred during the period, refers to the more recent marriage.
*Assumes*—does not neglect or desert wife or children; not unfaithful; not physically or mentally abusive to wife or children. Assumes economic responsibilities toward them. See ECONOMIC RESPONSIBILITY.

*Neglects*—fails to meet the above standard.

*Inapplicable*—offender is single, or separated, or divorced from wife prior to beginning of period judged and has no children.

## ATTITUDE OF RELATIVES TO OFFENDER

B, 3–18b (p. 88)

*Friendly*—fond of him and keep in touch.

*Indifferent*—do not make effort to keep in touch but are not openly hostile.

*Hostile*—show definite dislike or disapproval of him.

## ATTITUDE OF WIFE TO MARITAL RESPONSIBILITY

B, 3–24; C, 12b (p. 86)

If more than one marriage occurred during the period, refers to the more recent marriage.

*Assumes*—does not neglect or desert husband or children; not unfaithful; not physically or mentally abusive to mate or children. Carries on her household duties and meets her economic responsibilities. See definition of ECONOMIC RESPONSIBILITY.

*Neglects*—fails to meet the above standard.

*Inapplicable*—wife separated or divorced from offender prior to beginning of the period studied. Included here even though she has the custody of offender's children.

## ATTITUDE TO CHILDREN

B, 3–29a (p. 86–87)

This includes illegitimate children and step-children.

*Good*—fond of, cares for.

*Fair*—casual toward; or fond of but neglectful.

*Poor*—no affection, or no supervision, or is abusive.

If children, not living with offender, i.e., have been placed out or in institution or with wife:

*Good*—if he maintains an interest in them to the greatest extent possible within the limits of the particular situation.

*Fair*—if he at least keeps in touch with them, even only casually.

*Poor*—if he is entirely out of touch with children.

*Inapplicable*—if offender is in an institution throughout the period.

## ATTITUDE TO INVESTIGATION

C, 56 (p. 7)

The purpose of this is to guide the field investigators in these continuing five-year follow-ups. If offender is found to be very hostile, for example, every attempt will be made in the next follow-up to get the information needed without seeing offender personally.

**AVERAGE PERIOD OF TIME HELD JOB**

B, 3–43; C, 31; D, 28 (p. 99)
Refers to employment in legitimate occupation.

**AVERAGE WAGE—WEEKLY**

B, 3–41; C, 26; D, 23 (p. 101)
Refers to wage in legitimate employment. In a maintenance position $5 a week is added to wage to cover board and room.

**CAUSES OF DEATH**

B, 3–80 (p. 73)

**CHURCH ATTENDANCE**

C, 37; D, 34 (p. 106)
*Regular* means attending every Sunday.
*Irregular* means attending occasionally.

**COMPANIONSHIPS**

C, 34; D, 31 (p. 104–105)
*Harmful*—any with whom association might lead to delinquency, as street-corner loafers, cheap pool-room habitués, youths who live by their wits, habitual drinkers, professional gamblers, and so on.
*Harmless*—those whose influence, though not necessarily wholesome, is at least not harmful.

**COMPETENCE OF WIFE AS HOMEMAKER**

C, 12, c (p. 86)
If more than one marriage occurred during the period, refers to the more recent marriage.
*Good*—systematic, economical, clean, neat.
*Fair*—some of the qualifications of the good homemaker, but, because of low mentality or temperamental difficulties or other reasons, at times a poor homemaker.
*Poor*—wasteful, indifferent, careless.
*Inapplicable*—wife not living with offender since beginning of period studied.

**CONDUCT DURING FIFTEEN YEARS AFTER END OF REFORMATORY SENTENCE**

B, 3–69 (pp. 121–122)

**CONJUGAL RELATIONS**

B, 3–22; C, 12; D, 11 (pp. 85–86)
Refers to legal and common-law marriages. If more than one marriage, the conjugal relations of offender and his more recent wife are judged.
*Good*—living together compatibly without undue quarreling.

*Fair*—living together but grossly incompatible. Indifferent or hostile to each other but no open breach.

*Poor*—separation, desertion, divorce, or occasional desertion or separation during period studied.

*Inapplicable*—not living with wife at least since beginning of period studied.

DELINQUENCIES

C, 54; D, 45 (pp. 118–120)

*Non-delinquent*—no police or court record, or dishonorable discharge or desertion from army or navy, or unofficial misconduct for which he might be arrested, as drinking, abuse of family, stealing, and so on. See OFFICIAL RECOGNITION OF DELINQUENCY for definition. Technical automobile violations in the absence of any other misconduct are allowable in this category.

*Delinquent*—official or unofficial misconduct except technical auto violations in the absence of other delinquencies.

DELINQUENCY IN FIFTH YEAR

B, 3–57b (p. 119)

See DELINQUENCIES.

DELINQUENCY IN FIVE-YEAR PERIOD AND FIFTH YEAR IN COMBINATION

B, 3–61 (p. 119)

See OFFICIAL RECOGNITION OF DELINQUENCY for definition of *official* and *unofficial* misconduct.

DELINQUENCY OF CHILDREN

B, 3–29b (p. 120)

DEPENDENTS

C, 15; D, 14 (pp. 90–91)

Refers to wife, children (including illegitimate children), and parents (if they need his aid).

DISPOSITION OF EARNINGS

B, 3–34a; C, 16; D, 15 (p. 91)

ECONOMIC CONDITION

B, 3–33a; C, 17; D, 16 (pp. 89–91)

*Comfortable*—means having accumulated resources sufficient to maintain self and family for at least four months.

*Marginal*—means living on daily earnings and accumulating little or nothing; being on the border between self-support and dependency. Here are included instances in which temporary aid is resorted to occasionally in order to tide over a critical situation; for example, in case of illness or seasonal unemployment.

Aid may have been given for a few days or even a month, and with this little assistance the offender was able to manage his own problem.

*Dependent*—receiving aid continuously from public funds or from persons outside the immediate family. This means chronic dependency. Aid may have been given in the form of money, clothing, food, coal, or medical assistance. As here applied, dependency is due to reasons other than the economic depression of 1929–1933.

*Dependent on relatives*—receiving considerable or continuous aid from relatives, *not because of industrial depression.*

*Dependent on agencies or relatives*—receiving considerable or continuous aid *solely because of the economic depression.* This applies to men who would otherwise be self-supporting.

#### ECONOMIC RESPONSIBILITY TOWARD FAMILY

B, 3–31a; C, 21; D, 18 (pp. 92–94)

*Meets responsibility*—if single, separated, widowed, or divorced and is without legal dependents (wife, children, or parents) supports self even if by illegitimate employment and at least in *marginal* circumstances with only occasional public or private aid or sporadic assistance from relatives; if he has dependents (wife, children, or parents) makes every reasonable effort to support them at least in *marginal* circumstances. See ECONOMIC CONDITION, for definition.

*Fails to meet responsibility*—does not meet the above standard through his own fault, or contracts avoidable debts or receives frequent aid from social agencies or relatives when should be self-supporting.

*Inapplicable*—unable to meet his responsibilities through no fault of his own, as chronic physical or mental illness or defect, depression victim, and so on.

#### ECONOMIC RESPONSIBILITY IN FIFTH YEAR

B, 3–64 (p. 93)

See ECONOMIC RESPONSIBILITY

#### EDUCATIONAL ACTIVITIES

C, 38; D, 35 (p. 107)

As attendance at evening school, vocational classes, and so on.

#### ENVIRONMENTAL HISTORY IN FIFTH YEAR

B, 3–65a (p. 83)

See ENVIRONMENTAL JUDGMENT

#### ENVIRONMENTAL JUDGMENT

C, 9b; D, 8a (p. 83)

This is a composite picture of neighborhood influences (see NEIGHBORHOOD IN-FLUENCES for definition), physical aspects of the home (see HOME—PHYSICAL for definition), and moral standards (see MORAL STANDARDS OF HOME for definition).

If a person has been assigned to the *good* class in all three of these factors, he is here assigned to the *good* class.

If *fair*—fair.

If *poor*—poor.

If two *good*, one *fair* or *poor*—fair (except if neighborhood influences *fair*)—good.

Two *fair*, one *good*—fair.

Two *fair*, one *poor*—fair.

Two *poor*, one *fair*—poor.

Two *poor*, one *good*—fair.

One *good*, one *fair*, one *poor*—fair.

FAMILY RELATIONSHIPS

C, 14; D, 13 (pp. 88–89)

If offender is married, his relation to his wife and children is judged.

If offender is separated, divorced, or widowed, his relation to his children is judged.

If offender has no children, his relation to his parents and siblings is judged.

If offender is single, separated, divorced, or widowed before beginning of period studied and has no children, his relation to his parents and siblings is judged.

If the offender is single, his relation to his parents and siblings is judged.

If offender has a common-law wife, his relationship to her is judged as though she were his legal wife.

The standard of *socially acceptable conduct* in regard to family relationships adopted for our purposes is the following: The man must not be harming his family in any way deemed injurious to the institution of the family, that is, if married, he must not neglect or desert his wife or children during period judged, and must not be separated or divorced from his wife during the period judged, or have illicit relations with other women, or be abusive to his wife or children, or be continually away in the evening if this is not necessary to his business.

If single, separated, widowed, or divorced before beginning of period and living away from home, he must be in touch with his parents or nearest relatives. If single, separated, widowed, or divorced, and living at home, he must give evidence that he considers it more than merely a convenient place to sleep and eat in; for example, he must not be continually out in the evening if this is not necessary to his work, or live at home only when he is in need of funds.

A man is a failure in his *family relationships* if he does not meet the above standard.

FAMILY RELATIONSHIPS IN FIFTH YEAR

B, 3–63a (p. 88)

See FAMILY RELATIONSHIPS

FREQUENCY OF ARRESTS

B, 3–55; C, 41; D, 37 (pp. 109–110)

This is calculated on the basis of sixty months, from which is subtracted the length of time the offender spent in penal or non-penal institutions during this period. Into the time remaining is divided the number of arrests occurring in the sixty-month period.

FREQUENCY OF CONVICTIONS

B, 3–56; C, 45; D, 39 (pp. 114–115)

Calculated in same way as frequency of arrests. See FREQUENCY OF ARRESTS. *Files* are tabulated as convictions.

GANG LIFE

C, 35a (pp. 104–105)

A *gang* is distinguished from a *crowd* by being organized for a definite anti-social purpose (thieving, malicious mischief, and so on), and having specific leadership.

HABITS

B, 3–49; C, 43 (pp. 110–111)

This refers to any habits which might lead to conflict with the law, as drink, drugs, gambling, stealing, lying, illicit sexuality.

HAUNTS

C, 35; D, 32 (p. 105)

*Good*—places of recreation that are under strict and constructive supervision as public playgrounds, community centers, school recreation centers.

*Fair*—places in which there is no constructive supervision but where the influences are not necessarily harmful (as political clubs, bowling alleys, public dance-halls, skating rinks, beaches), since the great majority of patrons are not there for illicit purposes.

*Poor*—places that are distinctly harmful in character in that most of those who frequent them have an illicit purpose as their objective, i.e., houses of ill fame, gambling dens, bootlegging joints.

HIGHEST WAGE—WEEKLY

B, 3–42; C, 27; D, 24 (p. 101)

Refers to wage in legitimate employment.

In a maintenance position $5 a week is added to wage to cover board and room.

HOME—PHYSICAL

B, 3–12; C, 7; D, 6 (p. 79)

*Good*—adequate space (not more than two people, excluding infant, to a bedroom), light, ventilation, cleanliness, sufficient furniture.

*Fair*—more than one of the above advantages plus one unfavorable factor.

*Poor*—overcrowding, dirt, shabby furnishing, lack of ventilation, and so on. One or more of these factors and no advantages to offset them. Cases of extreme overcrowding belong in this class even if the home is good or fair in other respects.

*Varied*—here are included those the character of whose physical home changes from one type to another as described above. The predominant type is indicated, however.

HOUSEHOLD STABILITY

B, 3–17; C, 6; D, 5 (p. 78)

This refers to the number of changes in the household experienced by offender during the period studied. For example, if offender lives for a time with his parents and then goes away to work and lives alone this is counted as one change; if he then marries and lives with wife, this is two changes; if he leaves his wife to go to a mistress, this is three changes; if he leaves a mistress and returns to the parental home, this is four changes.

In a case in which offender has been living with his parents and marries, and the wife comes to live with offender in his parental home, this is not tabulated as a change, so that any additions to the household are not changes in the sense in which the term is used here. Commitments to institutions are not rated as changes.

ILLICIT OCCUPATION

C, 23; D, 20 (p. 98)

This refers to any occupation, engagement in which is illegal, as prostitution, bootlegging, deriving profits from prostitution, drug selling, disposing of stolen goods.

INDUSTRIAL HISTORY

B, 3–34b; C, 33; D, 30 (p. 103)

*Success*—work habits good, and offender a *regular* worker.

*Partial success*—work habits good, and offender either *fairly regular* or *irregular* worker; or work habits *fair* or *poor,* but offender works *regularly.*

*Failure*—work habits *poor,* and offender is a *fairly regular* or *irregular* worker or is engaged in illicit occupations to the exclusion of all, or almost all, legitimate work.

**INDUSTRIAL HISTORY IN FIFTH YEAR**

B, 3–63b (p. 103)
See INDUSTRIAL HISTORY

**INSTITUTIONAL EXPERIENCES (PENAL AND NON-PENAL)—BY TYPE**

C, 47 (p. 118)

**INSTITUTIONAL EXPERIENCES (PENAL AND NON-PENAL)—MEN WITH**

B, 3–7; C, 4; D, 3 (pp. 76–77)

**INSTITUTIONAL EXPERIENCES (PENO-CORRECTIONAL)—GEOGRAPHICAL SPREAD**

C, 48 (p. 118)

**INSURANCE**

C, 18 (pp. 89–90)
Refers to insurance of any type carried by the offender on himself or on members of his family.

**INSURANCE—PREMIUM PAID BY WHOM**

C, 19 (p. 90)

**INTERVIEW WITH**

C, 57 (p. 8)
Refers to persons interviewed in connection with field investigation.

**LEGITIMACY OF CHILDREN**

B, 3–27 (p. 87)

**LEISURE AND HABITS**

C, 39; D, 36 (pp. 107–108)
*Constructive*—member of a well-supervised social group as Y.M.C.A.; utilizes leisure to further himself culturally or vocationally (as by attendance at night school).
*Negative*—at least not engaging in harmful activities, even though not utilizing his time constructively.
*Harmful*—indulges in forms of recreation which might lead to criminal conduct (such as membership in gangs, association with bootleggers, prostitutes, loafers, drug addicts, drunkards, gamblers).

**LEISURE AND HABITS IN FIFTH YEAR**

B, 3–65b (p. 107)
See LEISURE AND HABITS

LENGTH OF TIME IN PRIVATE EMPLOYMENT

B, 3–36b (p. 95)

LONGEST PERIOD OF TIME HELD JOB

B, 3–44; C, 32; D, 29 (pp. 98–100)
Refers to legitimate employment only

MARITAL STATUS

B, 3–19; B, 3–20; C, 10; D, 9 (pp. 84–85)
If offender died before the end of the period judged, his marital status at the
time of his death is referred to.
An illegal marriage means that a ceremony has been performed although one
or both of the spouses were not free by law to marry.

MENTAL CONDITION

B, 3–6; C, 55
This refers to mental balance or mental abnormalities.
Although two or more of the conditions listed may be present, the person is
classified once in the order of precedence indicated in the code.
*Personality liabilities*—unusually strong emotional or conative traits such as
impulsiveness, lack of self-control, self-indulgence, egocentricity, fault-finding,
hypochondria, introspectiveness, jealousy, self-dramatization, obscenity, opin-
ionation, profanity, seclusiveness, self-pity, self-justification, vanity, asociality,
lack of foresight, irresponsibility.

MOBILITY

B, 3–15a; C, 5; D, 4 (pp. 77–78)
*Mobility*—changes in environment which indicate that the individual does not
take root and establish close associations in any one community. This is indicated by excessive moving within a city (more than once a year); or from city
to city on the average of once in two years; or by coming from or going to a
foreign country.

MONTHS IN COMMUNITY

B, 3–11; C, 3; D, 2 (p. 76)
Refers to the number of months out of the sixty-month period studied that the
offender is not under restraint and therefore freely able to commit crime. From
the sixty-month period is deducted the time offender spends in penal or non-
penal institutions (including hospitals for mental and physical diseases), or is
under the disciplinary restraint of the army, navy, or merchant marine.

MORAL STANDARDS OF HOME

B, 3–16a; C, 9a; D, 6a (pp. 79–80)
Refers to the atmosphere of the home in which offender lives during the period

judged. If he lives alone, the standards of his immediate physical environment are taken cognizance of. In making the judgment, the conduct and attitude of the offender himself are excluded.

*Good*—in offender's immediate environment there are thrift, temperance, wholesome ideals, conformity to sex standards, and no delinquency except for slight automobile violations or violations of license laws.

*Fair*—in offender's immediate environment although there is no delinquency among those comprising the immediate family, or, if offender living alone, among the persons in his nearest vicinity, there is an absence of thrift, temperance, and wholesome ideals, and there is no positive disapproval of criminal conduct.

*Poor*—in offender's immediate environment there is criminality, alcoholism, or other delinquency, or though no actual delinquency, such conduct is lightly regarded and even encouraged.

## NEIGHBORHOOD INFLUENCES

B, 3–14; C, 9; D, 8 (pp. 81–82)

*Good*—no street gangs, no centers of vice or crime within a radius of two square blocks in the city or a mile in the country; opportunity for constructive recreation (see LEISURE for definition) within easy walking distance—as public playgrounds, school or community centers, parks, and so on.

*Fair*—no street gangs, no centers of vice or crime within a radius of two square blocks in the city, or a mile in the country, but no opportunities for constructive recreation within walking distance.

*Poor*—corner gangs, centers of vice or crime within a radius of two square blocks in the city or a mile in the country, regardless of whether facilities for constructive recreation exist within walking distance.

## NEIGHBORHOOD—TYPE

B, 3–13; C, 8; D, 7 (pp. 80–81)

This refers to the predominant type of neighborhood in which offender is resident during the period judged.

A radius of two square blocks in the urban districts and of one mile in rural from the particular place of residence is judged and characterized as:

*Urban partly residential*—if it is a business, factory, or lodging house area.

*Urban residential*—if it is an area of tenements or private houses used mainly as permanent residences and not for house transients, and from which business or factory areas are more than two blocks distant.

*Suburban*—an outlying residential district of a city in which there are mainly detached houses with considerable open space.

*Rural or small town*—any town of five thousand population or under is classified here.

*Varied*—if a person has shifted during the period studied from a neighborhood of one type to another type, he is classified in this group but the type of neighborhood in which he has lived the most during the period studied is indicated.

**NUMBER OF ARRESTS**

C, 40a (p. 109)

**NUMBER OF CHILDREN**

C, 11; D, 10 (p. 87)

Refers to legitimate and illegitimate children *living* at the end of the period under consideration.

**NUMBER OF CONVICTIONS**

C, 44a (p. 115)

**NUMBER OF DEATHS**

B, 3–79a (p. 4)

**NUMBER OF DIFFERENT OCCUPATIONS**

B, 3–40a; C, 22a (pp. 97–98)

If change of occupation is within the same branch of employment it is not counted as a change. This does not mean number of different jobs but *different types* of work.

**NUMBER OF PENAL EXPERIENCES**

C, 46; D, 40 (p. 117)

**NUMBER OF SOCIAL SERVICE AGENCIES**

B, 3–35; C, 20; D, 17 (p. 91)

**OFFICIAL RECOGNITION OF DELINQUENCY**

C, 51 (pp. 111–112); D, 43 (p. 120)

*Official*—based on police or court records.
*Unofficial*—delinquency for which the person has not come to the attention of official agencies of the law.

**PERIOD STUDIED—END**

B, 3–1b

This refers to the date of the end of the third five-year period.

**PREDOMINANT OFFENSE**

C, 42; D, 38 (pp. 112–114)

This is a social category of offenses which is based on unofficial as well as official misconduct. See OFFICIAL RECOGNITION OF DELINQUENCY for definition of *official* and *unofficial*. The type of offense most characteristic of the offender is the predominant offense.

PRINCIPAL COMPONENT OF MISCONDUCT

B, 3–66 (p. 119); D, 42 (p. 120)

Each offender is categorized once, in the order indicated in the code.

RELATION TO NEAREST RELATIVES

C, 13; D, 12 (p. 87)

This refers to the ties existing between the offender and his nearest blood relatives, that is, to one or both parents if they are living, or to his siblings if one or both parents are not living.

SAVINGS

C, 16a (p. 89)

This refers to the savings of the offender if he is single, separated, widowed, or divorced before the beginning of the period judged, and to the joint savings of himself and his wife if he is living with her.

SKILL

C, 24; D, 21 (pp. 95–96)

This generally refers to the *usual* occupation. If it is difficult to determine the *usual* occupation, the highest degree of skill which the individual reflects in any of the occupations he holds during the period judged, is indicated.

The *unskilled laborer* does any kind of rough work to which he can be sent without any training whatever. Mere strength of hand or keenness of eye, untutored through any course of apprenticeship or training, serves for him.

The *semi-skilled* worker uses tools and processes requiring learning. He cannot take up the kind of work unless he has had a period of experience under guidance or of study. The processes, however, are not greatly complicated and the period of training is likely to be short (three days to three months, perhaps). The *skilled* worker uses tools and processes which are usable only by one who has given a long period of time, perhaps at least a year, to the acquiring of the skill.

SKILL IN FIFTH YEAR

B, 3–38b

See SKILL for definition

SOCIAL SERVICE NEEDS NOT MET

B, 3–60 (p. 92)

Refers to the needs of the offender if he is single and has no dependents or if he is separated or divorced from his wife before period judged and has no legal responsibility for any children.

Refers to the needs of himself and his wife and children if he is married and living with his wife, or though separated, has legal responsibilities toward her and their children during the period judged. If he has been separated or divorced from his wife before the beginning of the period judged but his children live with him or are dependent upon him for support, the needs in such a total situation are considered here.

The needs indicated are only the glaring ones. For example, those tabulated as *needing vocational guidance* are the men who in the period judged were very poor and irregular workers; those set down as *requiring recreational supervision* were the men who spent their leisure time harmfully and not merely negatively; those *in need of family guidance* are the ones who had serious marital difficulties or, in some instances, those who though unmarried were getting along poorly with nearest relatives. Those *in need of relief* were men in a state of total dependency. If their relatives were taking care of them they were not tabulated as needing relief.

See TYPES OF SOCIAL SERVICE AGENCIES.

### SOCIETY MEMBER

C, 36; D, 33 (p. 106)

Refers to any organization of which offender was a member during period, that offers opportunity for constructive use of leisure time, including church societies, lodges, Y.M.C.A., K.C., and so on.

### STEADINESS OF EMPLOYMENT

C, 30; D, 27 (p. 100)

*Regular*—very few breaks (not more than an average of two months of unemployment a year) in otherwise continuous employment.

*Fairly regular*—unemployment in excess of two months a year but compensated for by periods of sustained work.

*Irregular*—frequent or long-protracted periods of unemployment, and none of sustained employment.

### STREET LIFE

C, 35b (pp. 104–105)

This refers to hanging about on street corners.

### SUMMARY OF ARRESTS

C, 40 (p. 110)

Refers to arrests as officially recorded.

### SUMMARY OF ARRESTS—BY TYPE

C, 40b (pp. 110–111)

### SUMMARY OF DISPOSITIONS OF ARRESTS

C, 44 (p. 116)

SUMMARY OF DISPOSITIONS OF ARRESTS—BY TYPE

C, 44b (p. 116)

TIME IN PENAL INSTITUTIONS

B, 3–9 and 3–10; C, 49; D, 41 (p. 117)

TYPES OF SOCIAL SERVICE AGENCIES

C, 20a (pp. 91–92)

This refers to offender himself if he has no dependents, is single, widowed, divorced, or separated, and has no legal obligations to a wife or children during period under consideration; and refers to him, his wife, and children if he is married and living with them.

*Health, physical*—includes free hospital care, free clinic attendance, supervision by a hospital social service department or department of health.

*Health, mental*—includes free mental hospital or outpatient treatment, and schools for feebleminded.

*Relief*—includes not only aid in the form of money, but clothing, food, groceries, medicines, and so on.

*Family welfare*—has to do with adjusting problems of domestic relations, unemployment.

*Child or adolescent welfare*—includes all agencies of the non-punitive type dealing specifically with problems of childhood and adolescence, as the Society for the Prevention of Cruelty to Children, Children's Aid Society, Judge Baker Guidance Center, Division of Child Guardianship, and so on.

*Correctional*—any agencies dealing with delinquent minors, as state industrial schools, truant schools.

USUAL OCCUPATION

C, 22; D, 19 (pp. 96–97)

Refers to the type of occupation which is engaged in the longest during the period, or which is returned to the most frequently.

If it is impossible to determine the usual occupation because of the variety of work engaged in, tabulated as *varied*.

USUAL REASON FOR LEAVING WORK

C, 29; D, 26 (pp. 102–103)

This refers to the most frequent reason if possible; otherwise the last known.

*Fault of worker*—arrested; discharged for inefficiency, dishonesty, drink, and so on.

*Not fault of worker*—laid off because of slack work, left to marry, left because of illness.

WHEREABOUTS AT END OF PERIOD

C, 2 (pp. 73–74)

WITH WHOM LIVING

C, 1; D, 1 (pp. 74–76)

WORK HABITS

C, 28; D, 25 (pp. 101–102)

*Good*—refers to the person who is reliable, industrious, commended by employers. Is an asset to them.

*Fair*—refers to the person who has the qualifications of the good worker but who permits his work to be interrupted by periodic drinking, by the drug habit, by occasional vagabondage, by deliberate choice of irregular occupation such as longshoring, for the chief purpose of having leisure time.

*Poor*—refers to the worker who is unreliable, loafs, is lazy, dishonest, unstable, a vagabond and floater, ambitionless, wayward, or is engaged in illegitimate work.

WORK RELIEF

B, 3–39c (p. 95)

## DESCRIPTIVE TABLES: THIRD FIVE-YEAR
## FOLLOW-UP PERIOD

THE following tables refer to 439 of the 510 men (unless otherwise indicated) originally described in *500 Criminal Careers*, since 439 of the men were living at the beginning of the third five-year period. The table numbers correspond to those used in Section B of Appendix C of *Later Criminal Careers*, in which the status of the 454 men living at the beginning of the second five-year follow-up period is described (pages 299–328). If a table recorded in *Later Criminal Careers* is now omitted, it is because the data were not secured for the third five-year span. When the same data are given in the Period-Comparison Tables (Appendix C), the title of the table appears in Appendix B and the reader is referred to the corresponding table in Appendix C. Tables in which the breakdown is given in more detail in Appendix B are retained, as well as those which present data not given in the Period-Comparison Tables.

A few tables not appearing in Appendix C of *Later Criminal Careers* have been inserted in their proper order in the present work but have been designated in a way that does not interfere with the original numbering of the tables.

Definitions of the factors appear in Appendix A, in alphabetical order.

The figure 3 appearing before each table number designates the third five-year follow-up period.

Wherever a line appears beneath a category, it means that in the categories appearing below the line each case may have been recorded more than once. This is a *multiple* table and totals more than 439. The sum of the incidence of the categories "inapplicable," "unknown if any," and "none," if subtracted from the total cases involved, gives the number of cases actually represented by the remaining categories or sub-classes of the factor.

#### 3–1A. ALIASES (See Appendix C, 52)

#### 3–1B. PERIOD STUDIED—END

| | |
|---|---|
| 200 | 1936 |
| 239 | 1937 |

#### 3–2. AGE AT END OF PERIOD OR AT DEATH

| | | | |
|---|---|---|---|
| 0 | 21–25 | 106 | 41–45 |
| 0 | 26–30 | 45 | 46–50 |
| 60 | 31–35 | 14 | 51–55 |
| 211 | 36–40 | 3 | 56 and over |

### 3–3. WITH WHOM LIVING AT END OF PERIOD (See Appendix C, 1)

### 3–6. MENTAL CONDITION

| | | | |
|---|---|---|---|
| 28 | Psychosis (manic depressive, dementia praecox, paranoid, sex pervert) | 1 | Congenital syphilis |
| | | 3 | Question of mental disease |
| 44 | Psychopathic personality or traits | 61 | Emotional instability |
| 6 | Epilepsy (or epileptic characteristics) | 12 | Other personality liabilities |
| 51 | Alcoholism or delirium tremens | 123 | None |
| 9 | Drug addiction | 95 | Unknown |
| 6 | Neurasthenia | | |

### 3–7. INSTITUTIONAL EXPERIENCES (PENAL AND NON-PENAL), MEN WITH, BY TYPE OF EXPERIENCE

      3   Inapplicable
     40   Unknown if any
    221   None (in community throughout or no institutional experience up to time of death)
    175   Had institutional experiences
    _____
      0   School for feebleminded
     17   Hospital for mental diseases
      6   Hospital for chronic physical diseases
    157   Peno-correctional institutions
      3   Army

### 3–8. NUMBER OF PENAL EXPERIENCES (See Appendix C, 46)

### 3–9. TIME IN PENAL INSTITUTIONS

| | | | |
|---|---|---|---|
| 232 | None | 12 | 24–29 months |
| 32 | Less than 3 months | 8 | 30–35 months |
| 19 | 3–6 months | 13 | 36–47 months |
| 22 | 7–11 months | 11 | 48–59 months |
| 15 | 12–17 months | 14 | 60 months |
| 11 | 18–23 months | 50 | Unknown |

### 3–10. TIME IN PENAL INSTITUTIONS*

| | | | |
|---|---|---|---|
| 232 | None | 9 | 40–49 months |
| 45 | Under 5 months | 10 | 50–59 months |
| 19 | 5–9 months | 14 | 60 months |
| 26 | 10–19 months | 3 | Inapplicable (dead four years or more) |
| 20 | 20–29 months | 47 | Unknown |
| 14 | 30–39 months | | |

* The difference in the groupings of the same factor in tables 3–9 and 3–10 is necessitated by our desire to make these tables comparable with other studies.

### 3–11. MONTHS IN COMMUNITY

| | | | |
|---|---|---|---|
| 27 | None | 6 | 24–29 months |
| 3 | Less than 3 months | 18 | 30–35 months |
| 3 | 3–5 months | 32 | 36–47 months |
| 13 | 6–11 months | 72 | 48–59 months |
| 6 | 12–17 months | 210 | 60 months |
| 8 | 18–23 months | 41 | Unknown |

### 3–12. HOME—PHYSICAL

| | | | |
|---|---|---|---|
| 90 | Good | 7 | Varied—poor |
| 140 | Fair | 43 | Inapplicable as in institution throughout |
| 101 | Poor | | or in community for less than one year |
| 0 | Varied—good | 55 | Unknown |
| 3 | Varied—fair | | |

### 3–13. NEIGHBORHOOD—TYPE

| | | | |
|---|---|---|---|
| 117 | Urban partly residential | 8 | Small town |
| 117 | Urban residential | 42 | Varied (urban and rural) |
| 0 | Urban unspecified | 43 | Inapplicable as in institution throughout |
| 29 | Suburban | | or in community for less than one year |
| 32 | Rural (or semi-rural) | 51 | Unknown |

### 3–14. NEIGHBORHOOD INFLUENCES

| | | | |
|---|---|---|---|
| 34 | Good | 8 | Varied—poor |
| 186 | Fair | 43 | Inapplicable as in institution throughout |
| 109 | Poor | | or in community for less than one year |
| 0 | Varied—good | 55 | Unknown |
| 4 | Varied—fair | | |

### 3–15A. MOBILITY

| | |
|---|---|
| 208 | Not excessive |
| 33 | Excessive moving in one city area |
| 38 | Excessive moving in different parts of one city |
| 1 | Excessive moving in one city but localities unknown |
| 73 | Excessive moving to other cities, states, or countries |
| 43 | Inapplicable (institution throughout, or no excessive mobility in the less than one year in community) |
| 43 | Unknown |

### 3–15B. ENVIRONMENTAL JUDGMENT (See Appendix C, 9B)

### 3–16A. MORAL STANDARDS OF HOME

130 Good
108 Fair
92 Poor
1 Varied—good
4 Varied—fair

8 Varied—poor
43 Inapplicable (in institution throughout, or in community for less than one year)
53 Unknown

### 3–16B. FAMILY RELATIONSHIPS (See Appendix C, 14)

### 3–17. HOUSEHOLD STABILITY

7 One change
37 Two changes
18 Three changes
8 Four changes
8 Five changes
13 More than five changes

44 Several but exact number unknown
209 No change
43 Inapplicable (not in community at all, or during the less than one year in community, stability not determinable)
52 Unknown

### 3–18A. RELATION TO NEAREST RELATIVES (See Appendix C, 13)

### 3–18B. ATTITUDE OF RELATIVES TO OFFENDER

221 Friendly
101 Indifferent
10 Hostile or disgusted or disapprove
43 Inapplicable as in institution throughout or in community too brief to judge
5 Inapplicable as no relatives
59 Unknown

### 3–19. MARITAL STATUS AT BEGINNING OF PERIOD

157 Single
171 Married, living with wife
3 Married but offender in institution
1 Married, wife in institution, no separation prior to this
1 Illegally married—living with wife
1 Illegally married—separated
36 Separated
25 Divorced
8 Widowed
36 Unknown, or unknown if married or single

### 3–20. MARITAL STATUS AT END OF PERIOD

131 Single
181 Married, living with wife

  2  Married, wife in institution, no separation prior to this
  2  Married, wife unfaithful, offender in institution
 44  Separated
 30  Divorced
  8  Widowed
 41  Unknown, or unknown if married or single

## 3–22. CONJUGAL RELATIONS

131  Single
138  Good
 33  Fair
 42  Poor
  1  Marriage too brief to judge
 52  Inapplicable (separated, divorced, widowed before beginning of period and not remarried during period)
  3  Inapplicable as in institution throughout or dead
  3  Inapplicable as wife in institution at least four years
 36  Unknown if married or single

## 3–23. ATTITUDE OF OFFENDER TO MARITAL RESPONSIBILITY (See Appendix C, 12A)

## 3–24. ATTITUDE OF WIFE TO MARITAL RESPONSIBILITY

131  Single
179  Assume
 24  Neglect
 48  Inapplicable (separated from offender before beginning of period and does not have children for whom she is responsible in Period III)
  3  Inapplicable as husband in institution throughout or dead (over 4 of 5 years), no children
  3  Inapplicable as wife in institution 4 of 5 years
 15  Unknown
 36  Unknown whether married or single

## 3–26. COMPETENCE OF WIFE AS HOMEMAKER
### (See Appendix C, 12C)

## 3–27. LEGITIMACY OF CHILDREN

323  No children born during period
 63  Legitimate children—conceived in wedlock
  4  Legitimate children—conceived out of wedlock
  1  Unmarried with illegitimate children
  2  Married with illegitimate children
  0  Legitimate and illegitimate children (including children conceived out of wedlock)
 46  Unknown or inapplicable (dead, institution under strict supervision)

### 3–28. NUMBER OF CHILDREN (See Appendix C, 11)

### 3–29A. ATTITUDE TO CHILDREN

201    No children or none living
118    Good
30    Fair
40    Poor
8    Inapplicable (institution throughout or four of five years and no children)
42    Attitude unknown or unknown if any children

### 3–29B. DELINQUENCY OF CHILDREN (510)

122    None
21    Official delinquents
23    Unofficial delinquents
294    Inapplicable (children too young, or no children)
50    Unknown or unknown if any children

### 3–31A. ECONOMIC RESPONSIBILITY TOWARD FAMILY

131    Meets responsibility with legitimate earnings
11    Meets responsibility with illicit earnings
15    Meets responsibility with illicit and legitimate earnings
125    Fails to meet responsibility (through his own fault)
15    Unable to meet his responsibility because of chronic illness
50    Unable to meet his responsibility completely because of industrial condition though manifests willingness to do so
43    Inapplicable (not in community at all, or less than one year in community, responsibility not determinable)
49    Unknown

### 3–31B. SAVINGS (See Appendix C, 16A)

### 3–32A. INSURANCE (See Appendix C, 18)

### 3–32B. INSURANCE—PREMIUM PAID BY WHOM (See Appendix C, 19)

### 3–33A. ECONOMIC CONDITION

20    Comfortable
177    Marginal
69    Entirely or partially dependent on agencies or persons outside of immediate family (not because of depression)
44    Entirely or partially dependent on agencies or relatives (because of depression)
39    Entirely or partially dependent on relatives (not because of depression)

43 Inapplicable (institution throughout or in community for less than one year)
47 Unknown

## 3–33B. DEPENDENTS (See Appendix C, 15)

### 3–34A. DISPOSITION OF EARNINGS

164 Self only
153 Wife and/or children, no dependent parents
6 Wife and/or children, dependent parents
9 Dependent parents
59 Inapplicable (as no earnings either because in institution throughout or most of the time or idle with cause)
48 Unknown

### 3–34B. INDUSTRIAL HISTORY

62 Success
115 Partial success
130 Failure (including illegitimate occupation)
54 Inapplicable (never in community or unable to work for legitimate reasons, or in community too brief to judge)
33 Inapplicable as on work relief (and on straight relief for more than three years)
45 Unknown

### 3–35. NUMBER OF SOCIAL SERVICE AGENCIES (KNOWN TO SOCIAL AGENCIES, BY NUMBER OF AGENCIES)

145 None
68 One
59 Two
33 Three
22 Four
9 Five
9 Six
12 Seven and over
35 Inapplicable (institution throughout or too brief to judge)
47 Unknown if any

## 3–36. TYPE OF SOCIAL SERVICE AGENCIES (See Appendix C, 20A)

### 3–36B. LENGTH OF TIME IN PRIVATE EMPLOYMENT

39 Never in private employment
22 Less than 6 months
12 6–11 months
14 12–23 months
25 24–35 months
26 36–47 months
35 48–59 months

56  60 months
132  Off and on throughout, exact time unknown
37  Inapplicable (institution large part of time)
41  Unknown

## 3–37. USUAL OCCUPATION (See Appendix C, 22)

## 3–38A. SKILL (See Appendix C, 24)

### 3–38B. SKILL IN FIFTH YEAR

125  Unskilled
121  Semi-skilled
32  Skilled
118  Inapplicable (institution, chronic illness, idle, illicit occupation)
43  Unknown

## 3–39A. STEADINESS OF EMPLOYMENT (See Appendix C, 30)

## 3–39B. WORK HABITS (See Appendix C, 28)

### 3–39C. WORK RELIEF

347  No work relief or inapplicable or unknown
1  Work relief throughout
24  Work relief and some steady employment
10  Work relief and odd jobs
54  Work relief and straight relief (possibly odd jobs)
1  Work relief and unemployment
2  Work relief and illicit work (even if odd jobs)

### 3–40A. NUMBER OF DIFFERENT OCCUPATIONS

113  One
53  Two
25  Three
4  Four
1  Five or more
102  Odd jobs
97  Inapplicable (never in community, idle for cause, illicit occupation throughout or mostly on relief or work relief)
44  Unknown

### 3–41. AVERAGE WAGE—WEEKLY

| | | | |
|---|---|---|---|
| 17 | Less than $5 | 13 | $40 and over |
| 34 | $5–$9 | 77 | Inapplicable (never in community, or too brief to judge, or idle for good reason, or seldom worked) |
| 50 | $10–$14 | | |
| 38 | $15–$19 | | |
| 42 | $20–$24 | 20 | Inapplicable as in illicit occupation throughout |
| 21 | $25–$29 | | |
| 11 | $30–$34 | 110 | Incalculable or unknown |
| 6 | $35–$39 | | |

### 3–42. HIGHEST WAGE—WEEKLY

| | | | |
|---|---|---|---|
| 23 | Under $10 | 19 | $40–$44 |
| 40 | $10–$14 | 17 | $45 and over |
| 54 | $15–$19 | 142 | Inapplicable (incalculable, or unknown, or institution throughout) |
| 48 | $20–$24 | | |
| 38 | $25–$29 | 20 | Inapplicable as in illicit occupation throughout |
| 25 | $30–$34 | | |
| 13 | $35–$39 | | |

### 3–43. AVERAGE PERIOD OF TIME HELD JOB

| | | | |
|---|---|---|---|
| 119 | Less than 3 months | 77 | Inapplicable (never in community or too brief to judge, as unable to work) |
| 19 | 3–5 months | | |
| 12 | 6–8 months | 20 | Inapplicable as in illicit occupation throughout |
| 4 | 9–11 months | | |
| 8 | 12–23 months | 70 | Incalculable (on and off in one place for years or one long job, others short or in private employment less than 2 years) |
| 17 | 24–35 months | | |
| 1 | 36–47 months | | |
| 43 | 48–60 months | 49 | Unknown |

### 3–44. LONGEST PERIOD OF TIME HELD JOB

| | | | |
|---|---|---|---|
| 93 | Less than 3 months | 48 | 48 months and over |
| 15 | 3–5 months | 19 | Incalculable (as on and off in one place) |
| 24 | 6–9 months | 77 | Inapplicable (never in community or unable to work or too brief to judge) |
| 24 | 10–11 months | | |
| 25 | 12–23 months | 20 | Inapplicable as in illicit occupation throughout |
| 28 | 24–35 months | | |
| 19 | 36–47 months | 47 | Unknown |

### 3–45A. ILLICIT OCCUPATION (See Appendix C, 23)

### 3–45B. USUAL REASON FOR LEAVING WORK (See Appendix C, 29)

### 3–46A. LEISURE (See Appendix C, 39)

3–46B. SOCIETY MEMBER (See Appendix C, 36)

3–47A. CHURCH ATTENDANCE (See Appendix C, 37)

3–47B. EDUCATIONAL ACTIVITIES (See Appendix C, 38)

3–48A. COMPANIONSHIPS (See Appendix C, 34)

3–48B. HAUNTS (See Appendix C, 35)

### 3–49. HABITS IN CONFLICT WITH LAW

| | |
|---|---|
| 36 | Inapplicable (never in community or too brief to judge) |
| 56 | Unknown |
| 137 | None |
| 210 | Had bad habits |

| | |
|---|---|
| 99 | Sex |
| 49 | Stealing |
| 181 | Excessive drinking |
| 11 | Drugs |
| 39 | Gambling |
| 4 | Lying |
| 5 | Other |

3–50A. GANG LIFE (See Appendix C, 35A)

3–50B. STREET LIFE (See Appendix C, 35B)

3–51A. DELINQUENCIES (See Appendix C, 54)

3–51B. OFFICIAL RECOGNITION OF DELINQUENCY (See Appendix C, 51)

3–52. PREDOMINANT OFFENSE (See Appendix C, 42)

3–53. NUMBER OF ARRESTS (See Appendix C, 40A)

3–54. NUMBER OF CONVICTIONS (See Appendix C, 44A)

### 3–55. FREQUENCY OF ARRESTS AMONG THOSE ARRESTED MORE THAN ONCE

| | |
|---|---|
| 13 | One arrest in less than 3 months |
| 24 | One arrest in 3–5 months |
| 26 | One arrest in 6–8 months |

13 One arrest in 9–11 months
18 One arrest in 12–14 months
12 One arrest in 15–17 months
11 One arrest in 18–20 months
3 One arrest in 21–23 months
31 One arrest in 24 and more months
210 Incalculable (only one arrest or no arrests, or for other reasons incalculable)
33 Inapplicable (not in community throughout or too brief to judge)
45 Unknown or unknown if arrested

## 3–56. FREQUENCY OF CONVICTIONS AMONG THOSE CONVICTED MORE THAN ONCE

9 One conviction in less than 3 months
20 One conviction in 3–5 months
16 One conviction in 6–8 months
17 One conviction in 9–11 months
11 One conviction in 12–14 months
9 One conviction in 15–17 months
11 One conviction in 18–20 months
6 One conviction in 21–23 months
45 One conviction in 24 months and more
219 Incalculable (no arrests or only one arrest, or one conviction)
33 Inapplicable (not in community throughout or too brief to judge)
43 Unknown or unknown if arrested

## 3–57A. ASSOCIATES IN CRIME

123 Offenses committed alone
33 Offenses committed with one or two others
19 Offenses committed with three or more others
70 Unknown with whom offenses committed
120 Non-delinquent
33 Inapplicable (not in community or too brief to judge or delinquency doubtful)
41 Unknown if delinquent

## 3–57B. DELINQUENCY IN FIFTH YEAR

146 Non-delinquent
203 Delinquent
49 Inapplicable (non-penal institution, dead)
41 Unknown

## 3–58. SUMMARY OF ARRESTS—BY TYPE (See Appendix C, 40B)

## 3–59. SUMMARY OF DISPOSITIONS OF ARRESTS—BY TYPE (See Appendix C, 44B)

## 3–60. SOCIAL SERVICE NEEDS NOT MET

87   Inapplicable or unknown
61   All needs met
72   No needs present
219  Not all needs met
    89   Some needs not met
   130   No needs met
---
67   Vocational .
65   Recreational
44   Family welfare
 0   Relief
71   Health-mental
 3   Health-physical
 3   Child or adolescent welfare
158   Friendly supervision

## 3–61. DELINQUENCY IN FIVE-YEAR PERIOD AND FIFTH YEAR IN COMBINATION

120   Non-delinquent
208   Delinquent throughout
 20   Delinquent—upgrade
 21   Temporary lapse after many years of non-delinquency
 18   Penal institution throughout (or for first 4 years, and last year unknown)
  2   Institution throughout (but not entirely penal)
  9   Mental hospital throughout
 41   Unknown

## 3–63A. FAMILY RELATIONSHIPS IN FIFTH YEAR

184   Succeed
132   Fail
 78   Inapplicable (institution, dead, no family)
 45   Unknown

## 3–63B. INDUSTRIAL HISTORY IN FIFTH YEAR

81   Success
79   Partial success
108   Failure (including illicit occupation)
83   Inapplicable (institution, dead, ill)
43   Inapplicable as depression victim
45   Unknown

## 3–64. ECONOMIC RESPONSIBILITY IN FIFTH YEAR

137   Meets responsibility legitimately
13   Meets responsibility illegitimately
 8   Meets responsibility partly illegitimately

101 Fails to meet responsibility
40 Inapplicable as is victim of industrial depression
10 Inapplicable as has chronic illness
13 Inapplicable as dependent for other good reasons
72 Inapplicable (dead, institution throughout)
45 Unknown

### 3–65A. ENVIRONMENTAL HISTORY IN FIFTH YEAR

83 Good
138 Fair
93 Poor
72 Inapplicable (institution or dead or too brief to judge)
53 Unknown

### 3–65B. LEISURE AND HABITS IN FIFTH YEAR

8 Constructive
148 Negative
153 Harmful
72 Inapplicable (institution, dead)
58 Unknown

### 3–66. PRINCIPAL COMPONENT OF MISCONDUCT

18 Penal institution at least 55 months (or part of time and then mental hospital totalling 55 months) or sentence imposed during second five-year period and effective for part of third five-year period, and then non-delinquent
92 Conviction for serious offense; warrant out for serious offense; dishonorable discharge or desertion from Army or Navy
5 Unofficial serious delinquencies
3 Arrest for serious offense, not followed by conviction
105 Conviction for minor offense
31 Unofficial minor offense, or warrant out for minor
15 Arrest for minor offense not followed by conviction, or disposition unknown
120 Non-delinquent
9 Inapplicable (non-penal institution throughout)
41 Unknown, or delinquency doubtful

### 3–67. AGE AT REFORMATION (510)

| | | | |
|---|---|---|---|
| 1 | Under 18 | 20 | 33–35 |
| 24 | 18–20 | 9 | 36–38 |
| 23 | 21–23 | 9 | 39–41 |
| 22 | 24–26 | 2 | 42 and over |
| 24 | 27–29 | 316 | Inapplicable as did not reform |
| 19 | 30–32 | 41 | Unknown if reformed |

### 3–68. AGE AT CHANGE FROM SERIOUS TO MINOR DELINQUENCY SINCE SENTENCE TO REFORMATORY (510)

| | | | |
|---|---|---|---|
| 1 | Under 18 | 3 | 42–44 |
| 24 | 18–20 | 1 | 45 and over |
| 36 | 21–23 | 320 | Inapplicable as continued to be serious of- |
| 39 | 24–26 | | fender to death, or unknown if change |
| 40 | 27–29 | | from serious to minor, or did not |
| 23 | 30–32 | | change from serious to minor but to |
| 11 | 33–35 | | non-delinquency, or always minor of- |
| 7 | 36–38 | | fender |
| 5 | 39–41 | | |

### 3–69. CONDUCT DURING FIFTEEN YEARS AFTER END OF REFORMATORY SENTENCE (510)

135 Serious offender throughout
1 Minor offender throughout
121 Did not reform but became a minor offender
    9 Under 21 years
   44 At 21–26 years
   46 At 27–32 years
   22 At 33 years or older
140 Reformed
   18 Under 21 years
   38 At 21–26 years
   45 At 27–32 years
   39 At 33 years or older
5 Temporary lapse in conduct when under 33 years old after at least five years of non-delinquency
16 Temporary lapse in conduct when over 33 years old after at least five years of non-delinquency
50 Inapplicable (as died before beginning of third five-year span and continued to be serious offender to death)
1 Inapplicable (in mental hospital throughout almost entire span)
41 Unknown

### 3–79A. NUMBER OF DEATHS, BY PERIOD IN WHICH DEATH OCCURRED (98)

11 Died in Massachusetts Reformatory
22 Died on parole from Massachusetts Reformatory
23 Died in first five-year follow-up period
15 Died in second five-year follow-up period
27 Died in third five-year follow-up period

### 3–79B. AGE AT DEATH (98)

| | | | |
|---|---|---|---|
| 5 | Under 21 | 17 | 31–35 |
| 25 | 21–25 | 20 | 36–40 |
| 21 | 26–30 | 10 | 41 and over |

## 3–80. CAUSES OF DEATH (98)

| | | | |
|---|---|---|---|
| 24 | Tuberculosis | 3 | Intestinal infection |
| 21 | Accidents | 3 | After operation |
| 20 | Pneumonia or influenza | 2 | Suicide |
| 8 | Heart disease | 2 | Killed in brawls with police |
| 5 | Acute alcoholism | 6 | Other (Hodgkin's disease, cerebral hemorrhage) |
| 4 | Kidney disease | | |

3–H81A. INTERVIEW WITH (See Appendix C, 57)

3–H81B. WHEREABOUTS AT END OF PERIOD (See Appendix C, 2)

3–H82. ATTITUDE TO INVESTIGATION (See Appendix C, 56)

3–H107. INSTITUTIONAL EXPERIENCES (PENO-CORRECTIONAL)— GEOGRAPHICAL SPREAD (See Appendix C, 48)

3–H125. SUMMARY OF ARRESTS (See Appendix C, 40)

3–H126. SUMMARY OF DISPOSITIONS OF ARRESTS (See Appendix C, 44)

3–H139. INSTITUTIONAL EXPERIENCES (PENAL AND NON-PENAL)—NATURE OF, BY TYPE (See Appendix C, 47)

# PERIOD-COMPARISON TABLES

THE tables in this appendix are numbered to check with those in *Later Criminal Careers,* Appendix D, p. 329. Wherever tables have been inserted that do not appear in the latter work, they have been placed in their proper order and designated by letter. Although the purpose of this appendix is to present a mass comparison of the status of the men in follow-up Periods I, II, and III, wherever data were pertinent or available for the period prior to commission to the Reformatory, they are included even though not referred to in the text. Occasionally even data from the parole period have been inserted.

In each period are included the men who are living at the beginning of every span. The pre-Reformatory Period refers to 510 men, Period I to 477, Period II to 454, and Period III to 439. This differs from the presentation made in Appendix D of *Later Criminal Careers,* since in that appendix comparison was made between the 454 men living at the beginning of the second five-year period and the same 454 men in the first follow-up period and in the pre-Reformatory Period. Therefore, the percentages given are not the same in the two works.

Wherever a line appears beneath a category, it means that in the categories appearing below the line, each case may have been recorded more than once. This is a *multiple* table and totals to more than 510 in the prior period, 477 in Period I, 454 in Period II, and 439 in Period III. The sum of the incidence of the categories "inapplicable," "unknown if any," and "none," if subtracted from the total cases involved, gives the number of cases actually represented by the remaining categories or sub-classes of the factor.

When a space appears between categories, it means that the number immediately preceding the space has been distributed into the categories following it; that is, the sum of the number below the space equals the number above it.

## Environmental Factors

### 1. WITH WHOM LIVING

| | At time of commitment to Reformatory | | End of Period I | | End of Period II | | End of Period III | |
|---|---|---|---|---|---|---|---|---|
| | Number | Per cent | Number | Per cent | Number | Per cent | Number | Per cent |
| Inapplicable (as in institution or army, or dead) or whereabouts unknown or unknown with whom living | 14 | – | 161 | – | 137 | – | 138* | – |
| Parents ................. | 343 | 69.2 | 52 | 16.5 | 48 | 15.1 | 29 | 9.6 |
| Siblings ................. | 25 | 5.0 | 16 | 5.1 | 20 | 6.3 | 13 | 4.3 |
| Other relatives ............ | 30 | 6.1 | 4 | 1.3 | 3 | .9 | 7 | 2.3 |
| Wife and children ......... | 28 | 5.6 | 156 | 49.4 | 165 | 52.1 | 168 | 55.8 |
| Children ................ | 0 | – | 0 | – | 3 | .9 | 5 | 1.7 |
| Sweetheart .............. | 0 | – | 13 | 4.1 | 7 | 2.2 | 6 | 2.0 |
| Employer ............... | 0 | – | 3 | 1.0 | 7 | 2.2 | 6 | 2.0 |
| Alone .................. | 70 | 14.1 | 72 | 22.6 | 64 | 20.3 | 67 | 22.3 |

* Institution or army, 67; deceased, 27; unknown, 44.

### 2. WHEREABOUTS

| | End of Period I | | End of Period II | | End of Period III | |
|---|---|---|---|---|---|
| | Number | Per cent | Number | Per cent | Number | Per cent |
| Penal institution ............ | 85 | 17.8 | 55 | 12.1 | 49 | 11.2 |
| Non-penal institution ........ | 7 | 1.5 | 14 | 3.1 | 16 | 3.6 |
| Boston and vicinity .......... | 68 | 14.3 | 92 | 20.3 | 87 | 19.8 |
| Other cities in Massachusetts .. | 111 | 23.3 | 99 | 21.8 | 89 | 20.3 |
| Other states ............... | 81 | 16.9 | 108 | 23.8 | 117 | 26.7 |
| Foreign countries ........... | 7 | 1.5 | 6 | 1.3 | 5 | 1.1 |
| Fugitive from justice ......... | 31 | 6.5 | 3 | 0.7 | 1 | 0.2 |
| Drifting around ............ | 6 | 1.3 | 12 | 2.7 | 6 | 1.4 |
| Army or Navy .............. | 6 | 1.3 | 3 | .7 | 2 | .4 |
| At sea .................... | 6 | 1.3 | 0 | – | 0 | – |
| Dead .................... | 22 | 4.6 | 15 | 3.3 | 27 | 6.2 |
| Unknown for part of period ... | 20 | 4.2 | 14 | 3.1 | 4 | .9 |
| Completely unknown ........ | 27 | 5.5 | 33 | 7.1 | 36 | 8.2 |

### 3. MONTHS IN COMMUNITY

| | Period I | | Period II | | Period III | |
|---|---|---|---|---|---|---|
| | Number | Per cent | Number | Per cent | Number | Per cent |
| Unknown .................. | 49 | – | 54 | – | 41 | – |
| None ..................... | 13 | 3.0 | 30 | 7.5 | 27 | 6.8 |
| Less than 12 ............... | 29 | 6.8 | 22 | 5.5 | 19 | 4.8 |
| 12–23 ..................... | 33 | 7.7 | 25 | 6.3 | 14 | 3.5 |
| 24–35 ..................... | 37 | 8.6 | 22 | 5.5 | 24 | 6.0 |
| 36–59 ..................... | 108 | 25.2 | 80 | 20.0 | 104 | 26.1 |
| 60 ........................ | 208 | 48.7 | 221 | 55.2 | 210 | 52.8 |
| Average number of months in community of those in community at all ............. | 44.78 ± .53 | | 47.06 ± .51 | | 48.14 ± .46 | |

### 4. INSTITUTIONAL EXPERIENCES (PENAL AND NON-PENAL), MEN WITH

| | Prior Period | | Period I | | Period II | | Period III | |
|---|---|---|---|---|---|---|---|---|
| | Number | Per cent | Number | Per cent | Number | Per cent | Number | Per cent |
| Inapplicable, unknown ..... | 70 | – | 45 | – | 53 | – | 43 | – |
| No institutional experience .. | 162 | 36.8 | 217 | 50.2 | 231 | 57.6 | 221* | 55.8 |
| Institutional experience ..... | 278 | 63.2 | 215 | 49.8 | 170 | 42.4 | 175 | 44.2 |

\* In community throughout or no institutional experience up to time of death.

### 5. MOBILITY

| | Prior Period | | Period I | | Period II | | Period III | |
|---|---|---|---|---|---|---|---|---|
| | Number | Per cent | Number | Per cent | Number | Per cent | Number | Per cent |
| Inapplicable, unknown ..... | 0 | – | 88 | – | 94 | – | 86 | – |
| Mobility not excessive ....... | 277 | 54.3 | 178 | 45.8 | 191 | 53.1 | 208 | 58.9 |
| Mobility excessive .......... | 233 | 45.7 | 211 | 54.2 | 169 | 46.9 | 145 | 41.1 |

### 6. HOUSEHOLD STABILITY

| | Period I | | Period II | | Period III | |
|---|---|---|---|---|---|---|
| | Number | Per cent | Number | Per cent | Number | Per cent |
| Inapplicable, unknown ....... | 105 | – | 118 | – | 95 | – |
| No change ................. | 146 | 39.2 | 183 | 54.4 | 209 | 60.8 |
| One or two changes .......... | 90 | 24.2 | 43 | 12.8 | 44 | 12.8 |
| Three changes or more ....... | 136 | 36.6 | 110 | 32.8 | 91 | 26.4 |

### 7. HOME—PHYSICAL

| | Period I | | Period II | | Period III | |
|---|---|---|---|---|---|---|
| | Number | Per cent | Number | Per cent | Number | Per cent |
| Inapplicable, unknown ....... | 141 | – | 129 | – | 98 | – |
| Good .................... | 87 | 25.9 | 109 | 33.5 | 90 | 26.4 |
| Fair .................... | 128 | 38.1 | 116 | 35.7 | 143 | 41.9 |
| Poor .................... | 121 | 36.0 | 100 | 30.8 | 108 | 31.7 |

### 8. NEIGHBORHOOD—TYPE

| | Period I | | Period II | | Period III | |
|---|---|---|---|---|---|---|
| | Number | Per cent | Number | Per cent | Number | Per cent |
| Inapplicable, unknown ....... | 86 | – | 116 | – | 94 | – |
| Mostly urban .............. | 307 | 78.5 | 276 | 81.7 | 263 | 76.2 |
| Mostly rural ................ | 26 | 6.7 | 33 | 9.8 | 40 | 11.6 |
| Varied (urban and rural) ..... | 58 | 14.8 | 29 | 8.5 | 42 | 12.2 |

### 9. NEIGHBORHOOD INFLUENCES

| | Period I | | Period II | | Period III | |
|---|---|---|---|---|---|---|
| | Number | Per cent | Number | Per cent | Number | Per cent |
| Inapplicable, unknown ....... | 136 | – | 130 | – | 98 | – |
| Good .................... | 52 | 15.2 | 46 | 14.2 | 34 | 10.0 |
| Fair .................... | 149 | 43.7 | 164 | 50.6 | 190 | 55.7 |
| Poor .................... | 140 | 41.1 | 114 | 35.2 | 117 | 34.3 |

### 9A. MORAL STANDARDS OF HOME*

| | Period II | | Period III | |
|---|---|---|---|---|
| | Number | Per cent | Number | Per cent |
| Inapplicable, unknown ...................... | 120 | – | 96 | – |
| Good ................................... | 134 | 40.1 | 131 | 38.2 |
| Fair ................................... | 76 | 22.8 | 112 | 32.7 |
| Poor ................................... | 124 | 37.1 | 100 | 29.1 |

* Information not gathered in Period I.

### 9B.  ENVIRONMENT*

|  | *Period II* | | *Period III* | |
|---|---|---|---|---|
|  | Number | Per cent | Number | Per cent |
| Unknown, inapplicable | 127 | – | 99† | – |
| Good | 81 | 24.8 | 79 | 23.2 |
| Fair | 140 | 42.8 | 150 | 44.1 |
| Poor | 106 | 32.4 | 111 | 32.7 |

\* Information not available for Period I.

† In institution throughout or in community for less than one year and environmental judgment not possible, 43; unknown, 56.

### 10.  MARITAL STATUS*

|  | *At time of commitment to Reformatory* | | *End of Period I* | | *End of Period II* | | *End of Period III* | |
|---|---|---|---|---|---|---|---|---|
|  | Number | Per cent | Number | Per cent | Number | Per cent | Number | Per cent |
| Status unknown, unknown if married or single, dead ... | 2 | – | 42 | – | 44 | – | 41 | – |
| Single | 462 | 90.9 | 198 | 45.5 | 157 | 38.3 | 131 | 32.9 |
| Married | 46 | 9.1 | 237 | 54.5 | 253 | 61.7 | 267 | 67.1 |
| Legitimate marriage, living with wife | 27 | 5.3 | 176 | 40.5 | 177 | 43.2 | 185 | 46.5 |
| Separated | 12 | 2.4 | 38 | 8.7 | 42 | 10.2 | 44 | 11.1 |
| Divorced | 3 | .6 | 16 | 3.7 | 26 | 6.3 | 30 | 7.5 |
| Widowed | 4 | .8 | 7 | 1.6 | 8 | 2.0 | 8 | 2.0 |

\* Slight difference between this table and table in *Later Criminal Careers* because of additional information gathered in present investigation.

### 11.  NUMBER OF CHILDREN

|  | *At time of commitment to Reformatory* | | *End of Period I* | | *End of Period II* | | *End of Period III* | |
|---|---|---|---|---|---|---|---|---|
|  | Number | Per cent | Number | Per cent | Number | Per cent | Number | Per cent |
| Single | 462 | – | 198 | – | 157 | – | 131 | – |
| Unknown if married or unknown if any children | 0 | – | 39 | – | 49 | – | 41 | – |
| None | 6 | – | 76 | – | 64 | – | 73 | – |
| One | 18 | 56.3 | 79 | 48.2 | 68 | 37.0 | 72 | 37.1 |
| Two | 3 | 9.4 | 39 | 23.8 | 43 | 23.4 | 38 | 19.6 |
| Three | 10 | 31.3 | 20 | 12.2 | 33 | 17.9 | 32 | 16.5 |
| Four or more | 1 | 3.0 | 26 | 15.8 | 40 | 21.7 | 52 | 26.8 |
| Average number of children among those with children | 2.18 ± .11 | | 2.32 ± .08 | | 2.46 ± .11 | | 2.98 ± .09 | |

## 12. CONJUGAL RELATIONS

| | Prior Period | | Period I | | Period II | | Period III | |
|---|---|---|---|---|---|---|---|---|
| | Number | Per cent | Number | Per cent | Number | Per cent | Number | Per cent |
| Inapplicable, unknown, married too brief to judge, unknown whether married or single | 0 | – | 72 | – | 96 | – | 95 | – |
| Single | 462 | – | 198 | – | 157 | – | 131 | – |
| Good | 29 | 60.4 | 116 | 56.0 | 122 | 60.7 | 138 | 64.8 |
| Fair | 6 | 12.5 | 34 | 16.4 | 30 | 14.9 | 33 | 15.5 |
| Poor | 13 | 27.1 | 57 | 27.6 | 49 | 24.4 | 42 | 19.7 |

## 12A. ATTITUDE OF OFFENDER TO MARITAL RESPONSIBILITY

| | Period II | | Period III | |
|---|---|---|---|---|
| | Number | Per cent | Number | Per cent |
| Single | 157 | – | 131 | – |
| Unknown whether married or single | 37 | – | 36 | – |
| Assume | 125 | 62.2 | 137 | 65.2 |
| Neglect | 76 | 37.8 | 73 | 34.8 |
| Unknown (or marriage too brief to judge) | 13 | – | 8 | – |
| Inapplicable (as separated, divorced, or widowed before beginning of period and not remarried and did not have children to whom responsible in period) | 37 | – | 35 | – |
| Institution or dead (over 4 years) | 8 | – | 3 | – |
| Wife in institution 4 years or more | 1 | – | 3 | – |
| Inapplicable because of depression or illness. Does best he can | – | – | 13 | – |

## 12B. ATTITUDE OF WIFE TO MARITAL RESPONSIBILITY

| | Period II | | Period III | |
|---|---|---|---|---|
| | Number | Per cent | Number | Per cent |
| Single | 157 | – | 131 | – |
| Inapplicable (separated from offender before beginning of period and does not have children for whom she is responsible in Period III) | 37 | – | 48 | – |
| Assume | 174 | 89.7 | 179 | 88.2 |
| Neglect | 20 | 10.3 | 24 | 11.8 |
| Unknown | 20 | – | 15 | – |
| Husband in institution throughout | 8 | – | 3 | – |
| Unknown whether married or single | 37 | – | 36 | – |
| Wife in institution four of five years | 1 | – | 3 | – |

### 12C. COMPETENCE OF WIFE AS HOMEMAKER (LAST WIFE)*

| | Period II | | Period III | |
|---|---|---|---|---|
| | Number | Per cent | Number | Per cent |
| Inapplicable (as separated, widowed, or divorced before beginning of period or offender in institution, or wife in institution four of five years) | 45 | – | 58 | – |
| Single ..................................... | 157 | – | 131 | – |
| Unknown whether married or single .......... | 37 | – | 36 | – |
| Good ...................................... | 128 | 69.9 | 140 | 71.1 |
| Fair ...................................... | 41 | 22.4 | 44 | 22.3 |
| Poor ...................................... | 14 | 7.7 | 13 | 6.6 |
| Unknown ................................. | 32 | – | 17 | – |

\* Refers to legal marriages only.

### 13. RELATION TO NEAREST RELATIVES

| | Period I | | Period II | | Period III | |
|---|---|---|---|---|---|---|
| | Number | Per cent | Number | Per cent | Number | Per cent |
| Inapplicable, unknown ....... | 106 | – | 90 | – | 102* | – |
| In touch with, friendly ....... | 201 | 54.2 | 190 | 52.2 | 190 | 56.4 |
| In touch with because or when in need .................. | 83 | 22.4 | 71 | 19.5 | 54 | 16.0 |
| Rarely in touch ............. | 87 | 23.4 | 103 | 28.3 | 93 | 27.6 |

\* No relatives, 6; in institution throughout or in community less than one year, relation not determinable, 43; unknown, 53.

### 14. FAMILY RELATIONSHIPS

| | Prior Period | | Period I | | Period II | | Period III | |
|---|---|---|---|---|---|---|---|---|
| | Number | Per cent | Number | Per cent | Number | Per cent | Number | Per cent |
| Inapplicable or unknown .... | 77 | – | 96 | – | 94 | – | 96* | – |
| Succeed ................. | 137 | 31.6 | 198 | 52.0 | 180 | 50.0 | 186 | 54.2 |
| Fail .................... | 296 | 68.4 | 183 | 48.0 | 180 | 50.0 | 157 | 45.8 |

\* Never in community, or less than one year in community, relation not determinable, or wife in institution over four of five years, 46; unknown, 50.

## *Economic Responsibility*

### 15. DEPENDENTS

|  | Period I | | Period II | | Period III | |
|---|---|---|---|---|---|---|
|  | Number | Per cent | Number | Per cent | Number | Per cent |
| Inapplicable, unknown ....... | 73 | – | 92 | – | 83* | – |
| No dependents .............. | 132 | 32.7 | 112 | 30.9 | 98 | 27.5 |
| Dependents ................. | 272 | 67.3 | 250 | 69.1 | 258 | 72.5 |

* Never in community or in community less than a year, 43; unknown, 40.

### 16. DISPOSITION OF EARNINGS

|  | Period I | | Period II | | Period III | |
|---|---|---|---|---|---|---|
|  | Number | Per cent | Number | Per cent | Number | Per cent |
| Inapplicable, unknown ....... | 99 | – | 102 | – | 107 | – |
| Self only ................. | 204 | 53.9 | 188 | 53.4 | 164 | 49.4 |
| Wife and/or children, no dependent parents ........... | 137 | 36.3 | 147 | 41.8 | 153 | 46.1 |
| Wife and/or children, has dependent parents but does not support them ............. | 6 | 1.6 | 6 | 1.7 | 6 | 1.8 |
| Dependent parents, supporting or helping support ......... | 29 | 7.7 | 11 | 3.1 | 9 | 2.7 |
| Wife and children and supports dependent parents ......... | 2 | .5 | 0 | – | 0 | – |

### 16A. SAVINGS

|  | Period II | | Period III | |
|---|---|---|---|---|
|  | Number | Per cent | Number | Per cent |
| Inapplicable (institution mostly or chronic illness or for other legitimate reasons unable to work or dead four of five years) .................... | 41 | – | 43 | – |
| Yes ................................ ....... | 76 | 23.8 | 36 | 10.8 |
| No ....................................... | 243 | 76.2 | 298 | 89.2 |
| Unknown ................................ | 94 | – | 62 | – |

## 17. ECONOMIC CONDITION

| | Prior Period | | Period I | | Period II* | | Period III | |
|---|---|---|---|---|---|---|---|---|
| | Number | Per cent | Number | Per cent | Number | Per cent | Number | Per cent |
| Inapplicable or unknown .... | 63 | – | 76 | – | 109 | – | 90 | – |
| Comfortable .............. | 129 | 28.9 | 34 | 8.5 | 34 | 9.9 | 20 | 5.7 |
| Marginal ................ | 252 | 56.4 | 318 | 79.3 | 243 | 70.4 | 177 | 50.7 |
| Dependent ............... | 66 | 14.7 | 49 | 12.2 | 68 | 19.7 | 152 | 43.6 |

\* The slight change in figures and percentages from *Later Criminal Careers* is due to the fact that we have now added to the dependent group 8 men who were dependent because of the depression and whom we had previously included in the inapplicable group.

## 18. INSURANCE

| | Prior Period | | Period II | | Period III | |
|---|---|---|---|---|---|---|
| | Number | Per cent | Number | Per cent | Number | Per cent |
| Inapplicable or unknown ..... | 15 | – | 172 | – | 115* | – |
| No insurance .............. | 252 | 50.9 | 144 | 51.1 | 178 | 54.9 |
| Insurance ................. | 243 | 49.1 | 138 | 48.9 | 146 | 45.1 |

\* Never in community or less than a year, 43; unknown, 72.

## 19. INSURANCE—PREMIUM PAID BY WHOM

| | Prior Period | | Period II | | Period III | |
|---|---|---|---|---|---|---|
| | Number | Per cent | Number | Per cent | Number | Per cent |
| Inapplicable, unknown, no insurance, or unknown by whom paid .............. | 286 | – | 316 | – | 293* | – |
| Paid by self .............. | 14 | 6.3 | 110 | 79.7 | 121 | 82.9 |
| Paid by relatives or others ..... | 210 | 93.7 | 28 | 20.3 | 25† | 17.1 |

\* No insurance, 178; never in community or less than a year, 43; unknown if has insurance, 72.
† Paid by relatives, 21; paid by government or employer or social agency, 4.

## 20. KNOWN TO SOCIAL SERVICE AGENCIES

| | Prior Period | | Period I | | Period II | | Period III | |
|---|---|---|---|---|---|---|---|---|
| | Number | Per cent | Number | Per cent | Number | Per cent | Number | Per cent |
| Inapplicable, unknown ..... | 67 | – | 95 | – | 98 | – | 82 | – |
| Not known to agencies ..... | 189 | 42.7 | 285 | 74.6 | 210 | 59.0 | 145 | 40.6 |
| Known to agencies ......... | 254 | 57.3 | 97 | 25.4 | 146 | 41.0 | 212 | 59.4 |

## 20A. TYPE OF SOCIAL SERVICE AGENCIES
(Known to Social Service Agencies, by Type of Agency)

| | Period II | | Period III | |
|---|---|---|---|---|
| | Number | Per cent | Number | Per cent |
| Inapplicable (institution throughout or too brief to judge) .................................. | 35 | – | 35 | – |
| Not known to any agencies ................... | 210 | – | 145 | – |
| Unknown whether dealt with by agencies ....... | 63 | – | 47 | – |
| Dealt with by agencies ....................... | 146 | – | 212 | – |
| Health—physical ........................... | 74 | 50.7 | 68 | 32.1 |
| Health—mental ............................ | 14 | 9.6 | 20 | 9.4 |
| Relief .................................... | 90 | 61.6 | 172 | 81.1 |
| Family welfare ............................ | 11 | 7.5 | 6 | 2.8 |
| Child or adolescent welfare .................. | 20 | 13.7 | 17 | 8.0 |
| Correctional .............................. | 4 | 2.7 | 6 | 2.8 |
| Other (vocational) ......................... | 29 | 19.9 | 14 | 6.6 |
| Work relief ............................... | 0 | – | 63 | 29.7 |

## 21. ECONOMIC RESPONSIBILITY TOWARD FAMILY

| | Prior Period | | Period I | | Period II | | Period III | |
|---|---|---|---|---|---|---|---|---|
| | Number | Per cent | Number | Per cent | Number | Per cent | Number | Per cent |
| Inapplicable or unknown .... | 114 | – | 101 | – | 117 | – | 157 | – |
| Meets responsibility ........ | 70 | 17.7 | 249 | 66.2 | 215 | 60.8 | 157 | 55.7 |
| Fails to meet responsibility .. | 326 | 82.3 | 127 | 33.8 | 122 | 39.2 | 125 | 44.3 |

## *Industrial History*

## 22. USUAL OCCUPATION

| | Prior Period | | Period I | | Period II | | Period III | |
|---|---|---|---|---|---|---|---|---|
| | Number | Per cent | Number | Per cent | Number | Per cent | Number | Per cent |
| Inapplicable, unknown, varied, exact nature unknown .... | 61 | – | 88 | – | 100 | – | 102* | – |
| Mostly idle ............... | 0 | – | 0 | – | 15 | 4.2 | 16 | 4.7 |
| Illicit occupation ........... | 0 | – | 28 | 7.2 | 25 | 7.1 | 26 | 7.7 |
| Rough labor .............. | 101 | 22.5 | 85 | 21.9 | 83 | 23.5 | 101 | 30.0 |
| Trucking, teaming ......... | 62 | 13.8 | 55 | 14.1 | 42 | 11.9 | 28 | 8.3 |
| Factory work ............. | 112 | 24.9 | 61 | 15.7 | 44 | 12.4 | 39 | 11.6 |
| Farm hand ............... | 33 | 7.4 | 12 | 3.1 | 13 | 3.7 | 10 | 3.0 |
| Salesmen, store clerks ....... | 31 | 6.9 | 30 | 7.7 | 31 | 8.8 | 32 | 9.5 |
| Skilled trades ............. | 54 | 12.0 | 88 | 22.6 | 67 | 18.9 | 57 | 16.9 |
| Restaurant or hotel work .... | 56 | 12.5 | 18 | 4.6 | 21 | 5.9 | 15 | 4.5 |
| Other .................... | 0 | – | 12 | 3.1 | 13 | 3.6 | 13 | 3.8 |

* In institution at least four of five years, or did not work for legitimate reasons, 62; varied or unknown, 40.

### 22A. NUMBER OF DIFFERENT OCCUPATIONS

|  | Period II | | Period III | |
|---|---|---|---|---|
|  | Number | Per cent | Number | Per cent |
| Inapplicable (never in community, idle for cause, illicit occupation throughout or mostly on relief or work relief), unknown .................. | 173 | — | 141 | — |
| One ...................................... | 163 | 58.0 | 113 | 37.9 |
| Two ...................................... | 68 | 24.2 | 53 | 17.8 |
| Three or more ............................. | 50 | 17.8 | 132 | 44.3 |

### 23. ILLICIT OCCUPATION

|  | Period I | | Period II | | Period III | |
|---|---|---|---|---|---|---|
|  | Number | Per cent | Number | Per cent | Number | Per cent |
| Inapplicable, unknown ....... | 140 | — | 144 | — | 112* | — |
| No illicit occupation ......... | 262 | 77.7 | 237 | 76.5 | 260 | 79.5 |
| Illicit occupation part of time .. | 51 | 15.1 | 50 | 16.1 | 47 | 14.4 |
| Illicit occupation throughout .. | 24 | 7.2 | 23 | 7.4 | 20 | 6.1 |

* Never in community, or in community less than one year and not in illicit occupation, 43; unknown, 69.

### 24. SKILL

|  | Prior Period | | Period I | | Period II | | Period III | |
|---|---|---|---|---|---|---|---|---|
|  | Number | Per cent | Number | Per cent | Number | Per cent | Number | Per cent |
| Inapplicable, unknown ..... | 6 | — | 102 | — | 112 | — | 130* | — |
| Skilled .................. | 30 | 5.0 | 37 | 9.9 | 38 | 11.4 | 30 | 9.7 |
| Semi-skilled ............. | 194 | 38.5 | 193 | 51.5 | 169 | 50.9 | 139 | 45.0 |
| Unskilled ............... | 280 | 56.5 | 145 | 38.6 | 125 | 37.7 | 140 | 45.3 |

* Institution throughout or in community too brief to judge, or idle, or illicit occupation throughout, 84; unknown, 46.

### 26. AVERAGE WAGE—WEEKLY

|  | Period I | | Period II | | Period III | |
|---|---|---|---|---|---|---|
|  | Number | Per cent | Number | Per cent | Number | Per cent |
| Inapplicable, unknown, no legitimate work ............ | 262 | — | 233 | — | 207 | — |
| Under $15 .................. | 25 | 11.6 | 37 | 16.9 | 101 | 43.5 |
| $15–$24 .................... | 81 | 37.7 | 77 | 34.8 | 80 | 34.5 |
| $25–$34 .................... | 76 | 35.4 | 74 | 33.4 | 32 | 13.8 |
| $35 and over ............... | 33 | 15.3 | 33 | 14.9 | 19 | 8.2 |
| Average weekly wage ...... | $26.60 ± .43 | | $25.25 ± .44 | | $19.20 ± .57 | |

## 27. HIGHEST WAGE—WEEKLY

| | Prior Period | | Period I | | Period II | | Period III | |
|---|---|---|---|---|---|---|---|---|
| | Number | Per cent | Number | Per cent | Number | Per cent | Number | Per cent |
| Inapplicable, unknown, no legitimate work ......... | 422 | – | 188 | – | 190 | – | 162 | – |
| Under $15 ................ | 48 | 54.5 | 10 | 3.5 | 17 | 6.5 | 63 | 22.7 |
| $15–$24 ................. | 30 | 34.1 | 79 | 27.3 | 70 | 26.5 | 102 | 36.8 |
| $25–$34 ................. | 9 | 10.2 | 102 | 35.3 | 73 | 27.6 | 63 | 22.7 |
| $35 and over ............. | 1 | 1.2 | 98 | 33.9 | 104 | 39.4 | 49 | 17.8 |
| Average highest weekly wage | $19.30 ± .44 | | $30.30 ± .48 | | $32.00 ± .47 | | $23.70 ± .56 | |

## 28. WORK HABITS

| | Prior Period | | Period I | | Period II | | Period III | |
|---|---|---|---|---|---|---|---|---|
| | Number | Per cent | Number | Per cent | Number | Per cent | Number | Per cent |
| Inapplicable or unknown .... | 132 | – | 124 | – | 114 | – | 129* | – |
| Good ................... | 75 | 19.8 | 124 | 35.1 | 140 | 41.2 | 133 | 42.9 |
| Fair .................... | 105 | 27.8 | 115 | 32.6 | 112 | 32.9 | 79 | 25.5 |
| Poor .................... | 198 | 52.4 | 114 | 32.3 | 88 | 25.9 | 98† | 31.6 |

* Never in community or unable to work for good reason, or in community too brief to judge, 82; unknown, 47.

† Poor, 78; illicit occupation throughout, 20.

## 29. USUAL REASON FOR LEAVING WORK

| | Period I | | Period II | | Period III | |
|---|---|---|---|---|---|---|
| | Number | Per cent | Number | Per cent | Number | Per cent |
| Inapplicable, unknown, other .. | 152 | – | 162 | – | 149* | – |
| Steady worker, seldom changes | 52 | 16.0 | 54 | 18.5 | 60 | 20.7 |
| Not fault of worker, or to better self ..................... | 100 | 30.8 | 109 | 37.3 | 116 | 40.0 |
| Fault of worker ............. | 173 | 53.2 | 129 | 44.2 | 114 | 39.3 |

* Never in community, illicit occupation throughout, or unavoidably idle throughout, 97; unknown, 51; other, 1.

## 30. STEADINESS OF EMPLOYMENT

| | Prior Period | | Period I | | Period II | | Period III | |
|---|---|---|---|---|---|---|---|---|
| | Number | Per cent | Number | Per cent | Number | Per cent | Number | Per cent |
| Inapplicable, unknown ..... | 122 | – | 128 | – | 113 | – | 129* | – |
| Regular ................ | 84 | 21.6 | 80 | 22.9 | 96 | 28.2 | 62 | 20.0 |
| Fairly regular ............. | | | 125 | 35.8 | 116 | 34.0 | 105 | 33.9 |
| Irregular ................ | 304 | 78.4 | 144 | 41.3 | 129 | 37.8 | 143† | 46.1 |

* Never in community or unable to work for good reason, or in community too brief to judge, 82; unknown, 47.

† Irregular, 123; illicit occupation, 20.

### 31. AVERAGE PERIOD OF TIME HELD JOB

| | *Period I* | | *Period II* | | *Period III* | |
|---|---|---|---|---|---|---|
| | Number | Per cent | Number | Per cent | Number | Per cent |
| Inapplicable, unknown, incalculable ................... | 180 | – | 207 | – | 216 | – |
| Less than 3 months .......... | 133 | 44.8 | 100 | 40.6 | 119 | 53.4 |
| 3–11 months .............. | 70 | 23.6 | 47 | 19.0 | 35 | 15.7 |
| 12–35 months ............. | 64 | 21.5 | 50 | 20.2 | 25 | 11.2 |
| 36 months and more ......... | 30 | 10.1 | 50 | 20.2 | 44 | 19.7 |
| Average number of months held job ................. | $14.66 \pm .58$ | | $10.7 \pm .80$ | | $18.14 \pm .86$ | |

### 32. LONGEST PERIOD OF TIME HELD JOB

| | *Prior Period* | | *Period I* | | *Period II* | | *Period III* | |
|---|---|---|---|---|---|---|---|---|
| | Number | Per cent | Number | Per cent | Number | Per cent | Number | Per cent |
| Inapplicable, unknown, incalculable, illicit occupation throughout ............. | 47 | – | 157 | – | 190 | – | 163 | – |
| Less than 12 months ........ | 271 | 58.5 | 182 | 56.9 | 122 | 46.2 | 156 | 56.5 |
| 12–23 months ............. | 110 | 23.8 | 50 | 15.6 | 30 | 11.4 | 25 | 9.1 |
| 24–47 months ............. | 82 | 17.7 | 50 | 15.6 | 65 | 24.6 | 47 | 17.0 |
| 48–60 months ............. | 0 | – | 38 | 11.9 | 47 | 17.8 | 48 | 17.4 |
| Average number of months held job longest ......... | $14.54 \pm .35$ | | $18.38 \pm .63$ | | $23.3 \pm .77$ | | $20.90 \pm .76$ | |

### 33. INDUSTRIAL HISTORY

| | *Period I* | | *Period II* | | *Period III* | |
|---|---|---|---|---|---|---|
| | Number | Per cent | Number | Per cent | Number | Per cent |
| Inapplicable, unknown ....... | 105 | – | 116 | – | 132 | – |
| Good ..................... | 78 | 21.0 | 84 | 24.8 | 62 | 20.2 |
| Fair ..................... | 127 | 34.1 | 128 | 37.9 | 115 | 37.5 |
| Poor ..................... | 167 | 44.9 | 126 | 37.3 | 130 | 42.3 |

## *Leisure and Habits*

### 34. COMPANIONSHIPS

| | *Prior Period* | | *Period I* | | *Period II* | | *Period III* | |
| --- | --- | --- | --- | --- | --- | --- | --- | --- |
| | Number | Per cent | Number | Per cent | Number | Per cent | Number | Per cent |
| Inapplicable, unknown ..... | 2 | – | 124 | – | 116 | – | 107* | – |
| Harmless ................. | 27 | 5.3 | 110 | 31.2 | 125 | 37.0 | 147 | 44.3 |
| Harmful ................. | 481 | 94.7 | 243 | 68.8 | 213 | 63.0 | 185 | 55.7 |

\* Never in community or if in community less than a year, use of leisure harmless, 42; unknown, 65.

### 35. HAUNTS

| | *Period I* | | *Period II* | | *Period III* | |
| --- | --- | --- | --- | --- | --- | --- |
| | Number | Per cent | Number | Per cent | Number | Per cent |
| Inapplicable, unknown ....... | 132 | – | 129 | – | 104* | – |
| Harmless ................. | 110 | 31.9 | 125 | 38.5 | 151† | 45.1 |
| Harmful ................. | 235 | 68.1 | 200 | 61.5 | 184 | 54.9 |

\* Never in community or if in community less than a year, haunts harmless, 41; unknown, 63.
† Good, 39; fair, 112.

### 35A. GANG LIFE

| | *Period II* | | *Period III* | |
| --- | --- | --- | --- | --- |
| | Number | Per cent | Number | Per cent |
| Inapplicable (never in community, or if in community less than a year, no gang life) ......... | 38 | – | 42 | – |
| Member of gang ........................... | 20 | 7.0 | 10 | 3.5 |
| No gang but crowd, or unknown if gang, but crowd | 114 | 40.0 | 110 | 38.3 |
| No gang or crowd ......................... | 115 | 40.4 | 151 | 52.6 |
| No gang, but unknown if crowd ............. | 36 | 12.6 | 16 | 5.6 |
| Unknown ................................ | 131 | – | 110 | – |

### 35B. STREET LIFE

| | *Period II* | | *Period III* | |
| --- | --- | --- | --- | --- |
| | Number | Per cent | Number | Per cent |
| Inapplicable (never in community, or if in community less than a year, no street life) ......... | 38 | – | 42 | – |
| Yes ....................................... | 131 | 48.7 | 132 | 44.9 |
| No ....................................... | 138 | 51.3 | 162 | 55.1 |
| Unknown ................................ | 147 | – | 103 | – |

## 36. SOCIETY MEMBER

| | Prior Period | | Period I | | Period II | | Period III | |
|---|---|---|---|---|---|---|---|---|
| | Number | Per cent | Number | Per cent | Number | Per cent | Number | Per cent |
| Inapplicable, unknown ..... | 0 | — | 116 | — | 134 | — | 115* | — |
| Yes (wholesome) .......... | 81 | 15.9 | 14 | 3.9 | 15 | 4.7 | 9 | 2.8 |
| Yes (not wholesome) ....... | 0 | — | 29 | 8.0 | 29 | 9.1 | 38 | 11.7 |
| No ..................... | 429 | 84.1 | 318 | 88.1 | 276 | 86.2 | 277 | 85.5 |

\* Never in community, or if in community less than one year, not a society member, 43; unknown, 72.

## 37. CHURCH ATTENDANCE

| | Prior Period | | Period I | | Period II | | Period III | |
|---|---|---|---|---|---|---|---|---|
| | Number | Per cent | Number | Per cent | Number | Per cent | Number | Per cent |
| Inapplicable, unknown ..... | 50 | — | 188 | — | 179 | — | 123* | — |
| Regular ................. | 39 | 8.5 | 39 | 13.4 | 33 | 12.0 | 28 | 8.9 |
| Irregular ................ | 407 | 88.5 | 125 | 43.3 | 111 | 40.4 | 79 | 25.0 |
| None ................... | 14 | 3.0 | 125 | 43.3 | 131 | 47.6 | 209 | 66.1 |

\* Never in community, or in community less than one year, not a church goer, 42; unknown, 81.

## 38. EDUCATIONAL ACTIVITIES

| | Period I | | Period II | | Period III | |
|---|---|---|---|---|---|---|
| | Number | Per cent | Number | Per cent | Number | Per cent |
| Inapplicable, unknown ....... | 116 | — | 133 | — | 108* | — |
| Yes ..................... | 14 | 3.9 | 18 | 5.6 | 11 | 3.3 |
| No ..................... | 347 | 96.1 | 303 | 94.4 | 320 | 96.7 |

\* Never in community, or in community less than one year, no educational activities, 42; unknown, 66.

## 39. LEISURE AND HABITS

| | Prior Period | | Period I | | Period II | | Period III | |
|---|---|---|---|---|---|---|---|---|
| | Number | Per cent | Number | Per cent | Number | Per cent | Number | Per cent |
| Inapplicable, unknown ..... | 5 | — | 111 | — | 103 | — | 101* | — |
| Constructive ............. | 0 | — | 17 | 4.6 | 15 | 4.3 | 9 | 2.7 |
| Negative ................ | 18 | 3.6 | 95 | 26.0 | 105 | 29.9 | 135 | 39.9 |
| Harmful ................ | 487 | 96.4 | 254 | 69.4 | 231 | 65.8 | 194 | 57.4 |

\* Never in community, or in community less than one year, not harmful, 42; unknown, 59.

## Criminality

### 40. SUMMARY OF ARRESTS
(Arrests, by Type of Offense)

| | Prior Period | | Period I | | Period II | | Period III | |
|---|---|---|---|---|---|---|---|---|
| | Number | Per cent | Number | Per cent | Number | Per cent | Number | Per cent |
| Type of offense unknown ... | 10 | – | 0 | – | 3 | – | 0 | – |
| Against property ........... | 950 | 49.1 | 244 | 26.0 | 165 | 17.3 | 119 | 12.0 |
| Against chastity ........... | 18 | .9 | 60 | 6.3 | 17 | 1.8 | 23 | 2.3 |
| Against family and children .. | 14 | .7 | 35 | 3.7 | 39 | 4.1 | 37 | 3.8 |
| Against public health ....... | 495 | 25.6 | 168 | 17.9 | 164 | 17.2 | 174 | 17.7 |
| Drunkenness .............. | 279 | 14.4 | 388 | 41.4 | 488 | 51.3 | 568 | 57.7 |
| Drugs ................... | 10 | .5 | 12 | 1.3 | 11 | 1.2 | 11 | 1.1 |
| Against person ............ | 107 | 5.5 | 13 | 1.5 | 41 | 4.3 | 43 | 4.4 |
| Other .................... | 61 | 3.3 | 18 | 1.9 | 27 | 2.8 | 10 | 1.0 |
| Total ................. | 1944 | | 938 | | 955 | | 985 | |

### 40A. NUMBER OF ARRESTS
(Men Arrested, by Number of Arrests)

| | Period I | | Period II | | Period III | |
|---|---|---|---|---|---|---|
| | Number | Per cent | Number | Per cent | Number | Per cent |
| Inapplicable (not in community throughout or too brief to judge) or unknown ........ | 142 | – | 91 | – | 74* | – |
| Not arrested ................ | 108 | 29.3 | 163 | 44.9 | 157 | 43.0 |
| Arrested ................... | 227 | 69.7 | 200 | 55.1 | 208 | 57.9 |
| One arrest ................. | 99 | 26.9 | 51 | 14.1 | 155 | 14.5 |
| Two arrests ................ | 50 | 13.6 | 36 | 9.9 | 44 | 12.1 |
| Three arrests .............. | 55 | 14.9 | 28 | 7.7 | 26 | 7.1 |
| Four arrests ............... | | | 18 | 5.0 | 24 | 6.6 |
| Five arrests ................ | 14 | 3.8 | 16 | 4.4 | 6 | 1.7 |
| Six arrests ................. | | | 6 | 1.7 | 8 | 2.2 |
| Seven arrests .............. | 42 | 11.5 | 8 | 2.2 | 12 | 3.3 |
| Eight arrests and more ....... | – | – | 36 | 9.9 | 33 | 9.0 |
| Number unknown ........... | – | – | 1 | .2 | 2 | .5 |
| Average number of arrests among those arrested ...... | 3.3 ± .11 | | 3.71 ± .12 | | 3.56 ± .11 | |

* Not in community throughout or too brief to judge, 33; unknown if arrested, 41.

40B. SUMMARY OF ARRESTS—BY TYPE

(Men Arrested, by Type of Offense)

| | Period II | | Period III | |
|---|---|---|---|---|
| | Number | Per cent | Number | Per cent |
| Inapplicable (not in community or too brief to judge) .................................. | 34 | – | 33 | – |
| Unknown if arrested ........................ | 57 | – | 41 | – |
| No arrests ................................. | 163 | – | 157 | – |
| Arrested ................................. | 200 | – | 208 | – |
| Crimes against property ..................... | 86 | 43.0 | 74 | 35.6 |
| Crimes against chastity ..................... | 16 | 8.0 | 18 | 8.7 |
| Crimes against family and children ............ | 21 | 10.5 | 16 | 7.7 |
| Crimes against public health, safety and policy (except drink and drugs) ..................... | 88 | 44.0 | 93 | 44.7 |
| Drunkenness .............................. | 101 | 50.5 | 103 | 49.5 |
| Drugs ................................... | 7 | 3.5 | 8 | 3.9 |
| Crimes against person ...................... | 22 | 11.0 | 25 | 12.0 |
| Other .................................... | 11 | 5.5 | 5 | 2.4 |

41. FREQUENCY OF ARRESTS AMONG THOSE ARRESTED MORE THAN ONCE

| | Prior Period | | Period I | | Period II | | Period III | |
|---|---|---|---|---|---|---|---|---|
| | Number | Per cent | Number | Per cent | Number | Per cent | Number | Per cent |
| Unknown, inapplicable, incalculable as only arrested once | 160 | – | 299 | – | 303 | – | 288 | – |
| Arrested more than once and frequency calculable ...... | 350 | – | 178 | – | 151 | – | 151 | – |
| One arrest in less than 9 months ............... | 153 | 43.7 | 69 | 38.8 | 67 | 44.4 | 63 | 41.7 |
| One arrest in 9–17 months .. | 118 | 33.7 | 48 | 27.0 | 37 | 24.5 | 43 | 28.5 |
| One arrest in 18 months or more .................. | 79 | 22.6 | 61 | 34.2 | 47 | 31.1 | 45 | 29.8 |
| Average frequency of arrests in months among those arrested more than once .. | $12.80 \pm .27$ | | $13.94 \pm .42$ | | $12.5 \pm .45$ | | $12.92 \pm .41$ | |

## 42. PREDOMINANT OFFENSE

### (Official and Unofficial Delinquents, by Predominant Offense)

|  | Prior Period | | Period I | | Period II | | Period III | |
|---|---|---|---|---|---|---|---|---|
|  | Number | Per cent | Number | Per cent | Number | Per cent | Number | Per cent |
| Inapplicable, unknown, not determined ............. | 53 | – | 75 | – | 94 | – | 81* | – |
| Non-delinquent ........... | 0 | – | 89 | – | 118 | – | 120 | – |
| Delinquent (official or un-official) ............... | 457 | – | 313 | – | 242 | – | 238 | – |
| Crimes against property ..... | 279 | 61.1 | 101 | 33.3 | 50 | 20.7 | 44 | 18.5 |
| Crimes against chastity ...... | 15 | 3.3 | 16 | 5.3 | 14 | 5.8 | 11 | 4.6 |
| Crimes against family and children .................. | 2 | .4 | 12 | 3.9 | 8 | 3.3 | 16 | 6.7 |
| Crimes against public health | 33 | 7.2 | 40 | 13.2 | 31 | 12.8 | 53 | 22.3 |
| Drunkenness .............. | 44 | 9.6 | 78 | 25.7 | 90 | 37.2 | 86 | 36.1 |
| Drug using or selling ....... | 4 | .9 | 5 | 1.7 | 6 | 2.5 | 6 | 2.5 |
| Crimes against person ...... | 8 | 1.8 | 6 | 2.0 | 1 | .4 | 5 | 2.1 |
| Varied .................. | 72 | 15.7 | 45 | 14.9 | 42 | 17.3 | 17 | 7.2 |

* Not in community at all, 27; unknown if arrested, 41; unknown or not determinable or no predominant offense, 13.

## 43. DRUNKENNESS

### (Official and Unofficial)

|  | Prior Period | | Period I | | Period II | | Period III | |
|---|---|---|---|---|---|---|---|---|
|  | Number | Per cent | Number | Per cent | Number | Per cent | Number | Per cent |
| Inapplicable or unknown ... | 2 | – | 131 | – | 99 | – | 144 | – |
| No drunkenness ........... | 308 | 60.6 | 149 | 43.1 | 173 | 48.7 | 114 | 38.6 |
| Drunkenness .............. | 200 | 39.4 | 197 | 56.9 | 182 | 51.3 | 181 | 61.4 |

## 44. SUMMARY OF DISPOSITIONS OF ARRESTS

| | Prior Period | | Period I | | Period II | | Period III | |
|---|---|---|---|---|---|---|---|---|
| | Number | Per cent | Number | Per cent | Number | Per cent | Number | Per cent |
| Commitment ............. | 604 | 31.2 | 312 | 33.3 | 282 | 30.7 | 322 | 32.9 |
| Probation ............... | 549 | 28.4 | 128 | 13.6 | 125 | 13.6 | 170 | 17.4 |
| Fine .................... | 221 | 11.4 | 214 | 22.8 | 154 | 16.7 | 99 | 10.1 |
| Commitment for non-payment of fine ................. | 59 | 3.1 | 36 | 3.8 | 36 | 3.9 | 24 | 2.5 |
| File .................... | 237 | 12.3 | 118 | 12.6 | 136 | 14.8 | 114 | 11.7 |
| Restitution .............. | | | 3 | .3 | 1 | .1 | 1 | .1 |
| Released by probation officer | 263 | 13.6 | 0 | – | 50 | 5.4 | 51 | 5.2 |
| Nol prossed ............. | | | 15 | 1.6 | 11 | 1.2 | 18 | 1.8 |
| No bill .................. | | | 6 | .6 | 6 | .7 | 0 | – |
| Not guilty or released ...... | | | 106 | 11.4 | 119 | 12.9 | 179 | 18.3 |
| Disposition unknown or other or awaiting disposition ... | 11 | – | 0 | – | 35 | – | 7 | – |
| Total ............... | 1944 | | 938 | | 955 | | 985 | |

## 44A. NUMBER OF CONVICTIONS AMONG MEN ARRESTED

(Men Convicted, by Number of Convictions)

| | Period I | | Period II | | Period III | |
|---|---|---|---|---|---|---|
| | Number | Per cent | Number | Per cent | Number | Per cent |
| Inapplicable or unknown (not in community throughout or too brief to judge, or not arrested, or unknown if arrested or arrested but number convictions unknown) ............... | 217 | – | 259 | – | 233 | – |
| Arrested but not convicted .... | 27 | 10.4 | 19 | 9.7 | 22 | 10.7 |
| Convicted .................. | 233 | 89.6 | 176 | 90.3 | 184 | 89.3 |
| One conviction ............. | 98 | 37.7 | 56 | 28.7 | 60 | 29.3 |
| Two convictions ............ | 47 | 18.1 | 30 | 15.4 | 43 | 21.0 |
| Three convictions ........... | 31 | 11.9 | 26 | 13.3 | 19 | 9.3 |
| Four convictions ............ | 16 | 6.2 | 13 | 6.7 | 17 | 8.3 |
| Five convictions ............ | 8 | 3.1 | 15 | 7.7 | 10 | 4.9 |
| Six convictions ............. | 10 | 3.8 | 6 | 3.1 | 10 | 4.9 |
| Seven convictions ............ | 0 | – | 3 | 1.6 | 1 | .5 |
| Eight convictions ........... | 23 | 8.8 | 27 | 13.8 | 24 | 11.1 |
| Average number of convictions among those arrested .. | $2.43 \pm .09$ | | $3.05 \pm .12$ | | $2.79 \pm .11$ | |

## 44B. SUMMARY OF DISPOSITIONS OF ARRESTS—BY TYPE

(Men Arrested, by Type of Disposition)

|  | Period II | | Period III | |
|---|---|---|---|---|
|  | Number | Per cent | Number | Per cent |
| Inapplicable (or no arrests, or unknown if arrested) | 254 | – | 231 | – |
| Arrested and disposition known ............... | 200 | – | 208 | – |
| Commitment ............................... | 111 | 55.5 | 131 | 62.0 |
| Probation ................................. | 65 | 32.5 | 77 | 37.0 |
| Fine ...................................... | 76 | 38.0 | 59 | 28.4 |
| Commitment for non-payment of fine .......... | 18 | 9.0 | 13 | 6.3 |
| Filed ..................................... | 70 | 35.0 | 57 | 27.4 |
| Restitution ................................ | 0 | – | 1 | .5 |
| Released by probation officer ................. | 31 | 15.5 | 25 | 12.0 |
| *Nol prossed* .............................. | 9 | 4.5 | 14 | 6.7 |
| No bill ................................... | 6 | 3.0 | 0 | – |
| Not guilty or released ...................... | 79 | 39.5 | 87 | 41.8 |
| Disposition unknown ....................... | 22 | – | 6 | – |

## 45. FREQUENCY OF CONVICTIONS AMONG THOSE CONVICTED MORE THAN ONCE

|  | Prior Period | | Period I | | Period II | | Period III | |
|---|---|---|---|---|---|---|---|---|
|  | Number | Per cent | Number | Per cent | Number | Per cent | Number | Per cent |
| Inapplicable, unknown, unknown if arrested, incalculable ................. | 169 | – | 315 | – | 308 | – | 295 | – |
| Convicted more than once and frequency calculable ...... | 341 | – | 165 | – | 146 | – | 144 | – |
| One conviction in less than 6 months ............... | 44 | 12.9 | 35 | 21.6 | 44 | 30.2 | 29 | 20.1 |
| One conviction in 6–11 months | 103 | 30.2 | 35 | 21.6 | 28 | 19.2 | 33 | 22.9 |
| One conviction in 12–17 months ............... | 71 | 20.8 | 25 | 15.4 | 15 | 10.2 | 20 | 13.9 |
| One conviction in 18–23 months ............... | 39 | 11.4 | 23 | 14.2 | 23 | 15.8 | 17 | 11.8 |
| One conviction in 24 months and over .............. | 84 | 24.7 | 44 | 27.2 | 36 | 24.6 | 45 | 31.3 |
| Average frequency of convictions in months among those convicted more than once .................. | 16.34 ± .36 | | 16.58 ± .52 | | 15.65 ± .48 | | 17.06 ± .57 | |

### 46. NUMBER OF PENAL EXPERIENCES

(Men Who Had Peno-Correctional Experiences, by Number of Experiences)

| | Prior Period Number | Prior Period Per cent | Period I Number | Period I Per cent | Period II Number | Period II Per cent | Period III Number | Period III Per cent |
|---|---|---|---|---|---|---|---|---|
| Inapplicable, unknown if any | 38 | — | 49 | — | 55 | — | 50* | — |
| No penal experiences ....... | 192 | 40.7 | 242 | 56.5 | 252 | 63.2 | 232 | 59.6 |
| Penal experiences .......... | 280 | 59.3 | 186 | 43.5 | 147 | 36.8 | 157 | 40.4 |
| 1–2 ..................... | | | 139 | 29.1 | 95 | 20.9 | 99† | 22.6 |
| 3–4 ..................... | | | 32 | 6.7 | 34 | 7.5 | 39 | 8.9 |
| 5–6 ..................... | | | 12 | 2.5 | 7 | 1.5 | 8 | 1.8 |
| 7–8 ..................... | | | 1 | .2 | 5 | 1.1 | 6 | 1.4 |
| 9–10 .................... | | | 0 | — | 3 | .7 | 3 | .7 |
| 11–12 ................... | | | 2 | .4 | 3 | .7 | 2 | .5 |
| Average number of penal experiences ............. | | | $2.22 \pm .08$ | | $2.72 \pm .12$ | | $2.72 \pm .11$ | |

\* Inapplicable, 10; unknown if any, 40.
† One, 67; two, 32.

### 47. INSTITUTIONAL EXPERIENCES (PENAL AND NON-PENAL)—BY TYPE

| | Prior Period Number | Prior Period Per cent | Period I Number | Period I Per cent | Period II Number | Period II Per cent | Period III Number | Period III Per cent |
|---|---|---|---|---|---|---|---|---|
| Reformatories ............. | 76 | 12.6 | 38 | 10.5 | 7 | 1.7 | 2 | .5 |
| Prisons ................... | 22 | 3.6 | 95 | 26.3 | 98 | 23.3 | 97 | 25.1 |
| Jails, houses of correction, state farms .............. | 216 | 35.8 | 217 | 60.1 | 285 | 67.7 | 288 | 74.4 |
| Other (truant schools, schools for feebleminded, industrial schools, protectorates, other) | 290 | 48.0 | 11 | 3.1 | 31 | 7.3 | 0 | — |
| Total ................. | 604 | | 361 | | 421 | | 387 | |

### 48. INSTITUTIONAL EXPERIENCES (PENO-CORRECTIONAL)—GEOGRAPHICAL SPREAD

| | Period I Number | Period I Per cent | Period II Number | Period II Per cent | Period III Number | Period III Per cent |
|---|---|---|---|---|---|---|
| Massachusetts .............. | 264 | 73.1 | 300 | 71.3 | 246 | 63.6 |
| Other states .............. | 93 | 25.8 | 116 | 27.6 | 137 | 35.4 |
| Canada ................... | 1 | .3 | 2 | .4 | 1 | .3 |
| Europe ................... | 3 | .8 | 3 | .7 | 3 | .7 |
| Total ................. | 361 | | 421 | | 387 | |

### 49. TIME IN PENAL INSTITUTION

|  | Period I Number | Period I Per cent | Period II Number | Period II Per cent | Period III Number | Period III Per cent |
|---|---|---|---|---|---|---|
| Unknown, inapplicable ....... | 49 | – | 55 | – | 50 | – |
| None ..................... | 241 | – | 252 | – | 232 | – |
| Less than 20 months ......... | 101 | 54.0 | 69 | 46.9 | 90 | 57.3 |
| 20–29 months .............. | 26 | 13.9 | 17 | 11.6 | 20 | 12.7 |
| 30–39 months .............. | 23 | 12.3 | 14 | 9.5 | 14 | 8.9 |
| 40–49 months .............. | 13 | 7.0 | 12 | 8.2 | 9 | 5.7 |
| 50–59 months .............. | 17 | 9.1 | 17 | 11.6 | 10 | 6.5 |
| 60 months ................. | 7 | 3.7 | 18 | 12.2 | 14 | 8.9 |
| Average number of months ... | 23.70 ± .78 | | 27.50 ± .98 | | 23.30 ± .87 | |

### 51. OFFICIAL RECOGNITION OF DELINQUENCY

|  | Prior Period Number | Prior Period Per cent | Period I Number | Period I Per cent | Period II Number | Period II Per cent | Period III Number | Period III Per cent |
|---|---|---|---|---|---|---|---|---|
| Inapplicable, unknown ..... | 49 | – | 48 | – | 86 | – | 68* | – |
| No delinquency ........... | 4 | – | 89 | – | 118 | – | 120 | – |
| Official .................. | 434 | 95.0 | 302 | 88.8 | 202 | 80.8 | 215 | 85.7 |
| Unofficial ................ | 23 | 5.0 | 38 | 11.2 | 48 | 19.2 | 36 | 14.3 |

* Not in community at all or too brief to judge, 27; unknown, 41.

### 52. ALIASES

|  | Period I Number | Period I Per cent | Period II Number | Period II Per cent | Period III Number | Period III Per cent |
|---|---|---|---|---|---|---|
| Inapplicable, unknown, no arrests ..................... | 227 | – | 261 | – | 237* | – |
| Used aliases ............... | 95 | 38.0 | 77 | 39.9 | 57 | 28.2 |
| Did not use aliases .......... | 155 | 62.0 | 116 | 60.1 | 145 | 71.8 |

* Inapplicable as not in community at all, 25; inapplicable as no arrests, 164; unknown, 48.

### 53. ASSOCIATES IN CRIME*

|  | Prior Period Number | Prior Period Per cent | Period II Number | Period II Per cent | Period III Number | Period III Per cent |
|---|---|---|---|---|---|---|
| Inapplicable or unknown ..... | 15 | – | 311 | – | 264 | – |
| Offenses committed alone ..... | 202 | 40.8 | 82 | 57.3 | 123 | 70.3 |
| Offenses committed with others | 293 | 59.2 | 61 | 42.7 | 52 | 29.7 |

* Information not available for Period I.

### 54. DELINQUENCIES (OFFICIAL AND UNOFFICIAL), BY SERIOUSNESS OF OFFENSE

| | Prior Period | | During Parole | | Period I | | Period II | | Period III | |
|---|---|---|---|---|---|---|---|---|---|---|
| | Number | Per cent | Number | Per cent | Number | Per cent | Number | Per cent | Number | Per cent |
| Inapplicable or unknown .......... | 49 | — | 86 | — | 24 | — | 62 | — | 50* | — |
| Non-delinquent ...... | 4 | .9 | 126 | 30.5 | 90 | 19.9 | 118 | 30.1 | 120 | 30.8 |
| Delinquent, minor .... | 62 | 13.5 | 77 | 18.7 | 132 | 29.1 | 125 | 31.9 | 151 | 38.8 |
| Delinquent, serious ... | 395 | 85.6 | 210 | 50.8 | 231 | 51.0 | 149 | 38.0 | 118 | 30.4 |

\* Mental hospital throughout, 9; unknown, 41.

## Miscellaneous

### 55. MENTAL CONDITION

| | Prior Period | | Period II | | Period III | |
|---|---|---|---|---|---|---|
| | Number | Per cent | Number | Per cent | Number | Per cent |
| Unknown .................. | 126 | — | 96 | — | 95 | — |
| Normal .................. | 105 | 27.3 | 123 | 34.3 | 123 | 35.8 |
| Abnormal ................. | 279 | 72.7 | 235 | 65.7 | 221 | 64.2 |

### 56. ATTITUDE TO INVESTIGATION

| | Period II | | Period III | |
|---|---|---|---|---|
| | Number | Per cent | Number | Per cent |
| Inapplicable or unknown ..................... | 269 | — | 132 | — |
| Friendly ................................... | 167 | 90.2 | 289 | 94.1 |
| Indifferent ................................ | 9 | 4.9 | 1 | .3 |
| Hostile ................................... | 9 | 4.9 | 17 | 5.6 |

### 57. INTERVIEW WITH

| | Period I | | Period II | | Period III | |
|---|---|---|---|---|---|---|
| | Number | Per cent | Number | Per cent | Number | Per cent |
| Offender .................. | 193 | 40.5 | 225 | 49.6 | 235 | 53.5 |
| Near relatives (wife, in-laws, siblings, aunts, cousins) .... | 179 | 37.5 | 147 | 32.4 | 109 | 24.8 |
| Others (police, probation officers, employers, social agencies) .................... | 105 | 22.0 | 12 | 2.7 | 8 | 1.8 |
| Record data or correspondence only .................... | | | 70 | 15.3 | 87 | 19.9 |

# CASE-BY-CASE COMPARISON TABLES

THIS appendix is concerned with the 439 men who were living at the beginning of the third five-year follow-up period. Their status in Period III is here related case-by-case to their status in Period II.

The table numbers check with those used in Appendix E, *Later Criminal Careers*. This arrangement has been maintained for the convenience of the student who may wish quickly to refer to tables in the other work. Wherever tables not contained in *Later Criminal Careers* have been inserted in this appendix, they are designated by letters.

From the title of each table it is possible to refer to Appendix A, *Definition of Terms*, where the definition of the factor will be found.

Reading from left to right the percentages total to 100. Unknown and inapplicable categories in either one or the other, or in both, periods, though presented, are not included in the percentages.

THIRD FIVE-YEAR PERIOD

| SECOND FIVE-YEAR PERIOD | Parents Num-ber | Per cent | Siblings Num-ber | Per cent | Other relatives Num-ber | Per cent | Wife and children Num-ber | Per cent | Children Num-ber | Per cent | Sweet-heart Num-ber | Per cent | Employer Num-ber | Per cent | Alone Num-ber | Per cent | Insti-tution Num-ber | Per cent | Died during period Num-ber | Per cent | Total | Un-known | Grand total |
|---|---|---|---|---|---|---|---|---|---|---|---|---|---|---|---|---|---|---|---|---|---|---|---|
| Parents | 22 | 45.8 | 1 | 2.1 | 1 | 2.1 | 8 | 16.6 | 0 | – | 0 | – | 1 | 2.1 | 7 | 14.6 | 7 | 14.6 | 1 | 2.1 | 48 | 0 | 48 |
| Siblings | 0 | – | 6 | 30.0 | 1 | 5.0 | 4 | 20.0 | 0 | – | 0 | – | 0 | – | 6 | 30.0 | 3 | 15.0 | 0 | – | 20 | 0 | 20 |
| Other relatives | 0 | – | 0 | – | 0 | – | 1 | 25.0 | 1 | 25.0 | 0 | – | 0 | – | 1 | 25.0 | 0 | – | 1 | 25.0 | 4 | 0 | 4 |
| Wife and children | 3 | 1.8 | 0 | – | 3 | 1.8 | 129 | 78.7 | 1 | .6 | 2 | 1.2 | 0 | – | 7 | 4.3 | 6 | 3.7 | 13 | 7.9 | 164 | 0 | 164 |
| Children | 0 | – | 0 | – | 0 | – | 0 | – | 3 | 100.0 | 0 | – | 0 | – | 0 | – | 0 | – | 0 | – | 3 | 0 | 3 |
| Sweetheart | 0 | – | 0 | – | 0 | – | 3 | 42.8 | 0 | – | 1 | 14.3 | 0 | – | 1 | 14.3 | 2 | 28.6 | 0 | – | 7 | 0 | 7 |
| Employer | 0 | – | 0 | – | 0 | – | 1 | 12.5 | 0 | – | 0 | – | 3 | 37.5 | 3 | 37.5 | 0 | – | 1 | 12.5 | 8 | 0 | 8 |
| Alone | 2 | 3.3 | 2 | 3.3 | 2 | 3.3 | 8 | 13.1 | 0 | – | 2 | 3.3 | 0 | – | 34 | 55.7 | 9 | 14.7 | 2 | 3.3 | 61 | 4 | 65 |
| Institution | 2 | 2.8 | 3 | 4.2 | 0 | – | 11 | 15.5 | 0 | – | 1 | 1.4 | 1 | 1.4 | 4 | 5.6 | 40 | 56.3 | 9 | 12.8 | 71 | 2 | 73 |
| Unknown | 0 | – | 1 | – | 0 | – | 3 | – | 0 | – | 0 | – | 1 | – | 4 | – | 0 | – | 1 | – | 10 | 37 | 47 |

## 2. MONTHS IN COMMUNITY

### THIRD FIVE-YEAR PERIOD

| SECOND FIVE-YEAR PERIOD | Never in community | | Some time in community | | In community throughout | | Total | Inapplicable, unknown | Grand total |
|---|---|---|---|---|---|---|---|---|---|
| | Num-ber | Per cent | Num-ber | Per cent | Num-ber | Per cent | | | |
| Never in community ... | 15 | 50.0 | 15 | 50.0 | – | – | 30 | – | 30 |
| Some time in community | 11 | 8.1 | 93 | 68.9 | 31 | 23.0 | 135 | 2 | 137 |
| In community throughout | 1 | 0.5 | 47 | 21.4 | 172 | 78.1 | 220 | 3 | 223 |
| Inapplicable, unknown | 0 | – | 6 | – | 7 | – | 13 | 36 | 49 |

## 3. INSTITUTIONAL EXPERIENCES (PENAL AND NON-PENAL), MEN WITH

### THIRD FIVE-YEAR PERIOD

| SECOND FIVE-YEAR PERIOD | No institutional experience | | Institutional experience | | Total | Inapplicable | Unknown | Grand total |
|---|---|---|---|---|---|---|---|---|
| | Num-ber | Per cent | Num-ber | Per cent | | | | |
| No institutional experience .......... | 186 | 83.0 | 38 | 17.0 | 224 | 1 | 2 | 227 |
| Institutional experience | 29 | 18.1 | 131 | 81.9 | 160 | 2 | 2 | 164 |
| Inapplicable ........ | 0 | – | 0 | – | 0 | 0 | 0 | 0 |
| Unknown .......... | 6 | – | 6 | – | 12 | 0 | 36 | 48 |

## 4. MOBILITY

### THIRD FIVE-YEAR PERIOD

| SECOND FIVE-YEAR PERIOD | No mobility | | Mobility | | Total | Inapplicable | Unknown | Grand total |
|---|---|---|---|---|---|---|---|---|
| | Num-ber | Per cent | Num-ber | Per cent | | | | |
| Mobility not excessive | 157 | 86.3 | 25 | 13.7 | 182 | 7 | 1 | 190 |
| Mobility excessive .... | 40 | 28.2 | 102 | 71.8 | 142 | 11 | 7 | 160 |
| Inapplicable ........ | 3 | 20.0 | 12 | 80.0 | 15 | 24 | 1 | 40 |
| Unknown .......... | 8 | – | 6 | – | 14 | 1 | 34 | 49 |

### 5. HOUSEHOLD STABILITY
#### THIRD FIVE-YEAR PERIOD

| SECOND FIVE-YEAR PERIOD | No change Number | No change Per cent | Two or three Number | Two or three Per cent | Four or more Number | Four or more Per cent | Total | Inapplicable | Unknown | Grand total |
|---|---|---|---|---|---|---|---|---|---|---|
| No change ........ | 134 | 78.8 | 21 | 12.4 | 15 | 8.8 | 170 | 4 | 2 | 176 |
| Two or three changes | 23 | 79.4 | 3 | 10.3 | 3 | 10.3 | 29 | 1 | 1 | 31 |
| Four changes or more | 35 | 34.0 | 13 | 12.6 | 55 | 53.4 | 103 | 13 | 2 | 118 |
| Inapplicable ....... | 5 | 31.3 | 4 | 25.0 | 7 | 43.7 | 16 | 24 | 1 | 41 |
| Unknown ......... | 12 | – | 3 | – | 11 | – | 26 | 1 | 46 | 73 |

### 6. HOME—PHYSICAL
#### THIRD FIVE-YEAR PERIOD

| SECOND FIVE-YEAR PERIOD | Good Number | Good Per cent | Fair Number | Fair Per cent | Poor Number | Poor Per cent | Total | Inapplicable | Unknown | Grand total |
|---|---|---|---|---|---|---|---|---|---|---|
| Good ............ | 75 | 73.5 | 25 | 24.5 | 2 | 2.0 | 102 | 5 | 1 | 108 |
| Fair .............. | 8 | 7.3 | 83 | 76.2 | 18 | 16.5 | 109 | 2 | 2 | 113 |
| Poor ............. | 2 | 2.3 | 15 | 17.4 | 69 | 80.3 | 86 | 8 | 4 | 98 |
| Inapplicable ....... | 1 | 6.3 | 8 | 50.0 | 7 | 43.7 | 16 | 25 | 2 | 43 |
| Unknown ......... | 4 | – | 12 | – | 12 | – | 28 | 3 | 46 | 77 |

### 6A. MORAL STANDARDS OF HOME
#### THIRD FIVE-YEAR PERIOD

| SECOND FIVE-YEAR PERIOD | Good Number | Good Per cent | Fair Number | Fair Per cent | Poor Number | Poor Per cent | Total | Inapplicable, unknown | Grand total |
|---|---|---|---|---|---|---|---|---|---|
| Good .............. | 109 | 84.5 | 17 | 13.2 | 3 | 2.3 | 129 | 5 | 134 |
| Fair .............. | 9 | 12.3 | 52 | 71.2 | 12 | 16.5 | 73 | 2 | 75 |
| Poor .............. | 7 | 6.7 | 28 | 26.9 | 69 | 66.4 | 104 | 14 | 118 |
| Inapplicable, unknown | 6 | – | 15 | – | 16 | – | 37 | 75 | 112 |

## 7. NEIGHBORHOOD—TYPE
### THIRD FIVE-YEAR PERIOD

| SECOND FIVE-YEAR PERIOD | Urban Number | Urban Per cent | Rural Number | Rural Per cent | Varied Number | Varied Per cent | Total | Inapplicable | Unknown | Grand total |
|---|---|---|---|---|---|---|---|---|---|---|
| Mostly urban ...... | 233 | 92.5 | 3 | 1.2 | 16 | 6.3 | 252 | 15 | 4 | 271 |
| Mostly rural ....... | 4 | 12.5 | 27 | 84.4 | 1 | 3.1 | 32 | 0 | 2 | 34 |
| Varied (urban or rural) ......... | 6 | 21.4 | 6 | 21.4 | 16 | 57.2 | 28 | 1 | 0 | 29 |
| Inapplicable, unknown ........ | 20 | – | 4 | – | 9 | – | 33 | 27 | 45 | 105 |

## 8. NEIGHBORHOOD INFLUENCES
### THIRD FIVE-YEAR PERIOD

| SECOND FIVE-YEAR PERIOD | Good Number | Good Per cent | Fair Number | Fair Per cent | Poor Number | Poor Per cent | Total | Inapplicable | Unknown | Grand total |
|---|---|---|---|---|---|---|---|---|---|---|
| Good ........... | 25 | 56.8 | 15 | 34.1 | 4 | 9.1 | 44 | 2 | 2 | 48 |
| Fair ............. | 7 | 4.5 | 129 | 83.8 | 18 | 11.7 | 154 | 5 | 2 | 161 |
| Poor ............ | 0 | – | 22 | 22.4 | 76 | 77.6 | 98 | 8 | 6 | 112 |
| Inapplicable ....... | 1 | 6.3 | 8 | 50.0 | 7 | 43.7 | 16 | 25 | 2 | 43 |
| Unknown ......... | 1 | – | 16 | – | 12 | – | 29 | 3 | 43 | 75 |

## 8A. ENVIRONMENT
### THIRD FIVE-YEAR PERIOD

| SECOND FIVE-YEAR PERIOD | Good Number | Good Per cent | Fair Number | Fair Per cent | Poor Number | Poor Per cent | Total | Inapplicable, unknown | Grand total |
|---|---|---|---|---|---|---|---|---|---|
| Good .............. | 59 | 76.6 | 17 | 22.1 | 1 | 1.3 | 77 | 5 | 82 |
| Fair ............... | 12 | 9.3 | 98 | 76.0 | 19 | 14.7 | 129 | 7 | 136 |
| Poor .............. | 4 | 4.3 | 14 | 15.2 | 74 | 80.5 | 92 | 12 | 104 |
| Inapplicable, unknown | 4 | – | 21 | – | 17 | – | 42 | 75 | 117 |

| SECOND FIVE-YEAR PERIOD | Single | | Married, living with wife | | Separated, divorced | | Illegal marriage, living with wife | Illegal marriage, separated | Widowed | | Total | Inapplicable, unknown, or unknown if married or single | Grand total |
|---|---|---|---|---|---|---|---|---|---|---|---|---|---|
| | Num-ber | Per cent | Num-ber | Per cent | Num-ber | Per cent | Number | Number | Num-ber | Per cent | | | |
| Single ............... | 126 | 82.4 | 24 | 15.7 | 2 | 1.3 | 0 | 0 | 1 | .6 | 153 | 3 | 156 |
| Married, living with wife ....... | 0 | – | 145 | 87.3 | 21 | 12.7 | 0 | 0 | 0 | – | 166 | 2 | 168 |
| Separated, divorced ........... | 0 | – | 10 | 17.2 | 46 | 79.3 | 0 | 0 | 2 | 3.5 | 58 | 3 | 61 |
| Illegal marriage, living with wife | 0 | – | 5 | 100.0 | 0 | – | 0 | 0 | 0 | – | 5 | 0 | 5 |
| Illegal marriage, separated ..... | 0 | – | 0 | – | 0 | – | 0 | 0 | 0 | – | 0 | 0 | 0 |
| Widowed ................ | 0 | – | 0 | – | 2 | 28.6 | 0 | 0 | 5 | 71.4 | 7 | 0 | 7 |
| Inapplicable, unknown, unknown if married or single ......... | 4 | – | 2 | – | 3 | – | 0 | 0 | 0 | – | 9 | 33 | 42 |

## 10. NUMBER OF CHILDREN
### THIRD FIVE-YEAR PERIOD

| SECOND FIVE-YEAR PERIOD | No children Number | No children Per cent | Children Number | Children Per cent | Total | Number unknown, unknown if any | Grand total |
|---|---|---|---|---|---|---|---|
| No children .......... | 194 | 91.5 | 18 | 8.5 | 212 | 3 | 215 |
| Children ............. | 3 | 1.7 | 172 | 98.3 | 175 | 3 | 178 |
| Number unknown, unknown if any ....... | 9 | – | 4 | – | 13 | 33 | 46 |

## 11. CONJUGAL RELATIONS
### THIRD FIVE-YEAR PERIOD

| SECOND FIVE-YEAR PERIOD | Good Number | Good Per cent | Fair Number | Fair Per cent | Poor Number | Poor Per cent | Total | Inapplicable, unknown, single | Grand total |
|---|---|---|---|---|---|---|---|---|---|
| Good .............. | 102 | 86.4 | 8 | 6.8 | 8 | 6.8 | 118 | 3 | 121 |
| Fair .............. | 5 | 17.9 | 14 | 50.0 | 9 | 32.1 | 28 | 0 | 28 |
| Poor .............. | 4 | 16.0 | 4 | 16.0 | 17 | 68.0 | 25 | 22 | 47 |
| Inapplicable, unknown, single ............ | 27 | – | 7 | – | 8 | – | 42 | 201 | 243 |

## 12. RELATION TO NEAREST RELATIVES
### THIRD FIVE-YEAR PERIOD

| SECOND FIVE-YEAR PERIOD | In touch with, friendly Number | In touch with, friendly Per cent | In touch when in need Number | In touch when in need Per cent | Rarely in touch Number | Rarely in touch Per cent | Total | Inapplicable, unknown | Grand total |
|---|---|---|---|---|---|---|---|---|---|
| In touch with, friendly | 151 | 88.3 | 5 | 2.9 | 15 | 8.8 | 171 | 15 | 186 |
| In touch when in need | 7 | 11.5 | 38 | 62.3 | 16 | 26.2 | 61 | 8 | 69 |
| Rarely in touch ...... | 18 | 23.1 | 8 | 10.3 | 52 | 66.6 | 78 | 20 | 98 |
| Inapplicable, unknown | 14 | – | 3 | – | 10 | – | 27 | 59 | 86 |

### 13. FAMILY RELATIONSHIPS

#### THIRD FIVE-YEAR PERIOD

| SECOND FIVE-YEAR PERIOD | Succeed | | Fail | | | Inapplicable, | Grand |
|---|---|---|---|---|---|---|---|
| | Number | Per cent | Number | Per cent | Total | unknown | total |
| Succeed .............. | 151 | 87.8 | 21 | 12.2 | 172 | 4 | 176 |
| Fail ................. | 27 | 18.4 | 120 | 81.6 | 147 | 24 | 171 |
| Inapplicable, unknown .. | 8 | – | 16 | – | 24 | 68 | 92 |

### 14. DEPENDENTS

#### THIRD FIVE-YEAR PERIOD

| SECOND FIVE-YEAR PERIOD | No dependents | | Dependents | | | Inapplicable, | Grand |
|---|---|---|---|---|---|---|---|
| | Number | Per cent | Number | Per cent | Total | unknown | total |
| No dependents ........ | 69 | 67.6 | 33 | 32.4 | 102 | 8 | 110 |
| Dependents ........... | 15 | 6.6 | 212 | 93.4 | 227 | 14 | 241 |
| Inapplicable, unknown .. | 14 | – | 13 | – | 27 | 61 | 88 |

## 15. DISPOSITION OF EARNINGS
### THIRD FIVE-YEAR PERIOD

| SECOND FIVE-YEAR PERIOD | Self mostly | | Wife and/or children, has no dependent parents | | Wife and/or children, has dependent parents | | Dependent parents | | Total | Inapplicable, unknown | Grand total |
|---|---|---|---|---|---|---|---|---|---|---|---|
| | Num-ber | Per cent | Num-ber | Per cent | Num-ber | Per cent | Num-ber | Per cent | | | |
| Self mostly .................... | 127 | 79.9 | 25 | 15.7 | 1 | .6 | 6 | 3.8 | 159 | 25 | 184 |
| Wife and/or children, no dependent parents | 11 | 8.4 | 118 | 90.1 | 2 | 1.5 | 0 | – | 131 | 11 | 142 |
| Wife and/or children, dependent parents .. | 1 | 16.7 | 4 | 66.6 | 1 | 16.7 | 0 | – | 6 | 0 | 6 |
| Dependent parents ........... | 3 | 33.3 | 2 | 22.3 | 1 | 11.1 | 3 | 33.3 | 9 | 2 | 11 |
| Inapplicable, unknown ....... | 22 | – | 4 | – | 1 | – | 0 | – | 27 | 69 | 96 |

359

## 16. ECONOMIC CONDITION
### THIRD FIVE-YEAR PERIOD

| SECOND FIVE-YEAR PERIOD | Comfortable | | Marginal | | Dependent | | Total | Inapplicable, unknown | Grand total |
|---|---|---|---|---|---|---|---|---|---|
| | Number | Per cent | Number | Per cent | Number | Per cent | | | |
| Comfortable ......... | 17 | 50.0 | 13 | 38.2 | 4 | 11.8 | 34 | 0 | 34 |
| Marginal ........... | 3 | 1.4 | 135 | 61.4 | 82 | 37.2 | 220 | 15 | 235 |
| Dependent .......... | 0 | – | 9 | 13.4 | 58 | 86.6 | 67 | 4 | 71 |
| Inapplicable, unknown | 0 | – | 20 | – | 8 | – | 28 | 71 | 99 |

## 17. KNOWN TO SOCIAL SERVICE AGENCIES
### THIRD FIVE-YEAR PERIOD

| SECOND FIVE-YEAR PERIOD | Not known to agencies | | Known to agencies | | Total | Inapplicable, unknown | Grand total |
|---|---|---|---|---|---|---|---|
| | Number | Per cent | Number | Per cent | | | |
| Not known to agencies .. | 112 | 59.3 | 77 | 40.7 | 189 | 12 | 201 |
| Known to agencies ..... | 18 | 13.3 | 117 | 86.7 | 135 | 9 | 144 |
| Inapplicable, unknown .. | 15 | – | 18 | – | 33 | 61 | 94 |

## 18. ECONOMIC RESPONSIBILITY TOWARD FAMILY

### THIRD FIVE-YEAR PERIOD

| SECOND FIVE-YEAR PERIOD | Meets responsibility legitimately | | Meets responsibility illegitimately | | Fails to meet responsibility due to own fault | | Unable to meet responsibility | | Total | Inapplicable, unknown | Grand total |
|---|---|---|---|---|---|---|---|---|---|---|---|
| | Number | Per cent | Number | Per cent | Number | Per cent | Number | Per cent | | | |
| Meets responsibility legitimately .... | 103 | 59.9 | 4 | 2.3 | 26 | 15.1 | 39 | 22.7 | 172 | 5 | 177 |
| Meets responsibility illegitimately .... | 7 | 25.0 | 14 | 50.0 | 4 | 14.3 | 3 | 10.7 | 28 | 3 | 31 |
| Fails to meet responsibility due to own fault .......... | 7 | 6.7 | 2 | 1.9 | 80 | 76.2 | 16 | 15.2 | 105 | 13 | 118 |
| Unable to meet responsibility ....... | 2 | 18.2 | 1 | 9.1 | 2 | 18.2 | 6 | 54.5 | 11 | 0 | 11 |
| Inapplicable, unknown ........... | 12 | – | 5 | – | 13 | – | 1 | – | 31 | 71 | 102 |

I9. USUAL OCCUPATION

THIRD FIVE-YEAR PERIOD

| SECOND FIVE-YEAR PERIOD | Idle through own fault | | Illicit occupation | | Rough labor | | Trucking, teaming, chauffeuring | | Factory hand | | Farm hand | | Salesmen and store clerks | | Skilled trades | | Restaurant work | | Total | Inapplicable, varied, unknown, other | Grand total |
|---|---|---|---|---|---|---|---|---|---|---|---|---|---|---|---|---|---|---|---|---|---|
| | Number | Per cent | Number | Per cent | Number | Per cent | Number | Per cent | Number | Per cent | Number | Per cent | Number | Per cent | Number | Per cent | Number | Per cent | Total | other | total |
| Idle through own fault ... | 5 | 41.7 | 2 | 16.6 | 5 | 41.7 | 0 | – | 0 | – | 0 | – | 0 | – | 0 | – | 0 | – | 12 | 2 | 14 |
| Illicit occupation ........ | 1 | 6.3 | 10 | 62.5 | 3 | 18.6 | 0 | – | 0 | – | 0 | – | 1 | 6.3 | 1 | 6.3 | 0 | – | 16 | 8 | 24 |
| Rough labor .......... | 7 | 9.7 | 1 | 1.4 | 50 | 69.5 | 1 | 1.4 | 6 | 8.3 | 0 | – | 2 | 2.8 | 2 | 2.8 | 3 | 4.1 | 72 | 8 | 80 |
| Trucking, teaming, chauffeuring ............. | 0 | – | 2 | 5.6 | 5 | 13.9 | 22 | 60.9 | 1 | 2.8 | 1 | 2.8 | 2 | 5.6 | 2 | 5.6 | 1 | 2.8 | 36 | 4 | 40 |
| Factory hand ........... | 0 | – | 1 | 2.4 | 9 | 22.0 | 1 | 2.4 | 25 | 61.0 | 0 | – | 0 | – | 5 | 12.2 | 0 | – | 41 | 2 | 43 |
| Farm hand ............ | 0 | – | 0 | – | 4 | 36.4 | 0 | – | 0 | – | 7 | 63.6 | 0 | – | 0 | – | 0 | – | 11 | 3 | 14 |
| Salesmen, store clerks .... | 1 | 3.8 | 5 | 19.2 | 1 | 3.8 | 0 | – | 1 | 3.8 | 0 | – | 18 | 69.4 | 0 | – | 0 | – | 26 | 6 | 32 |
| Skilled trades .......... | 1 | 1.8 | 0 | – | 7 | 12.5 | 2 | 3.6 | 1 | 1.8 | 0 | – | 3 | 5.4 | 40 | 71.3 | 2 | 3.6 | 56 | 10 | 66 |
| Restaurant work ........ | 0 | – | 1 | 5.9 | 2 | 11.8 | 1 | 5.9 | 1 | 5.9 | 0 | – | 2 | 11.8 | 1 | 5.9 | 9 | 52.8 | 17 | 4 | 21 |
| Inapplicable, varied, unknown or other ........ | 1 | – | 4 | – | 15 | – | 1 | – | 4 | – | 2 | – | 4 | – | 6 | – | 0 | – | 37 | 68 | 105 |

### 20. ILLICIT OCCUPATION

#### THIRD FIVE-YEAR PERIOD

| SECOND FIVE-YEAR PERIOD | No illicit occupation Number | No illicit occupation Per cent | Illicit occupation part of time Number | Illicit occupation part of time Per cent | Illicit occupation throughout Number | Illicit occupation throughout Per cent | Total | Inapplicable, unknown | Grand total |
|---|---|---|---|---|---|---|---|---|---|
| No illicit occupation ....... | 209 | 93.7 | 11 | 4.9 | 3 | 1.4 | 223 | 13 | 236 |
| Illicit occupation part of time | 17 | 43.6 | 16 | 41.0 | 6 | 15.4 | 39 | 10 | 49 |
| Illicit occupation throughout | 1 | 6.7 | 5 | 33.3 | 9 | 60.0 | 15 | 8 | 23 |
| Inapplicable, unknown ..... | 33 | – | 15 | – | 2 | – | 50 | 81 | 131 |

### 21. SKILL

#### THIRD FIVE-YEAR PERIOD

| SECOND FIVE-YEAR PERIOD | Unskilled Number | Unskilled Per cent | Semi-skilled Number | Semi-skilled Per cent | Skilled Number | Skilled Per cent | Total | Inapplicable, unknown | Grand total |
|---|---|---|---|---|---|---|---|---|---|
| Unskilled .......... | 92 | 91.1 | 9 | 8.9 | 0 | – | 101 | 19 | 120 |
| Semi-skilled ........ | 34 | 23.4 | 108 | 74.5 | 3 | 2.1 | 145 | 19 | 164 |
| Skilled ............ | 0 | – | 10 | 28.6 | 25 | 71.4 | 35 | 3 | 38 |
| Inapplicable, unknown | 14 | – | 12 | – | 2 | – | 28 | 89 | 117 |

### 23. AVERAGE WAGE—WEEKLY

#### THIRD FIVE-YEAR PERIOD

| SECOND FIVE-YEAR PERIOD | Less than $25 Number | Less than $25 Per cent | $25–$34 Number | $25–$34 Per cent | $35 and over Number | $35 and over Per cent | Total | Inapplicable, unknown | Grand total |
|---|---|---|---|---|---|---|---|---|---|
| Less than $25 ....... | 79 | 91.9 | 6 | 7.0 | 1 | 1.1 | 86 | 27 | 113 |
| $25–$34 ............ | 32 | 59.3 | 16 | 29.6 | 6 | 11.1 | 54 | 16 | 70 |
| $35 and over ........ | 7 | 28.0 | 8 | 32.0 | 10 | 40.0 | 25 | 8 | 33 |
| Inapplicable, unknown | 63 | – | 2 | – | 2 | – | 67 | 156 | 223 |

## 24. HIGHEST WAGE—WEEKLY
### THIRD FIVE-YEAR PERIOD

| SECOND FIVE-YEAR PERIOD | Less than $25 Num-ber | Per cent | $25–$34 Num-ber | Per cent | $35 and over Num-ber | Per cent | Total | Inappli-cable, unknown | Grand total |
|---|---|---|---|---|---|---|---|---|---|
| Less than $25 ........ | 67 | 84.8 | 10 | 12.7 | 2 | 2.5 | 79 | 8 | 87 |
| $25–$34 ............. | 28 | 46.7 | 25 | 41.7 | 7 | 11.6 | 60 | 13 | 73 |
| $35 and over ........ | 27 | 32.9 | 21 | 25.6 | 34 | 41.5 | 82 | 17 | 99 |
| Inapplicable, unknown | 43 | – | 7 | – | 6 | – | 56 | 124 | 180 |

## 25. WORK HABITS
### THIRD FIVE-YEAR PERIOD

| SECOND FIVE-YEAR PERIOD | Good Num-ber | Per cent | Fair Num-ber | Per cent | Poor* Num-ber | Per cent | Total | Inappli-cable, unknown | Grand total |
|---|---|---|---|---|---|---|---|---|---|
| Good ............. | 99 | 84.6 | 13 | 11.1 | 5 | 4.3 | 117 | 20 | 137 |
| Fair ............... | 20 | 20.2 | 51 | 51.5 | 28 | 28.3 | 99 | 14 | 113 |
| Poor* ............. | 6 | 9.1 | 7 | 10.6 | 53 | 80.3 | 66 | 18 | 84 |
| Inapplicable, unknown | 8 | – | 8 | – | 12 | – | 28, | 77 | 105 |

* Includes those engaged in illicit occupation throughout.

## 26. USUAL REASON FOR LEAVING WORK
### THIRD FIVE-YEAR PERIOD

| SECOND FIVE-YEAR PERIOD | Steady worker, seldom changes Num-ber | Per cent | Fault of worker Num-ber | Per cent | Not fault of worker or to better self Num-ber | Per cent | Total | Inappli-cable, unknown | Grand total |
|---|---|---|---|---|---|---|---|---|---|
| Steady worker, seldom changes .......... | 33 | 67.3 | 7 | 14.3 | 9 | 18.4 | 49 | 3 | 52 |
| Fault of worker ...... | 5 | 5.2 | 70 | 72.2 | 22 | 22.6 | 97 | 29 | 126 |
| Not fault of worker or to better self ....... | 16 | 16.7 | 13 | 13.5 | 67 | 69.8 | 96 | 10 | 106 |
| Inapplicable, unknown | 6 | – | 24 | – | 18 | – | 48 | 107 | 155 |

## 27. STEADINESS OF EMPLOYMENT

### Third Five-Year Period

| Second Five-Year Period | Regular | | Fairly regular | | Irregular | | Illicit | | Total | Inapplicable, unknown | Grand total |
|---|---|---|---|---|---|---|---|---|---|---|---|
| | Number | Per cent | Number | Per cent | Number | Per cent | Number | Per cent | | | |
| Regular .................. | 49 | 56.3 | 27 | 31.0 | 9 | 10.4 | 2 | 2.3 | 87 | 8 | 95 |
| Fairly regular ............ | 11 | 11.5 | 52 | 54.2 | 30 | 31.3 | 3 | 3.0 | 96 | 18 | 114 |
| Irregular ................ | 0 | – | 9 | 10.5 | 72 | 83.7 | 5 | 5.8 | 86 | 17 | 103 |
| Illicit .................... | 1 | 7.1 | 1 | 7.1 | 2 | 14.3 | 10 | 71.5 | 14 | 9 | 23 |
| Inapplicable, unknown ... | 1 | – | 16 | – | 10 | – | 0 | – | 27 | 77 | 104 |

## 28. AVERAGE PERIOD OF TIME HELD JOB

### Third Five-Year Period

| Second Five-Year Period | Less than 3 months | | 3–11 months | | 12–35 months | | 36 months and over | | Total | Inapplicable, unknown, incalculable | Grand total |
|---|---|---|---|---|---|---|---|---|---|---|---|
| | Number | Per cent | Number | Per cent | Number | Per cent | Number | Per cent | | | |
| Less than 3 months ...... | 70 | 95.9 | 2 | 2.7 | 0 | – | 1 | 1.4 | 73 | 27 | 100 |
| 3–11 months ............ | 7 | 29.2 | 13 | 54.2 | 3 | 12.5 | 1 | 4.1 | 24 | 20 | 44 |
| 12–35 months ........... | 4 | 14.3 | 6 | 21.4 | 10 | 35.7 | 8 | 28.6 | 28 | 21 | 49 |
| 36 months and over...... | 2 | 5.1 | 3 | 7.7 | 8 | 20.5 | 26 | 66.7 | 39 | 10 | 49 |
| Inapplicable, unknown, incalculable | 36 | – | 11 | – | 4 | – | 8 | – | 59 | 138 | 197 |

## 29. LONGEST PERIOD OF TIME HELD JOB
### Third Five-Year Period

| Second Five-Year Period | Less than 3 months | | 3–11 months | | 12–35 months | | 36 months and over | | Total | Inapplicable, unknown | Grand total |
|---|---|---|---|---|---|---|---|---|---|---|---|
| | Number | Per cent | Number | Per cent | Number | Per cent | Number | Per cent | | | |
| Less than 3 months .............. | 44 | 75.9 | 9 | 15.5 | 4 | 6.9 | 1 | 1.7 | 58 | 18 | 76 |
| 3–11 months ................. | 14 | 38.9 | 13 | 36.1 | 8 | 22.2 | 1 | 2.8 | 36 | 11 | 47 |
| 12–35 months ............. | 10 | 17.9 | 15 | 26.8 | 14 | 25.0 | 17 | 30.3 | 56 | 14 | 70 |
| 36 months and over ......... | 2 | 3.3 | 7 | 11.7 | 12 | 20.0 | 39 | 65.0 | 60 | 9 | 69 |
| Inapplicable, unknown ......... | 23 | – | 19 | – | 15 | – | 9 | – | 66 | 111 | 177 |

## 30. INDUSTRIAL HISTORY
### THIRD FIVE-YEAR PERIOD

| SECOND FIVE-YEAR PERIOD | Good | | Fair | | Poor | | | Inapplicable, unknown | Grand total |
|---|---|---|---|---|---|---|---|---|---|
| | Number | Per cent | Number | Per cent | Number | Per cent | Total | | |
| Good .............. | 47 | 62.7 | 24 | 32.0 | 4 | 5.3 | 75 | 8 | 83 |
| Fair ............... | 12 | 11.8 | 61 | 59.8 | 29 | 28.4 | 102 | 23 | 125 |
| Poor .............. | 2 | 2.1 | 12 | 12.6 | 81 | 85.3 | 95 | 28 | 123 |
| Inapplicable, unknown | 1 | – | 18 | – | 16 | – | 35 | 73 | 108 |

## 31. COMPANIONSHIPS
### THIRD FIVE-YEAR PERIOD

| SECOND FIVE-YEAR PERIOD | Harmless | | Harmful | | Total | Inapplicable, unknown | Grand total |
|---|---|---|---|---|---|---|---|
| | Number | Per cent | Number | Per cent | | | |
| Harmless ............. | 108 | 91.5 | 10 | 8.5 | 118 | 4 | 122 |
| Harmful ............. | 28 | 15.6 | 152 | 84.4 | 180 | 26 | 206 |
| Inapplicable, unknown .. | 11 | – | 23 | – | 34 | 77 | 111 |

## 32. HAUNTS
### THIRD FIVE-YEAR PERIOD

| SECOND FIVE-YEAR PERIOD | Harmless | | Harmful | | Total | Inapplicable, unknown | Grand total |
|---|---|---|---|---|---|---|---|
| | Number | Per cent | Number | Per cent | | | |
| Harmless ............. | 110 | 90.9 | 11 | 9.1 | 121 | 1 | 122 |
| Harmful ............. | 23 | 13.5 | 147 | 86.5 | 170 | 24 | 194 |
| Inapplicable, unknown .. | 18 | – | 26 | – | 44 | 79 | 123 |

## 33. SOCIETY MEMBER
### THIRD FIVE-YEAR PERIOD

| SECOND FIVE-YEAR PERIOD | No | | Yes (wholesome) | | Yes (not wholesome) | | | Inapplicable, unknown | Grand total |
|---|---|---|---|---|---|---|---|---|---|
| | Number | Per cent | Number | Per cent | Number | Per cent | Total | | |
| No ............... | 223 | 93.3 | 1 | .4 | 15 | 6.3 | 239 | 25 | 264 |
| Yes (wholesome) ..... | 2 | 13.3 | 8 | 53.4 | 5 | 33.3 | 15 | 0 | 15 |
| Yes (not wholesome) .. | 11 | 37.9 | 0 | – | 18 | 62.1 | 29 | 2 | 31 |
| Inapplicable, unknown | 41 | – | 0 | – | 0 | – | 41 | 88 | 129 |

### 34. CHURCH ATTENDANCE
#### THIRD FIVE-YEAR PERIOD

| SECOND FIVE-YEAR PERIOD | Regular | | Irregular | | None | | Total | Inapplicable, unknown | Grand total |
|---|---|---|---|---|---|---|---|---|---|
| | Number | Per cent | Number | Per cent | Number | Per cent | | | |
| Regular ............. | 21 | 70.0 | 7 | 23.3 | 2 | 6.7 | 30 | 2 | 32 |
| Irregular ........... | 7 | 7.0 | 58 | 58.0 | 35 | 35.0 | 100 | 11 | 111 |
| None .............. | 0 | – | 6 | 5.0 | 113 | 95.0 | 119 | 11 | 130 |
| Inapplicable, unknown | 0 | – | 8 | – | 59 | – | 67 | 99 | 166 |

### 35. EDUCATIONAL ACTIVITIES
#### THIRD FIVE-YEAR PERIOD

| SECOND FIVE-YEAR PERIOD | Yes | | No | | Total | Inapplicable, unknown | Grand total |
|---|---|---|---|---|---|---|---|
| | Number | Per cent | Number | Per cent | | | |
| Yes ................. | 9 | 52.9 | 8 | 47.1 | 17 | 2 | 19 |
| No ................. | 2 | .7 | 268 | 99.3 | 270 | 24 | 294 |
| Inapplicable, unknown .. | 0 | – | 44 | – | 44 | 82 | 126 |

### 36. LEISURE AND HABITS
#### THIRD FIVE-YEAR PERIOD

| SECOND FIVE-YEAR PERIOD | Constructive | | Negative | | Harmful | | Total | Inapplicable, unknown | Grand total |
|---|---|---|---|---|---|---|---|---|---|
| | Number | Per cent | Number | Per cent | Number | Per cent | | | |
| Constructive ......... | 8 | 53.3 | 6 | 40.0 | 1 | 6.7 | 15 | 24 | 39 |
| Negative ........... | 1 | 1.0 | 92 | 90.2 | 9 | 8.8 | 102 | 0 | 102 |
| Harmful ............ | 0 | – | 29 | 14.9 | 166 | 85.1 | 195 | 28 | 223 |
| Inapplicable, unknown | 0 | – | 8 | – | 18 | – | 26 | 49 | 75 |

### 37. FREQUENCY OF ARRESTS AMONG THOSE ARRESTED MORE THAN ONCE
#### THIRD FIVE-YEAR PERIOD

| SECOND FIVE-YEAR PERIOD | One arrest in less than a year | | One arrest in one to two years | | One arrest in two years and over | | Total | Inapplicable, unknown | Grand total |
|---|---|---|---|---|---|---|---|---|---|
| | Number | Per cent | Number | Per cent | Number | Per cent | | | |
| One arrest in less than a year ............ | 41 | 75.9 | 11 | 20.4 | 2 | 3.7 | 54 | 25 | 79 |
| One arrest in one to two years ............. | 17 | 60.7 | 8 | 28.6 | 3 | 10.7 | 28 | 18 | 46 |
| One arrest in two years and over .......... | 3 | 33.3 | 3 | 33.3 | 3 | 33.4 | 9 | 13 | 22 |
| Inapplicable, unknown, incalculable ....... | 15 | – | 20 | – | 25 | – | 60 | 232 | 292 |

THIRD FIVE-YEAR PERIOD

| Second Five-Year Period | Non-delinquent | | Crimes against property | | Crimes against chastity | | Crimes against family and children | | Crimes against public health, safety, and policy | | Drunkenness | | Drug using or selling | | Crimes against person | | Varied | | Total delinquencies | Inapplicable, unknown | Grand total |
|---|---|---|---|---|---|---|---|---|---|---|---|---|---|---|---|---|---|---|---|---|---|
| | Number | Per cent | Number | Per cent | Number | Per cent | Number | Per cent | Number | Per cent | Number | Per cent | Number | Per cent | Number | Per cent | Number | Per cent | | | |
| Non-delinquent | 91 | 82.7 | 3 | 2.7 | 0 | – | 4 | 3.6 | 6 | 5.5 | 4 | 3.6 | 0 | – | 1 | .9 | 1 | .9 | 110 | 6 | 116 |
| Crimes against property | 4 | 11.4 | 22 | 62.8 | 1 | 2.9 | 0 | – | 4 | 11.4 | 1 | 2.9 | 0 | – | 0 | – | 3 | 8.6 | 35 | 12 | 47 |
| Crimes against chastity | 3 | 23.0 | 0 | – | 4 | 30.8 | 0 | – | 4 | 30.8 | 1 | 7.7 | 0 | – | 0 | – | 1 | 7.7 | 13 | 1 | 14 |
| Crimes against family and children | 1 | 14.3 | 0 | – | 0 | – | 6 | 85.7 | 0 | – | 0 | – | 0 | – | 0 | – | 0 | – | 7 | 2 | 9 |
| Crimes against public health, safety and policy | 7 | 24.1 | 0 | – | 0 | – | 0 | – | 19 | 65.5 | 3 | 10.4 | 0 | – | 0 | – | 0 | – | 29 | 2 | 31 |
| Drunkenness | 5 | 5.7 | 3 | 3.5 | 0 | – | 1 | 1.1 | 10 | 11.5 | 67 | 77.1 | 0 | – | 1 | 1.1 | 0 | – | 87 | 1 | 88 |
| Drug using or selling | 0 | – | 0 | – | 0 | – | 0 | – | 0 | – | 1 | 16.7 | 5 | 83.3 | 0 | – | 0 | – | 6 | 0 | 6 |
| Crimes against person | 0 | – | 0 | – | 0 | – | 0 | – | 0 | – | 0 | – | 0 | – | 1 | 100.0 | 0 | – | 1 | 0 | 1 |
| Varied | 5 | 13.2 | 6 | 15.8 | 2 | 5.3 | 3 | 7.9 | 3 | 7.9 | 8 | 21.1 | 0 | – | 1 | 2.5 | 10 | 26.3 | 38 | 2 | 40 |
| Inapplicable, unknown | 4 | – | 10 | – | 4 | – | 2 | – | 7 | – | 1 | – | 1 | – | 1 | – | 2 | – | 32 | 55 | 87 |

### 39. FREQUENCY OF CONVICTIONS AMONG THOSE CONVICTED MORE THAN ONCE

#### THIRD FIVE-YEAR PERIOD

| SECOND FIVE-YEAR PERIOD | One conviction in less than a year | | One conviction in one to two years | | One conviction in two years and over | | Total | Inapplicable, unknown, incalculable | Grand total |
|---|---|---|---|---|---|---|---|---|---|
| | Number | Per cent | Number | Per cent | Number | Per cent | | | |
| One conviction in less than a year ........ | 35 | 76.1 | 6 | 13.1 | 5 | 10.8 | 46 | 23 | 69 |
| One conviction in one to two years ...... | 11 | 50.0 | 6 | 27.3 | 5 | 22.7 | 22 | 15 | 37 |
| One conviction in two years and over ..... | 5 | 27.8 | 7 | 38.9 | 6 | 33.3 | 18 | 18 | 36 |
| Inapplicable, unknown, incalculable ....... | 11 | – | 18 | – | 29 | – | 58 | 239 | 297 |

### 40. NUMBER OF PENAL EXPERIENCES

#### THIRD FIVE-YEAR PERIOD

| SECOND FIVE-YEAR PERIOD | None | | One or more | | Total | Inapplicable, unknown | Grand total |
|---|---|---|---|---|---|---|---|
| | Number | Per cent | Number | Per cent | | | |
| None ................ | 196 | 83.4 | 39 | 16.6 | 235 | 8 | 243 |
| One or more .......... | 29 | 20.6 | 112 | 79.4 | 141 | 5 | 146 |
| Inapplicable, unknown .. | 7 | – | 6 | – | 13 | 37 | 50 |

### 41. TIME IN PENAL INSTITUTIONS

#### THIRD FIVE-YEAR PERIOD

| SECOND FIVE-YEAR PERIOD | None | | Less than 20 months | | Twenty months and more | | Total | Inapplicable, unknown | Grand total |
|---|---|---|---|---|---|---|---|---|---|
| | Number | Per cent | Number | Per cent | Number | Per cent | | | |
| None .............. | 202 | 84.2 | 34 | 14.2 | 4 | 1.6 | 240 | 4 | 244 |
| Less than twenty months | 23 | 34.8 | 30 | 45.5 | 13 | 19.7 | 66 | 2 | 68 |
| Twenty months and over ............ | 7 | 9.1 | 20 | 26.0 | 50 | 64.9 | 77 | 2 | 79 |
| Inapplicable, unknown | 0 | – | 6 | – | 0 | – | 6 | 42 | 48 |

### THIRD FIVE-YEAR PERIOD

| SECOND FIVE-YEAR PERIOD | Non-delinquent | Penal institution at least four of five years | Conviction for serious offense | Warrant out for serious offense | Dishonorable discharge or desertion from Army or Navy | Unofficial, serious | Arrest for serious, not followed by conviction | Conviction for minor | Unofficial, minor | Arrest for minor, not followed by conviction | Unknown, inapplicable (non-penal institution throughout) | Grand total |
|---|---|---|---|---|---|---|---|---|---|---|---|---|
| Non-delinquent | 93 | 0 | 2 | 0 | 0 | 1 | 1 | 10 | 5 | 2 | 0 | 114 |
| Penal institution at least four of five years | 0 | 7 | 13 | 0 | 0 | 1 | 1 | 1 | 1 | 0 | 1 | 25 |
| Conviction for serious offense | 5 | 11 | 58 | 0 | 0 | 2 | 1 | 17 | 6 | 3 | 2 | 105 |
| Warrant out for serious offense | 0 | 0 | 0 | 0 | 0 | 0 | 0 | 0 | 0 | 0 | 3 | 3 |
| Dishonorable discharge or desertion from Army or Navy | 0 | 0 | 1 | 0 | 0 | 1 | 0 | 1 | 0 | 0 | 0 | 3 |
| Unofficial, serious | 3 | 0 | 6 | 0 | 0 | 0 | 0 | 3 | 1 | 0 | 2 | 15 |
| Arrest for serious, not followed by conviction | 0 | 0 | 1 | 0 | 0 | 0 | 0 | 1 | 0 | 0 | 1 | 3 |
| Conviction for minor | 8 | 0 | 3 | 0 | 0 | 0 | 0 | 47 | 8 | 8 | 1 | 75 |
| Unofficial, minor | 6 | 0 | 5 | 0 | 0 | 0 | 0 | 15 | 9 | 1 | 2 | 38 |
| Arrest for minor, not followed by conviction | 4 | 0 | 0 | 0 | 0 | 0 | 0 | 5 | 1 | 1 | 1 | 12 |
| Unknown, inapplicable (non-penal institution throughout) | 1 | 0 | 3 | 0 | 0 | 0 | 0 | 5 | 0 | 0 | 37 | 46 |

* In this table percentages have not been given because the categories are so fine.

### 43. OFFICIAL RECOGNITION OF DELINQUENCY
#### THIRD FIVE-YEAR PERIOD

| SECOND FIVE-YEAR PERIOD | *Official* Number | *Official* Per cent | *Unofficial* Number | *Unofficial* Per cent | *Non-delinquent* Number | *Non-delinquent* Per cent | *Total delinquent* | *Inapplicable, unknown* | *Grand total* |
|---|---|---|---|---|---|---|---|---|---|
| Official ............. | 148 | 81.4 | 17 | 9.3 | 17 | 9.3 | 182 | 14 | 196 |
| Unofficial .......... | 24 | 57.2 | 9 | 21.4 | 9 | 21.4 | 42 | 4 | 46 |
| Non-delinquent ...... | 17 | 14.8 | 7 | 6.1 | 91 | 79.1 | 115 | 0 | 115 |
| Inapplicable, unknown | 26 | – | 3 | – | 3 | – | 32 | 50 | 82 |

### 44. ALIASES
#### THIRD FIVE-YEAR PERIOD

| SECOND FIVE-YEAR PERIOD | *Used aliases* Number | *Used aliases* Per cent | *Did not use aliases* Number | *Did not use aliases* Per cent | *Total* | *Inapplicable, unknown* | *Grand total* |
|---|---|---|---|---|---|---|---|
| Used aliases ........... | 33 | 63.5 | 19 | 36.5 | 52 | 23 | 75 |
| Did not use aliases ..... | 8 | 9.5 | 76 | 90.5 | 84 | 32 | 116 |
| Inapplicable, unknown .. | 16 | – | 50 | – | 66 | 182 | 248 |

### 45. DELINQUENCIES (OFFICIAL AND UNOFFICIAL) BY SERIOUSNESS OF OFFENSE
#### THIRD FIVE-YEAR PERIOD

| SECOND FIVE-YEAR PERIOD | *Non-delinquent* Number | *Non-delinquent* Per cent | *Delinquent, minor* Number | *Delinquent, minor* Per cent | *Delinquent, serious* Number | *Delinquent, serious* Per cent | *Total* | *Inapplicable, unknown* | *Grand total* |
|---|---|---|---|---|---|---|---|---|---|
| Non-delinquent ...... | 92 | 78.6 | 21 | 17.9 | 4 | 3.5 | 117 | 0 | 117 |
| Delinquent, minor .... | 17 | 14.5 | 92 | 78.6 | 8 | 6.9 | 117 | 5 | 122 |
| Delinquent, serious ... | 9 | 8.4 | 31 | 29.0 | 67 | 62.6 | 107 | 13 | 120 |
| Inapplicable, unknown | 2 | – | 7 | – | 21 | – | 30 | 50 | 80 |

# INDEX

Accident, role of, in reform of offenders, 284
Activities, constructive, of offenders, 106–107
Adolescence and antisocial behavior, 184
Affectional ties of offenders, as differentiator of success and failure, 209
Age of offenders
and behavior
during parole, 157, 247–250
during peno-correctional treatment, 151–156
during probation, 156, 238–240
during probation under suspended sentence, 156, 240–243
in Army or Navy, 158, 276–280
in correctional schools, 157, 258–259
in jails, 158, 272–276
in Navy or Army, 158, 276–280
in prisons, 158, 267–270
in reformatories, 158, 263–266
and concept of maturation, 250
and response to peno-correctional treatment, 148, 151–159
as constituent of prediction tables, 185
as differentiator of success and failure, 211
at beginning to work, 6
at change from serious to minor offender, prediction of, 226–227
at change in behavior, 121–122
at death, 73 $n1$
at end of fifteen-year follow-up span, 70
at end of first follow-up period, 3
at end of second follow-up period, 3
at entrance to Massachusetts Reformatory, 5
at first conflict with school and society, 6
at first delinquency, as differentiator of success and failure, 211–212
at leaving home, as differentiator of success and failure, 209
at reformation, 226–227, 284
Alexander, F., 289 $n10$
Alias, use of, by offenders, 114
American Law Institute, 251 $n4$
Antonio, case of ("A 'Normal' Youth Who Found His Proper Niche in Life"), 65–69, 231–232, 246–247, 256, 263, 293
"Appeal" in Massachusetts criminal court practice, 31 $n8$
Argow, W. W., 217 $n2$

Armand (and Robert), cases of ("Varied Fruits of the Same Tree"), 28–40, 245, 254, 261, 293
Army or Navy
behavior in
at various age levels, 158, 276–280
prediction of, 275–280
service in, as form of treatment, 158
successes and failures in, compared, 202–205
Arrests of offenders, 109–111
dispositions of, 115–116
early, 6
Arthur, case of ("The Mental Defective in a Protected Environment"), 40–47, 229–230, 245, 255, 262, 264, 293
Assistance by social service agencies, 91–92
as differentiator of success and failure, 207
Associates in crime, 114

Background and characteristics of offenders
related to post-treatment behavior, 285
related to success and failure, 206–212
Behavior of offenders
acceptable, in various institutions, 154 $n7$
age at which change occurred, 121–122, 226–227, 284
and emotional control, 184
at various age levels, 151–156. See also Age of offenders
background and characteristics as chief determinants of, 285
criminal, during three periods, 109–124
during extramural treatment, 162–165, 172–185, 234–251
during fifteen-year follow-up period, 121, 215–218
during intramural treatment, 166–169, 186–205, 252–283
during intra- and extramural treatment, 150
during peno-correctional treatment, 151–159
during third five-year follow-up period, 120–121
environmental vs. biologic factors in, 132–133, 184, 185, 188, 193, 212, 294
in Army or Navy, 158, 202–205, 275–280
See also Criminal conduct of offenders; Prediction of behavior of offenders; Success